THE
WIDENING SCOPE
OF PSYCHOANALYSIS:

COLLECTED ESSAYS OF
BERTRAM KARON

THE
WIDENING SCOPE
OF PSYCHOANALYSIS:

COLLECTED ESSAYS OF
BERTRAM KARON

EDITED BY:
MARTIN COSGRO, PH.D. AND
ANMARIE WIDENER, LCSW-C, PH.D.

IPBOOKS.net
International Psychoanalytic Books

International Psychoanalytic Books (IPBooks)
New York • http://www.IPBooks.net

International Psychoanalytic Books (IPBooks)
Queens, New York
Online at: www.IPBooks.net

Book design by Dan Williams

ISBN: 978-1-7320533-3-5

CONTENTS

FOREWORD

All that patients need, including patients diagnosed with schizophrenia, is a competent therapist. They do not need shock treatment or even medication. These papers share what I think a competent therapist can use. I hope that competent therapists can make use of this book, as well as those who are not yet competent therapists but who aspire to become one. I think that Drs. Cosgro and Widener have done an excellent job in selecting the papers for this compilation. I have spent more than half a century as a professional psychoanalytic psychologist. This book is a compilation of what I have learned in a lifetime.

INTRODUCTION

It is our honor and privilege to edit the work of Dr. Bertram P. Karon into this collected volume. Each of us have gotten to know Bert Karon well over the years. As students of his during our undergraduate and graduate educations, we hung on his every word during lectures. It was obvious to us as students that we were in the presence of a great teacher then; and we have thought back on those meaningful lectures ever since. We were among many to later to become colleagues and friends of his. It truly has been a joy to reflect back on the impact he's had on each of us as we poured over his six decades of professional contributions to the fields of Psychology and Psychoanalysis.

Publishing his first article in 1955—the first of well over a hundred more to come, Bert Karon's writings cover a broad range of topics. He is most known for his insights into the successful treatment of persons suffering from psychosis. His book, *Psychotherapy of Schizophrenia: The Treatment of Choice,* (co-authored with Gary VandenBos in 1981), is still considered by many today to be the most important and influential text on how to treat persons with psychosis. This seminal contribution has illuminated the path for many clinicians in their efforts to help clients struggling with psychological conflict. We hope this new volume of his collected papers will be equally as useful.

Bert Karon is a third generation Freudian, meaning he was trained by someone (Richard Sterba) who was directly trained by the father of Psychoanalysis, Sigmund Freud. As a third generation Freudian, Dr. Karon is intimately familiar with the classical psychoanalytic understanding of human psychology. Richard Sterba once told Bert that the popular translators of Sigmund Freud's work into English did not do him justice, that Freud was a much more kind, gentler person than his translated writings conveyed. Luckily for the reader, Dr. Karon's writings do not require a translator and so we are able to see first-hand, through his writings, the compassion and common sense that is too seldom found in published literature on psychological theory and technique. His keen ability to make sense of highly complex clinical phenomena and express that understanding in simple, everyday terms gives every reader the opportunity to understand these complicated aspects of the human condition.

Throughout his career, Bert Karon has worked tirelessly to give hope both to those struggling with serious emotional issues as well as the therapists that work to help them. He gives hope that there is a better way, a better future, and indeed that there is a cure for those who struggle with the most difficult psychological sequelae. Publishing his insights via a diverse array of journals, books, DVDs, and book chapters—in multiple countries and multiple languages—has allowed readers everywhere to glean much from those insights. To say that he is passionate about the real attainable good outcomes for people who have previously been told they were suffering from an incurable disorder and would need to take medication for the rest of their lives is an understatement. Bert Karon has spent a lifetime advocating for those who have no voice. In continually publishing his work, he has given us all the opportunity to learn how to truly help those who are suffering.

In compiling these articles, we tried to sequence them to make this volume as readable as possible and thus they are not arranged in chronological order. We selected papers on the basis of our perception of their broad impact and timelessness, though certainly the case could easily be made for the inclusion of many others. Though primarily known for his effective work with people struggling with severe emo-tional disturbance, Dr. Karon has also effectively treated people with a variety of clinical problems. We have included some of these papers, with topics such as suicide, depression, phobias, smoking cessation techniques, obsessions and compulsions. Needing to keep in mind a "reasonable length" for the volume, excellent papers were left out by necessity. However, we have included his entire bibliography for those wishing to further explore his diverse writings.

We hope that our editorial efforts have done justice to Dr. Bert Karon's long career encompassing hundreds upon hundreds of hours of direct therapeutic work with patients; thousands upon thousands of teaching hours with students at every stage in their career; and over half a century of passionate devotion to better understand the human condition. We believe that that the reader will be as moved and positively impacted by his insights as we have over the years.

Martin Cosgro, Ph.D. and
Anmarie Widener, LCSW-C, Ph.D.

Section 1:
ESSAYS ON PSYCHOSIS

Section 1: Essays on Psychosis

CHAPTER 1
Who Am I To Treat This Person?
What It Feels like to Treat a Seriously Disturbed Patient

Who am I to treat this person? That is what came to mind when I saw my first seriously disturbed patient. That is what comes to mind over and over again whenever I treat any seriously disturbed patient.

I don't know enough. I don't know enough to treat this patient. I don't know what he or she is doing or what it means. On the other hand, from very early in my training, it was helpful to ask myself what kind of treatment will this patient get if I don't treat him or her. If Sigmund Freud or Harry Sullivan or Frieda Fromm-Reichmann or Sandor Ferenczi were available, of course the patient would get better treatment. But they are not available. All I had to do at that time or since, was to ask what kind of treatment, or therapist (if the patient would get a therapist), the patient would actually receive if I did not treat him or her. In most cases the alternative was clearly awful.

Furthermore, I had hang-ups. I had anal issues from my childhood, problems with anger, and even sexual problems. Potentially violent people made me anxious. The patient needed someone without those problems. But the truth is there are no therapists without hang-ups. Luckily, patients do not need perfect therapists. They just need therapists who do the best they can do. Of course, our personal psychotherapy or psychoanalysis helps greatly. At the very least, it makes it possible to discuss issues that make us uncomfortable. Real therapists, unlike researchers, cannot avoid issues that trouble us. We must work with whatever issues the patient needs to have understood.

Some therapists who have not yet had therapy do excellent work. Some therapists even with many years of personal therapy never become very helpful. Most of us learn in our own therapy to be more helpful with some problems. But we learn to tolerate and be effective in dealing with issues that are important to the patient that make us uncomfortable and to do so without undue anxiety. Therapists as well as patients deserve to live comfortably.

Feelings of the Therapist

While I worked with severely disturbed patients, I often felt scared. But I learned that was because the patient felt scared. I felt angry, depressed, overwhelmed, and a myriad of unpleasant feelings at times. While these were not always the patient's feelings, they frequently were, and I learned to consider any unpleasant feeling something the patient might be feeling and to raise that possibility with the patient if I felt it would be helpful.

You cannot help but be confused. The patients do not understand what is going on. But, in addition, they do not communicate even what they do understand. They do not trust us. Why should they? Most of what they have to transfer is awful. They could not be that sick unless the people on whom they depended made them feel awful. Moreover, even the mental health people whom they should have been able to trust and receive help from sometimes were untrustworthy or hurtful and destructive. When patients tell us about abuse from mental health professionals, usually patients are being truthful. They expect us to be equally destructive, or at the very least to approve of what other mental health professionals have done, even if it was harmful. When patients describe being abused, we can let them know that we believe they were abused and that it was unjustifiable. All we have to do is tell the truth. In those few cases where it did not happen, the two of you will discover this as you work. Discussing it as if it was real makes the discovery that it was not real easier.

Memories of Abuse

Early in my training, I was taught to consider memories of abuse and trauma as probably delusional. But that teaching was wrong. Most reports by patients of abuse in childhood or adulthood turn out to be true. When they are not true, they are usually disguised versions of real abuse or trauma.

In general, If you treat a delusion as if it is true, and teach the patient how you would think about and cope with such problems if they happened to you, you will teach them how to think rationally about real problems and how to cope with them. They will learn from you how to think rationally and how to learn as much as possible about coping with real problems. They will then discover with you whether and to what extent any of their problems are delusional. They get excited when their lives makes sense.

Creating Hope

You will at times feel hopeless. That is because these patients feel hopeless. Nothing in their life, and probably nothing that previous mental health professionals have told them, would give them hope. It is up to you to give them rational hope. That you can do by sharing what you know realistically. The patients will not believe you, but they begin to consider it possible that you know what you're talking about.

A long time ago Thomas French (1952) talked about the importance of hope for normal functioning. You are the only one who will share a feeling of hope with the patient. We do not have to be unrealistic. The world we live in has many bad things in it, but it is not as horrible as the world seriously disturbed patients believe in.

You know that long-term studies (Ciompi, 1980; Harding, 1995) show that 30% of schizophrenics have full recoveries spontaneously within 25 years, and another third have social recoveries. You know that 80% of depressives get better within two years spontaneously (Postemak et al., 2006; Rennie, 1942; Schuyler, 1974). You know that outcome for patients who receive meaningful psychotherapy is much better than that. In fact, most patients with meaningful psychotherapy do very well, even if they are very disturbed to begin with.

Benedetti and Furlan (1987) found that 80 percent of severe schizophrenics had a very good outcome with 2 to 10 years of treatment, two to five times per week, median length of treatment was five years and median frequency was three times per week.. Karon and VandenBos (1981) blindly evaluated schizophrenic patients randomly assigned to psychoanalytic psychotherapy, to medication without psychotherapy, or to combined treatment. An average of 70 sessions of psychoanalytic psychotherapy without medication led to greater improvement in the thought disorder, shorter hospitalization, much shorter long term rehospitalization,, as well as better ability to hold a job, take care of their children, and live reasonable lives as compared to patients only on medication. Best results were achieved with psychoanalytic psychotherapy without medication at all or with initial medication which was withdrawn as the patients could tolerate it. Medication plus psychotherapy was better than medication alone, but not as good in the long run as psychotherapy alone or psychotherapy plus medication that was withdrawn. But most of the readers of this book will be familiar with these or other studies with similar results, or with their own clinical observations.

Of course, a good supervisor or knowledgeable colleagues can help provide the novice therapist with rational hope. But the best basis for rational hope is your own experience with severely disturbed patients who get better. Once one such patient has shown dramatic improvement, the therapist learns that therapy is difficult, but doable. One never has to doubt the reality of one's own experience.

Most patients are likely to have been told by mental health professionals that they have a genetic incurable disease. With the best of modem treatment (by which is usually meant medication) they can be made barely acceptable to other people most of the time. There is very little in such false information to give a patient hope.

It is important to remember that with schizophrenics underneath everything else is terror. The patient who is menacing is also scared. The patient who is mute and catatonic is scared that if he or she says something or moves he or she will be killed. It is helpful to most schizophrenics to say to them that you will not let anyone kill them. Professionals who have observed me interviewing a new patient have reported that they could see the patient react to this statement, even if they did not seem to be reacting to anything else. I have even been asked by professionals who knew the patient how I knew the patient was afraid of dying, because they had forgotten to tell me. But Bruno Bettelheim many years ago described the fact that all acute cases of schizophrenia have a conscious terror of dying.

Not Understanding

We do not have to understand everything patients say or do. Indeed it is impossible. If we understand anything, patients are impressed. In their experience most mental health professionals have not listened very carefully, or understood much of anything. For research purposes Norman Kagan recorded one session of a schizophrenic patient whom I was treating under observation by a graduate seminar of mental health professionals (using a one-way screen). I left the room, and Kagan played the tape of the session, stopping at every pause, and asking the patient what was going on. His thoughts were complex and fascinating. At the end of their discussion, Kagan asked the patient, "Does Karon understand this?" "Of course he does."

But of course I did not. I understood the fragments that he had told me as best I could. But I did not understand most of what was going on in his mind. Since then, I have found that this is very general. When patients say they feel understood, it is not necessarily because we correctly understand them. They are responding to our trying to understand them. That is a very good thing. We cannot promise to always correctly understand our patients, but we can do our damnedest to try and understand our patients. And that is all they need.

There are some advantages to not understanding. You then know that you will have to act on imperfect knowledge. My first schizophrenic patient, a man in his 30s, had been psychotic for16 years, and treated unsuccessfully at expensive hospitals. In my first session he sat on his bed, unmoving and making clicking sounds. I did not know what it meant or what to do. Later in the therapy I would learn that the clicking sound was short for "best" which was short for "three four infinity best." He had the number three come to mind hundreds of times each day which he would change to four. We learned that three stood for penis and four stood for a world without penises and sexuality, where his mother would love him. He did not know these meanings consciously, and when we discovered them together, and discussed them, his delusions concerning the number four disappeared. But that took many months, and there was no way I could guess what was going on until then.

I reached out to him, and he fell off the bed as if he were rigid. I reached out to him, and he ran to the furthest comer of the room. I followed, and he ran to another comer. I followed. He yelled, "Don't hit me, don't hit me."

I said, "I won't hit you. I promise I won't hit you." "Not you. Him." He pointed to the center of the room where he apparently saw someone terrifying.

Not knowing what to do, I used threatening language that I had read in a book on Malay magic that witch doctors used in threatening evil spirits and demons, that I would kill "him" horribly if he did not leave this boy alone, or harmed this boy in any way. The patient suddenly relaxed. He was then ready to talk to me for the first time. We had the beginning of a therapeutic alliance. The only problem it caused, which was trivial, was that he complained that I wanted to analyze his hallucinations and delusions when I knew how to make them go away the easy way. That was the only patient with which I ever used that technique, because that was the only patient for whom it seemed appropriate. It was only possible to do the right thing, because I did not know what to do. Again and again, not knowing has led to improvisation which has led to therapeutic progress.

A chronically catatonic patient had a history of emerging violently from his catatonic state. He had broken the jaws of several attendants at previous hospitals. When I worked with him, I was scared of him, found him disgusting, and did not like him. Being scared of him was rational. He was dangerous. Being disgusted with him was also rational. He was urinally and anally incontinent. But, in addition, I did not like him.

This was not a rational feeling. On reflection I became aware that he reminded me of "dirty little bastards" who picked on me when I was a child. When I grew bigger, they stopped picking on me, but picked on other children. At this point it was clear to me that it was unfair to hate him for what others had done to me in my childhood (or in psychoanalytic terms, my counter-transference).

But then I began to think. "Dirty little bastards." They were not big guys. Maybe they were scared. The patient was not big either, but he was very muscular. The next time this patient seem to be getting angry, I said to him, "I know how scared you are. Why don't you use my strength to protect you." The patient quieted down immediately and was responsive in psychotherapy.

The attendants at that institution, all of whom had been college football players, thought this was very funny. "Your strength. Do you know what he could do to you?" Of course, they were right. I would have been no match for him in a fistfight. But his violence was never a problem after that. The same reassurance from me always worked.

Learning to reassure patients against death or violence was a very useful general lesson. This is not magic. In general, the dangers they fear are not realistic, but based on transference. Only a therapist can help. If they are in realistic danger, telling you as much as they know will permit you to help them take whatever realistic actions are indicated. Even paranoids are sometimes in realistic danger. If they act rationally (with your help) to cope with the dangers, they will discover if the dangers are not realistic and be ready to investigate their meaning.

Delusions and Hallucinations

Paranoid delusions should be investigated by encouraging the patient to give us as much detail as possible. Again, we can share the way we would think about these issues if they affected us. We can share with them sources of information, and rational ways of investigating issues. You should try not to humiliate the patient.

Paranoid patients often combine fears of danger with unrealistic actions that make the probability much greater that they will be harmed. Thus a female patient described a strange man of whom she was frightened walking around her neighborhood at night. When he rang her doorbell and asked to be let in, she opened the door and let him in, even though she was terrified. She said she was afraid that he would get angry at her if she did not let him in. She was surprised to be told that she should never let anyone in her apartment that she was afraid of, that letting him into her apartment increased her danger. She was further surprised when she was told that if she was afraid of a stranger walking around her neighborhood, she should call the police. She objected that if she did not let him in, or if she called the police, they might think she was crazy. When at a later time she called the police when there was a strange prowler in her neighborhood, she was surprised to find that the police investigated him and found him not dangerous, and told her so. They also acted as if calling them to investigate was exactly the proper thing to do.

Of course, this is often a transference reaction from a dangerous parent, who hurt the child or seemed about to hurt the child, but punished the child or humiliated the child for acting as if the parent was dangerous.

A patient had out of body experiences. He described them in his first hour. Then he said that he thought I didn't believe him. I did not want to put him down or enrage him, nor did I want to lie to him. Moreover, I am generally too transparent to successfully hide my feelings. What I did say was that I found it improbable, but I wasn't there, and he was. Tell me about it. That was sufficient honesty and acceptance for him to be able to work with me.

Six months later, after we had developed a therapeutic relationship and discussed many issues, he described rising out of his body to the moon, which looked like a large face smiling down at him.

"I have an idea."

"What?"

"It's not your way of understanding it."

"What is it?"

"It's not your way of understanding it."

"Cut it out. What is it?"

"As you described it, it felt like a child...

He interrupted, "being lifted in his mother's arms to her face."

He got excited, and began to translate this experience into a childhood experience, and to reconsider his other experiences as repetitions of childhood. He was excited that his experiences now made better sense to him.   Always ask patients to describe a delusion in as much detail as they can. Then you can help them discover its meaning. In general, delusions have four bases. The most common is transference to the world at large of childhood experiences, and that should be your first consideration. The second basis is a defense against pseudo-homosexual anxieties, as described by Freud (1911/1950). Patients usually need to be told that we all need friends of both sexes, that having the best friend of the same sex is normal, and that homosexual thoughts are not usually about homosexuality. Almost always they need to learn that all thoughts are acceptable, that only actions and words can be bad because they have effects on other people, and that thoughts in general cannot be controlled. But it will be a long time for the patient to accept this. The third basis of delusions are strange ways of thinking that are specific to their families, but which the patient believes are general to other people. The fourth basis for delusions is the attempt by the patient to make sense of their life despite having bizarre experiences, including both symptoms and strange real-life experiences. Patients always try to be as realistic as their defenses allow, which is helpful to us when they realize that our way of understanding things makes their lives make more sense to them than their previous understanding.

Hallucinations should be used like dreams in therapy. Most patients preferred to talk about voices rather than hallucinations, finding the word hallucinations demeaning. We should follow their wishes.

Always ask for associations if the patient is able and willing to provide them. "What comes to mind when…" Even if the patient will not or cannot associate, it is often easy to guess at the meaning of the hallucination, since the motivation has to be stronger to hallucinate when you are wide awake. All of us can hallucinate when we are asleep.

The patient can be told that voices are like dreams and that therapists use dreams to help in therapy. The main difference between hallucinations and dreams, aside from waking or sleeping, is that most schizophrenic hallucinations are voices, while most dreams are visual. That is because schizophrenia is an interpersonal disorder.

One paranoid schizophrenic told me that "Bridie Murphy said she would kill you."

"Why do you want to kill me?"

"You can't blame me for what Bridie Murphy says."

Since we had been working together for several months and he knew to a large extent how I thought, I said, "Do I blame you for what Bridie Murphy said?"

"No."

"What do I blame you for?"

"For believing her."

I then gave him my schedule —where I would be every hour for that day and the next day, and told him to tell Bridie Murphy. If Bridie Murphy killed me, we could stop therapy. If she did not, we would double his hours.

"None of your god damned bets."

We could then explore the meaning of his hallucination.

Hallucinations of God should be treated tactfully. Early in my career I was assaulted by patients when I told them that their voice was not God. How would you feel if you had a direct line to God, and someone tried to take it away from you? Crusades have been fought for less. Of course, if God tells them to do something destructive like killing themselves or someone else, you must tell them that the voice is not God because God is not a sadist.

The Place of Theory

When we first try to talk with and understand a severely disturbed patient what we hear is largely chaos, and we do not understand. But psychoanalytic theories are invaluable. With their help much of what the patient says seems to make sense. It is not that all psychoanalytic theories are accurate. Indeed, it is the fact that psychoanalytic theories are continuously developed on the basis of clinical experience that makes them so powerful. When we read a psychoanalytic theory, we do not necessarily accept it as the truth. But when a patient talks about it, we know that it is true for him or her, although it may have additional meanings which we will discover. Without psychoanalytic theories, we hear chaos. With psychoanalytic theories we hear form and order and a first approximation.. But there is still chaos, areas that don't make sense, and areas where the implications seem to be contradictory. But this first approximation is invaluable. It gives us a place to begin. And we begin to listen around the areas that don't make sense or where the implications are contradictory.

Castration anxiety seemed an abstract concept to me until a patient yelled, "Don't cut them off, dad!" while he covered his genitals with his hands. For him castration anxiety was obviously a reality. However, another patient, when I interpreted that he might have been afraid his father would castrate him, said, "He wouldn't castrate me, he'd kill me!"

Of course, we both accepted his version of reality.

The patient's statements should always be taken seriously. But even when they are consistent with theory, they are often only the beginning. Thus, fears of castration by the father may in part be a defense against the even more frightening fear of castration by mother who may have made such threats in connection with childhood masturbation, or against the terror of the inside of the body being drained through the penis (Karon and Rosberg, 1958). When in doubt about the psychodynamic meaning of material, with severely disturbed patients it is generally good procedure to emphasize problems from the oral phase and problems concerning survival.

One can over emphasize the importance of theory, especially of a particular theory. Therapists of different theoretical orientations, psychoanalytic, psychological, or psychiatric, who have worked with seriously disturbed patients understand each other. It is notable at the meetings of the International Society for the Psychotherapy of the Schizophrenias and Other Psychoses that therapists using different theories who have worked with seriously disturbed patients readily understand each other. The words used, and some of the relevant abstractions, are different. But each of them understands what the problems are with which the other therapist is trying to cope. Some of the techniques may be different. But they understand each other, and what the other therapist is trying to do. This is different from the reactions of professionals who have only read about these patients, or possibly done some research, or processed for patients superficially, but have no real feel for what it is like to try to be helpful to people in such dire psychological states.

Transference

As usual in any psychotherapy, the transference is an essential part of the therapeutic process. It is an invaluable source of information about the patient's past and the sources of his or her problems. At the same time it represents the most important of the resistances, the difficulties in the treatment process. As mentioned above, since their lives have been worse than those who are neurotic, the transference tends to be more negative. The blank screen will inevitably turn into a monster. We should try to be unambiguously helpful, although it is difficult for the patient to perceive it.

We are accustomed to continually ask ourselves," Am I the patient's mother or father?" But we also may be any important figure in the patient's past. We may be a sibling, grandparent, or any important figure. We may even be a destructive mental health professional in the patient's past. Nonetheless, it is true that for most patients the most important figures are mother and father, and both are transferred to the therapist whether the therapist is a man or a woman.

Particularly when the patient treats us badly and we are confused, it is often because the patient is not treating us as if we were his or her mother or father, but treats us the way the destructive parent treated the patient. These are frequently sessions that are hard to take.

But if we are not crushed by the patient's reactions, we are already being helpful. They learn that it is possible to endure mistreatment. If we react in a reasonable self protective way without hurting them, they learn that it is possible to protect oneself, without doing harm to oneself or to others. If, in addition, we can relate what happened in the session to what must have happened to them, the therapy moves forward even more.

Therapeutic Change

Therapeutic change in psychoanalytic therapy seems to be primarily the result of two things: understanding and the internalization of the therapist. The patient learns to understand themselves, their agonies, and maladaptive reactions from the material of the therapy and the therapist's interpretations. It is helpful to present interpretations as, "I wonder if...", so that the interpretation does not become a contest of wills. Since even neurotic patients hear every interpretation as an accusation, it is useful to phrase interpretations as, "Anyone would feel..." or "It would only be human to feel..." The patient does not need anyone else in his or her life to add to their humiliation.

The internalization of the therapist is crucial. It goes on without explicit discussion in most psychotherapies. Nonetheless, the patient internalizes the therapist as a new superego, kinder and more rational than the superego figures of the patient's life before therapy. The patient internalizes the therapist into the ego, as a model for how a human being might be. This concerns us as therapists, since we do not want the patient to adopt our weaknesses or hangups. But we provide a better model of a human being than most of the people the patient has used as models. Moreover, the patient, as a result of growing in psychotherapy, is very much like the adolescent. They will internalize the therapist, but continue to grow and reject the parts of the therapist which are not helpful.

Feelings

Feelings are at the center of any meaningful psychotherapy. In fact, they are the center of any meaningful experience. It is one of the great mistakes of psychology that for a long time we treated feelings as if they were irrational. But emotions are a central part of rational thinking, as Tomkins (2008) most clearly pointed out. Feelings are summary statements of what is going on.

Freud said that emotions are what psychoanalysis is all about, what else could it possibly be about? (R. Sterba, personal communication, 1980). Carl Rogers (1961) and his colleagues demonstrated the centrality of feelings and of paying careful attention to feelings for successful psychotherapy and for successful living in general.

If we are scared, there is something to be scared of. If we are sad, there is something to feel bad about. If we are angry, something is hurting us. If it is not something of which we are aware, it is unconscious. If it is not in the present, it is in the past and something in the present is symbolic of it. If we feel good, there is something to feel good about.

Patients believe that their feelings are irrational. With our help they learn that their feelings make good sense and that they are bearable. Even the negative affect of shame is useful to understand. As Tomkins pointed out, one cannot feel ashamed unless one wants a relationship with someone else and feels that it is not possible. But you can help the patient understand that wanting a relationship is healthy, and even if it is not possible in some instances immediately, it will be possible eventually. In fact, a relationship with their therapist is possible immediately. While the patient may denigrate this relationship, it is always very important to them.

Depression

Depressed patients tend to be unique in two ways. The first is that they are geniuses at making you depressed. Obviously they are depressed about themselves and their lives. Any possibility, they can assure you, will not work and will not help them. Moreover, anything you say or have said has not and will not help them. They are often good at badmouthing you in general. They are very convincing.

It is not surprising that you will find yourself angry at them. Mental health professionals in general feel angry at depressed patients, but feel they shouldn't be angry. Consequently, it is not surprising that mental health professionals sometimes feel relieved when bad things happen to a depressed patient, as long as it cannot be interpreted as a bad thing that they have done to the patient. At one psychiatric hospital it was observed that the residents, nurses, and attendants laughed whenever a depressed patient with whom they had worked was assigned to ECT. They did not laugh when any other patient was assigned to ECT, or when the depressed patient was assigned to psychotherapy and/or medication.

When you are angry at them, it is useful to remember that this is evidence that their depression is at least in part based on anger. Of course, depressed patients are not usually aware of their anger and the part it plays in their depression, but everyone who deals with them feels it and tends to dislike them for it. This only makes the depression worse.

However, no matter how good they are at proving that they are worthless and that you and the psychotherapy are worthless, they unconsciously hope that they will not succeed in convincing us. Moreover, they often will not tell us about an improvement, because they are afraid we will punish them or take it away from them. After all, when they tried to convince you that you and your work are worthless, they were only acting out in the transference what has been done to them.

The second way in which depressed patients are different is in their use of isolation as a defense mechanism. They do not connect things which seem obviously connected. It is not unusual when you ask a depressed patient what happened before their depression started to be told, "Nothing."

"Something must have happened, you were alive."

"Nothing important."

If you persist, they will eventually tell you things that would depress anyone, but which they did not connect with their depression. In my experience, every endogenous depression has very good reasons for being depressed. As Viggo Jensen (personal communication, 1970) once said, "An endogenous depression is a very severe depression in someone whom you haven't talked to long enough to find out why they are depressed."

It would be easy to exaggerate the difference between severely depressed patients and schizophrenic patients. Every depressed patient has to cope with massive terror, and every schizophrenic patient has severe depressions. As Michael Teixeira (personal communication, 1990) has pointed out, the basic therapeutic approach is the same with both sets of patients, as well as with patients who have both sets of symptoms. The most useful paper on the treatment of manic-depressive psychoses (severe bipolar disorders) is that of Teixeira (1992).

Of course, just because a patient is diagnosed as depressive, does not mean that he she necessarily feels depressed. They may feel sad, guilty, scared, angry, or have no feelings at all. You do not know what they feel unless you ask them and they tell you. The most severely depressed patients do not feel sad, they feel nothing at all. When they begin to feel sad or cry, they are usually getting better. The dead feelings are a defense against unbearable affect.

Suicide

Patients who are suicidal obviously make us uncomfortable. We don't want them to die. But every seriously disturbed patient considers suicide at some point in their treatment. In my experience meaningful psychotherapy is the most effective way to keep them alive. Patients who threaten to kill themselves should be taken seriously. They should be asked to talk about it..

Patients who describe killing themselves in fanciful and elaborate ways that do not seem practical are not likely to be dangerous, but patients who describe themselves committing suicide in practical ways with available weapons are much more dangerous.

The most dangerous thing a therapist can do is to do nothing. Jensen and Petty suggested that suicidal patients project their superego on to someone else, whom they implicitly ask, "Do I deserve to live or die?" That is why suicidal patients almost always tell someone. If that someone does nothing, the patient concludes they deserved to die. If that someone is the therapist, the therapist certainly must do something that indicates the therapist does not think the patient deserves to die.

A psychology intern early in her career was supervised by a well published psychologist. A patient brought a gun to the therapy hour and said that he was going to kill himself with it. Not knowing what to do, the intern reacted rationally.

"No, you're not." She took his gun and put it in a drawer, and closed the drawer. Her supervisor told her that she could not do that. It was interfering with the patient's autonomy. Further, the gun was the patient's property, and she had no right to take it away from him. Despite her qualms, she followed her supervisor's advice and returned the gun. The patient shot himself after he left her office. Obviously, he interpreted the return of the gun as a message of what he should do.

If the supervisor had been knowledgeable enough to have read Jensen and Petty, he would have done the right thing. The intern, without knowing what to do, used her own judgment, and did the right thing. But the supervisor with some sophistication used the wrong set of abstract principles, and the patient died. If you do not know what to do as a therapist, act like a human being. It will almost always lead you to do the right thing.

One of the things the therapist can do is to interpret the meaning of the wish to commit suicide. The most common wish is to hurt someone else. This wish may be conscious or unconscious, but the therapist can make it conscious by saying, "Some people kill themselves to get even with someone else. I wonder if you want to get even with..." or "I wonder if there is someone you want to get even with." I recommend adding, "but it is stupid." If that someone does not like the patient, they will be happy when the patient dies. If that someone, like a parent, might feel unhappy, they will feel unhappy a little, not the agony the patient hopes for, and not the agony the patient will inflict on themselves.

One ambulatory schizophrenic, who was suicidal after his wife left him, said after a session in which such interpretations were made, "I'm not going to let her piss on my grave." He did not kill himself, but continued psychotherapy. Another patient who began a telephone call by declaring her intention to kill herself continued for a full session on the phone which ended with, "Damn you, Karon. I always felt that if worst came to worst, I could always kill myself. But now you've taken that away from me." She was furious at me, but she did not kill herself, and continued her treatment.

Hopelessness is a necessary but not a sufficient condition for suicide. But the therapist can arouse realistic hope. After all, most of the reasons people commit suicide are solvable. It is possible to find a new love, a new job, or to live on a lower income. Only in infancy do we have one love, our mother, who can never be replaced.

One thing we can and must do is give the patient the relationship with us as one relationship on which they can depend.

It is well known that some depressed patients commit suicide when they seem to be getting better. This is usually explained on the basis that the patient didn't have enough energy to commit suicide, but as they get better they have enough energy to kill themselves. This is not what is going on. As Atwood (1972) learned by listening to patients, some depressed patients decide to solve their problems by killing themselves. Since they think they have a solution, they seem to get better. Then they carry out their solution and kill themselves.

If depressed patients are genuinely getting better, they have more insight into why they are depressed. They also talk more about the future. If the therapist raises the issue of suicide, they will discuss it. If depressed patients seem to be getting better because they have decided to kill themselves, they do not have any more insight into why they are depressed. They do not talk about the future because they don't have any. If the therapist raises the issue of suicide, they will either not discuss it, or unemotionally tell you that they intend to kill themselves.

If all three of these indices are in the right direction, the depressed patient is getting better. If all three of these indices are in the wrong direction, the depressed patient intends to kill him or herself, and the therapist needs to do something about it.

In addition to psychotherapy, there are realistic measures which sometimes are very helpful. A locked ward can be temporarily helpful. But I have known patients who found ways of killing themselves in a locked ward or by escaping the locked ward. (None of these patients were in intensive psychotherapy.) I have known patients in solitary confinement in a reformatory who managed to hide a piece of metal or a glass sliver with which they intended to kill themselves. (They had begun psychotherapy and did not kill themselves, although they did make cuts on their body before they stopped.)

Having someone stay with a patient or keep an eye on a patient who is suicidal is very helpful. This is kinder and more helpful in most cases than a locked ward, if there are relatives or friends were willing to take on this burden.

The Thematic Apperception Test (TAT) can be useful with suicidal patients. The more cards you use, the easier it is to make accurate predictions. Card 3 BM, card 12 M (12 F if both the therapist and the patient are female), card 14, and card 16 should always be included, for both men and women. Usually, if 6 to 12 cards are used, it is usually possible to estimate not only the danger, but the conditions under which the patient will or will not commit suicide.

Unfortunately, some few patients manage to commit suicide under any circumstances. It is often clear that the patient intended to set the therapist up to feel like a failure. Some therapists have been badly damaged by such patients. It is always useful to consult with a colleague and/or a therapist to discuss what happened, if a patient does kill him or her self.

One is tempted to use antidepressant medication with a patient who is suicidal. But recent data suggest that antidepressants do not effectively prevent suicide (Breggin, 2008b; Breggin & Cohen, 2008; Jackson, 2008). Apparently, 30% of normal volunteers become acutely suicidal with antidepressant medication, which disappears when the drug wears off. Most people, depressed or not, will not kill themselves, and an even smaller group will kill other people. But antidepressant medication seems to increase the rate of suicide and of homicide. If patients are taking antidepressant medication, it is useful to warn them that if they feel like killing themselves or someone else, it is not them it is the medication. They should get immediate help in changing or reducing the medication appropriately, and hopefully get psychotherapy.

Homicide

Homicidal threats are even more scary to therapists than suicidal threats. Again, the patient should be taken seriously. Get the patient to describe their intentions in as much detail as possible. Again, fantastic or unrealistic murder techniques are not likely to be dangerous but realistic ones might well be.

Each state has legal standards of procedure that have to be obeyed. Their purpose like ours is to try to make sure that the murder does not take place. But it has been my experience that the best preventative is competent psychotherapy.

Thus, one multiple murderer was in a reformatory on a minor charge. His psychiatrist tried to turn him in, only to discover that the only way the patient could be convicted was if he confessed. In many ways he was psychotic, but he had no intention of confessing. His therapist, with whom he would no longer work, recommended maximum sentence. This would have only kept him in jail for two years, after which he would return to society as a better trained criminal.

He was thoroughly unlikable. But treating him was the only way to protect society. Six months of psychoanalytic therapy ended his symptomatic murders. He now felt guilty about his murderers and about his beatings of innocent victims. On my recommendation, he was paroled with mandatory psychotherapy as a condition of parole. He did not commit any more murders. He did return to jail for breaking and entering. We did not have enough time to deal with his irrational way of earning a living, unfortunately, but both he and I felt that his not murdering was well worth the time and work.

In my experience murderers are always people who cannot stand conscious anger. They can kill, but they cannot tolerate feeling angry. They either act on their anger immediately or, more commonly, do not feel the anger at all.

Thus, it is helpful to teach the patient to feel angry, but not to kill. Get them to tell you who they want to kill and why. Encourage them to feel angry and even validate that this person deserves to die, if that judgment seems rational. But then add that it would be stupid to kill them, because it would ruin the patient's life.

The patient needs to know that it is alright to want to kill anyone, but it is not alright to kill anyone, except under unusual circumstances like realistic self-defense. They need to know that it is all right to think anything, to feel anything, that only actions are subject to moral judgment, and that you will discuss anything that they need to think about, no matter how bad they think it is.

Medication

The Michigan State Psychotherapy Research Project (Karon and VandenBos, 1981) found that schizophrenic patients responded to psychoanalytic therapy best if they were not on medication. Initial medication which was withdrawn as rapidly as the patients could tolerate was nearly as effective. Maintenance medication combined with psychotherapy was better than medication alone, but not as effective in the long run as psychotherapy alone or psychotherapy with initial medication that was withdrawn. The most dramatic difference was the improvement in the thought disorder with psychotherapy, the ability to think logically when you want to. This seemed to have increasing impact on their way of life, and consequent ability to stay out of the hospital, as time went by.

Consequently, our recommendation is that patients should be treated by psychotherapy alone if the patient, the therapist, and the setting (e.g., hospital, family, or other living arrangement) can tolerate it. If any one of these three cannot tolerate it, the patient should be started on medication with psychoanalytic therapy to produce initial behavioral control. But the patient should be withdrawn from medication as rapidly as they can tolerate it. While the Michigan Psychotherapy Project (Karon and VandenBos, 1981) studied only severe schizophrenics, the same recommendations would be made for other serious mental patients. Continuing medication indefinitely slows the improvement in the thought disorder. Moreover, we are learning that there are serious medical risks in maintaining psychiatric medication indefinitely, as well as poor long-term outcomes (Whitaker, 2010). However, if the patient has been on medication for a long time, it seems clear that one must withdraw the patient slowly. Breggin and Cohen (2007) is a brief, convenient, and accurate source for information about the known side effects of psychiatric medications, the known withdrawal effects of current medications, and recommended procedures for safely withdrawing patients from currently used psychiatric medications.

Of course, the optimal use of medication is a legitimate source of disagreement among helpful professionals. There are those who always medicate their patients, those who never medicate their patients, those who temporarily medicate their patients, or use medication to cope with crises. Serious mental health professionals disagree, and each of us must take our own clinical experiences seriously. .Nonetheless, this is my recommendation.

In many settings, particularly those in which younger professionals work, the therapist may have little choice about whether and to what extent medication is used. In that case, one can only do the best work possible under the circumstances. As one gets better known, even among one's immediate colleagues, it is typical to find one's clinical judgments increasingly respected.

For detailed summaries of the currently known down sides to current psychiatric medications, see Breggin (2008b) and Jackson (2009).

Electroconvulsive Therapy

Unfortunately, patients who have received ECT improve very slowly during psychoanalytic psychotherapy as compared to patients of equal severity who have never received ECT. Other therapists have estimated that it takes 3 to 6 times as much work to produce similar progress. I was startled to discover how rapidly some psychotic patients improve when I first worked with patients who had never received ECT.

The books by Andre (2009), Morgan (1999), and Breggin (2008a) detail the evidence that electroconvulsive therapy probably leaves permanent brain damage, which undoubtedly is related to the difficulty in making use of psychotherapy by patients who have received ECT. In any event I would strongly recommend that psychoanalytic psychotherapy, or other sensible psychotherapy, be tried before, rather than after, ECT. Of course, it is the experience of most psychotherapists that ECT will not be necessary if meaningful psychotherapy is available.

Summary

It is my recommendation that one should not treat only seriously mentally ill patients.. There is no single group of patients that I believe we treat best if we treat only that one kind of patient. Both the patients and the therapists do better if we treat a varied group of patients, so that the defenses and the issues vary. Of course, despite the differences in process and in resistances, the basic issues remain the same for all patients, which is how best to be a human being.

Working with severely disturbed patients is difficult. It is tiring, it is demanding, it is scary, and sometimes depressing. But most patients respond, and when severely disturbed patients respond to psychotherapy, the change is not subtle. When patients who will not eat, begin to eat, when patients who hear voices, no longer believe they are real, and eventually do not hear them as external, but have them merge with their other thoughts, when patients who were not logical, become logical, when patients who are too sick to work, are able to work, when patients who cannot adequately take care of their children, take care of their children, it would be hard to miss that something important has happened. It is a benign trauma for the therapist from which we never recover.

REFERENCES

Andre, L. (2009). Doctors of deception: What they don't want you to know about shock treatment. New Brunswick, NJ & London: Rutgers University Press.

Atwood, G. (1972). Note on a relationship between suicidal intentions and the depressive mood. Psychotherapy, Theory, Research and Practice, 9, 284 285.

Breggin, P.R. (2008a). Brain disabling treatments in psychiatry: Drugs, electric shock, and the psychopharmaceutical complex. New York: Springer.

————— (2008b/ Medication madness.. New York: St. Martin's Press.

————— & Cohen, D. (2007). Your drug may be your problem. Cambridge, MA: Perseus.

Ciompi, L. (1980). Catamnesic long-term study on the course of life and aging of schizophrenics. Schizophrenia Bulletin, 6, 606–617.

French, T.M. (1952). The integration of behavior (Vol.l). Chicago: University of Chicago Press.

Freud, S. (1911). Psychoanalytic notes upon an autobiographical account of a case of paranoia (dementia paranoides). Collected Papers (Vol. 3), pp. 316–357. London: Hogarth and the Institute for Psychoanalysis, 1950.

Harding, C, M. (1995). The interaction of biopsychosocial factors, time, and course of schizophrenia. In C. L. Shriqui & H. A. Nasrallah (Eds.), Contemporary issues in the treatment of schizophrenia (pp. 653–681). Washington, DC: American Psychiatric Press,

Jackson, G.E. (2009). Drug-induced dementia: A perfect crime. Bloomington, IN: AuthorHouse.

Karon, B, P. & Rosberg, J. (1958). The homosexual urges in schizophrenia. Psychoanalysis and the Psychoanalytic Review, 45, 50–56.

————— & VandenBos, G. R. (1981). Psychotherapy of schizophrenia: The treatment of choice. New York: Aronson.

Morgan, R. F. (Ed.). (1999). Electroshock treatment over four decades: The case against. Phoenix AZ: Morgan Foundation Publishers International.

Postemak, M. A., Solomon, D. A., Leon, A. C., Mueller, T. I., Shea, M. T., Endicott, J., & Keller, M. B. (2006). The naturalistic course of unipolar major depression in the absence of somatic therapy. Journal of Nervous and Mental Diseases, 194, 324–329.

Rennie, T. A. C. (1942). Prognosis in manic-depressive psychoses. American Journal of Psychiatry, 98, 801–814.

Rogers, C. R. (1961). On becoming a person. Boston: Houghton Mifflin.

Schuyler, D. (1974). The depressive spectrum. New York: Jason Aaronson.

Teixeira, M. (1992). Psychoanalytic theory and therapy in the treatment of manic-depressive disorders. Psychoanalysis and Psychotherapy, 11, 81–96.

Tomkins, S. S. (2008) Affect, imagery, consciousness: The complete edition. New York: Springer.

Whitaker, R. (2010). Anatomy of an epidemic: Magic bullets, psychiatric drugs, and the astonishing rise of mental illness in America. New York: Crown.

CHAPTER 2
The Fear of Understanding Schizophrenia
Bertram P. Karon, PhD

It is generally believed that a treatment that is more effective than its alternatives will be used, but psychological treatments for schizophrenic and other psychotic reactions have been avoided despite the evidence for their effectiveness from the time of "moral treatment" to the present. Less effective (or even destructive) treatments have been seized upon, in part because they do not require understanding these patients. Understanding schizophrenic persons means facing facts about ourselves, our families, and our society that we do not want to know, or to know again (in the case of repressed feelings and experiences). The central role of terror in producing symptoms, and the genesis and psychological handling of symptoms, including delusions and hallucinations, are briefly described.

It is ordinarily believed that if a treatment is more helpful than its alternatives it will be used. Yet, an early psychologically based treatment for schizophrenics—moral treatment—was tried out, found to be successful, then abandoned (Alexander & Selesnick, 1966; Bockoven, 1972; Whitaker, in press).

In our time, psychoanalytic psychotherapies for schizophrenia are not fashionable; not because they are not helpful, but because they make therapists,as well as the public at large, so uncomfortable. It is usual to assume that this discomfort is felt because schizophrenic people are extremely different from the rest of us, but the truth is just the opposite. What makes both professionals and the general public alike uncomfortable with schizophrenic people is not so much their difference from us, but their similarity. We do not want to know what they have to teach us about the human condition (Deikman, 1971).

In the 1930s, Harry Stack Sullivan and Frieda Fromm-Reichmann consistently helped schizophrenics. The treatment was arduous, but patients improved (Fromm-Reichmann, 1950; Sullivan, 1953). The well-known novel, *I Never Promised You a Rose Garden* (Greenberg, 1964), described that early treatment. The author, who had been a patient of Fromm-Reichmann, used an assumed name. It was only after later novels under her own name became popular that she finally attached her name to this book, which not only describes such treatment, but demonstrates the kind of recovery that allowed the patient to write so well. Yet there are many professionals who act as if they have never heard of psychotherapy with schizophrenics or as if it was demonstrated long ago to be unhelpful and inferior to somatic treatment.

Of course, there are economic, sociological, political, ideological, and apparently scientific motives for turning away from understanding schizophrenics. But we would be remiss to ignore the fundamental emotional bases of these motives. Whenever, in the course of treatment, something about a schizophrenic person has come to light, it has illuminated the human condition in general; and whatever psychoanalysis or psychology has learned about the general human condition has illuminated schizophrenia as well and is helpful in its treatment.

To understand schizophrenic persons is to grasp painful facts about the human condition that we would rather not know, or, more frightening, to be reminded of painful facts we once knew, but repressed.

Even the sociological data about schizophrenia remind us of unpleasant realities. For example, a disproportionately greater incidence and prevalence of schizophrenic disorders is associated with low socioeconomic status (Hollingshead & Redlich, 1958), and cannot be accounted for by downward drift. This suggests, and psychotherapeutic experience makes vivid, the physical and psychological pain, humiliation, and physical danger associated with being very poor in our society—realities which those of us who are not very poor do not like to perceive or remember. Similarly, schizophrenic disorders are more common among those who are the victims of prejudice and discrimination (Karon, 1975). Thus, the psychotherapist, to be effective, will often be confronted with the ugliness of the economic, racial, ethnic, and religious discrimination which have contributed to these disorders. And the fact that the long-term prognosis for schizophrenics is better in non-literate cultures (Sartorius, Jablensky, & Shapiro, 1978) reminds us of the relative lack of kindness in our "civilization."

Many schizophrenics have talked about incest, sexual abuse, and physical abuse; but such talk nearly always has been dismissed as the ravings of lunatics (Rieger, 1896). Freud, referring specifically to conversion hysterics, reported that the incest memories they related in psychoanalysis were revealed more often to be fantasies than real events, although in many cases, according to Freud, they were undoubtedly real:

> Phantasies of being seduced are of particular interest, because
> so often they are not phantasies but real memories. Fortunately,
> however, they are nevertheless not real as often as seemed at

first to be shown by the findings of analysis

.... You must not suppose, however, that sexual abuse of a child by its nearest male relatives belongs entirely to the realm of phantasy. Most analysts will have treated cases in which such events were real and could be unimpeachably established . . . (Freud, 1917, p. 370)

Psychology, psychiatry, and psychoanalysis (but not Freud) falsely generalized that all such memories of all patients were only fantasies, because it was believed incest was a rare event (e.g., J. Strachey and E. Jones as cited by Masson, 1984, p. 213). (Masson's book is in part a reaction to the widely held belief by professionals that Freud denied the reality of child sexual abuse. Interestingly enough, in every published instance cited by Masson where Freud retracts his seduction theory of hysteria, Freud mentions that some seductions are undoubtedly real.)

Therapists and researchers who worked with schizophrenics (e.g., Lidz, 1973), however, reported that the incest fantasies related by those patients more often reflected real events rather than fantasies, as did their memories of child abuse. The ugly realities of child abuse— psychological, physical, and sexual (including incest)—in our society are only now evident to most mental health professionals. It is now known, for example, that one out of six women, and perhaps one out of three, have been sexually abused (Finkelhor, 1979; Gagnon, 1965; Russell, 1983).

The fantasies of schizophrenics help to illuminate the fantasies which all people share. Psychotherapeutic work with schizophrenics (Karon & Rosberg, 1958) revealed that they often wish to be their own mother. This wish, consciously or unconsciously, may underlie many symptoms. But Kestenberg 1975), on the basis of her observation and treatment of children, reported that at the age of 2 years nearly every child goes through a stage where he or she wants to be a mother. Girls want to be a mother to a little girl, and boys want to be a mother to a little boy, so it is clear whose mother they want to be. Schizophrenics simply continue this need into adulthood.

In order to help a postpartum schizophrenic (Rosberg & Karon, 1959), it was necessary to learn (in her psychotherapy) about the fantasy that anything that filled the body was food. But Michel-Hutmacher (1955) found that normal children under 7 regularly reported that belief.

Schizophrenic patients (Karon & Rosberg, 1958; Rosberg & Karon, 1958) revealed clearly the existence of a terrifying fantasy of having the inside of their body emptied out and drained, a terror originating in early infancy and augmented or diminished by later experiences. This fantasy takes various symptomatic forms; some male patients fear being emptied or drained through the penis, which is often experienced as more frightening than castration. Thus some patients attempt to cut off their penises as the lesser evil. Knowledge of this fantasy allows the therapist to recognize the subtle evidence of it that occurs in some relatively normal men whose impotence is derived from this fear and, consequently, to help these non-schizophrenic impotent patients as well.

Common Misconceptions About Schizophrenia

What happens when a therapist talks to a schizophrenic? Usually the therapist at least feels uncomfortable, depressed, and/or angry, because the patient does not react the way the therapist wants him or her to react; the patient often does not show the therapist respect. What the therapist knows does not seem to work. But, in addition, the therapist feels scared and does not know why.

One of the reasons for these uncomfortable feelings is that these are the patient's feelings. One of the great mistakes made in evaluating schizophrenia, a mistake that even Eugen Bleuler made, is to assume, because they look as if they have no feeling, that they have no feelings. In fact, schizophrenic persons have very intense feelings, although they may mask or even deny them. The primary or most basic affect is fear, actually terror.

It is not an accident that the most illuminating discussions of negative countertransference have come from therapists who have worked with schizophrenics (e.g., Searles, 1965). Sometimes the therapist may, all too successfully, empathize with the schizophrenic patient's terror and tend to withdraw in terror just like the patient.

Human beings are not easily able to tolerate chronic, massive terror. All of the symptoms of schizophrenia may be understood as manifestations of chronic terror and defenses against the terror. The chronic terror tends to hide other feelings. Nonetheless, the schizophrenic frequently experiences, in addition to fear—whether chronically or intermittently—anger, hopelessness, loneliness, and humiliation.

If it is believed that schizophrenics have no affect, then it becomes a puzzle why the major tranquilizers and similar drugs, which are known to greatly diminish affect, should be helpful. But once the centrality of terror in schizophrenia is understood, then their utility makes sense. All the medications that are of some use to schizophrenics are drugs which, among other things, damp down the affect system and, therefore, diminish the fear. (It was a public relations coup to relabel major tranquilizers as "antipsychotic medication," implying that they are as specific and effective for psychosis as Vitamin C is for scurvy. Unfortunately, there is no "antipsychotic" medication in that sense.)

But someone living with a loss of affect has some handicaps in adjusting to life. For example, in most big cities, there are gangs of teenage hoods who prey on medicated patients who are unable to be alert and self-defensive. Patients die of the effects of multiple muggings.

Fundamentally, we do not want to know about schizophrenia because we do not want to feel terror at that intensity. All of us have the potential for schizophrenic symptoms if there is enough stress; the only differences seem to lie in the quantity and qualitative nature of the necessary stress.

The myths of the lack of meaning of schizophrenic symptoms, the irrelevance of understanding, and the incurability of schizophrenic disorders are still with us. A psychologist at a state hospital in another state consulted me about some problems in the treatment of a schizophrenic patient who had been hospitalized for 15 years. After a year of hard and insightful psychotherapeutic work by the psychologist, the patient left the hospital. The staff psychiatrist said, "I guess the medication finally took hold."

Deikman and Whitaker (1979) instituted a regimen of almost purely psychological treatment on one "experimental" ward of a psychiatric hospital. Despite dire warnings that their failure to medicate constituted malpractice, their ward program resulted in decreased need for re-hospitalization, and there were no suicides, suicide attempts, or elopements during the 11 months in which the ward was fully operative. A comparison ward that was more fully staffed and practiced expert psychopharmacology had three suicides in the same period, despite sending its more disturbed patients to a long-term state hospital. The experiment was discontinued and never imitated in spite of its success.

Among the problems with *The Diagnostic and Statistical Manual of Mental Disorders* (3rd ed.; DSM-III; American Psychiatric Association, 1980) are its rationalization of bad treatment and preservation of the myth of the incurability of schizophrenia. Thus, it states that a diagnosis of Schizophrenic Disorder, Residual Type, In Remission "should be used when an individual with a history of Schizophrenia, now is free of all signs of the illness" (American Psychiatric Association, 1980, p. 193), denying curability. Moreover, the very same symptom picture is diagnosed as "brief reactive psychosis," "schizophreniform psychosis," or "schizophrenia," solely dependent on whether the patient recovers in less than 2 weeks, more than 2 weeks but less than 6 months, or more than 6 months, irrespective of type or adequacy of treatment (American Psychiatric Association, 1980, pp. 181–193, 199–202).

In the 1950s, as Senior Clinical Psychologist at a reformatory for male adolescents, I instituted a policy of psychotherapy for all psychotic reactions. Patients had daily psychotherapy sessions without medication for 5 days before transfer to the state hospital was considered. Psychotherapy was continued at a minimum of one session per week. During a 6–month period, no state hospital transfers for reason of psychosis were necessary. The usual procedure before and after that 6–month period was to transfer psychotic patients to the state hospital; the usual length of stay in the 1950s was approximately 2 years before they were returned to the reformatory. But DSM–III makes that comparison seem irrelevant. According to DSM–III, as it were, only "brief reactive psychoses" occurred during the 6 months when psychotherapy was available, whereas before and after that period, the state hospital treated true "schizophrenics", from the same population.

Kraepelin (1907) taught the field that schizophrenia was a chronic disorder, that it might have remissions, but that the outlook was poor in the long run. But he followed only hospitalized patients. Recently, Ciompi (1980) published 40 years' follow-up data for patients in Switzerland, beginning in 1900. There are only four other studies which followed schizophrenics for more than 25 years. All five studies, summarized by Harding, Zubin, and Strauss (1987), found that 30% fully recovered in the long run, and that 60% to 70% became self-sufficient. Moreover, using DSM–III diagnoses made no difference in the long-term prognosis in Harding's study.

Harding (1988) pointed out that although many of the professionals who have encouraged patients to take their medication have been well meaning, in her study the patients who fully recovered were among the 50% who had stopped taking their medication.

There has never been a lack of treatments which do more harm than good. They have in common that they do not require understanding the human condition. In this light one can grasp why Freud, who laid the basis for most modern psychotherapy, never was awarded a Nobel prize. Instead, the Nobel prize was presented to the neurosurgeon Egas Moniz, the pioneer of prefrontal lobotomy, an operation that is now illegal in many countries and is rarely practiced in the remainder because of its destructive effects, but only after tens of thousands of brains were destroyed. Lobotomy allowed one to treat these people without having to understand them at all. It got them so they would not bother anyone.

Electric shock treatment is still practiced despite clear evidence that it too, produces brain damage (cf. Breggin, 1979; Morgan, 1991). But if a psychiatrist who has given shock treatments becomes a patient, the first thing he does is beg not to be shocked: and the more people he has shocked himself, the stronger he begs.

The predominant treatment which does not require understanding today is medication, which does reduce disturbing affect and some of its immediate consequences. Patients' behavior improves, and they become more compliant, which is sometimes very helpful because other people are almost always afraid of schizophrenics. People in general, and hospital staff in particular, tend to be cruel when they are afraid. Because cruelty makes schizophrenic people more schizophrenic, there are advantages to making schizophrenic people less frightening.

However, there are many problems with psychiatric medication. Breggin's (1983, 1990) reviews of the literature on brain-damaging effects of psychiatric medication are troubling because they suggest that the mental health system, which right now relies on medication, is creating a population of brain-damaged people. Not only are the patients given medication, but they are told they must take the medication for the rest of their lives. There are professionals who think psychotherapy with schizophrenics is finding out why they do not take their medication; but if they are good patients and take their medication, in the long run at least 40% of them are going to be demonstrably brain damaged (Breggin, 1990; Breggin, 1991, pp. 68–91).

Suddath, Christison, Torrey, Casanova, and Weinberger (1990) studied the brains of 15 pairs of monozygotic twins discordant for schizophrenia, and found brain abnormalities of unknown origin in the schizophrenic twin as compared to the non-schizophrenic twin. Although they concluded that this could not be due to the medication because the correlations of lifetime medication dosage with measures of brain damage did not reach the conventional 5% level of statistical significance, in fact the data show that they reached the 6% level; the correlations of abnormalities (e.g., enlarged ventricles) with lifetime medication dosage were as high as .50 within the schizophrenic twin sample, all of whom had been medicated; and as any statistician knows, the correlations of brain abnormalities with medication would be higher if the range of lifetime medication dosage were extended downward to zero, as none of the non-schizophrenic twins had been medicated. Examination of the data reveals that the findings of brain abnormalities in the schizophrenic twin as compared to the non-schizophrenic twin would disappear if these differences were statistically corrected for medication dosage. In other words, the simplest explanation of their findings is that the medication produced the brain abnormalities.

Enlarged ventricles result from the medication. And, the excess dopamine receptors found in the brains of schizophrenics have been demonstrated to be the result of the medications (Porceddu, Giorgi, Ongini, Mele, & Biggio, 1986; Porceddu, Ongini, & Biggio, 1985).

The only thing that is keeping us from doing more damage is that patients sometimes lie. The medication is unpleasant: Men are often made impotent by it, women often cannot enjoy sex, and the feeling of not having feelings is unpleasant. Some studies (Boczkowski, Zeichner, & DeSanto, 1985; Irwin, Weitzel, & Morgan, 1971; Willcox, Gillan, & Hare, 1965), as well as clinical experience, suggest that up to 60% of patients who are believed to be taking maintenance medication lie about it. Why patients lie when they stop taking their medication is illustrated by a patient interviewed as part of an inservice training session for psychiatric residents. When asked why he was in the hospital, he replied, "Because I stopped taking my medication."

This seemed to be a chance to teach him something useful. So the patient was told, "Now that's nonsense. Nobody would put you in the hospital because you stopped taking your medication. What happened is that you stopped taking your medication, and then you did something. The something you did upset people so much that they put you in the hospital. What did you do?" The patient did not say. Afterward, several members of the staff said that the patient had told his psychiatrist, "I stopped taking my medication," and that the patient was put in the hospital for that reason alone. The message was, "How dare you think you can make decisions about yourself (unless you lie to me)."

Medication has been so popular and so well advertised that the current generation of psychiatrists have been trained almost exclusively in treating patients by means of medications, and have neglected their training in psychotherapy. Indeed, it has been proposed that departments of psychiatry should not teach psychotherapy at all

(Black et al.,1987). Unfortunately, the medications do not live up to their advertisements: They are only partially effective, they habituate, and they have serious side effects (Breggin, 1991; Fisher & Greenberg, 1989). Thus as the disadvantages of medication are finally being learned, some psychiatrists are going back to administering shock treatments, which are more quickly and grossly brain damaging. If a psychiatrist instead changes from medicating people to practicing psychotherapy, he or she has three problems: (a) Psychotherapy is a difficult skill; (b) it requires experiencing all kinds of very unpleasant feelings; (c) and the psychiatrist's income is going to drop dramatically.

Sometimes it is argued that research shows psychotherapy is not helpful. But when the Michigan State Psychotherapy Project (Karon & VandenBos, 1981) randomly assigned schizophrenic patients to (a) an average of 70 sessions of psychoanalytic psychotherapy per patient, (b) medication, or (c) a combination of the two, blind evaluation showed that psychotherapy alone, or with initial medication that was withdrawn as the patients could tolerate it, led to earlier discharge from the hospital, kept the patients out of the hospital, and improved their thought disorders more than medication did, and the patients lived a more human life in a variety of ways. Psychotherapy with maintenance medication was better than medication alone, but not as good in the long run as psychotherapy alone or with initial medication that was withdrawn. (The experienced therapist who combined medication with psychotherapy withdrew the medication as rapidly as the patients could tolerate the withdrawal, whereas the inexperienced therapists who combined medication with psychotherapy maintained the medication.) Because of the hospitalization and particularly re-hospitalization findings, psychotherapy was less expensive in the long run, saving nearly half the usual (medication) treatment costs in a 4-year period.

Unfortunately, decision makers are not interested in saving money over 4 or more years. In that length of time there will be a different political administration, a different head of this hospital, or of this department of an insurance company. The decision makers want to save money within 6 months, or at most 1 or 2 years, and that is unfortunate.

In the Michigan study, the experienced therapists had over 10 years of experience in treating schizophrenics with psychoanalytic therapy, were knowledgeable about treating Black and lower socioeconomic patients (characteristic of most of the inner city patients in this study), and were considered effective by their colleagues. The inexperienced therapists wanted to learn how to do this kind of therapy, valued their supervisors, were paid for their time, and were given careful training and supervision.

The Michigan study is different in these respects from the most widely cited controlled studies conducted in this country (i.e., Grinspoon, Ewalt, & Shader, 1972; May, 1968). These studies found that psychotherapy was not as effective as medication. (Understandably, a drug company distributed widely free copies of May's book.) Although these studies have many methodological flaws, the most important is that they involve so-called psychotherapists and supervisors who have never treated a schizophrenic patient by psychotherapy before. They either have little training in any psychotherapy or have training in treating a different kind of patient with a different kind of therapy, like a psychoanalyst experienced only in treating upper middle class neurotic outpatients on a couch.

If the therapist does not know how to do therapy, it is true that medication works better than psychotherapy. If bicycle riding were studied the same way, using only people who had never ridden a bicycle before, it would be concluded that human beings clearly cannot ride bicycles.

Of course, there is nothing about the medical degree per se which precludes psychotherapeutic competence. Thus, Benedetti and Furlan (1987) reported from Italy and Switzerland a series of 50 severe schizophrenic cases treated with intensive psychoanalytic therapy (two to five sessions per week) for 3 to 10 years by supervisees, who were psychiatrists, with very good results in 80% of the cases. My review (Karon, 1989) of all available studies found by a computer search, found that the effectiveness of psychoanalytic therapy is supported by empirical data. In Finland, Alanen (1991) demonstrated what a real community mental health system providing psychotherapy for psychotics can do.

Psychotherapy has been discouraged by the supposed evidence from adoption studies which claimed there is a strong genetic basis for schizophrenia. However, the Danish adoption studies conducted by Kety, Wender, and Rosenthal (Kety, Rosenthal, Wender, & Schulsinger, 1968; Wender, Rosenthal, Kety, Schulsinger, & Weiner, 1974; Wender, Rosenthal, Zahn, & Kety, 1971) suffer from fatal scientific flaws and misleading reporting, as revealed in the critiques by Lidz, Blatt, and Cook (1981), by Lidz and Blatt (1983), and in the book, *Not in Our Genes*, by Lewontin, Rose, and Kamin (1984). But there is a careful, extensive adoption study from Finland, reported by Tienari (1991), which found that the most potent predictor of schizophrenia in adopted children is Communication Deviance (cf. Wynne & Singer, 1963), measured in the interaction between the adopting parents; that children of schizophrenics are more vulnerable; but that children of normals or of schizophrenics only become schizophrenic in disturbing adoptive families. No study is perfect, and this study included adoptions as late as 4 years of age. (See also Tienari et al., 1985, for an earlier preliminary report,) But the Tienari data are by far the best available.

Moreover, as M. Bleuler (1978) first reported, only 20% of the children of schizophrenics who live with their schizophrenic parents, with both genetic and environmental factors working in the same direction, ever become schizophrenic. Any adoption study with higher rates therefore must be scientifically suspect.

Clinical experience also leads one to be skeptical of genetic factors. Of course, hospital records and superficial examinations often make the disorder seem uncaused. But if one dares to listen carefully, the disorder always makes psychological sense, and seems inevitable in terms of the life as experienced.

A favorite example was provided by the residents in psychiatry at a state hospital who endured a seminar with me which made them uncomfortable because they were told that shock treatment was destructive, psychosurgery was destructive, and medication was of limited benefit. They were encouraged to talk to their patients. That was not what the rest of their supervisors told them. The residents, in reaction, asked me to interview a patient.

Most schizophrenics are not dangerous, but the residents chose someone with a history of repeatedly assaulting strange men, who himself was big, muscular, and moved very fast. I insisted that the residents sit in the same room during the interview, knowing that they had never been that close to anybody who moved that fast or was that dangerous. The patient had been hospitalized for 10 years, but there was nothing in the case records which would account for his disorder. The only apparent major stresses were that he was poor, his father was an alcoholic, he had developed a speech disorder (stutter) as an adolescent which did not respond to speech therapy, and he had reported to sick call in the army with a venereal disease, whose site was his mouth, just before his first assault on a stranger.

He was grossly incoherent and, when he became coherent, he stuttered very badly. All the residents could have done to choose a more difficult psychotherapy prospect would have been to choose someone who did not speak English at all.

In my value system, which most patients share, one deals first with homicidal danger; secondly, suicidal danger; and thirdly, anything else. This patient would creep up behind other patients and choke them. The attendants would see feet waving in the air. The patient had not killed anyone (he dropped the victim when the victim was unconscious), but the attendants were worried that he might.

Therefore, I kept bringing up this symptom during the first session. Finally, the patient and I worked out what seemed to be going on—that when the patient was a little boy, his mother, for minor offenses like not eating, would put a cloth around his neck and choke him. After that first session he stopped choking other patients. (It is a useful clinical rule of thumb that when you get a dramatic improvement in a symptom, you are probably doing the right thing.) Now this is not the kind of difficulty with which even people with difficult mothers have had to cope.

A second fact came to light in a transference reaction. The patient began a therapy hour by yelling, "Why did you do it to me, Dad?" It is not difficult to recognize a transference reaction when a schizophrenic patient calls the therapist "daddy" or "mommy."

"What did I do?"

"You know what you did!"

When asked how old he was, he said, "You know I was 8 years old." Bit by bit he revealed that "you" had come home drunk and anally raped him. This was not an ordinary alcoholic father.

The patient's terrible stutter was also revealed to have an extraordinary cause. In the middle of his stutter there were words in Latin. When asked if he had been an altar boy, he said, "You swallow a snake, and then you stutter. You mustn't let anyone know." He was extremely ashamed and guilty. Apparently, he had performed fellatio on a priest.

He was reassured that it was all right, and it was interpreted orally: "Anyone as hungry as you were would have done the same thing." (With schizophrenic patients much of what seems sexual really has to do with orality, that is, infantile feelings, survival, and the early mother-child relationship. A penis, for example, may represent a mother's breast, and the breast represents love.) At that point the stuttering stopped. When he started to stutter in later sessions, it was only necessary to repeat the interpretation, and the stuttering immediately ceased.

But look at this poor man's life. He turned to mother, and mother was terrible. If mother is terrible, one ordinarily turns to father, but his father was terrible. He turned to God, and the priest was destructive. Would not that drive anyone insane? Yet examination of 10 years of ordinary hospital records revealed no basis for his psychosis.

Of course, most parents of schizophrenics are not consciously destructive people, but often admirable people who will go to great lengths to attempt to get help for their children. Sometimes the destructive life experiences have nothing to do with the parents at all; in other instances hurtful parenting is the result of bad professional advice, or the repetition of bad parenting that they endured from their own idealized parents, or the result of unconscious defenses which are uncontrollable until brought into awareness.

Understanding The Dramatic Symptoms Of Schizophrenia

Let us consider what can be learned about the human condition from the most bizarre symptoms of schizophrenia. Take the catatonic stupor, in which the patients sit in the corner and do not move, and they are either absolutely rigid or waxily flexible. They may stay in one position for hours or for days.

Frornm-Reichmann (1950) reported a long time ago that catatonic patients see and hear everything that is going on around them, even though they do not react. They look like they are in a stupor, but they are not: They feel as if they will die if they move. Fromm-Reichmann understood this because the patients told her when they finally came out of the stupor.

Some years ago, Ratner (Ratner, Karon, VandenBos, & Denny, 1981) investigated animals in a state that used to be called animal hypnosis. If one turns an animal upside down and presses it, it becomes rigid or waxily flexible. Rabbits, lions, tigers, alligators, 70 species of birds, fish, octopuses, in fact, just about every species of animal, fish, bird, and insect tested, show this response. The animals will not move, even if great pain is inflicted. After the passage of time the animals come into rapid violent motion unpredictably, which is like human catatonic excitement.

Classical conditioning experiments, pairing two stimuli while the animals are rigid, lead to learning that can be demonstrated after the animals come out of the rigid state, so during it they must be fully conscious of external stimuli. In fact, this state is identical with the catatonic stupor.

Ratner discovered its meaning. Most animals are prey for some predator. Every species has a species-specific sequence of behaviors when it is under attack by a predator—sham death, cries of distress to warn the others in the group, and so on. The last stage seems to be this state of rigidity. Most predators, if they are not hungry, will kill their prey and save it for later. Some predators will not even attack something that does not move, but most predators will. When the animal goes into this catatonic-like state, most predators act as if they think it is dead. In an experiment with ferrets and frogs, for example, a ferret ate the eye out of one frog in this state and the frog did not flinch. The ferret crunched up the foreleg of another in its teeth, and it did not flinch either. In this experiment with ferrets and frogs, 70% of the frogs survived. According to Ratner, if even 30% survive to one mating, the effect on evolution is massive.

So the catatonic stupor is a life and species preservative strategy that is built into just about all living animals, including human beings. The biological evidence is consistent with the clinical evidence from Fromm-Reichmann, who genuinely listened to her patients. That needs to be said because there are many "experts" on schizophrenia who have never listened to any one of their patients for more than half an hour.

But we do not want to know that you and I would go catatonic if we were terrified enough, nor do we want to know what it feels like to be that terrified.

Schizophrenic patients as well as professionals like to say that nobody understands hallucinations. But hallucinations are entirely understandable by Freud's (1900, 1917, 1933) theories of dreams, with a few additions. Today, the concept of the collective unconscious seems scientifically untenable; it was based on the then-accepted biological theory of the inheritance of acquired characteristics, no longer acceptable to biologists. There is no evidence of universal symbols; there are only symbols which are used frequently with a given meaning. But there are always people who will use any symbol with an entirely different meaning.

Unlike most people, schizophrenics hallucinate while they are wide awake. Everyone hallucinates when asleep. Dreams may take any sensory modality, but the predominant experience is visual. Schizophrenics also may hallucinate in any sensory modality, but the predominant modality is auditory. Whatever other hallucinations they have, they almost always hear voices. This is different from toxic psychoses, in which the hallucinations are primarily visual. (That is why LSD research was irrelevant. LSD produces phenomena which are primarily visual, like any other toxic psychosis, but not at all like schizophrenia.)

Why predominantly auditory hallucinations? Because basically schizophrenia is an interpersonal disorder. If someone is blind, they are more physically incapacitated than someone who is deaf, but in terms of the probability of emotional disorders, deafness is more likely to cause emotional problems because it tends to cut an individual off from other people (Corbin & Eastwood, 1986; Gelder, Gath, & Mayou, 1989, pp. 457–458; Thomas, 1981).

But is the capacity to hallucinate while wide awake restricted to schizophrenics? Not at all. It is well known that starving people start seeing food. It is a human capacity if the motivation is strong enough; luckily, most of us will never be desperate enough to have to hallucinate. A trivial example illustrates the meaning of hallucinations. In the middle of a therapy session, a patient asked,

"What's that bell?"

"I didn't hear a bell."

"Well, I did."

"It may well be. There are a lot of funny noises in this building. I work here all the time and maybe, like a lighthouse keeper, I just don't pay attention to them anymore. What did the bell sound like?"

"It sounded like a telephone bell, only very loud."

"That's surprising. A telephone bell I would have heard. What comes to mind when you think of a telephone bell?"

"Trying to get through to somebody." "I think I know what's happening. I've been talking about what I thought was important, but you know I'm off somewhere; and you wish I would get through to you and talk about what is really going on here."

And then the patient smiled. She was too intimidated to tell the therapist he did not understand and ask why he was talking about irrelevancies when there were some things that were important. The most she could do was wish that somehow he would get through to her; and even that was too frightening to deal with consciously, so she had to have it come through in disguise, as an hallucination.

As mentioned earlier, attempts to understand delusions would lead to considering incest, sexual abuse of children, and physical abuse of children as serious problems in our society. What else do we not want to know?

There are four major bases for delusions. The most important source of delusions is transference (Freud, 1912): reliving feelings, fantasies, and experiences from the past with no awareness that it is the past. Of course, Freud thought schizophrenics did not form a transference; he was mistaken because he did not talk to schizophrenics. According to people who knew him, Freud said schizophrenic patients scared him. He certainly had enough work to do without schizophrenic patients, but even Freud's inferences are unlikely to be accurate unless they are based on clinical observations.

Freud originally thought of transference as a phenomenon occurring only in psychoanalysis, as the chief resistance, which by understanding he was able to transform into its most potent therapeutic tool. Ferenczi (1909/1950) first pointed out, and Freud accepted, that transference, like other resistances, was a defense used to cope in ordinary life. What was unique about transference in therapy was not its occurrence, but that it was studied.

But schizophrenics, if listened to, are not subtle in their transferences. It is not pleasant to be reminded of the varieties of misery which are inflicted on children in our society. Even more troubling than the awareness of obviously hurtful or neglectful treatment of children is the insight that parents of admirable character and with the very best of intentions may harm their children, either because their hurtful interactions are unconscious (Karon, 1960; Meyer & Karon, 1967) or because the parents are misinformed about the consequences of their actions.

A young woman alarmed the hospital staff by repeatedly cutting and burning herself. When asked about her religion, she said,

"I was raised a Catholic."

"Oh, you were raised a Catholic, but you're not now."

"Actually, I'm a Satanist."

"Why don't you tell me about it."

"I used to feel I had to save people. I had to save all the people inBeirut."

"That's a marvelous image. Beirut, that's a marvelous image. You know who the people in Beirut are, don't you?"

She started to say yes and then she said, "Well, no."

"What's Beirut? Beirut is a city where people kill each other, and then they declare peace. But when you look, they are still killing each other. Then they find out why they are killing each other, and try to deal with those problems and solve them; but they go on killing each other. Then they have a truce, but still go on killing each other. What a marvelous image—your family must have been like that."

She became very interested at that point. "Satan says that if I hurt myself, he'll keep me with him. That's what he says."

She was very scared. She described Satan's voice and his appearance. She described his face in considerable detail. When asked whether she knew anybody who looked like that, she thought and said,

"Yes; he doesn't look like it now, but he used to."

"Who?"

"My father."

Indeed, according to later information from the family, her father used to beat her mother, and her mother eventually left the house. One can understand a little girl's belief that pain is the price of not being abandoned.

That hallucination disappeared. All one had to do was to ask the patient to describe her experience, and ask what it could possibly mean.

The second source of delusions was described by Freud (1911) on the basis of insights derived from his reading of Schreber's (1903/1955) book. As is widely cited, Freud derived many paranoid delusions from the fear of homosexuality, viewing them as different ways of contradicting the implicit guilt-producing feeling (for a man), "I love him." Thus, (a) I do not love him, I love me—megalomania; (b) I do not love him, I love her—erotomania; (c) I do not love him (using projection), she loves him—delusional jealousy; (d) I do not love him (using projection), he loves me—the delusional threat of being endangered by homosexuals; (e) I do not love him (using reaction formation), I hate him—irrational hatred; or, most common, (f) I do not love him (using reaction formation), I hate him, but I cannot hate him for no reason, so (using projection) he hates me, which is why I hate him, and if I hate him, obviously I do not love him—delusional feelings of persecution.

However, secondary sources almost never mention one part of Freud's insight that is most meaningful and essential for therapeutic effectiveness. In the language of libido theory, Freud (1911, p. 70) said that the patient with schizophrenia feels withdrawn from emotional relatedness to everybody. Consequently (again in the case of a man), he wants to be able to relate to someone again. In addition to the hunger for approval from the father, people of the same sex are more like us than are those of the opposite sex, and, in growing up, it is usual to feel comfortable in relating closely to peers of the same sex before becoming comfortable with the opposite sex. When one feels withdrawn from everybody, there is a strong urge to get close to people of the same sex. Unfortunately, the patient fearfully interprets this self-curative tendency as "homosexuality."

But is the schizophrenic different from the normal adolescent who is having trouble with the opposite sex? Time spent with friends of the same sex leads to becoming more comfortable both with them and with the opposite sex. This is the normal developmental sequence. With normals and neurotics, too, the fear of homosexuality can lead to withdrawing from friends of the same sex, and that makes relating to the other sex even more difficult. Hence, the generally useful advice for adolescents (or adults) having trouble with the opposite sex is to spend more time with same sex friends, instead of withdrawing from them.

Even the specific dynamics of paranoid feelings as defenses are mirrored in the dynamics of some similar feelings in people who are not schizophrenics.

It is usually helpful to let schizophrenic patients with symptoms based on the fear of homosexuality know that their fear of being homosexual is unfounded (if, as is usually the case, it is unfounded), that they are simply lonely, that their loneliness is normal, and that we all need friends of both sexes. Unless they have had a meaningful and benign homosexual relationship, schizophrenics are not helped by reassurances concerning the increased acceptability of homosexuality, but they always feel understood when their therapist talks of loneliness.

Of course, Freud's views on paranoid delusions have been criticized, fairly and unfairly. The fair criticism is that they account for only some delusions, not all. The unfair criticism is that persecutors in the delusions of women are usually men. But the first to point out this apparent contradiction was Freud (1915) who noted that when a woman is first psychotic, the persecutor is female, and is changed to a male persecutor as a later development of the delusion, illustrating the general human condition that feelings about men are not necessarily based on experiences with men, nor are feelings about women necessarily based on experiences with women.

The third basis for delusions is that some families actually teach strange ideas. The study of schizophrenic patients (Lidz, 1973) revealed how human beings depend on their families to teach them the categories of thought and the meaning of those categories. Children (and adults) assume that other people use concepts in the same way that they do, unless confronted with understandable contradictions. For example, if a person believes that "I love you" includes in its meaning "I hurt you, physically assault you, occasionally even try to kill you," that person is unlikely ever to be able to relate closely to another in a loving relationship. It has been noted (Lidz, 1973; Searles, 1965) that families with disturbed children have a tendency to discourage the use of people outside the family as sources of information and corrective identification. Patients from very disturbed families who do not become schizophrenic are inevitably found to have remedied the defects in their nuclear families with relationships outside that nuclear family. This is a normal mechanism. Nobody ever had a perfect mother or father, nor can parents provide every kind of nurturance needed. Most children, as well as adults, use people outside the family to correct any problems in their family.

When parents interfere with this mechanism, any problem in the family is enormously magnified in its destructive impact. The parents, of course, do not do this to be hurtful; they are unaware that it has any harmful consequences. Indeed, they may even believe that it is good for the child.

Parents who discourage extra familial identifications are spared the normal discomfort of having their values and beliefs challenged by their children. But these challenges, whether or not communicated overtly, partially shield the child from the impact of the inevitable parental mistakes.

The last basis for delusions is the general human need for a more or less systematic explanation of our world. Most people share similar systematic understandings. One who believes the world is flat is normal if the year is 1400, and is suspect if the year is 1992. The belief is the same; it is the relationship to others' beliefs that makes it normal or suspect. Schizophrenic people have had strange experiences. In part, their symptoms are strange experiences by ordinary standards. In addition, their lives often include unusual real events. Therefore, their systematic explanations of their world seem strange. But they demonstrate a need to be as realistic as their anxieties permit. Insofar as discrepancies between their understanding and reality become apparent to them, and as dynamic balances change, the patients continually revise their understanding.

The more intelligent patients are more apt to develop a systematic understanding that is adequate enough to obviate the need for more deteriorated symptoms and, hence, to be diagnosed as paranoid or paranoid schizophrenic. The less intelligent are less likely to develop as functionally adequate a "paranoid system."

Because the paranoid system is not an abnormal process, but a normal process used to cope with unusual problems, it is possible for a non-frightened, non-humiliating therapist to share the patient's systematic understanding, to respectfully call attention to inconsistencies, and to helpfully supplement the patient's understanding with the therapist's knowledge of the world, of other people and, more importantly, of the workings of the human mind.

The best description of what it feels like to be schizophrenic came from a catatonic man whom it took 8 weeks of psychotherapy (without medication) to get out of the hospital and back to work. One of his symptoms was bowing. When asked why he bowed, he said,

"I don't bow."

"Yes, you do."

"No, I don't bow."

"Wait a minute. You do this [the therapist bowed]. This is bowing; you bow."

"No, I don't bow."

"But you do this."

"That's not bowing."

"What is it?"

"It's balancing."

"What are you balancing?"

"Emotions."

"What emotions?"

"Fear and loneliness."

That is, when he was lonely, he wanted to get close to people (so he leaned forward). When he got close to people, he got scared and had to pull away (so he straightened up). But then he was lonely again.

Balancing between fear and loneliness is the best description of what it feels like to be schizophrenic. But that is what the rest of us do not want to understand.

ACKNOWLEDGMENTS

This article was delivered as the Presidential address, Division of Psychoanalysis (Division 39), American Psychological Association, on August 15, 1991, San Francisco.

I thank Drs. Leighton C. Whitaker and Gary R. VandenBos, both of whom have influenced the content of this article, and Anmarie Widener for editorial assistance.

CHAPTER 3
Psychotherapeutic Technique and the Economically Poor Patient

Bertram P. Karon & Gary R. Vandenbos

Abstract

Psychotherapy with the poor patient is no different from good psychotherapy with anyone. The intertwining of reality and psychodynamics must be dealt with in all its complexity. But reality problems elicit prototypic counter-transferences. The therapist from lower class origins may perceive the patient as his bad self, himself as failure. The upper class therapist may avoid guilt over never facing such difficulties, or idealize poverty. Such problems need to be dealt with consciously.

Therapy can fail because the patient is awed and does not want to reveal his own "inadequacy" or "criticize" the authority by saying that he does not understand the therapist or that the therapist does not understand him. Failure in treating schizophrenics is as often a function of their socio-economic status as of their pathology.

The therapist must also educate the patient as to what therapy is all about, and why it should be helpful. When appropriate, crisis intervention, or repeated crisis intervention, can be as effective as continuous therapy.

Whether to help the patient adapt to being lower class or to escape, is ideology, not therapy. The therapist must help the patient evaluate the alternatives in the light of his reality and psychodynamics, and then to act.

The therapist must learn to be a therapist: to know about psychopathology, dynamics, therapeutic technique, be motivated to be helpful, effectively use supervision, and have the continuing need to learn about his patients and himself as an integral part of his professional way of life.

Psychotherapists are typically far from excited at the prospect of working with the economically poor patient. It is often assumed that the economically poor are not (and cannot be) psychologically-minded, that reality problems preclude dynamic psychotherapy, and that poor patients cannot understand what psychotherapy is about.

That is not our experience. The above assumptions are only true when the patients are inappropriately treated by therapists uninformed about poor patients. To treat poor patients effectively in psychotherapy, therapists need to know about the special difficulties (resistances and counter-transferences) to be encountered in doing such treatment with poor patients and how to deal with these special difficulties.

In what ways are poor patients different? In brief, they are poor; reality problems are greater. We are not using the word "poor" to mean temporary financial distress. Primarily, we mean people who have been poor all their lives, whose parents were poor, and who have a high probability of remaining poor. It is thus a social as well as an economic condition. This definition of "poor" does not have sharp boundaries, but includes the unemployed, partially employed, and the lower income members of the working class.

Poor patients tend to be less educated, hence less verbally fluent and less knowledgeable about many matters, including what real psychotherapy is about. They are more likely to be accustomed to being treated authoritarianly, both in childhood and adult life. Hence, they tend to be more compliant, but also more distrustful and resentful of authorities, including so-called helping professionals. Either they do not freely voice their complaints or questions, or they tend to voice them in a way that gets both the patient and his complaints rejected.

In what ways are the therapist's reactions to poor patients different? In brief, the therapist tends to be more pessimistic, less interested, more fearful of the time commitment involved, more apprehensive about over-dependency, and find it harder to identify with the patient; hence, they tend to believe the patients to be not psychologically-minded, nor capable of being psychologically-minded, or to be in a situation where increased insight would be of no value.

Ordinarily, if the therapist is attentive and reflective, the experience of doing therapy is a process which teaches him whatever he does not already know that he needs to know to be helpful, especially if the patient is unusual or difficult. This feedback process may not happen in psychotherapy with poor patients because the special communication problems may prevent it, and even prevent the therapist from being aware that there is a communication problem. In fact, the problem of communication with the poor patient is so central that the failure of the therapist to appreciate this difficulty may by itself account for negative treatment results.

All of these problems in treating the poor patient in psychotherapy and the consequent appropriate procedures to overcome them will be discussed more fully below.

Background

Even such otherwise sophisticated authors as Hollingshead and Redlich (1954) are doubtful that psychotherapy is of much value for poor patients. Nor are they alone. It is reported that such patients are less likely to be referred for psychotherapy (Kahn, Pollack, & Fink, 1957; Galagher, Sharaf, & Levinson, 1965), less likely to be accepted for psychotherapy if referred (Rosenthal & Frank, 1958; Cole, Branch, & Allison, 1962), more likely to be seen as uninteresting, and hence referred to the least trained and least experienced member of the staff (Schaffer & Myers, 1954; Carlson, Coleman, Errera, & Harrison, 1965). Hence, it is not surprising they are reported more likely to reject psychotherapy or to terminate prematurely (Rubenstein & Lorr, 1956; Yamamoto & Goin, 1966).

On the other hand, if such patients are offered treatment in a manner that allows them to see its value, they are reported to benefit (Frank, Gliedman, Imber, Nash, & Stone, 1957; Goin, Yamamoto, & Silverman, 1965; Gould, 1967; Riessman & Scribner, 1965; Jones, 1974; Lorion, 1973, 1974). Therapists, considered better by their supervisors, (Terstman, Miller & Weber, 1974) and therapists with personal therapy (Baum, Felzer, D'Zmura, & Schumaker, 1966; Siassi, 1974) are reported as more successful with poor patients, suggesting that the factors which affect treatment with the poor are the same as those which affect treatment with anyone.

Therapists are cited as reporting that such patients are hard to empathize with, do not permit appropriate therapeutic procedure, insist on exclusively symptom relief, use "unbearably" crude language, engage in sexual and aggressive behavior of which the staff disapproves, and are apparently apathetic with regard to treatment (e.g. Auld & Myers, 1954; Brill and Storrow, 1960).

However, these and similar difficulties seem to be problems of therapist attitude or lack of understanding rather than patient treatability. Thus, for example, Baum & Felzer (1964) reported that lower socio-economic class patients remained in therapy more often following the introduction of staff briefings about the life style, needs, and expectations of such patients, and the continued discussion of these issues in supervision as related to specific cases.

Thus, it seems that the basic problem is the therapist: his emotional reactions, his lack of understanding, and his assumption that if something is going wrong, it must be the patient's fault rather than there is something to be learned.

Economically poor patients have been found not to understand what therapy is about (Heine & Trasman, 1960; Overall & Aronson, 1964) and attempts outside of therapy and before therapy at altering the patient's expectations (Strupp & Bloxom, 1973; Hoehn-Saric, Frank, Imber, Nash, Stone, & Battle, 1964; Orne & Wender, 1968) have proved useful. However, such procedures, while they demonstrate that poor patients are not unworkable, are cumbersome. Moreover they are often perceived by patients as another roadblock to wear them out. Remember, lower class patients do not believe that the purpose of elaborate procedures is to give them anything; all too often in their lives they have found the purpose of elaborate procedures was, in fact, to wear them out, and, when they have persisted, they were provided little or nothing in the end.

There are two important drawbacks to the practical application of this research. The patient is more likely to respond and take seriously individual attention from a concerned human being than from an impersonal procedure. Thus, it is better for the therapist to do the educating of the patient continuously and as a part of the psychotherapy process. Moreover, separate "pre-training" procedures continue to deflect the therapist from thinking about his own contribution to the impasse.

Socio-Economic Counter-Transference Fantasies

If defenses, motivations, or inhibitions central to the therapist's felt integration are threatened by working with a particular patient, the patient will not be treated (and, most typically, the "fault" will be viewed as lying in the patient). Thus, when working with unusual or difficult patients of any sort, it is important to consider one's own psychological needs as they relate to attempting to treat such patients. There are some common counter-transference difficulties in working with poor patients which can be described.

There are, after all, only therapists who come from two kinds of backgrounds: those from lower class backgrounds who were socially upwardly mobile, and those who came from at least upper-middle class backgrounds. Each have difficulty working with poor patients. Obviously, there are no therapists from lower class environments who were comfortable there.

The upwardly mobile therapist has escaped by means of education, impulse control, and hard work. The therapist's need to maintain his view of how awful his life would have been had he not escaped (in order to justify to himself the hard work and sacrifice that went into upward mobility) may interfere with doing psychotherapy with poor patients. In a sense, the patient may acquire the unconscious meaning of the therapist's "bad self," that is the therapist who was lazy, self-indulgent, and unsuccessful. (Of course, such impulses are common to everyone). The projection of the therapist's rejected impulses can lead to an exaggerated view of the patient's weaknesses. The patient has not escaped, and usually cannot escape by

the same techniques that the therapist did. The therapist cannot conceive of either living without escape, or of other ways of escaping.

The therapist from an upper-middle class background frequently cannot conceive of how one can live in the manner and circumstances of the poor patient. The inequity between the therapist's life and the patient's life is dramatically apparent. This therapist may also feel guilty, about the suffering he has never experienced. Or, he may feel inadequate at the thought that he could not cope if he had to live under such conditions. To relieve his guilt or inadequacy he may seize on behavioral characteristics of the poor patient which "justify" or explain the inequity. In a sense, the patient may acquire the unconscious meaning of this therapist's "bad self," too, that is, the therapist as exploiter or as inadequate victim, immoral, and without social conscience. (Of course, these impulses are also common to everyone). The projection of the therapist's rejected impulses may lead to an exaggerated view of the "badness" of the patient's behavior.

The therapist may fail to see these patient traits as either results of or as attempts at adjustment to the patient's environment. The therapist may not conceive of the possible, even necessary, function in a different milieu of behavior which would be maladaptive or in-comprehensibly "bad" in the therapist's own milieu.

There is a less frequent reaction to the poor patient which may occur for therapists of any socio-economic background, that is to "romanticize" the poor patient. For example, the freer expression of aggression (adaptive or neurotic) permitted the poor patient may lead to the therapist subtly supporting such behavior, without evaluating it in terms of the real consequences for the patient. Such inappropriate therapeutic involvement with the patient's aggressive behaviors is a defense not only against the rage the therapist himself would feel if he lived in such circumstances, but is also a displacement of rage from his own emotionally and/or economically unsatisfying childhood circumstances. By "romanticizing" the poor, the therapist may feel that "they" are compensated for the inequities of life, or may express his unconscious idealization of the child vs. the parent (the rich one in the family).

But, even the well-intended therapist may romanticize the poor out of respect for the patient's individuality or cultural heritage. The therapist may ponder such questions as what the goal of therapy should be with poor patients to provide new values, to motivate them, to develop new behavior patterns, to make them "happy poor," or to make them "non-poor." But such questions "look in the wrong place." A resolution in favor of one simple alternative or another is for the most part defensive rationalization. The questions assume the therapist makes the decision for the patient or tells the patient how to behave or what to choose.

Real therapy consists of making the alternatives thinkable, and choice as rational as possible in the light of both personal wants and social demands, always with the understanding that one's choices may be different as one's wants, social circumstances, and accidental external circumstances change. The solution as in any therapy, is to emphasize realistic consequences for the patient, evaluated from the patient's point of view, given the added knowledge of the therapist and the therapeutic dissolution of neurotic and psychotic distortions of reality. Not to raise a possibility for benign change to the patient is never a service; the patient in real therapy is always free to reject what does not make sense nor seem useful. Whatever its reasons, "romanticizing" can lead to discouraging or not encouraging changes that would improve the patient's life, including change in socio-economic status. These "romanticizations" are just other ways of not empathizing with the patient, and are no different from the counter-transference difficulties to be dealt with in any psychotherapy.

It is understandably painful for therapists to empathize with poor patients living under circumstances the therapist would not willingly (and perhaps could not) endure. The easiest way to avoid such painful fantasies is to not accept such patients, to unconsciously maneuver the patient into dropping out of treatment, or to not do real therapy but only aid with a misery-abatement plan or escape plan (i.e., only deal with "reality problems.")

Like all fantasies of the therapist, the fantasies about the poor patient described above do not interfere with treatment if they are conscious and attended to in staff meetings, supervision, and training, rather than unconscious and acted out or defended against by pseudo-therapeutic maneuvers.

Length Of Treatment And Dependency

However, the reluctance to closely examine the physical and psychological realities of the poor patient's life, based on such unexamined counter-transferences, is not what therapists talk about when voicing their reservations about working with poor patients. Usually therapists mention their concerns about the length of treatment and/or dependency. Two views are commonly stated: either the poor patient will require such inordinate expenditures of time as to make therapy unfeasible and/or will expect the therapist to do everything, or the poor patient won't stay long enough to make any difference and/or will not allow the therapist to do anything. Paradoxically, both convictions are frequently voiced by the same therapists on different occasions.

However, problems of over-dependency or counter-phobic independence and overly long treatment or overly brief treatment are not really different with poor patients than with any other patient. The poor patient is more likely to appear more extremely compliant or non-compliant, than other patients, reflecting his feelings of having less power with respect to authority figures. These behaviors are not necessarily unsatisfiable over-dependence or unmanageable resistance. Poor patients' demands and resistances often enrage and/or frighten prospective therapists. Therapists need to know how to understand the seemingly more extreme reactions of poor patients and how to respond to them.

Some poor patients do seem to expect or even demand perpetual treatment, which may not be indicated, and is unfeasible in any agency. Such patients are demanding from a therapist the all-pervading acceptance and care that they feel vaguely entitled to and deprived of, but which is too threatening to consciously connect with their childhood and family, particularly mother. It is less threatening to demand it from and be angry at a "non-giving" therapist. It also may have the function of proving (unconsciously) that the patient's parent was not defective, since the patient's demands are so excessive no one, including the therapist, can meet them. When described, it is obvious that these same problems occur in other patients but they are not acted out so intensely.

Client Attraction and Distress

It is the therapist's task to help the patient become aware of this by sharing the therapist's understanding with him; of course, the interpretation should be made in a way that the patient can utilize—it must be understandable and sufficiently tactful that it cannot be misinterpreted as an accusation.

However, agencies often reinforce the staffs' displacement of concern about time and dependency by arbitrary rules imposing rigid procedures for ultra-brief "therapy" (not even meaningful crisis intervention) or simple-minded and single-minded behavioral goals that make little sense from the perspective of the patient's well being or from the nature of psychotherapy and of symptoms. It is, of course, well known that the presenting symptom is usually the last straw that pushed the patient into seeking help, not the sole or even the most important symptom. The poor patient is more likely to either accept such an arbitrary definition of his problem without overtly raising his objections, or else leave without explanation.

The relationships between time and psychotherapy are complex. However, one relationship is very simple. If an agency is only open from 8-5, poor patients won't be able to use it, unless they are unemployed or too disturbed to work.

Poor patients can frequently be helped by crisis intervention or brief psychotherapy. Indeed, they may accept only crisis intervention, because from their perspective psychotherapy seems like a luxury unless one is overwhelmed. However, patients in crisis truly make good use of therapeutic time because of their high level of motivation for change and understanding during the crisis. It has become increasingly obvious that, for patients of any socioeconomic class, crisis intervention can be of real and lasting value (if appropriately carried out). Mann (1973) has written an excellent book on the technique of such short-term psychotherapy.

Surprisingly enough, we have found repeated crisis intervention can be as effective as continuous psychotherapy for patients who will accept help only on such a basis (Karon & VandenBos, 1972). Since this is not well known, when the economically poor patient chooses not to continue treatment, even an effective therapist may inappropriately feel ineffective, as well as rejected. If the patient reappears with a new crisis, or several repeated crises for intervention at irregular intervals, the therapist may inappropriately conclude this proves his interventions were certainly useless.

Nonetheless, just because the patients may request short term treatment does not mean that they are inappropriate for long-term treatment or will necessarily reject it once the therapist has explained why he makes such a recommendation. Poor patients are often psychologically-minded and are eager to talk once they know you are interested and that there is something they can gain by talking.

Authority And Communication

Economically poor patients have special difficulty in dealing with psychotherapists. They are intimidated by us, just as they are by all doctors and indeed, all authority figures, and this leads to and perpetuates a problem in communication. As we said before, this is so serious a difficulty that psychotherapy will fail if it is not dealt with directly. All therapists use a language with which poor patients are not familiar, in part because of our own socio-economic class, education, and broader knowledge of the world, but even more because of our technical training. The patients may also use a language (of their ethnic, socio-economic, and geographic group) with which we are not familiar. Any such language barrier not only prevents both parties from giving or understanding meaningful information; it may even prevent us from asking meaningful questions.

What makes this communication problem more important with the lower-class patient is that he is more intimidated by us. He feels that if he does not understand us, or we do not understand him, he is at fault. Unfortunately, most human beings try to hide their inadequacies. He feels inadequate and does not want to reveal this inadequacy by telling us we did not understand him or asking us what we meant. The feeling that one should not ask if one does not know what is going on, or correct an authority's misunderstanding of one, is obviously a transference problem, as well as a reality problem.

It is well known that lower-class parents are apt to stress unquestioning obedience more than middle-class parents. Parents do get angry and act as if the child is defective. Unfortunately, most authority figures (e.g., teachers, police officers, employers, etc.) in later life act similarly, and this transference reaction is so convenient for the authority figures that it will be encouraged. It may be comfortable, unconsciously gratifying to us, and in some ways even useful, to be a frightening authority figure. But it is not only inappropriate, it is incompatible with psychotherapy except when it is discussed as a resistance.

Poor people do have a realistic basis for distrusting authorities. Frequently in the patient's lives, authorities have acted in the best interest of some system, institution, or person other than the patient while claiming to be acting in the patient's best interest. Authorities do use information furnished by the patient against their best interests. For example, parole and probation officers may use information inadvertently revealed to convict clients of parole violations. Social agencies may make information available to collection agencies. Social agencies, schools, and hospitals may use information given with a supposition of trust to deny the client privileges, services, and financial support.

Thus, poor patients in one big city psychiatric hospital believed that if one had been a previous admission to that or any other psychiatric hospital, or had an alcohol or drug problem, one would not be given careful consideration for first-rate treatment (which in this case meant psychotherapy). They were right. They characteristically lied about these matters; if they trusted the hospital and did not lie, they were obviously punished by not being given treatment.

A way of dealing with the communication problem is to simply and straightforwardly tell the patient that sometimes we talk in ways that are "funny" and hard to understand and that, in addition, we have difficulty understanding people. We tell the patient he must help us by telling us when he doesn't understand, and we will try to tell him when we can't understand him. We let him know that people frequently think they understand each other or are being understood, when they aren't. We make it clear that in psychotherapy it is important to be sure that we know what each of us is talking about.

The therapist makes it clear that he expects and, in fact, desires questions, thereby making the contrast with the parents and other authority figures more apparent and facilitating the discussion of previous experiences in communicating with authority figures. Of course, the patient will still transfer and still believe such things as "I would have been told if I was supposed to know," or that to ask for information implies a criticism of the therapist (which will be resented), or that his asking will be viewed (and condemned) as presumptuous. But a clear statement early in therapy (and repeated) provides an opening wedge for the therapeutic work.

Another issue which must be directly addressed is trust/mistrust of the therapist, particularly since other authorities may not have been trustworthy. We specifically tell patients they don't have to believe anything we say; in fact, there is no reason why they should. We invite them to do what they will do anyway, distrust us; but, we encourage them to check us out. We might say "Nothing is true just because I say it. Check me out. I personally distrust anyone who says never doubt me. If they are telling the truth, they can stand being doubted. And I can stand being doubted."

Understanding us involves more than just a problem of language; we do have a set of concepts which justify our therapeutic procedures. The patient needs to know what we are doing and why, if he is to be a working participant in the therapy. Lower-class patients generally have little idea what to expect and no idea at all why cooperating with psychotherapy should be helpful.

Why should talking be of help? What does the therapist have to offer other than advice? (Implicit in the patient's views are that if they are good people they should not need advice, and that their options are limited all too often to unquestioned acceptance or secretive rejection). Even more fundamental is conveying to the patient the knowledge that his specific symptoms are such that psychotherapy might be of use to him. Indeed, even the fact that his problems might be symptoms that could be helped rather than simply facts of existence is important and even startling information.

Sometimes, of course, the symptoms are such that they might be psychogenic, but we cannot be sure even after appropriate diagnostic procedures. Then, as with any patient, one is direct and says that the symptom may or may not be psychogenic, but a trial period of therapy is the best way to find out.

As long as the patient believes that what he experiences is a fact of life, there is no hope and no motivation for change. Hence, we explain psychological functioning and the therapeutic process.

Educative Comments

This does not mean we give an extended lecture. What one explains and when is always governed by what you think is relevant. Assuming one is practicing a psychoanalytic therapy, the patient needs to be educated about the unconscious, repression, resistance, transference, free association, dreams, and any procedures with which you expect the patient to cooperate. A few sentences at a time, as it becomes relevant, we teach the patient what therapy and psychological functioning are all about. We do this, as we do all therapy, using bits of their thoughts or behavior, to as vividly as possible convey our meaning to aid them in understanding themselves concretely, and to demonstrate dramatically psychological principles.

It may be helpful to share some of the specific comments we might make to patients. When it becomes relevant to some specific behavior, or ideation, we have said such things as:

a) "You know, we can't fight an enemy we can't see. If we see it, it may scare us; but, we can handle it, particularly since you don't have to handle it alone. You have me on your side." "There's a part of the mind we know nothing about that nonetheless pushes us around and causes problems, and we don't know why. Down there are all the memories, conflicts, and feelings that were too scary, or guilt-provoking, or made us too angry, or that we couldn't handle. It's sort of like a sewer, and we put things there that stink too much, that we can't or don't want to see or handle. We all do it. And that's OK, if it works. But when we do things we don't want to do and can't stop, it usually involves something from the unconscious, and we have to find out what."

b) "What's in the unconscious is there for a reason—you couldn't handle it any other way at the time. Now things may be different, but the unconscious doesn't know. What is unconscious doesn't change. When it is conscious, you can change it, if you want to."

"Everybody in treatment starts doing things to get in the way of learning more about themselves, even though they want to learn. Even consciously we may find ourselves not wanting to find out. But unconsciously we all don't want to find out. That's why we shoved it in the unconscious to begin with. But, if we deal with the difficulties at looking at ourselves, we will always be dealing with the right thing. What makes it difficult to talk about things here, makes it difficult to think about them when you're away from here."

"Sometimes you're going to be angry at me, and to think I'm rotten, mean, and out to hurt you, and sometimes you're going to think I'm a lot better than I really am. Whatever you feel about me is important to our work, and you will find talking about it will help you learn about your life. Let me assure you I can take it, and I will only use it to help you understand what is going on. You and I can talk about anything. It's an essential part of what's going on here."

There is nothing special about these words. What is special is that the therapist talks to the patient in a way that is both factually correct and is as likely as possible to be understood. What we are emphasizing is that one of our goals in the early sessions of psychotherapy is to teach the patient about the process of therapy. This education is not the only goal nor even the most central goal. But patients, particularly poor patients, need to have a rationale for understanding themselves and treatment if they are to be motivated to stay in treatment and if they are to be "partners" in treatment rather than weak, submissive recipients of advice. It should be obvious by this time that we do not assume the patient will necessarily believe the first or even the tenth time we say anything, but a basis for examining the discrepancies has been laid.

Differentiating Reality and Psychological Problems

When an economically poor patient discusses a "reality" problem, it often happens that the therapist either responds to it as solely a reality problem or solely a psychological problem. Neither is optimally helpful, because neither one is truly realistic! One of the tasks of a therapist is to deal with the intertwining of reality problems and psychological problems, a clinical skill seldom discussed in graduate school or medical school.

Indeed, reality problems are often taken to be a counter-indication for psychotherapy. Yet when Freud was asked whether he would treat someone whose reality situation was so bad that neurosis might be considered the best solution, his judgment was that he would still analyze the patient: "It is better to go down in a fair fight with destiny than to be a neurotic." It is our experience in the psychotherapy of the poor that the patient does not go down.

The therapist must be, first of all, that dependable person who is reliable no matter what difficulties the patient encounters or arranges in life, and who expects and accepts anxiety, rage, and any other feelings. But the therapist is also someone whose gaze is firmly fixed on reality, insofar as it is known to him. In other words, the task of the therapist is to accept and talk about any feelings or thoughts whatsoever, but also to help the patient clearly evaluate actions in the light of reality, that is, the consequences of his own action.

Of course, the therapist must also introduce the possibility of psychodynamic factors. With the acceptance of the patient's realistic and unrealistic feelings and the acceptance of the reality factors in the patient's problems, whatever discrepancies exist between "reality" and the patient's reaction tend to become clear, and the transference (or other psychodynamic) basis of the discrepancies can then be dealt with in a context that makes sense to the patient.

In any event, the therapist should direct the patient's attention to and review in therapy the events that actually occurred. It is important to convey to the patient the attitude of always starting with the relevant information that one's own experience provides, and to encourage gathering relevant information (i.e., asking questions about what will happen and why). By "gathering relevant information" we mean focusing the patient's attention on his and others' behavior. Exploration of the patient's feelings and fantasies are obviously important, but we do not let it obscure the first task of getting the facts of what actually happened. This approach stands in contrast to merely discussing the patient's interpretations and abstractions without checking against whatever information or observations might be available to both the patient and therapist.

Consider, for example, the poor patient who presents in psychotherapy his difficulties in dealing with the welfare department. What are the reality and psychodynamic aspects of the dilemma?

First of all, one needs to appreciate the realistic anxiety and anger resulting from such extraordinary dependence on a bureaucratic agency. Often, what seems to the agency to be a minor delay may mean the difference between real suffering and its alleviation. In addition, the poor patient has little knowledge of the internal functioning of the agency: what needs to happen, why, how long it should take, and what is likely to go wrong in the process.

The patient's handling of the current reality situation may be complicated by the patient's reservoir of anger based on a lifetime of varied frustrations. From his experiences in his family, the patient expects that anyone he depends on will frustrate him, that expressing his frustrations or anger will only lead to more frustration, and that questions will only elicit anger and rejection.

The therapist should share whatever specific knowledge he has of the agency with which the patient is having difficulty. If the therapist does not know the specific agency, he does at least know agencies in general and can convey a sense of what the process may be about and why it is progressing as it is. The therapist should encourage the patient to ask relevant questions of the agency personnel. Only by direction of the patient's attention to what he knows (and to a lesser extent, what the therapist knows) can you make the patient aware of the critical difference between the events and his interpretation of them.

Of course, at first the patient will simply be aware that the discrepancy is between his interpretations of events and yours. Eventually he will learn that your interpretations of events and causal sequences lead to more predictable and/or more satisfactory consequences. He may account for this discrepancy by attributing it to your being a better person. But, with your continued focus on the descriptions of actual events, gathering and seriously considering relevant information, and considering the possibility of transference or other psychological distortions, the patient will eventually learn that such a way of approaching and understanding events leads to more realistic consequences. The therapist must help the patient learn what constitutes relevant or irrelevant information in any particular situation, and, of course, begin the central, difficult, but most helpful process of sorting out the reality and transference elements in current difficulties. (Indeed, one could readily argue that that is in essence what psychotherapy is all about).

Often the patient's experience, even with the added experience of the therapist, is not sufficient to permit an immediate understanding and solution. The therapist must teach the attitude of being able to tolerate not knowing. The patient needs to learn to live with uncertainty rather than leaping to premature closure and that, in most instances, further observation of one's experience will eventually clarify what is going on.

There are many areas of living that the patient knows far better than the therapist. It is not the therapist's task to teach the patient everything he needs to know to live. Only a fool would presume to tell the patient how to deal with situations remote from the therapist's experience. The therapist helps the patient take his own judgment seriously, act on it, and learn from his action, especially his mistakes.

For example, when a poor patient says "I fight too much," the middle-class therapist is apt to advise the patient to talk out any personal difficulties and to apply that to all situations. But, in some situations, it is appropriate to fight, and it is the proper role of the therapist to help the patient use his own feelings, judgments, and coping abilities and to consider whether a given situation could be dealt with differently.

The therapeutic task in this example is to help the patient to assess his unique situation. It may be that he is provoking fights when they are not in his best interest or that he is always looking for a challenge; then one would help him to explore the psychological reasons for this aspect of his behavior. But there are many times when the fighting is important, and the task of therapy is to help the patient to more accurately assess when he should fight and when he might wish to consider alternative ways of handling the situation. The therapeutic task is to help the patient be aware of the complex feelings that are involved, including fear, the role his fighting plays in handling and/or provoking internal stress, and its relationship to his past.

In general, even when a patient has an appropriate coping strategy, he may feel it is inappropriate. It is important for him to learn that it is his guilt, feelings of inadequacy, or anxiety which is inappropriate rather than his coping strategy or understanding in such cases. (Usually there is someone in the patient's current life whose inappropriate negative judgment the patient is accepting on a transference basis). Of course, it is important to learn that inappropriate strategies are inappropriate. However, therapists sometimes act as if only the latter task is important and ignore the former.

To take a dramatic example, consider the patient who says someone is going to kill them. One first directs the patient's attention to relevant information: Who wants to kill them? Why? Has there been any threat? Does the dangerous person own a gun? Has the supposed murderer ever killed or seriously injured anyone?

In some instances, the fear is realistic. A male delinquent talks about an ex-friend he has beaten severely in a quarrel over a girl; the ex-friend has made threats, carries a gun, and has physically injured people in the past. The patient's strategy of avoiding that city is not phobic.

In other instances, the fear is not realistic. A gas station attendant has short-changed a patient five cents, and the patient is afraid to ask for the change. "He'll murder me. He nearly did anyway." The patient needs to know murder was not at hand and is highly improbable under the circumstances. But the projection of her rage and the transference of her parents (who had actually made murder attempts on each other and her) must be dealt with, because this feeling of being in danger of being murdered by a stranger over trivia can be guaranteed to recur, unless it is dealt with therapeutically. The patient will agree to discuss it, because this fear has recurred and/or will recur inevitably. Moreover, the therapist is well advised to deal with it before it is re-experienced as the stranger called "therapist" who is the assassin.

In still other instances the fear is unrealistic, but is a disguised representation of a realistic fear, handled unrealistically. Take the case of the patient whose husband does not have a gun, has not made a threat, and has never been violent, but the patient "knows" that he is going to kill her. It seemed likely that the husband was thinking of leaving her ("getting rid of her,") which he had not directly said. Upon investigation, this turned out to be the case. She was dealing with this reality issue of separation psychotically as "he's going to murder me." This not only expressed her transference fears, i.e., separation equals death, but also served to avoid the reality problem of a husband who's tired of the trouble and expense of a psychotic wife. At some level, it was intended to get the therapist to reassure her "It's not going to happen," when in fact, the husband would leave unless this delusion was seen as reflecting a reality problem, and the avoided issue dealt with. (Adjunctive interviews with the husband will in some cases suffice to deal with his anxieties, and lead him to tolerate the temporary discomfort of his marriage while his wife received further help. If it does not, it would be important to help her cope with the separation.)

Extension To Schizophrenics

The comments in this paper on communication, reality problems, and the need to separate and respond to both reality factors and psychodynamic factors are particularly pertinent for the so-called schizophrenic. As is well known, such patients are far more frequent in the lower socio-economic classes, primarily because life in the lower socio-economic class is much harder, not only for the patient, but for those family members on whose resources, emotional and otherwise, the patient would ordinarily depend. Of course, it is also true that psychopathology itself interferes with the economic status of the individual.If the patient is severe enough to be considered schizophrenic, he is likely to assume that his difficulties happen only to him, are specifically directed at him, and that something he is doing caused it. Such beliefs typically have been encouraged by his family (Lidz, 1974). The families of most schizophrenics have, throughout life, systematically discouraged the use of people outside the family as sources of information and help; that is, those extra-familial relationships and identifications which most of us use to correct the impact of ineffective hurtful identifications, misinformation, and other harmful consequences of the emotional limitations of our families of origins. Therefore, giving accurate information, teaching the patient to direct his attention to relevant knowledge and information, and to possible transference become even more critical.

However, it should never be forgotten that even our psychotic patients know a lot about their reality. It is just as important to get a psychotic patient to take his own knowledge, perception, and judgment seriously as it is to help him unravel his distortions of reality. No one completely distorts reality. The patient's family frequently has imposed their distortions on him, so that he does not trust his own judgment even when it is demonstrably correct.

Some Special Practical Considerations

Sometimes a poor patient has urgent practical needs that he or she is incapable of dealing with for realistic or symptomatic reasons, and which require immediate action, e.g., no food for a baby, critical medical needs, no place to sleep. It then may be necessary for the therapist or some other staff member to help directly with that urgent practical problem. Similarly, the therapist must act for the patient who asks for and needs protection from his own impulses:

"Lock me up so I can't kill (or hurt) someone."

Such a patient is using the therapist or the institution as an ego-extension to bolster his own absolutely necessary defenses.

The rule of thumb is that you never do for a patient what they are capable of doing for themselves, but of what they are capable is always a clinical judgment. As we noted earlier, in many instances someone looks incapable because they lack information about reality or the nature of feelings, and simply giving information in a single therapeutic interview (as described above) makes it possible for them to handle the situation. However, if at the end of the interview the individual still seems genuinely incapable of action, and the consequence of inaction is likely to be irreversible (e.g., fatal), the therapist must act.

Sometimes it is not primarily the patient's emotional disorder which is preventing action, but the nature of the agency or personnel of the agency (e.g., welfare, parole, police, prosecutors, etc.) from whom the patient is seeking assistance, and the agency may be more responsive to a call from the (higher status) therapist. Such help should be temporary. Direct practical intervention does not mean we stop talking to the patient. Emphasis should be placed as far as possible on teaching the patient what needed to be done, how such crises can be avoided, and discovering what in the patient prevents him or her from taking such actions.

A further practical step which was occasionally taken in the Michigan State Psychotherapy Project (Karon & VandenBos, 1972) was to provide money for transportation and/or baby-sitting expenses (e.g., $5/session). This permitted the patients to remain in psychotherapy on a regular basis without undue realistic hardship (and hardship never facilitates treatment). The cost of such reimbursements are minimal as compared to the cost of staff time. We would recommend this option to be available whenever the therapist feels it would be helpful.

Summary

Psychotherapy with the poor patient is, in fact, no different from good psychotherapy with anyone. There are usually more severe reality problems, and they need to be seriously considered; the intertwining of reality and psychodynamic problems must be dealt with in all its complexity. But these reality problems may touch off prototypic counter-transference problems, which impede empathy. The socially mobile therapist from lower class origin may perceive the patient as his bad self, i.e., himself as a failure. The upper class therapist may need to avoid guilt over never having had to face such realistic difficulties, or tend to idealize poverty. Such problems are to be dealt with as counter-transference is always dealt with (i.e., consciously).

Therapy can easily founder because of lack of meaningful communication, particularly if the therapist does not know there is no real communication occurring. Usually, the patient is awed by authority, and does not want to reveal his own "inadequacy" or criticize the authority, by bringing up the fact that he does not understand the therapist, or that the therapist does not understand him. It is up to the therapist to spot and undo such a communica-tion gap. Of course, there is also an information gap. It is up to the therapist to educate the patient as to what therapy is all about, and why it should be helpful. Only then is it reasonable to expect a cooperative patient, i.e., a "therapeutic alliance."

As a general strategy, the therapist must help the patient untangle reality and psychodynamics: The therapist starts with "facts" and the patient's feelings about them, moves towards gathering additional relevant information, and reinforcing accurate perceptions and analyzing the discrepancies that careful attention to one's life eventually reveals. The views that psychotherapy can deal only with reality problems, or intra-psychic events, or social change doom the therapy, and more importantly, the patient, to less than that of which he is capable.

The dilemma of whether the therapist should help the patient adapt to being lower class or to escape it has to do with ideology, not therapy. The therapist must help the patient evaluate the alternatives available to him in the light of reality, and of his psychodynamics, and then to act and live as effectively as possible in the light of his own decisions (which, of course, can be changed).

It is a mistake to believe that therapists for the economically deprived are genetically endowed, or are the result of extensive training programs. Such views are themselves resistance against making therapy available. What is required is a therapist who is motivated to be helpful, who is willing to learn from his patients and his own reactions to them, and from supervisors. Supervisors with successful experience with such patients are obviously of great value, as are continuing in-service training, seminars, and/or informal discussions of such patients and the difficulties in dealing with them. The therapist's life experience before becoming a therapist can be a help or a hindrance depending on how the therapist is able to learn from it.

Of course, the therapist must learn to be a therapist, that is, to know about psychopathologic dynamics, therapeutic technique, and have the continuing need to learn about his patients and himself as an integral part of his professional way of life.

The good therapist for the economically poor is well described by Strupp, Fox, and Lessler (1969) in summarizing how patients in general who have been helped view their therapists: "a keenly attentive, interested, benign, and concerned listener—a friend who is warm and natural, is not averse to giving direct advice, who speaks one's language, makes sense, and rarely arouses intense anger."

REFERENCES

Auld, F. & Myers, J.K. Contributions to a theory for selecting psychotherapy patients. Journal of Clinical Psychology, 1954, 10, 56-60.

Baum, O.E. & Felzer, S.B. Activity in initial interviews with lower-class patients. Archives of General Psychiatry', 1964, 10, 345-353.

————, Felzer, S.B., D'Zmura, T. & Schumaker, E. Psychotherapy, dropouts, and lower socioeconomic patients. American Journal of Orthopsychiatry, 1966, 38, 629-635.

Brill, N.O. & Storrow, H.A. Social class and psychiatric treatment. Archives of General Psychiatry, 1960, 3, 340-344.

Carlson, D.A., Coleman, J.B., Errera, P. & Harrison, R.W. Problems in treating the lower class psychotic. Archives of General Psychiatry, 1965, 13, 269-274. Cole, N. J., Branch, C.H. & Allison, R.B. Some relationships between social class and the practice of dynamic psychotherapy. American Journal of Psychiatry, 1962, 118, 1004-1012.

Frank, J.D., Gliedman, L.H., Imber, S.D., Nash, E.H. & Stone, A.R. Why patients leave psychotherapy. Archives of Neurology & Psychiatry, 1957, 77, 283-299.

Galagher, E.B., Sharaf, M.R. & Levinson, D.J. The influence of patient and therapist in determining the use of psychotherapy in a hospital setting. Psychiatry, 1965, 28, 297-310.

Goin, M.K., Yamamoto, J. & Silverman, J. Therapy congruent with class-linked expectations. Archives of General Psychiatry, 1965, 13, 133-137.

Gould, R.E. Dr. Strangleclass: Or how I stopped worrying about the theory and began treating the blue-collar workers. American Journal of Orthopsychiatry, 1967, 37, 78-86.

Heine, R.W. & Trosman, H. Initial expectations of the doctor-patient interaction as a factor in continuance in psychotherapy. Psychiatry, 1960, 23, 275-278.

Hoehn-Saric, R., Frank, J.D., Imber, S.D., Nash, E. H., Stone, A. R. & Battle, C.C. Systematic preparation of patients for psychotherapy. Journal of Psychiatric Research, 1964, 2, 267-281.

Hollingshead, A.B. & Redlich, R.C. Schizophrenia and social structure. American Journal of Psychiatry, 1954, 110, 695-701.

Jones, E.E. Social class and psychotherapy. Psychiatry, 1974, 37, 307-320.

Kahn, R.L., Pollack, M. & Fink, M. Social factors in the selection of therapy in a voluntary mental hospital. Journal of the Hillside Hospital, 1957, 6, 216-228.

Karon, B.P. & VandenBos, G.R. The consequences of psychotherapy for schizophrenic patients. Psychotherapy: Theory, Research & Practice, 1972, 9, 111-119.

Lidz, T. The Origin and Treatment of Schizophrenic Disorders. New York: Basic Books, 1974.

Lorion, R.P. Socioeconomic status and traditional treatment approaches reconsidered. Psychological Bulletin,

———— Patient and therapist variables in the treatment of low-income patients. Psychological Bulletin, 81, 344-354.

Mann, J. Time-Limited Psychotherapy. Cambridge, Mass.: Harvard University Press, 1973.

Orne, M. T. & Wender, P. H. Anticipatory socialization for psychotherapy: method and rationale. American Journal of Psychiatry, 1968, 124, 1202-1212.

Overall, P. & Aronson, H. Expectations of psychotherapy in patients of lower socioeconomic class. American Journal of Orthopsychiatry, 1963, 33, 421-430.

Riessman, F. & Scribner, S. The underutilization of mental health services by workers and low income groups: causes and cures. American Journal of Psychiatry, 1965,121, 798-801.

Rosenthal, D. & Frank, J.D. The fate of psychiatric clinic outpatients assigned to psychotherapy. Journal of Nervous & Mental Disease, 1958, 127, 330-343.

Rubenstein, E.A. & Lorr, M.A. A comparison of terminators and remainers in outpatient psychotherapy. Journal of Clinical Psychology, 1956, 12, 345-349.

Schaffer, L. & Myers, J.K. Psychotherapy and social stratification. Psychiatry, 1954, 17, 83-93.

Siassi, I. Psychotherapy with women and men of lower classes. In Franks, Violet, & Burtle (Eds.) Women In Therapy, New York: Brunner/Mazel, 1974.

Strupp, H.H., Fox, R.E. & Lessler, K. Patients view their psychotherapy.

Baltimore: John Hopkins Press, 1969.

——— & Bloxom, A. L. Preparing lower-class patients for group psychotherapy: development and evaluation of a role-induction film. Journal of Consulting & Clinical Psychology, 1973, 41, 373-384.

Terstman, N., Miller, D. & Weber, J. Blue collar workers at the psychoanalytic clinic. American Journal of Psychiatry, 1974, 131,261-266.

Yamamoto, J. & Goin, M.K. Social class factors relevant for psychiatric treatment. Journal of Nervous and Mental Diseases, 1966, 142, 332-339. INTERNATIONAL

CHAPTER 4
Is There Really A Schizophrenogenic Parent?
Bertram P. Karon and Anmarie J. Widener

Understandably, parents of schizophrenics find the classification of schizophrenogenic parent offensive. No one wants to believe that they could have caused, even inadvertently, such terrible suffering in someone they love. But therapists who treat schizophrenics generally report a parenting interaction different from that usual to neurotic patients (although there are cases where relevant noxious life events have nothing to do with parents; in other cases, both parents and child are tragic victims of bad or absent professional advice). Communication deviance, measured from parental interaction, the Rorschach Inkblot Test (Rorschach, 1932), and the Thematic Apperception Test (TAT; Murray, 1943) has been found to characterize parents and adoptive parents of schizophrenics. Expressed emotion (intrusive hostility) of parents increases re-hospitalization. Genetic factors, at most, represent increased vulnerability.

Pathogenesis, based on clinical observations, is measured from the TAT and is defined as the degree to which the parent, when there is a potential conflict between the needs of the child and the needs of the parent, unconsciously acts in terms of the parent's needs without regard to the potentially conflicting needs of the child. Pathogenic parents, as well as their children, are victims in the same way that any patient who suffers psychological symptoms based on unconscious factors is a victim and not a culprit. In a series of studies, mothers of normals averaged 35% pathogenic. Mothers of schizophrenics averaged 65% pathogenic. Fathers of schizophrenics are nearly as high. Most convincing are clinical observations. Clinical examples of the meaning of pathogenesis are provided.

Parents of schizophrenics usually find the label of schizophrenogenic parent offensive. To cause, even inadvertently, such terrible suffering in someone you love seems unbelievable and insulting. One of the reasons for emphasizing heredity and disturbed physiology is to avoid the guilt engendered by focusing on the possible mistakes of the parent.

But all parents make mistakes. No one knows how to be a perfect parent, as even a cursory reading of childrearing texts reveals. There are islands of knowledge, with the gaps filled in by the "expert" from his or her own childhood or from what is fashionable. Most parents worry about how they have raised their children; the children go through crisis periods that seem irretrievable. In most cases, parents see their children live through these crises and continue to psychological maturity. But parents of schizophrenics do not see their children weather crises well; their children do not move toward maturity.

Parents generally believe that they have a great deal to do with how their children turn out; when children do not turn out well, parents have to cope with the question, "What did I do?" Because our knowledge is so inexact, the answers are apt to be wrong. A parent guided by an incorrect theory makes the situation worse rather than better. Anyone who has worked with delinquents has heard, "He [she] was no good. Nothing worked. No matter how much I hit him [her], he [she] never learned to behave decently."

Parents expect disapproval if their children do not turn out well and expect psychotherapists to disapprove of them. But what they are coping with is their own belief that someone must be censured if something goes wrong. This represents either their own values or their parents' values. They assume that therapists think as they do. However, a biological theory, genetic and purely physiological (a "chemical imbalance"), provides a way out for the majority of parents who are as much a victim of their child's schizophrenia as is the child.

It also provides a way out for the minority of parents of schizophrenics who have done something that most parents would recognize as destructive (e.g., physical, sexual, or verbal abuse). These parents can better live with themselves if they can believe that the abuse made no difference: If their child's disorder is genetic and physiological, then their child was doomed in any event; their mistakes, they believe, were the result of an abnormal child. Even child abuse can be rationalized by the parent, as it so often is, as the seductive child "seduced me" or the provocative child "made me" beat him or her.

Of course, the majority of parents of schizophrenics are not child abusers and do not knowingly do gross things that are obviously outside the pale of normal childrearing. But therapists generally report a parenting interaction different from the one typical of neurotic patients, even though there are cases where the relevant noxious life events have nothing to do with parents. Thus, a psychotic reaction to terrifying battlefield experiences may occur, even in individuals with a relatively healthy childhood (Grinker & Spiegel, 1965). Unfortunately, some civilian environments and experiences are as terrifying as the battlefield. In other cases, both parents and children are tragic victims of bad or absent professional advice. For example, an infant was operated on for removal of a tumor, and the mother was not permitted to stay in the hospital. The operation was carried out without anesthesia, as was standard practice because the use of anesthesia with young infants was considered too risky. The mother should have been told (but was not) that it was normal for an infant under such circumstances to reject the mother—as an expression of anger—when they were reunited, that her child really wanted her to keep reaching out despite the rejection, and that normal emotional relatedness would eventually be resumed. Not having been told, the mother felt that either the child or she was defective; she withdrew defensively and told her child for many years, "You could never love me." Both mother and child desperately longed for the relationship each thought was impossible—a relationship that was established only when the adult child finally entered psychoanalytic therapy, reconstructed the trauma, understood it, and reached out to the mother.

The child's subjective view of a parent is not the same as that parent being objectively viewed. When children are very young, they perceive everything that happens to them as being caused directly by the parent, especially the mother. Thus, it is a common observation that when a child is teething, the child will bite his or her thumb just as before, but now it will hurt. Usually, the infant will turn its face reproachfully to the mother, seeming to express, "How could you do this to me?" Not yet understanding the newly formed teeth, the child believes, "Mother did this to me. Mother hurt me." After all, mother is omnipotent and controls everything, good or bad (or the good mother and the bad mother are omnipotent and control everything). To be helpful, a therapist has to uncover the child's subjective experience as it was (and not what it would be if he or she had adult knowledge and reasoning capacity and were an unusually fair, rational, and objective observer). Parents have trouble understanding that good therapy must uncover and validate the child's actual experience, no matter how objectively "unfair." Patients will usually make the fair adult reappraisal, but that comes later.

When parents ask about their role or the cause of their child's schizophrenia, the only honest answer is that the therapist does not know. For example, "I do not know what caused your child's schizophrenia and will not know until the therapy is over. Usually, something small happened in infancy which changed the way the infant understood what happened next, something then happened which changed how the child understood what happened next, and so forth. A lifetime of many small things probably caused the disorder. But sometimes crises occur. What do you think may have contributed to your child's problems?" This is discussed more fully in Karon & VandenBos, 1981, pp. 129-133.). Alanen (1992) and his colleagues began every therapy of a psychotic with a family session, which has the aim of obtaining "more information of the patient's course of life of how he/she was taken ill and of the factors which precipitated the admission" (p. 241). Thus, the family, the patient, and the therapist become co-workers in the process of discovery.

Adoption, Communication Deviance, and Expressed Emotion

The widely cited Danish adoption studies (Kety, Rosenthal, Wender, & Schulsinger, 1968; Wender, Rosenthal, Kety, Schulsinger, & Welriei, 1974; Wender, Rosenthal, Zahn, & Kety, 1971) suffer from fatal scientific flaws and misleading reporting, as described in the critiques by Lidz, Blatt, and Cook (1981), Lidz and Blatt (1983), and Lewontin, Rose, and Kamin (1984). We mention only four of the most striking problems from these studies. First, the increase in schizophrenia among biological relatives as compared to adoptive relatives is mainly attributable to half-siblings who, in those studies, were significantly more likely to be schizophrenic than full siblings, biological parents, or adoptive relatives. Second, the definition of schizophrenia spectrum disorders was changed in each successive sub-study to maximize the apparent effect of genetic factors. Third, the higher frequency of psychiatric hospitalization of adoptive parents whose adoptees later became schizophrenic was not reported. Finally, these authors did not publish the finding that Margaret Singer (Wynne, Singer, & Toohey, 1976) was able to differentiate blindly (without error) adoptive parents whose children were schizophrenic from those whose adoptive children were not schizophrenic using the Rorschach communication deviance score (discussed hereafter).

Tienari (1992) and his co-workers in their Finnish adoption study presented the most rigorous data available so far on genetic factors. Their findings were that (a) genetic factors are not sufficient in themselves to produce schizophrenia but may represent increased vulnerability to unfavorable life experiences, (b) unfavorable family experiences are related to schizophrenia and serious psychopathology, and (c) the most potent predictive factor for serious psychopathology is disturbed communication (communication deviance) between the adoptive parents. The interaction between adoptive parent-child conflict and the genetic factor (i.e., schizophrenic mother vs. normal biological mother) accounts for half as much variance as does communication deviance; and then, accounting for only half as much variance as that, the interaction between (lack of) empathy and the genetic variable. It is worth noting that Tienari found that the best single predictor of psychopathology was communication deviance measured from the interaction between the adoptive parents without the child present, which showed that it clearly was not a reaction to a disturbed child.

No research is perfect. The major flaw in this study was the inclusion of adoptions of children as old as 4 years of age so that the study would be comparable to the Danish adoption studies. But the Finnish data are far more careful and reliable than anything hitherto available.

Tienari's work follows up on, and is perhaps the most important of, the body of research that used Wynne and Singer's (1963a, 1963b; Singer & Wynne, 1965a, 1965b) concept of communication deviance, which can be measured from family interactions, the Rorschach Inkblot Test (Rorschach, 1932), or the Thematic Apperception Test (TAT; Murray, 1943). Communication deviance may be defined roughly as a "fuzziness," a lack of clarity in communication, particularly about potentially conflicting issues, or, as Miklowitz et al. (1991) paraphrased it, the inability to establish and maintain a shared focus of attention in communicating with a listener. In their original research, Wynne and Singer (1963a, 1963b; Singer & Wynne, 1965a, 1965b) found increased communication deviance in the family interactions, Rorschachs, and TATs of parents of schizophrenics as compared to other parents.

These scoring systems are complex and subtle, and they are not easy to learn. When the research group at University of California, Los Angeles (Doane, West, Rodnick, Goldstein, & Jones, 1980) wanted to use the TAT scoring system for their family studies, it took one year of repeated consultations with Dr. Singer to develop a scoring manual that bright graduate students could use reliably.

Wender, Rosenthal, Zahn, and Kety (1971) changed the communication deviance scoring system (apparently without being aware of it) and found that the changed scoring system did not differentiate adoptive parents of schizophrenics from adoptive parents of normals. When they sent the randomly intermixed Rorschachs to Margaret Singer, she was able to pick out, on the basis of the Rorschach communication deviance score alone, every adoptive parent whose adoptive child became schizophrenic, with no false positives and no false negatives (Wynne et al., 1976). Wender et al. (1971) did not refer to her Rorschach findings, but instead falsely reported that psychological tests did not differentiate adoptive parents of schizophrenics. When challenged (Karon, 1975a, 1975b, 1976), Wender, Rosenthal, and Kety (1975) said the Singer finding was meaningless because the Rorschach was only one test, and they had not found anything on the Minnesota Multiphasic Personality Inventory (Dahlstrom & Welsh, 1960), the Word Association Test (Rosanoff, 1927), or the TAT. Of course, they did not send Singer the TAT protocols, but they used their own mis-scoring as they had done with the Rorschach.

The University of California group produced one of the few prospective studies in the literature (Doane, West, Goldstein, Rodnick, & Jones, 1980). Families of teenagers who were disturbed but not psychotic were studied. Those who had families characterized by both communication deviance and so-called high expressed emotion were either psychotic or borderline five years later, although none of them were when first studied.Those adolescents whose families were characterized by neither communication deviance nor so-called high expressed emotion were not psychotic or borderline five years later. Those whose family was characterized by one but not both of these predictors had an intermediate frequency of serious pathology.

The high expressed emotion variable was found earlier to characterize families of schizophrenics who were more likely to relapse than those whose families were characterized as low expressed emotion (Leff & Vaughn, 1985; Vaughn & Leff, 1976). It is our view that the expressed emotion index is really better described as intrusive hostility. So-called high expressed emotion does not consist of statements like, "I'm really glad to see you," "I really like you," or "I'm really proud of you," but rather "You ought to be ashamed of yourself," "You ought to know better than that," and so forth. There is a kind of puritanism in the naming of expressed emotion, as if feelings per se were dangerous. Indeed, Leff recently reported1 that expressions of positive affect by the family are helpful to the adjustment of schizophrenic patients.

Pathogenesis

On the basis of clinical experience with schizophrenics and observations of their parents, it became obvious that there were no simple behaviors that consistently differentiated parents of schizophrenics from parents of normals (Karon & Rosberg, 1958). Many of the descriptions of parenting in the literature were oversimplified. Even variables like the double-bind did not fit with clinical experience. As Potash (1964/1965) found in his research, double-bind cognitive problems are tougher for everyone to solve than non-double-bind problems, and schizophrenics have more trouble solving any problem than non-schizophrenics, but there is no interaction or special vulnerability to double-binds. Most schizophrenic patients feel that they are in a "single bind": their very existence is their crime.

The parents of schizophrenics are often admirable people with respect to their actions that are under conscious control (particularly those parents who go to great length to try to get adequate treatment for their children). Problems in parenting, however, usually have unconscious bases and are better understood as symptoms or coping devices developed in order to come to terms with the parents' own childhood (Karon, 1960; Karon & Rosberg, 1958). The specifically hurtful parental behaviors are different in different families, but these behaviors are not behaviors a child could teach a parent. Just as schizophrenic patients are also widely differing people, so are the. parents of schizophrenic patients.

However, what seems consistent across families is an unconscious dynamic or defense, pathogenesis: When the needs of the parent and the needs of the child are in conflict, the parent of a pre-schizophrenic child, more often than other parents, acts in terms of the parent's need without regard to the conflicting need of the child. Of course, all parents do this some of the time; it just seems more frequent in parents of pre-schizophrenics. Furthermore, this is not a conscious choice by the parent; the parent is typically unaware of the potential conflict of needs (Karon, 1960; Karon & Rosberg, 1958).

To test this, a pathogenesis score was operationally defined from the TAT (Meyer & Karon, 1967). Stories were scored pathogenic if there was an interaction between a dominant and a dependent character with potentially conflicting needs, and the dominant character did not take the dependent person's needs into account. An easily scored pathogenic story is "One person murders another." Clearly, the dominant person is not considering the dependent person's needs. A story is scored as benign if the dominant person takes into account the need of the dependent person. An easily scored benign story is "Parents force a child to do something; the child is unhappy; they change." Stories were scored as unscoreable if it was not possible to tell whether it was pathogenic, benign, or if there was no interaction. The pathogenesis score is the number of pathogenic stories, divided by the total number of stories scored either pathogenic or benign; in other words, it is the percentage of the total number of scoreable stories that were scored pathogenic.

Meyer (Meyer & Karon, 1967) tested six mothers of schizophrenics and six mothers of normal boys who were of the same age and social class. The TAT stories were intermixed and scored blindly by Karon, and a theoretically generated scoring key was transcribed during the initial scoring (using themes from the sample of stories as specific instances of the scoring categories). When the protocols were reassembled, there was practically no overlap: Mothers of schizophrenics varied from 65% to 89% pathogenic, and control mothers varied from 23% to 69% pathogenic. The findings were clearly statistically significant (p = .003) even with this small number of cases. In the same study, Kevin Mitchell, using this scoring key, was able to score blindly the intermixed stories, and his scoring again discriminated between the samples, so it was a useable scoring key.

Mitchell (1968) then gathered samples of 20 mothers in each group and replicated Meyer's findings. He found that blind scoring on average differentiated mothers of schizophrenics from mothers of normals using this unconscious variable. Mothers of normal children average pathogenesis scores of about 35%. No one is perfect, but children do not require perfect mothers. If the TAT is representative, mothers of normals ignore the conflicting needs of their children about one third of the time. Mothers of schizophrenics average pathogenesis scores of 75%; mothers of schizophrenics do not always ignore the conflicting needs of their children, but the more consistent problem makes children vulnerable. Singer and Wynne made available to Mitchell their TAT data from their National Institute of Mental Health study (Singer & Wynne, 1965b), and Mitchell found again that blindly scored TATs differentiated mothers of schizophrenics from mothers of normals (Mitchell, 1974).

He also found that fathers of schizophrenics were more pathogenic than normal fathers (although scoring not quite as high as mothers), and the difference between fathers of normals and fathers of schizophrenics was not statistically significant with this small sample. Interestingly enough, the blindly scored pathogenesis ratings discriminated the parents of schizophrenics from the parents of normals in that study slightly better than Singer and Wynne's (1965a) communication deviance measure.

Nichols (1970) found that the pathogenesis score of mothers of adult male schizophrenics correlated significantly with the severity of pathology and severity of thought disorder of their sons. Within the normal range, Leigh (1986/1987) found that pathogenesis scores of mothers and fathers correlated with grades and school adjustment of adolescent girls—the best predictor being the average pathogenesis score of both parents. To attempt to deal with the issue of whether pathogenesis was a learned trait that resulted from the inordinate demands of a sick child (so that the parent learned in self-defense not to respond), Beavers (1976) investigated the TATs of mothers of mentally retarded children and found no increase in pathogenesis over mothers of normal children.

Clinical experience suggests that schizophrenics usually have two parents who are not helpful enough (unless they do not have two parents). As described in Karon and VandenBos (1981), usually there are two pathogenic parents or one parent who is pathogenic and one parent who is either physically absent or emotionally so weak as not to serve as an effective alternative.

The TAT of one such emotionally weak parent scored high on pathogenesis: This apparent parental weakness seemed to be expressing pathogenesis by proxy. The other parent's hurtfulness expressed this parent's hurtful needs without his having to actively acknowledge them. Of course, withdrawing rather than facing a conflict with a spouse over the treatment of a child is solving one's own need for marital harmony at the expense of the child's needs. The parental "solid front," advocated by many child care experts, is overvalued. Frequently, schizophrenic patients recount incidents where it would have been helpful if the other parent had intervened or at least overtly said that he or she disagreed with the parent who was being hurtful.

Because therapy, like parenthood, involves an interaction between a dominant person and a dependent person for the dependent person's good, a pathogenic therapist would not be very helpful. VandenBos and Karon (1971) tested this and found that pathogenesis scores of therapists (from TATs obtained before the Michigan State schizophrenia therapy research project, Karon & VandenBos, 1981, pp. 406-408, began) correlated between .48 and .73 with patient gain scores: in the first 6 months of treatment on measures of thought disorder and of overall functioning (i.e., Clinical Status Interview Ratings).

The Clinical Status Interview Ratings were based on careful clinical status interviews conducted by an experienced psychoanalytic psychiatrist who was familiar with psychotic patients but not connected with or aware of the specific treatment (aside from spontaneous remarks by the patient during the interview). The interview was conducted with the aim of eliciting information with respect to ability to take care of self, ability to work, sexual adjustment, social adjustment, absence of hallucinations and delusions, degree of freedom from anxiety and depression, amount of affect, variety and spontaneity of affect, satisfaction with life and self, achievement of capabilities, and benign versus malignant effect on others. The interviews were recorded on audio tape (with any mention of type of treatment deleted) and then rated blindly for emotional health by two clinical psychologists. Their ratings were quantified by a scaling technique, and the ratings were averaged.

There have been studies of child-abusive parents compared with normal parents (Evans, 1976; Melnick & Hurley. 1969). As might be expected, the child-abusive parents are elevated on pathogenesis, but their scores tend not to be as high as the parents of schizophrenics. The meaning of this is that the child-abusive parent, when he or she is being abusive, is more gruesome than the typical parent of a schizophrenic. However, the child-abusive parent is not consistently so insensitive to the conflicting needs of the child. The pressures that lead to schizophrenia tend to be more subtle, not so obvious to the parent or the child, but definitely more consistent.

Clinical Observations

The most convincing data are the evidence from clinical experience. In every case of schizophrenia that Karon has treated, facts have come to light that, as subjectively experienced, would have driven anyone crazy. Insofar as they concern externally observable events, it has been possible to verify what has been reconstructed in the treatment whenever the parents or siblings were still alive and cooperative with the treatment (and sometimes even when they were not cooperative). Often the parent would say, if the matter were something about which a parent might well be reticent, "Didn't I tell you about that?" or "I meant to tell you about that, but I forgot," or "I didn't think that was important," or even "I was ashamed to tell you about that."

Of course, some psychoanalysts believe that parents cannot have anything to do with schizophrenia; they have had neurotic patients whose parents were every bit as difficult to live with as the parents with whom schizophrenic patients have lived. But in Karon's experience as a clinician, when neurotic patients have parents who are that difficult to live with, there is always someone outside the immediate family who provided the corrective identifications, information, and support that was lacking in the immediate family. As Searles (1965) and Lidz (1973), among others, have pointed out, one of the premorbid risk factors for schizophrenia is a family that discourages the use of friends and adults outside the family to correct the faults in the family. Of course, parents do not know this is dangerous, and professionals do not tell them. Some parents discourage extrafamilial contacts to minimize an experience that no American parent is spared and that no American parent enjoys—the child who says, "Mary can do it, Henry can do it, so why can't I do it?" Parents handle this as best they can. They say, "If they can do it, you can do it," or "I don't care what they can do, you're living with me," or they check with Mary and Henry's parents, find out Mary and Henry can do it, and they give their permission. Perhaps they check with Mary and Henry's parents and find out that nobody has permission, but all of the children are saying, "Everybody else can do it, why can't I?" At this point as a parent, one has to realize that one of the prices of having healthy intelligent children is that they will outsmart us from time to time.

No matter how this parent-child interaction is handled, parents are usually uncomfortable. Nonetheless, it is good for the children; they are comparing their parents with the rest of the world. Even if parents handle things wrong, which inevitably will happen once in awhile, it is not that the children are rebels against God and the universe; they simply think, "That's the way my old man or my mom is, and I when I grow up, it will be different." These corrective identifications outside the family are the normal mechanism that all children use in growing up, for no one has had an ideal family. But when corrective identifications are discouraged or prevented, the normal corrective mechanism for parental mistakes is removed and problems in the family are enormously magnified in their destructive impact.

Of course, even when a patient's life has been blatantly hurtful, it may not be in the clinical record. For example, the voluminous psychiatric: and social work records on a patient who had been hospitalized for 10 years showed no reason for his illness (Karon & VandenBos, 1981, pp. 35-40). The only apparently hurtful factors were that his family was economically poor, his father was an alcoholic, and he grew up in the city of Detroit. As a teenager, he developed a stutter, and he did not respond to speech therapy. In the army, he reported to sick call with a venereal disease, and the site of infection was his mouth. Shortly thereafter, he assaulted a stranger and nearly killed him. Eventually, he was given a general discharge. The rest of his life consisted of assaulting strange men, becoming grossly incoherent, and being hospitalized. When he wasn't incoherent, he stuttered very badly. He was muscular, dangerous, and fast moving.

A class of psychiatric residents chose him to be interviewed by Karon, undoubtedly because he had made them anxious by suggesting that they talk to their patients, inasmuch as lobotomy (still occasionally practiced at that hospital) and shock treatments were destructive and medications were of limited benefit. Karon (expressing his own retaliatory sadism) insisted that the residents sit in the same room while he interviewed this dangerous and unpredictable man.

The patient had the peculiar symptom of choking other patients in the ward. He never killed anyone; he always released his victim as soon as the victim fell unconscious. In the first interview, Karon kept returning to this symptom. What seemed to come to light was that, for minor offenses like not eating, his mother would wrap a cloth around his neck and choke him. After this interview, there was an immediate change in this long-standing symptom, indicating (as a rule of thumb) the reconstruction to be accurate. By reenacting the trauma symbolically, he was reassuring himself that his mother would not kill him. Such a symbolic act reduces anxiety temporarily, but the problem cannot be overcome until it is understood consciously and connected with the past.

A second fact came to light when he yelled in a later session:

"Why did you do it to me, Dad?"

"What did I do?"

"You know what you did."

"How old were you?"

"You know I was 8 years old."

Eventually it became clear that "you" (his father) had come home drunk and anally raped him.

His stutter was a serious problem for therapy. In one session, he stuttered and then spoke a few words of real Latin. Where had this uneducated man learned Latin?

"Were you an altar boy?"

"You swallow a snake and then you stutter. You mustn't let anyone know."

His guilt was intense, and so the therapist guessed it was the priest rather than another altar boy. When it was interpreted that he had performed fellatio on a priest, and that "It's all right. Anyone as hungry as you were would have done the same thing," his stutter immediately stopped. When in later sessions it returned, it would immediately cease with the same interpretation. Even with a life history so unusually and blatantly destructive, none of these facts had come to light in 10 years of professionals (who perhaps didn't want to know).

In the famous case of Schreber (Niederland, 1984; Schatzman, 1973), what professional would have considered seriously that his father, a world famous pediatrician whose books on how to raise children were widely read, could have tortured his child (although the father honestly believed these were not tortures but were good for his son)? Schreber, in his delusion, talked of God fastening a metal band around his head and tightening it lovingly until it hurt. Schreber's pediatrician father believed posture was very important for children, so he invented chairs, beds, and tables with metal rods and metal bands that were tightened around the child's head "lovingly" so that the child would have to sit or lie perfectly straight. In his delusion, Schreber said that God wanted to castrate him and make him a woman. Schreber's pediatrician father thought masturbation was bad for children and invented anti-masturbation devices consisting of a ring with little spikes on the inside that were slipped over the little boy's penis; if he began to have an erection, the spikes would penetrate. Is it any wonder Schreber concluded that his father wanted to castrate him?

Usually the childhood pressures are much subtler and unconscious. Thus, a male paranoid schizophrenic showed obvious signs of an "oral" trauma (Karon 1960). He was afraid of being poisoned, sometimes talked of poisoned milk, sometimes went on hunger strikes, and hallucinated the "Athenian girls taunting [him] with their poisoned breasts." His mother, who had been psychoanalyzed and who was going to great lengths to get help for him—including taking care of the treatment house in which he lived—was proud of the fact that she had breastfed him for a year and had gradually weaned him. One day she said to him, "Didn't I give you enough milk?" "The cow gave her calf milk and then kicked it," he said. "She shouldn't do that. It's something that happened hundreds of times in the history of the world."

This continuing pressure was observed by the attendants over a 6-month period. If she cooked a meal and he ate it, there was always a quarrel between them afterwards. If she did not cook, but the attendants did, there was no quarrel. If she cooked, but he did not eat, as when he was on a hunger strike, there was no quarrel. The quarrel was never about food or eating. The mother was totally unconscious of this invariant sequence: The demand, "Feed me, mother me," made her anxious; when she was anxious, she became angry, and when she was angry, anything became the cause of a quarrel. Poison is simply something you eat that hurts you, and when mother consistently gets angry after she feeds you, that hurts. It is the oral trauma underlying delusions of poisoning and poisoned milk.

We cite one last example: A patient, termed "incurably schizophrenic" by the staff of the treating hospital, was brought to Karon's office (over the hospital's objections) after his wife had refused to permit electro-convulsive therapy and had withdrawn him from the hospital on the senior author's advice. He was not eating, he was not sleeping, and he was continuously hallucinating. He was from a middle-class family and had considered himself lucky to have had such good parents, particularly such a good mother However, even before his psychotic break, he could not remember his child hood before the second year of high school, and he did not think that was abnormal.

In the course of his treatment, some of the events that came to light and that he was able to confirm included being dressed in white clothes as a young child and then sent out to play, but being beaten if he got his clothes dirty. He was not of Italian descent, but his family lived in an Italian neighborhood in New York City. His mother would tell him to go out and play, but not with those Italian kids because they were very dangerous and he would get hurt (although every neighborhood child was Italian). Among his hallucinations was burning in Hell. When asked about the scar on his hand, he said,

"There's a story my mother tells. When I was 5 years old, we were in a store and she asked me where I had gotten the toy in my hand. I said the lady gave it to me. She asked the lady, who hadn't given it to me. She made me put it back, and she made me apologize to the lady. She then took me by the hand and we walked home."

"How far was that?"

"Five blocks. And then we went upstairs to the third floor. And she turned on the gas burner, and held my hand in it to teach me not to steal.

It left a scar. But it had no effect on me, because I don't remember it."

"I have a different view. What you can't remember has the most effect on you. Most of us can only imagine burning in Hell, but you have actually been there."

He is now internationally renowned in his field. He recently sent me a magazine article about a prestigious award he received for his scholarship, and a note that said, "Somehow, it's a shame that my deepest feelings of gratitude for returning a life to me have gone unexpressed."

One of the precipitants of his psychotic break was that he finally achieved his fantasied proof of being good enough (i.e., finishing his PhD) and immediately being promoted to a tenured position, with a substantial raise. He called his parents, but neither of them acted impressed. His father said, "Is that all you're making? I've been telling people you make more than that already." His defenses unraveled, and he regressed despite being on medication combined with psychotherapy with a psychiatrist; he was then hospitalized and declared "hopeless."

Remembering this, Karon wrote him:

Congratulations. It is good to have your work recognized appropriately. From time to time I have heard from people in your field about your accomplishments, and from your students about your teaching, and it has always been a source of satisfaction that I was available when you needed me.

But it is easier to be a psychoanalyst who deals consciously with most of a limited relationship than to be a full-time parent, dealing with all the needs, demands, conflicts, and fantasies of real life, only a small part of which are conscious.

REFERENCES

Alanen, Y.O. (1992). Psychotherapy of schizophrenia in community psychiatry. In A. Werbart & J. Cullberg (Eds.), Psychotherapy of schizophrenia: Facilitating and obstructive factors (pp. 237-253). Oslo, Norway: Scandinavian University Press.

Beavers, W.J. (1976). A study of the mothers of retarded children and the concept of pathogenesis utilizing the Thematic Apperception Test. Dissertation Abstracts International, 3b, 6369B. (University Microfilms No. 76-13, 989).

Dahlstrom, W.G., & Welsh, G.S. (1960). An MMPI handbook: A guide to use in clinical practice and research. Minneapolis: University of Minnesota Press.

Doane, J.A., West, K.L., Goldstein, M.J., Rodnick, E.H., & Jones, J.E. (1980). Parental affective style and communication deviance as predictors of subsequent schizophrenia spectrum disorders in vulnerable adolescents. Department of Psychology, University of California, Los Angeles, Los Angeles, CA.

Evans, A.L. (1976). Personality characteristics of child-abusing mothers. (Doctoral dissertation, Michigan State University, 1977). Dissertation Abstracts International, 37, 6322E-6323B. (University Microfilms No. 77-11, 642).

Grinker, K.R., & Spiegel, J.P. (1965). Men under stress. New York: McGraw-Hill.

Karon, B.P. (1960). A clinical note on the significance of an "oral" trauma. Journal of Abnormal and Social Psychology, 61, 480-481.

——— (1975a). All in the family [Review of The origin and treatment of schizophrenic disorders]. Contemporary Psychology, 20, 203-209.

——— (1975b). "You've got to look in the right place": A response to Wender, et a., Contemporary Psychology, 20, 987.

——— (1976). "You still have to look in the right place": A further reply. Contemporary Psychology, 21, 74.

——— & Rosherg, J. (1958). Study of the mother-child relationship in a case of paranoid schizophrenia. American Journal of Psychotherapy, 12, 522-533.

——— & VandenBos, G.R. (1972). The consequences of psychotheray for schizophrenic patients. Psychotherapy: Theory, Research, and Practice, 9, 111-120.

———— & VandenBos, G.R. (1981). Psychotherapy of schizophrenia: The treatment of choice. New York: Aronson.

Kety, S.S., Rosenthal, D., Wender, P.H., & Schulsinger, F. (1968). The types and prevalence of mental illness in the biological and adoptive families of adopted individuals who have become schizophrenic. In D. Rosenthal & S. S. Kety (Eds.), The transmission of schizophrenia (pp. 345-362). Oxford, England: Pergamon.

Leff, J., & Vaughn, C.E. (1985). Expressed emotion in families: Its significance for mental illness. New York: Guilford.

Leigh, L.D. (1987). The relation between "Pathogenesis" in parents and Rorschach indices of ego functioning in preadolescent daughters. (Doctoral dissertation, Michigan State University, 1986). Dissertation Abstracts International, 48, 3684B.

Lewontin, R.C., Rose, S., & Kamin, L.J. (1984). Schizophrenia: the clash of determinisms. In R.C. Lewontin, S. Rose, & L.J. Kamin (Eds.), Not in our genes (pp. 197-232). New York: Pantheon.

Lidz, T. (1973). The origin and treatment of schizophrenic disorders. New York: Basic.

———— & Blatt, S. (1983). Critique of the Danish-American studies of the biological and adoptive relatives of adoptees who became: schizophrenic. American Journal of Psychiatry, 140, 426-435.

————, Blatt, S., & Cook, B. (1981). Critique of the Danish-American studies of the adopted-away offspring of schizophrenic patients. American Journal of Psychiatry, 138, 1063-1068.

Melnick. B., & Hurley, J.R. (1969). Distinctive personality attributes of child-abusing mothers. Journal of Consulting Clinical Psychology, 33, 746-749.

Meyer, R.G., & Karon, B.P. (1967). The tichizophrenogenic mother concept and the TAT Psychiatry, 30, 173-179.

Miklowitz, D.J., Velligan, D.I., Goldstein, M.J., Nuechterlein, K.H., Gitlin, M.J., Ranlett, G., & Doane, J.A. (1991). Communication deviance in families of schizophrenic and manic patients. Journal of Abnormal Psychology, 700(2), 163-173.

Mitchell, K.M. (1968). An analysis of the schizophrenogenic mother concept by means of the Thematic Apperception Test. Journal of Abnormal Psychology, 73(6), 571-57 4.

———— (1974). Relationship between differential levels of parental "pathogenesis" and male children's diagnosis. Journal of Clinical Psychology, 30.

Murray, H.A. (1943). Thematic Apperception Test manual. Cambridge, MA: Harvard University Press (149-50).

Nichols, N. (1970). The relationship between degree of maternal pathogenicity and severity of ego impairment in schizophrenic offspring. (Doctoral dissertation, University of Michigan, 1970). Dissertation Abstracts International, 31, 5003B.

Niederland, W.G. (1984). The Schreber case: Psychoanalytic profile of a paranoid personality. Hillsdale, NJ: The Analytic Press.

Potash, H. (1965). Schizophrenic interaction and the double bind. (Doctoral dissertation, Michigan State University, 1964). Dissertation Abstracts International, 25, 6767B.

Rorschach, H. (1932). Psychodiagnostik: Methodik und ergebnisse wines wahrnehmungsdiagnostischen experiments. Bern, Switzerland: Huber.

Rosanoff, A.J. (1927). Manual of psychiatry. New York: Wiley.

Schatzman, M. (1973). Soul murder: Persecution in the family. New York: Random House.

Searles, H.F. (1965). Collected papers on schizophrenia and related subjects New York: International Universities.

Singer, M., & Wynne, L, (1965a). Thought disorder and family relations of schizophrenics: III. Methodology using projective techniques. Archives of General Psychiatry, 12, 187-200.

Singer, M., & Wynne, L. (1965b). Thought disorder and family relations of schizophrenics: IV. Results and implications. Archives of General Psychiatry, 44, 13-20.

Tienari, P. (1992). Interaction between geneticulnerability and rearing environment. In A. Werbart & J. Cullberg (Eds.), Psychotherapy of schizophrenia: Facilitating and obstructive factors (pp. 154-172). Oslo, Norway: Scandinavian University Press.

Tienari, P., Sorri, A., Lahti, I., Naarala, M., Wahlberg, K., Ronkko, T., Pohjola, J., & Moring, J. (1985). The Finnish adoptive study of schizophrenia. Yale Journal of Biology and Medicine, 58, 227-237.

VandenBos, G.R., & Karon, B.P. (1971). Pathogenesis: a new therapist dimension related to therapeutic effectiveness. Journal of Personality Assessment, 35, 252-260.

Vaughn, C.E. & Leff, J.P. (1976). The influence of family and social factors on the course of psychiatric illness: A comparison of schizophrenic and depressed neurotic patients. British Journal of Psychiatry, 129, 125-137.

Wender, P.H., Rosenthal, D., & Kety, S.S. (1975). "Distorted picture." Contemporary Psychology, 20. 986-987.

————, Rosenthal, D., Kety, S.S., Schulsinger, F., & Weiner, J. (1974). Cross-fostering: A research strategy for clarifying the role of genetic and experiential factors in the etiology of schizophrenia. Archives of General Psychiatry, 30, 121-128.

————., Rosenthal, D., Zahn, T., & Kety, S. (1971). ITie psychiatric adjustment of the adopting parents of schizophrenics. American Journal of Psychiatry, 127, 1013-1018.

Wynne, L. & Singer, M. (1963a). Thought disorder and family relations of schizophrenics: I. A research strategy. Archives of General Psychiatry, 9, 191-198.

———— & Singer, M. (1963b). Thought disorder and family relations of schizophrenics: II. A classification of forms of thinking. Archives of General Psychiatry, 9, 199-206.

————, Singer, M.T., & Toohey, M.L. (1976). Communication of the adoptive parents of schizophrenics. In J. Jorstad & E. Ugelstad (Eds.), Schizophrenia 75: Psychotherapy, family studies, research (pp. 413-450). Oslo, Norway: Universitetsforlaget.PSYCHOANALYTIC PSYCHOLOGY, 1989, 6(2), 169-185

CHAPTER 5
On the Formation of Delusions
Bertram P. Karon, PhD

Abstract

Four principles are identified that account for most delusion formation. The most important of these is transference—transference to the world at large. The second is the defense against pseudo-homosexual impulses as described by Freud (and generally misunderstood). The third is the learning within the family of bizarre meanings of concepts which are assumed erroneously to be the meanings other people use. The fourth is the need to have a more or less consistent understanding of one's life and experiences. Therapeutic implications are drawn.

The Michigan State Psychotherapy Project (Karon & VandertBos, 1981) found that psychoanalytic psychotherapy was effective with schizophrenic patients—and it was far more effective than medication. In brief, patients who received psychotherapy (either without medication or with initial medication from which the patient was gradually withdrawn) had significantly less thought disorder, were discharged from the hospital earlier, were far less likely to be re-hospitalized, and lived a more human life. The longer one followed the patients, the more difference it made whether the patient had received psychotherapy.

Of course, such findings are discrepant from the prevailing ethos in American psychiatry and from a number of widely cited American studies (Grinspoon, Ewalt, & Shader, 1972; May, 1968; May, Tuma, Yale, Potepan, & Dixon, 1976). Although there are many methodological problems in each of the available studies (Karon & VandenBos, 1975), a consistent picture nonetheless emerges from them. When psychoanalytic psychotherapy is carried out by inexperienced therapists (May, 1968) or by therapists experienced with other patients but inexperienced with schizophrenics (Grinspoon et al., 1972), it is hard to demonstrate effectiveness, but when it is carried out by psychoanalytic psychotherapists experienced in working specifically with schizophrenics or by motivated novices supervised by such experienced psychotherapists, it is more helpful than medication (Karon & VandenBos,1981). A Swedish study (Sjostrom & Sandin, 1981) using a very experienced therapist had similar findings.

Most recently, the Boston psychotherapy study (Gunderson et al.. 1984; Karon, 1984; Stanton et at, 1984) found that expressive insight-oriented psychotherapy as compared to supportive therapy produced more improvement in some aspects of ego functioning, but was not as effective at improving occupational functioning. For most criteria used, the treatments were not different. Although these findings are apt to be cited (often eliminating the ego-functioning differences), what is not cited is that medication levels were not reduced for insight-oriented therapy patients, that only approximately one fourth of the patients both stayed in treatment and allowed themselves to be assessed, and that patients with severe thought disorders (symptoms which are particularly apt to improve with psychoanalytic psychotherapy, Karon & O'Grady, 1969) were screened out.

Such research, however, is less convincing than clinical experience (Furlan & Benedetti, 1985) to most psychoanalytic therapists. Unfortunately, clinical experience will vary with the circumstances and the supervision under which the treatment of schizophrenic patients has been undertaken.

Effective psychoanalytic psychotherapy is, of course, always based on an understanding of the psychopathology. Among the most central symptoms, for schizophrenic patients, are delusions. An understanding of delusion formation is essential to effective treatment of schizophrenic patients. This view clearly differs from the perspective that, although delusions may be understandable on the basis of psychoanalytic theories, such an understanding is merely an interesting intellectual exercise that does not provide a basis for effective treatment.

Four bases for understanding delusions are described. In each instance, the understanding of the delusions leads directly to meaningful clinical intervention which also is described.

Terror, Psychosis, And Objective/Subjective Reality

To understand delusions, one must first understand that schizophrenia consists of a state of chronic terror and the defenses that the individual uses to cope with that terror (cf. Bcttelheim, 1956). Schizophrenic symptoms can only be understood in relationship to the whole life history of a given patient—from infancy onward. The worse one's early infancy, the less objectively terrifying one's later life has to be to produce schizophrenic symptoms. Conversely, the better one's early life, the more terrifying one's later experience must be to eventuate in a psychotic solution.

Such a view of schizophrenia is also controversial. It is consistent with the views of most other psychodynamic theorists, but not with those of most biologically oriented theorists, despite the fact that the medications which produce symptomatic improvement massively interfere with the affect system, dampening down terror and anger. Nor is the evidence for genetic factors as persuasive as secondary sources suggest. For example, early adopted-away offspring of schizophrenics only became schizophrenic if the adoptive families were disturbing in the way that Wynne and Singer (1963) described (Tienari et al., 1985; Wynne, Singer,&Touhey, 1976). At most, genetic factors increase vulnerability; it is the psychic life history which provides the basis for understanding specific symptoms and for therapeutic intervention.

The psychological life of all individuals consists of a set of fantasies, conscious and unconscious, which are formed on the basis of actual experience, as given meaning by the preexisting conscious and unconscious fantasies. Actual experience, of course, does not necessarily mean experience as it would be recorded by an outside observer, but as it was consciously experienced by the individual. Thus, an infant may feel that "mother tortures me" either because an abusive mother actually tortured the infant, or because the six-month-old infant was separated from the mother in order to be hospitalized for a necessary operation. In the infant's experience, these two experiences are identically terrifying, even though objectively the second mother is trying to help the child. Of course, "mother tortures me" is not experienced in words, but these feelings have to be put into words in order for us to discuss them (both in the psychotherapy situation and in scientific discussions).

In almost all situations involving schizophrenic psychopathology, there arc problems in the early mother-child relationship which are then relived in successive editions in the oral, anal, and genital battlegrounds (as well as later stages of development). Thus, for the schizophrenic, the problems of early infancy tend to be repeated and amplified by later experiences, whereas in normal development the later experiences, both with the original objects (the parents) and with new objects (people outside the immediate family), reduce the destructive impact of earlier experiences.

Insofar as destructive parental interactions are involved, they tend to be based on unconscious parental defenses (Meyer & Karon, 1967; Mitchell, 1968, 1969) or on conscious interactions which the parent does not know are hurtful. In either ease, the destructive interactions are continued, either because the parent is unaware of them, or because he or she has no conscious reason to change. Consciously, most parents of schizophrenics are decent, kind parents.

A Brief Clinical Example

A 35-year-old male chronic paranoid schizophrenic patient complains, for example, of a fear of being poisoned, sees "the Athenian girls taunting me, saying that their breasts are poisoned," goes on hunger strikes periodically, and makes sucking noises that turn out to be short forms of the word "best" (which itself, according to the patient, is a short form of "make die world best," which eventually is revealed by his associations to mean "make the world into a good breast"). Clearly, this is a patient with "oral" problems! Yet, this patient's mother breast-fed him for a full year and gradually weaned him. Where could the oral trauma have been?

As always, clinical material from the patient provided the answer (Karon, 1960; Karon & Rosberg, 1958). In this case, the nature of the trauma was revealed by his delusion of the cow. He said: "The cow gave her calf milk, and kicked it. She shouldn't do that. It is something that happened hundreds of times in the history of the world." Clearly the history of the world is his life history and he was saying that when his mother fed him, she became angry and hurt him. Poison is simply something that hurts one after eating it. Spitz (1965) showed how the quality of the movements of the angry mother hurts the infant, even if it is not apparent to the observer (without high-speed photography) nor to the conscious awareness of the mother.

But this same sequence was observable even when this patient was 35 (and his mother was in her late 50s). She took care of the treatment house, supposedly to save expenses. Whenever she cooked a meal and the patient ate it, they quarreled afterwards. The fight was never about eating. If someone else cooked, or if she cooked but he was on a hunger strike and did not eat there was no quarrel. This was observed for a 6-month period. The mother was not consciously aware of it. The demand "mother me/feed me" made her anxious. When she was anxious, she became angry. When she was angry, any pretext became the occasion for a quarrel. Thus, the early infantile traume was relived throughout life, and there was no chance to undo the damage (Karon, 1960; Karon & Rosberg, 1958). This illustrates the usual basis foi poisoned milk fantasies (and poisoning fantasies in general), namely, the mother who got angry after feeding her child.

The First Basis For Delusions: Transference

The single most important basis for the formation of delusions is also illustrated by the previous clinical example (viz., transference). Delusions are always meaningfully related to the individual's life history and defenses.

It is well-known that Freud believed that schizophrenic patients did not form a transference and, therefore, were not amenable to psychoanalytic therapy, although he felt that this was a technical difficulty that someone might find a way around. However, Freud did not treat schizophrenic patients because, as he told those close to him, they frightened him. Certainly, he had enough work to do for one lifetime, even without seeing schizophrenics. Nonetheless, psychoanalytic conclusions, even Freud's, are accurate only when they are based on patient observations.

Freud originally talked about transference as if it occurred uniquely in the psychoanalytic situation. But, as Ferenczi (1909/1950) pointed out in an early paper which Freud accepted, transference is something that human beings do all the time. What is unique in psychoanalysis is that it is studied and made conscious.

It is well-known that what appear as resistances in psychoanalytic therapy are the defense mechanisms that the individual uses to cope with life and impulses outside of the therapeutic hour. So, too, transference is a defense regularly used in everyday life. One may well ask, "If it is a defense, what is it a defense against?" Drs. Walter Poznanski and Jean Chambers (personal communication, February 16, 1984) pointed out that it is a defense against separation anxiety.

The claim that transference is primarily a defense against separation anxiety is obviously controversial and may strike the reader as an oversimplification. Indeed, other psychic processes may well be involved, for example, undoing, displacement, working through, attempts at mastering traumas, and repetition compulsion (a descriptive rather than explanatory concept). Nonetheless, that transference is primarily a defense against separation anxiety is a clinically powerful idea, which explains its ubiquity in ordinary life as well as pathology.

Schizophrenic patients do form a transference to their therapist, but what they have to transfer is awful. In our experience, the life history of every schizophrenic patient, as subjectively experienced by that patient, is adequate to the symptoms. Insofar as schizophrenics have very severe symptoms, one would expect (and one finds) a severe and painful life history. Consequently, the transference to the therapist is of destructive and hurtful expectations.

The problem, thus, is not how to get the schizophrenic to form a transference, but how to get the transference to be therapeutically useful. Developing a therapeutic alliance in the face of malevolent transferences is the technical problem. The following advice is controversial, but effective. The therapeutic alliance is fostered by the therapist's attempt to make clear that he or she is helpful, protective, and truly on the patient's side. The therapist must make it directly and explicitly clear that he or she will not allow the patient to be killed or severely injured, that the therapist believes that the patient can get better, that the symptoms are meaningful (although neither the patient nor the therapist need know the specific meaning to begin work), and that improvement and change only require a great deal of hard psychotherapeutic work (in which the therapist is willing and able to assist).

But the transference of the patient to the world at large is even more important. It is the single most important basis for delusional material. This is well illustrated in the classic case of Schreber (Niederland, 1959), where the delusion that God was "lovingly" tightening a metal band around his head until it hurt referred to actual experiences with his father. His father was a famous pediatrician whose books on child care were widely read. It contained such "good advice" as "bad habits" (i.e., masturbation) should be dealt with firmly and they will disappear by the age of 4, never to return—noting as evidence that he had done this with his own sons and there were no bad aftereffects. One of his sons committed suicide, and the other is the most famous paranoid schizophrenic who ever lived.

The father believed that exercise and posture were important for children, and he invented devices that consisted of rods and metal bands attached to chairs, tables, and beds so that the child must sit or lie perfectly straight. These metal bands, he advised, should be tightened lovingly. What Schrcber experienced God doing to him in his delusions and hallucinations was merely what his real father had actually done to him as a child. Yet, few psychiatrists of his time would have considered that a famous pediatrician could possibly have tortured his own sons. (Although the father, of course, did not think of it as torture, but as something he did for the child's good.)

In attempting to understand a delusion, therefore, one should first consider whether (and in what way) it might be a transference. If patients feel that people spy on them, did they feel that their parents spied on them? If patients feel that people want to kill them, did they feel that their parents wanted to kill them? If they feel that people are conspiring against them, did they feel that their parents (and siblings) conspired against them? If a patient feels that people hate him or her when they come near, and like the patient when they go away, is it because the patient tried to believe that the patient's parents liked the patient, but when they came close, the patient could feel their hostility? If patients are concerned about a war between two superpowers, did they feel caught in the war between their parents? If American patients have delusions about the Civil War, did they feel that if they loved their mother they must hate their father—or if they love their father, they have to hate their mother? The logic should be clear. The principle that transference accounts for the phenomena not only makes the delusion understandable to the therapist, but can also make it understandable to the patient and, hence, therapeutically useful.

Of course, the patient will initially deny that the delusion has any relationship to his or her past life. As the patient with the cow delusion said when it was first interpreted, "I want to talk about history, and you just want to tell dirty stories about me and my mother." But if the interpretation is presented as a possible explanation which makes meaningful what otherwise seems inexplicable, it will eventually reduce anxiety and be accepted. This assumes that the interpretation is presented tactfully within the confines of a warm, benign, protective relationship with a dependable therapist.

Therapeutic Handling Of Religious Delusions

One set of transference based delusions that must be handled with great tact are those concerned with God. Failure to do so has led to violent assaults on the author more often than any other mistake. Il is therefore worth describing appropriate therapeutic interventions. One should never say, "That voice is not God." Think of how anyone would feel if they had a direct line to God and someone tried to take it away from them. They might well get violent. The therapist should simply use the information presented in the delusion, such as by asking, "I wonder if your mother (or father) said or did . . . (what God said or did)?" If naming one parent does not work, the therapist should try the other. Once the therapist has discovered the identity of God, it can be relied upon in understanding later material. Frequently, the patient will respond with "How did you know that?" Eventually, the patient will discover the therapist's source of information, but that discovery indicates that it is no longer too threatening to the patient.

Unfortunately, the voice of God is sometimes so malevolent that it is necessary to disagree immediately, as when God says "You must kill yourself." Then the therapist should say: "I doubt that that is God, because God is not a sadist." If the patient is a Christian, the therapist can add: "The whole New Testament is about forgiveness. If you do not believe me, read it again." Usually the patient will say "That's not how I was taught." The therapist should have no hesitation in telling the patient authoritatively, but kindly, that the patient does not understand his religion, and that any "reasonable" minister/ priest of his denomination will agree with the therapist. If the patient insists that his or her childhood minister/priest disagrees, the therapist should tell the patient that the minister/priest really does not understand his or her denomination. Sometimes, one can also say that people often attribute to God things which really belong to their parents. "I have to think that your parents must have made you feel that they wanted . . . (whatever sadistic thing that God supposedly wants)."

Obviously, this is a recommendation that the therapist have no hesitation in talking theology of any religion authoritatively with schizophrenic patients. At some level, the patients want to be able to live with their religions beliefs and are grateful for a reinterpretation that makes their religion humanly bearable. Lovinger (1984) is a useful source for denominational information for therapists. Frequently, one is lucky enough to know a clergyman of the appropriate denomination who will cooperate in helping the patient arrive at a helpful (rather than a hurtful) version of his or her religion.

It is assumed the patient does not immediately accept the therapist's views and the therapist does not require agreement. But the therapist so often proves right about issues that seem outlandish to the patient, that the patient considers the therapist's views seriously, even if overtly rejecting them, and this produces eventual agreement and sufficient immediate doubt as to usually forestall precipitate destructive acting out.

The Second Basis For Delusions:
Loneliness And The Fear Of Pseudo Homosexuality

Freud described the second basis for understanding delusions, specifically paranoid delusions, in the case of Schreber (Freud, 1911). It is interesting that secondary sources report everything that Freud said, except what is fundamental and therapeutically useful. As is well-known and usually reported, many paranoid delusions may be understood as a defense against homosexual impulses. If one considers the different ways in which one could contradict the feeling "I love him," one derives many typical delusions. "I do not love him, I love me (megalomania)." "I do not love him, I love her (erotomania)." "I do not love him, she loves him (delusional jealousy)." "I do not love him, he loves me (projecting the homosexuality, producing a delusional homosexual threat)." "I do not love him, I hate him (reaction formation)." And, finally, most common, projecting the delusional hatred as "He hates me, hence, it is alright for me to hate him (and if I hate him, 1 do not love him)."

This understanding by itself might lead one to reassure a paranoid patient that he or she is merely homosexual, that such impulses are alright, and that homosexuality is an increasingly acceptable alternate way of life. The patient would undoubtedly feel insulted and might well physically assault the therapist.

What Freud actually said (in the language of libido theory) that is omitted is that the patient felt withdrawn from emotional contact with others. In addition to the father fixation was a regression to a pre-heterosexual object choice. Because as children we were comfortable with peers of the same sex before we became comfortable with opposite-sex peers, and because people of the same sex are more like us than people of the opposite sex, when we feel withdrawn from everyone, we are attracted to someone of the same sex. Unfortunately, the patient becomes aware of this attraction, misinterprets it as homosexuality, and this sets off the defenses just described. These paranoid delusions are, thus, the paradoxical result of the self-curative tendency to attempt to relate to other people.

This reading of Freud leads to reasonable interpretations. "You are simply lonely, and we all need friends of both sexes." Every schizophrenic understands and feels understood v/hen the therapist speaks of loneliness.

The therapist might even say (if, as is usual, the patient is not an overt homosexual), "You are not a homosexual although you may be afraid that you might be." The patient is grateful if the therapist lessens the taboo on close relations with people of the same sex; differentiates thoughts, fantasies, and dreams (for all of which morality is irrelevant) from actions; and clarifies the dynamics of sporadic, childhood, or forced homosexual experiences.

Of course, satisfying overt homosexual relationships would not be discouraged or denied (although their meanings will eventually be explored if the patient stays in long-term therapy), but they are rarely characteristic of patients with these kinds of paranoid delusions.

Freud's view of paranoid delusions has been criticized on three grounds. First, it does not account for many delusions. However, the most important determinant of delusions has already been discussed (viz., transference). Other bases are discussed later. Second, it does not account for the systematic nature of delusions; this is also discussed later. Third, it does not explain the observation that the persecutor in the delusions of female paranoids tends to be male. A number of writers have made this observation, but the first was Freud himself (Freud, 1915). He accounted for this by pointing out that when the female patient first had psychotic delusions, the persecutor was female and that, as the delusions developed, the persecutor's gender was changed as a further stage of disguise.

This latter point is a special case of two phenomena. The first is that delusional systems keep developing, and in the psychotherapy of a patient who has been delusional for a long time, the delusions do not simply disappear. Typically, earlier and earlier versions of the delusions reappear as the patient gets better. Often when the patient describes the delusions as they were at the time of the first psychotic break, the therapist is startled by how clear everything seems and wonders why the original treatment personnel never understood what, at a later time, has taken so much work to reveal clearly. The second phenomenon is that women's attitudes towards men (or the father) often are disguised representations of what was originally an attitude towards the mother. After all, the mother is the most important person in the world for the infant and child (male or female) in most families and cultures.

The Third Basis F:or Delusions:
Family-Specific Meanings

The third basis for delusions is a straightforward teaching by the family of strange beliefs about the world and other human beings. As Lidz (1973) pointed out, children depend on their family to teach them the categories that they use to think about the world and to communicate with other human beings. If their family teaches the children strange or atypical categories (or strange and atypical meanings to concepts that the children believe other people share), then their mode of thinking will be delusional by ordinary standards. An example that Lidz gave and is frequently seen in patients is related to the concept of love. If one thinks that love means "I hurt you and try to kill you from time to time," it is very difficult (and terrifying) to try to establish a close and loving relationship with another human being. The insidious part of teaching the child atypical meanings of concepts and categories is that the child assumes that people outside the family think and use language in the same way that the child has been taught. Furthermore, schizophrenics rarely are exposed to experiences which both require and allow them to relearn more appropriate and realistic meanings of the concepts that they use.

Normally, human beings correct for the inadequacies in their own family by using people outside the family as sources of corrective information, corrective experiences, and corrective identifications. Of course, no one has ever had (or been) a "perfect" parent, so such corrective experiences are important to everyone. Freud, who did not treat psychotics, did not emphasize this because his patients had such corrective experiences. Sullivan (1953), who worked with schizophrenics, emphasized the importance of these relation-ships or the lack of them. It has been noted by a number of psychotherapists who work with schizophrenics (e.g., Searles, 1965) that often the parents ac-tively discourage the use of people outside the family as sources of information and corrective identification. As one mother of a schizophrenic teenager said with a proud smile, when she was advised that it would be important for her daughter to visit with her friends upon release from the hospital, "You don't understand, doctor, we are not that kind of people. We never visit anyone, and no one ever visits us."

It must not be thought that the parents intend to hurt the child. The parent has no idea that this is destructive. The motive can be understood by considering an interaction that no American parent has ever been spared, or that any parent has ever enjoyed. The child says "Henry cart do it, Jean can coit, why can't I do it?"

Parents handle this situation as well as they can, but almost always with discomfort. They may say "If Henry and Jean can do it, you can do it." They may say, "I don't care what Henry and Jean can do, you are living with me and these are the rules here." They may check with Henry and Jean's parents, and then say "Alright," or they may check with Henry and Jean's paren: and discover that no one has permission, but that everyone is saying that others have permission. (If a parent wants a child who never outsmarts him or her, then the parent must have either a mentally defective child or a schizophrenic child. A healthy and intelligent child will outsmart a parent occasionally.)

But this sequence, beginning with the question, "They can do it, why can'tI do it?" (which makes parents uncomfortable), is very good for the child'sdevelopment, no matter how the specific issue is handled by the parent. Thechild is comparing the way things are done in their household with the way-other people do things. Even if the specific issue is inappropriately handled,at worst, the child thinks this is just my "nutty" parents and not that it isa "God-given" rule and that the child is evil for disagreeing with the parent!,.

However, if one interferes with the use of people outside the family, one'squestionable beliefs and values are never questioned. Although such a lackof questioning reduces the parents' anxiety, the unintended potential harm-ful effect on the child can be enormous. Unfortunately, any problem withinthe family is greatly magnified in its effect on the child when this normalcorrective mechanism is not available.

When discussing the parental pressures that lead to a vulnerability to schizophrenic symptoms, many psychoanalytic colleagues argue that parental pressures cannot be a primary cause of schizophrenic disorders, because they have had neurotic patients whose parents were every bit as difficult to live with as those of schizophrenic patients. Psychoanalytic experience with neurotic patients readily confirms this. But, in every case in my experience, there was someone outside of the immediate family who provided the child with the emotional relationship and corrective experiences that were lacking in the relationship with his or her parents.

Treatment centers for schizophrenics, such as Ronald Laing's Philadelphia Society in England and Soteria House in the United States, where patients live with non-punitive and acceptant peers, and the traditional treatment in Gheel, Belgium, where patients lived with healthy families, have their therapeutic action by reinstating I he normal process of extra-familial corrective emotional experience.

The Fourth Basis For Delusions:
The Need For Systematic Understanding

The fourth basis for delusions, particularly paranoid delusions, becomes increasingly clear when one asks, "Why are the delusional systems systematic?" The realization that all schizophrenic patients have systematic paranoid delusions is a key. The catatonics do not reveal their delusions until they begin talking. The therapist does not understand the hebephrenics; when the therapist does, hebephrenics have a delusional system. The patients who are diagnosed as paranoid seem to be the brighter ones. When one examines Wechsler IQ test scores, one finds that the pure paranoids are the brightest, the paranoid schizophrenics the next brightest, and the other schizophrenics less bright (Albert I. Rabin, personal communication, November 12, 1962, unpublished data on 1,000 consecutive admissions to the one public hospital in a small state for 2 years). Thus, the brighter one is, the more a delusional system seems to suffice as a symptom; and the less bright one is, the more one seems to need additional, more deteriorated symptoms.

The real insight came when I realized that all human beings have a more or less systematic understanding of the world in which they live. The only reason that people do not believe that most others are paranoid is because they share more or less the same systematic understanding of the world (and, if they differ, they can at least understand why they came to different conclusions). Thus, if one believes the world is flat, one is normal if it is 1400, but is at least suspect today.

This central ego function of understanding one's self and the world in which one lives is so obvious that it is easy to overlook. The paranoid or schizophrenic patients have had weird and unusual experiences. Their symptoms themselves are frequently strange experiences that other people do not have. Their life history, aside from symptoms, usually involves experiences which are not part of the life histories of other people. Like all human beings, they try to understand what is happening (and has happened) to them. Insofar as their experiences are strange, their explanations may well be strange. The brighter patients are able to come up with better explanations which serve to protect them to some extent from a need for more deteriorated symptoms.

One of the persistent myths is that delusions are unchanging and inchangeable. It persists because delusions are so different from the way most people think that superficially they seem unchanged. But rarely do they entirely fit reality, and the patient is constantly repairing them. If now an interested and sympathetic therapist considers them and tries to follow their logic, the repair work can get frantic.

The therapist must be on the patient's side, fostering the therapeutic alliance by considering seriously the probability of what is related, helping the patient to think clearly about the issues, and helping the patient to evaluate the evidence, remembering that just because something is improbable does not mean it is necessarily untrue, and even paranoids may be in actual danger of being killed.

The therapist should always ask for as much detail about the delusions as possible, but should do it in a kindly manner. Not only will this provide the material necessary for accurate interpretive work, but it will lead the patient to become aware of the inadequacies of his or her delusions as explanations and, hence, amenable to interpretation (i.e., to an alternative explanation).

Therapeutically, it is often useful to tell the patient, "That is a brilliant explanation." The patient is generally startled that any professional would treat his or her ideas seriously.

"You mean you think it is true?"

If, as is usually the case, the therapist believes that the patient can tolerate it, the therapist might usefully say: "No, but that is because I know some things about the human mind which you don't know yet, and I'll tell you if you're interested. But, given what you do know, that is a brilliant explanation." With such a non-humiliating approach to the patient, it is often possible to get the most suspicious paranoid to consider what might be going on and its real meaning as an attempt to solve the terrifying dilemmas of his or her symptoms and life history.

Thus, one male patient was sure that a large corporation for which he had worked was out to kill him. Indeed, he had left his job and fled that part of the country for several months before returning and seeking treatment. In particular, he was sure that one foreman was bent on his destruction. (His father had been a foreman for the same company.) When asked what made him think the corporation wanted to kill him, he reported that he had discovered erroneous data required by the federal government. Thinking it was simply a mistake, he had reported this to his foreman, who reported it upwards. Shortly afterwards, the foreman seemed to be in trouble with his superiors, and the patient was assigned away from the job he liked (where he had discovered the erroneous data) to more arduous, dangerous, and unpleasant work assignments. He became convinced that he was being harassed because the data was not a mistake but had been intentionally falsified. Shortly after, he felt that they would kill him and left.

"That sounds scary as hell!"

"It sure is," the patient said.

"You've got good reason to be scared. Some large corporations have killed people to cover up things. Karen Silkwood did exist."

"That's right."

"But in the past, this corporation has harassed people who were inconvenient and attempted to frighten them, but there are several well-known cases of large financial settlements to people whom it would have been cheaper to kill."

"But they were better known than me. Nobody knows me. I'd like to believe this is just paranoia, and you probably think so, but I don't think it is."

"I don't think so either. I believe you discovered faked data, and they harassed you to cover it up. I just don't think they'd kill you over it. By this time the data's gone, and no one could check."

"And no one would believe me now, anyway."

Eventually, the patient was able to contact the company to collect his last wages, and when no violence occurred, to investigate and deal with his childhood fear of his father's violence.

Lifelong, Chronic, And Acute Delusions

Delusions may be lifelong or they may occur acutely. Obviously, those delusional beliefs based on having learned strange facts or categories of thought within the family are lifelong. Those based on the denial of homosexual (or pseudo-homosexual) impulses and projection are most likely to be acute, although they may be enduring, and those based on transference may have any temporal configuration. As the life experience of the patient, as given meaning by his or her conscious and unconscious fantasies, increases in terror, the dynamic balance is upset. New delusions are created in the attempt to reestablish a dynamic equilibrium. When the level of terror decreases, with or without psychotherapy, or if a different symptom is developed to cope with it, a delusion may disappear. Acutely appearing delusions are more likely to disappear quickly. Sometimes, when a delusional belief is no longer needed, it is rejected as something the individual used to believe, but which he or she now' knows not to be true. Often, the acute occurrence of a delusion is remembered as m event which occurred in the past.

Of course, chronic delusions are frequently maintained, bur the patient has the good sense to not tell other people, including mental health professionals, because of their expected reactions.

The Reconstruction Of The Psychic Life History

There are some analysts who talk as if the patient's fantasies bear no relationship to their life history and any coherent narrative would do if the patient accepts it. This is not my view. The fantasies are formed in relationship to the actual experiences of the life history. As the therapist works with a patient, suddenly everything falls into place, makes sense, and the patient improves. This is because what has been reconstructed is what the life history, as experienced by the patient, really was.

Wrong interpretations are certainly not as effective as correct interpretations, even when ardently believed by the therapist. (As a therapist who has ardently believed in plausible, consistent, but incorrect formulations, I can attest to their therapeutic un-helpfulness.)

The patient actually did live a life, and wants to know what that life actually was. It is very helpful if the therapist and the patient together can reconstruct it.

It has been my experience that the reconstruction from therapy, with even psychotic patients, is very accurate and can be validated by external information when it is available. That does not mean that it is accurate the first time the patient presents it. But, after the patient and the therapist have worked over the material, the reconstruction is far more accurate than the initial accounts of the supposedly well member of the family. Often after the reconstruction, the other family members, if directly asked, will say "Of course, that happened. Didn't I tell you about that?" or 'I did not think that was important" or "I was ashamed to tell you about that."

The one distortion which remains is that what is reconstructed as a single event or memory is usually a summary of a series of events with similar meaning. There may also be some issues where it is not dear what actually happened and what was a fantasy. Even putting that uncertainty into words is helpful to the patient. The patient may achieve more insight at a later time in therapy, or later without the therapist's help, or the patient may feel that he or she does not need further clarification but that the therapist's putting the residual uncertainty into words is helpful.

The preverbal period poses a special problem. This is a critical period in any patient's life, and particularly in the lives of people who develop very serious disorders. But the experiences were not conceptualized in words. They may be relived in symptoms, dreams, delusional and hallucinatory experiences, and transference reactions, but the patient does not have words to capture them. Here, there is some arbitrariness to the reconstruction. Because of the uncertainties of our knowledge, different psychoanalytic schools use different theoretical concepts to describe the experiences of the preverbal period. But any psychoanalytic therapist provides the patient with a vocabulary of concepts with which to describe and understand these early experiences and their symptomatic reliving in the present, even though the therapist cannot be sure that his or her favorite conceptual school is the most adequate one. The patient will change the therapist's approximations of the patient's experience to make them fit more closely the patient's own subjective experiences.

Summary

Of course, everything that one knows as a psychoanalyst about primary process thinking, about development, and about intrapsychic events is relevant to understanding delusions. It may be noted that projective processes, including projective identification, are given less prominence in the previous discussion than is currently fashionable. That is true because most delusions based on projective processes involve transference repetitions of early experiences with a parent who blurred the distinction between parental identity and child identity as well as repetitions of that early period of infancy when such blurring is normal. Thus, most delusional material may be understood by the four relatively simple notions which are presented. .Although these principles may seem overly simple, it is my experience that they do allow the therapist to understand the vast majority of delusions and, hence, they provide the basis for effective psychoanalytic therapy with even the most severely disturbed patients.

ACKNOWLEDGMENTS

This article is a revised version of a paper presented to the Norwegian Psychoanalytic Association, Oslo, Norway, on March 13, 1984.

I express my gratitude to Gary R. VandenBos, PhD, who helped clarify these ideas.

REFERENCES

Bettelheim, B. (1956). Schizophrenia as a readior to extreme situations. American Journal of Orthopsychiatry, 26, 507-518.

Ferenczi, S. (1950). Introjection and transference. In E. Jones (Ed. and Trans.), Sex in psychoanalysis: Selected papers. Volume I (pp. 35-93). New York: Brunner/Mazel. (Original work published 1909)

Freud, S. (1911). Psycho-analytic notes on an autobiographical account of a case of paranoia (dementia paranoides). S.E., 12, 9-82.

———— (1915). A case of paranoia running counter to the psycho-analytic theory of the disease. S.E., 14, 261-272.

Furlan, P.A., & Benedetti, G., (1985). The individual psychoanalytic psychotherapy of schizophrenia: Scientific and clinical approach through a clinical discussion group. Yale Journal of Biology and Medicine, 58, 337-348.

Grinspoon, I., Ewalt, J.R. & Shader, R.I. (1972). Schizophrenia, pharmacotherapy and psychotherapy. Baltimore: Williams & Wilkins.

Gunderson, I.G., Frank, A.F. Katz, 11. M., Vannicelli. M. L., Frosch, J. P., & Knapp, P. H. (1984). Effects of psychotherapy in schizophrenia: II. Comparative outcome of two forms of treatmenl. Schizophrenia Bulletin, 10, 564-598.

Karon, B. P. (1960). A clinical note on the significance of an "oral" trauma. Journal of Abnormal and Social Psychology, 61, 480-481.

———— (1984). The fear of reducing medication, and where have all the patients gone? Schizophrenia Bulletin, 11, 613-617.

———— & O'Grady, P. (1969). Intellectual test changes in schizophrenic patients in the first six months of treatment. Psychotherapy: Theory, Research, and Practice. 6. 88-96.

———— & Rosberg, J. (1958). Study of the mother-child relationship in a case of paranoid schizophrenia. American Journal of Psychotherapy, 12, 522-533.

———— & VandenBos, G.R. (1975). Issues in current research on psychotherapy vs. medication with schizophrenics. Psychotherapy: Theory, Research, and Practice, 12, 143-148.

———— & VandenBos, G.R. (1981). The psychotherapy of schizophrenia: The treatment of choice. New York: Aronson.

Lidz, T. (1973). The origin and treatment of schizophrenic disorders. New York: Basic Books.

Lovinger, R.I. (1984). Working with religious issues in therapy. New York: Aronson.

May, P.R.A. (1968). Ireatmenl of schizophrenia: ,4 comparative study of five treatment methods. New York: Science House.

———, TUma, H. H., Yale, C., Potepan, R. & Dixon, W.J. (1976). Schizophrenia: A follow-up study of results of treatment. Archives of General Psychiatry, S3, 481 –486.

Meyer, R.M., & Karon, B.P. (1967). A study of the schizophrenogenic mother concept and the TAT. Psychiatry, 30, 173 179.

Mitchell, K.M. (1968). An analysis of the schizophrenogenic mother concept by means of the TAT. Journal of Abnormal Psychology, 73, 571–5 7 4.

——— (1969). Concept of "pathogenesis" in parents of schizophrenic and normal children. Journal of Abnormal Psychology, 74, 423–424.

Niederland, W.G. (1959). Schreber: Father and son. Psychoanalytic Quarterly, 11. 151–169.

Searles, H.F. (1965). Collected papers on schizophrenia and related subjects. New York: International Universities Press.

Sjostrom, R., Sandin, B. (1981, September). Effects of psychotherapy in schizophrenia—A retrospective study. Paper presented at the First European Conference of Psychotherapy Research, Trier, Federal Republic of Germany Psychiatric Research Center, Utleraker Hospital S-750, 17 Uppsula, Sweden.

Spitz, R. (1965). The first year of life. New York: International Universities Press.

Stanton, A.H., Gunderson, J.G., Knapp, P. FI., Frank, A.F., Vannicelli, M. 1... Schnitzer, R , & Rosenthal, R. (1984). Effects of psychotherapy in schizophrenia: I. Design and implementation of a controlled study. Schizophrenia Bulletin, 10, 520–563.

Sullivan, H.S. (1953). The interpersonal theory of psychiatry. New York: Norton.

Tienari, P., Sorri, A., Lahti, I., Naarala, M. Wall I berg, K., Ronkko, T., Pohjola, J. & Moring, J. 11985). The Finnish adoptive study of schizophrenia. Yale Journal of Biology and Medicine, 58, 227–237.

Wynne, L., & Singer, M. (1963). Thought disorder and family relations of schizophrenics. 11. A classification of forms of thinking. Archives of General Psychiatry, 9, 199–206.

————, Singer, M., & Touhey, M. (1976). Communication of the adoptive parents of schizophrenics, in J. Jorstad & E. Ugelstad (Eds.), Schizophrenia 75 tpp. 413–451). Oslo, Norway: University of Oslo Press. CASE REPORTS

CHAPTER 6
The Use of Hallucinations in the Treatment of Psychotic Patients
Bertram P. Karon, PhD

"No one understands hallucinations,"

The speaker might have been a psychiatrist or psychologist, but, in fact, he was a patient. Patients like to say that.

But hallucinations are simply wide-awake dreams, readily understandable by Freud's psychology of dreams, with minor modifications. Hallucinations are at least as useful in the treatment of psychotics as dreams are in the treatment of neurotics. After all, psychotics are more puzzling and are less likely to communicate clearly. They are also less likely to report dreams until they stop hallucinating. The capacity to hallucinate while wide awake, however, is not restricted to psychotics. All of us knew, long before we were therapists, that starving people hallucinate food, and people dying of thirst hallucinate water. These are obvious wish-fulfillments; the need simply has to be stronger to dream while you are wide awake.

A British study (Breheny, 1990) found that of the many people who hear voices, only 40% had ever been treated by a mental health specialist. Those whose voices were particularly terrifying, destructive, and overpowering found this helpful; those whose voices were comforting resented the interventions of the professional. Those who had talked to a clergyman or friend reported it as more consistently helpful. Twenty-four percent did not talk about it to anyone. This was because they did not want the voice to go away. The voice started when they were under stress, for example, after a parent or spouse died: the voice says, "You're doing fine," "It's okay," or some other comforting words from someone they wish were still around. They did not need Freud to tell them this was a wish fulfillment.

Psychotic hallucinations also may mean that the patient is lonely; the voices represent somebody who cares about them. But even malevolent voices are better than being alone. Any child would rather be punished than ignored; and all adults, sick or well, still carry the seeds of their childhood within them.

In primitive cultures, hallucinations are not uncommon but the well adjusted hear and see them only under culturally appropriate circumstances, while the emotionally disturbed hear and see them under culturally inappropriate circumstances.

Schizophrenics may hallucinate in any sensory modality but, as Eugen Bleuler (1950) pointed out, almost all schizophrenics hear voices. Predominantly visual hallucinations, particularly moving animals in color, suggest a toxic psychosis. These patients should be asked about their use of alcohol and other drugs. This relationship between visual hallucinations and toxic psychosis was ignored by researchers who tried to tie schizophrenia to LSD and other chemical substances (Karon & Vandenbos, 1981). But these chemically induced psychoses had all the characteristics of toxic psychoses, that is, a predominance of visual phenomena.

The predominance of auditory hallucinations, on the other hand, means that schizophrenia is basically an interpersonal disorder. People who are deaf tend to have more psychological problems than people who are blind. Blind people are more physically incapacitated, but deaf people are more cut off from other human beings. The voice is the most general connection to other people. The problems that lead to schizophrenia are the result of disturbed relations with other people, and it is these disturbed relations that the patient is trying to resolve.

Hallucinatory material—whether auditory, visual, odoriferous, or any other—should be treated like a dream; that is, it should be described, associated to, made sense of, and brought meaningfully into the context of the patient's problem. Nearly as common as the myth that no one knows what hallucinations mean is the secondary myth, that whatever they mean ought not to be disclosed to the patient, and that the very search for meaning is destructive. Many mental health professionals, including some psychoanalysts, believe that the patient should be directed toward reality and not encouraged to explore their hallucinations. Sometimes this is combined with the idea that the unconscious is already conscious in schizophrenics and that there is no need to seek beyond the hallucination for its meaning, if there is any meaning to it at all. Such views are mistakes. Not analyzing hallucinations is like not analyzing dreams; you are throwing away an extraordinarily valuable tool.

But it can be bewildering to deal with a hallucination. How does one talk to such a patient?

I was called as a consultant because a young woman alarmed her parents and the staff of a very good hospital by repeatedly cutting and burning herself despite years of hospitalization. The ward chief told me they had tried everything—and reported the 20 different medications (his idea of "everything").

When I talked to the patient, I told her that she did not have to talk to me, I was not her therapist, I was not even on the staff of the hospital. But her parents and the staff were worried because she hurt herself, and I would like to help her if I could. As I usually do, I said:

"Let's start with the tough questions. How old are you?"

"How far did you get in school?

"What's your religion?"

She said, "I was raised a Catholic."

"Oh, you were raised a Catholic, but you're not one now."

"Actually, I'm a Satanist."

I started to go on, and then realized she had something important.

"Tell me about it."

"I used to feel I had to save people. I had to save all the people in Beirut." (At that time there was continuous warfare and bloodshed among various factions in Lebanon.)

"What a marvelous image. Beirut, a marvelous image. You know who the people in Beirut are, don't you?"

She started to say yes and then said, "Well, no."

"What's Beirut? Beirut is a city where people kill each other, and then declare peace. But when you look, they are still killing each other. Then they find out why they are killing each other, and try to deal with those problems and solve them; but they go on killing each other. Then they have a truce, but still go on killing each other. What a marvelous image—your family must have been like that."

She became very interested at that point. "Satan says that if I hurt myself, he'll keep me with him. That's what he says." She was very scared. She described Satan's voice and his appearance. She described his face in considerable detail. When asked whether she knew anybody who looked like that, she thought and said, "Yes; he doesn't look like it now, but he used to."

"Who?"

"My father."

Indeed, according to later information from the family, her father used to beat her mother, and her mother eventually left the house. One can understand a little girl's belief that pain is the price of not being abandoned.

That hallucination disappeared. All one had to do was to ask her to describe her experience, and ask what it could possible mean.

As a therapist, you can not deal with what you do not know. The first thing to do is ask the patient to tell you what they see or hear, and to try to get the patient to describe it in as much detail as possible. Even if the material seems incomprehensible, it is important to listen and tolerate it. A therapist may feel scared either because disorganized material is scary or because the content (conscious or unconscious) is scary or because the feeling that the therapist should understand and does not is scary. Of course, the patient may not tell you about their hallucinations for some time. This is because they may not trust you or your perception of reality. The hallucinations may even say, "Do not tell him this." It is helpful to accept the patient's distrust and to tell him or her how sensible it is not to trust you; for example, "It is always safe to doubt someone who is telling the truth; I know I'm telling the truth, but you don't, and there are lots of people who have lied to you. And nothing is true just because I say it, even if I'm honest—I may be wrong." It is important that you let the patient know that you believe their experience and you do not consider them defective for hallucinating. Some patients do not like the word "hallucinations" and will lie or be uncooperative if you use it, but will talk freely about the voices.

It is even more important to teach a schizophrenic to pay careful attention to all of their own perceptions and judgments—including their hallucinations—than it is to teach them that some of their perceptions and judgments are hallucinatory and delusional. When they can pay careful attention to their perceptions, then they can learn to distinguish between fantasy and reality.

Most mental health professionals point out the patient's errors, but, paradoxically, we need to teach our psychotic patients that their subjective experience is their best guide to reality. There are, after all, only two bases to reality for any child: what you perceive and what your parents tell you. But destructive parents substitute their judgment for the child's judgment in all cases. As one mother of a schizophrenic patient said, "It's like training a child. It doesn't matter what he feels. You tell him what he feels and after a while, he feels it." This undercuts the child's ability to use his or her own experience to understand reality. It is up to the therapist to undo this mind control.

If the patient hallucinates during the hour, it is useful to let them know that you can't perceive it.

In the middle of a therapy session, a patient asked:

"What's that bell?"

"I didn't hear a bell."

"Well I did."

"It may well be. There are a lot of funny noises in this building. I work here all the time and maybe, like a lighthouse keeper, I just don't pay attention to them anymore. What did the bell sound like?"

"It sounded like a telephone bell, only very loud,"

"That's surprisingA telephone bell I would have heardWhat comes to mind when you think of a telephone bell?"

"Trying to get through to somebody-"

"I think I know what's happeningI've been talking about what I thought was important, but you know I'm off somewhere; and you wish I would get through to you and talk about what is really going on here."

And then the patient smiled. She was too intimidated to tell me I didn't understand and ask why I was talking about irrelevancies when there were some things that were important. The most she could do was wish that somehow I would get through to her; and even that was too frightening to deal with consciously, so she had to have it come through in disguise as a hallucination.

Sometimes patients will stop and appear to be looking at something or listening to something without talking about it. You should ask them, "Do you see something there?" or "Do you hear someone talking to you besides me?" Frequently they will say no, but sometimes they will tell you.

My first schizophrenic patient had been psychotic for 16 years. He sat cross-legged in the middle of his bed; his arms were folded. He was making a clicking noise with his tongue. When I touched him gently on the shoulder, he fell off the bed as if he were made of stone, and he was still rigid when he hit the floor. Whenever I approached him, he would get up, run to the farthest corner, and yell, "Don't hit me! Don't hit me! Don't hit me!"

"I won't hit you. I promise you I won't hit you," I replied.

"Not you, him," he said, pointing to the center of the room.

I began arguing with the hallucinated "him."

"You! Get out of here or I'll kill you. If you hurt him, you'll have to deal with me and I'll kill you!"

I went through the motions of arguing and threatening, all the while keeping one eye on the patient. When the patient relaxed, I turned toward him and said, "You see, he's gone."

The patient agreed and was ready to talk about his problems to the therapist who he now thought would protect him. He could face the omnipotent malevolent figures of his schizophrenic world now that he had an omnipotent benevolent figure (from the psychoanalytic standpoint, an omnipotent benevolent parent-figure) in the form of the therapist. With this security he could afford to neglect his own magical defenses and try to understand his sickness.

To use the patient's words, "They [the people of his hallucinations] said there wasn't any real world, that I didn't have to pay any attention to anything in the outside world. But they lied to me because they're afraid of you. When you talk, they run away."

The only difficulty in the therapy engendered by the use of this semi-magical technique was that occasionally the patient complained that he didn't understand why I insisted on analyzing hallucinations when "you can get rid of them the easy way." But at least he talked to me.1

Patients may not see any connection between their hallucinations and their current problems in life, any more than patients ordinarily see the connection between their dreams and their current difficulties. It is useful to say to the patient, "You know therapists use dreams. Hallucinations are even better than dreams. What comes to mind when you think of. . . ?"

As with dreams, you should attempt to get associations to the elements of the hallucination, or to the hallucination as a whole, or to a dramatic element of the hallucination. As with dreams, any way of getting associations will lead to the same conclusions.

Some very disturbed patients are unable or unwilling to associate, but many patients will, even when very disturbed. And, of course, even when the patient thinks they are not associating, or that they have changed the subject, the next material is an association whether or not we understand it. When the patient does not associate, you can fall back on your knowledge of the patient and of symbolism to make a good clinical guess. It is usually much easier to interpret an hallucination than it is to interpret a dream, because the motivation to hallucinate has to be much stronger.

It may be useful to review, albeit all too briefly, Freud's theory of dreams, which is equally applicable to hallucinations. The dream has the purpose of keeping the dreamer asleep in the face of disturbances, the most important of which for therapy are conscious, preconscious, and unconscious wishes. The hallucinations, too, consist of wish fulfillments. The dream is constructed from memories of the previous day and earlier memories going back to childhood.

In psychotherapy, after a while the dream takes on a new function as a medium of communication of what needs to be worked on from the patient's unconscious to the therapist (Richard Sterba, personal communication). This can be seen as a special case of Ferenczi's (1953) insight that when a patient has an urge to tell a dream to someone, that person is involved in some way in the dream.

Obviously, the hallucination does not preserve sleep, but it does deal with disturbing impulses. Freud's distinction between manifest and latent content is critical. The manifest content of a hallucination is the hallucination as it is experienced or as it is remembered; the latent content is what it is all about. In asking for associations, I always tell my patients, "It doesn't have to make sense, and there aren't any bad thoughts; what comes to mind?"

Wishes that are acceptable to the patient will be expressed openly in the hallucination. In general, the more unacceptable to the hallucinating patient or their superego (conscience) is their impulse, the more disguised is its expression.

The distortions in transforming the latent content into the manifest content of a dream (or hallucination) were summarized by Freud as condensation, displacement, and visual representation.

Condensation refers to many elements of the latent content being represented by a single element of the manifest content, or its converse, many elements of the manifest content representing a single element of the latent content. Thus, a patient feels her body is "hard, it feels like it's made of wood." Her associations reveal that this experience, which may appropriately be described as either a delusion or a hallucination, relates to at least the following latent thoughts: (a) if you are hard, you can't be hurt, (b) men's bodies are hard like wood, (c) penises are hard like wood, (d) she wishes she were a man, (e) her mother and father would prefer a son, (f) sex is all right if you are a man and dangerous if you are a woman,

(g) anger makes you hard, and hence strong, safe, and good, (h) men are angry, (i) sex and anger are the same thing.

Displacement refers to something that belongs in one place being expressed in the wrong place or in connection with the wrong thing.

For example, one patient warned me: "Bridey Murphy says she is going to kill you today."

I said, "Why do you want to kill me?"

He responded defensively, "I don't want to kill you, Bridey Murphy does. You can't hold me responsible for what she says."

Since he had been in therapy with me a while, I said, "Do I hold you responsible for what she says?"

"No."

"What do I hold you responsible for?"

"For believing her."

"That's right, you can't help hearing voices. That's not under your control. But you can control whether you accept it as real, or whether you treat it as something to be understood, something caused by your unconscious which has a lot of useful information. Hallucinations are even better than dreams, because they often lead to the conflicts much more directly." He said, "But suppose it is real?"

"All right, I'll tell you what. If it's real—when did she say that she was going to kill me? Here's my schedule for today. Make sure you tell her, and if I'm dead, we can stop therapy. But if I'm not dead, we'll double the length of the therapy sessions."

"None of your goddamn bets."

"It doesn't sound as if you really believe her."

"Well, none of your goddamn bets anyway."

"What comes to mind when you think of Bridey Murphy?"

Bridey Murphy turned out to be a condensation of two people, himself and his mother, both of whom were very, very angry at me. After all, his paranoid delusions had preserved his life, or so he believed, and I was asking him to give them up. His mother was hostile to me because his paranoid delusions and sickness played a role in maintaining her own functioning, and she was being called upon to change her adjustment as he got better. Moreover, his awareness of his mother's hostility to me was related to his feelings of her hostility to his father and to his belief that she had caused his father's death (although it was not interpreted on this level at that time). What was interpreted at that time was only his anger and his mother's anger.

Visual representation referred to expressing an abstract idea, in a visual or concrete form, often seeming like a bad pun. An 8-year-old girl, whose family characteristically paid careful attention to the television set and ignored her, interrupted her mother with her hallucination: "People are trying to put television sets on top of me!" (Modrow, 1992, p. 80)

Freud's concept of secondary elaboration, making further changes in the manifest content as you remember or tell the dream so that the manifest content makes more sense, applies to the hallucination as well.

Symbolism is usually misunderstood. There are no universal symbols. One always uses the patient's associations, if they are obtainable. Obtained associations to classical symbols frequently yield the usual symbolic meaning. When the patient cannot, or will not, give associations, then as Freud pointed out, we can surmise that the associations would be disturbing and use symbols to arrive at probable meanings. These are good guesses based on clinical experience that are frequently right but sometimes wrong.

Because of the nature of the human genitals, the male genitals will frequently be symbolized by the number three (because of the three parts), elongated objects, piercing objects, weapons, guns, or snakes (which are roughly penis-shaped, capable of elongation, and frequently dangerous); the female genitalia will frequently be symbolized by caves, containers, boxes, jars, vases, and so forth. Children will be represented by small things, small animals, insects, or even worms. Parents may be symbolized by giants or politically powerful figures like generals, presidents, kings, and queens.

Because of the frequency of the number three as a penis symbol, the number four will often represent escape to a world without penises and without sexuality. In the words of a patient: "Perfection is turning three's into four's" (Karon, 1958).

Running water may represent urine, and coming out of the water, birth. This is, in part, because of the frequency with which children, unfamiliar with the concept of semen, conceive of intercourse as the man urinating inside the woman (French, 1954)*

Language styles and slang expressions shape the symbols patients use. In Vienna where "bird" was a slang expression for penis, it was a frequently used dream symbol for penis; in England and the United

States, where "bird" usually has feminine connotations, it is rarely used as a penis symbol. (Although some English-speaking patients who are impressed with the elongated neck of some birds do use the bird as a penis symbol.)

Even the snake, used as a phallic symbol in many cultures as well as by many patients, may have other meanings. It may symbolize a biting creature—whether one's own wish to bite, or the mother, or women in general. It may represent a combination of the devouring mother and the sexually threatening father, and, for at least one patient (H. V. McLean, cited in French & Alexander, 1941), it symbolized his wife, whom he thought of as "a snake in the grass."

How a terrifying hallucination might be a wish-fulfillment is explained by the same principles that Freud used to explain the nightmare.

The wish-fulfillment refers to the latent content and not to the manifest content.

The dream (or hallucination) is an attempted wish-fulfillment, but the attempt may fail. In the case of the nightmare, the anxiety may wake up the patient, and the wish-fulfillment may be the awareness "It's only a dream," a reassurance that unfortunately is only partially true. In those patients who are aware that they hallucinate, the awareness "It's only a hallucination" may similarly be reassuring.

The terrifying hallucination, like the repetitive traumatic nightmare, can reflect a real experience whose horror the patient is trying to master. Like the repetitive traumatic war dream, for some patients it may also be an unconscious reassurance (Irving Alexander, personal communication)—"I went through this Hell and I didn't die then and I'm not going to die now."

The wish may be a wish for punishment.

A lesser fear may be substituted for a greater one. Thus, a male patient was terrified of a hallucinated middle-aged woman, outside the barred window of his room. He had no associations, and she was a total stranger. But the wish was that he were afraid of a strange woman outside his window instead of being afraid of his mother, who has access to his room, even in the hospital.

The major exception to the general rule that the more unacceptable a wish is to the dreamer, the more disguised will be its expression: An unacceptable impulse may be expressed directly if it is accompanied by sufficient anxiety. The intense negative affect serves the purpose of disguise. If it is so unpleasant, it surely cannot be the patient's wish!

A terrifying hallucination or a recurrent nightmare is a symptom in its own right, and proper interpretive work will relieve that symptom as the issues are dealt with consciously.

The patient was an incarcerated delinquent adolescent male.

"I get these nightmares," he said. "I keep getting the same dream over and over every night, my stepmother beating me with a stick. I wake up and it keeps on going. I still get the nightmare. She keeps on beating me after I wake up. What I want to know is, if I run away from here and kill her, will it stop?"

"What a bitch! A woman like that deserves to die.

"But it would be stupid to kill her because it would ruin your life."

We went on to discuss his life and his stepmother who, indeed, was an extremely cruel woman. Within a week, he was not hallucinating. Of course, at some level he had expected me to play the superego and tell him not to run away and not to kill his stepmother; instead, I validated his experience and dealt with his anger.

It is, of course, extremely important to help the patient see that hallucinations are not real, that they do not represent real persons, but rather material from his unconscious. The patient at first will not accept such a view, but when he finally does, the therapist has already undercut some of the function of the hallucinations, and the patient is already moving toward health.

In some cases, patients hallucinate my voice giving interpretations. I become aware of this when patients tell me strange things I had supposedly said: "If you believe in God, you don't need to understand anything else"; or mentioned that I spoke when I wasn't with the patient—"You said it when I was in my bedroom."

Sometimes patients hallucinate the therapist giving interpretation during the therapeutic hour. This may make therapy chaotic. It may take a long time before this comes to light. Unfortunately, hallucinatory interpretations are almost always wrong. But when patients do have such hallucinations, you can infer and interpret childhood experiences with a significant parental figure, most typically the mother.

What do you communicate to the patient about a hallucination? Communicate whatever part of your understanding you feel the patient can make use of.

A psychotic woman, age 20, whose father's death occurred six months previously, hallucinated seeing a priest and having a conversation with him, even though the priest was 500 miles away. It was easy to interpret, "You must have wanted him to be here." She then revealed having seen and talked to her father, for which the same interpretation was offered.

This opened up the issue of her longing for her father, her longing to be accepted by a father-figure, her loneliness, her fear of death, and the fact that she handled this by hallucinatory wish fulfillments, which could then be talked about. Eventually the hallucinations disappeared.

The voice of God is a hallucination to be dealt with tactfully. Direct challenges that the voice really is not God can provoke violent attacks. After all, God represents everything good. You seem to be trying to take God away from the patient, and crusades have been fought for less.

Listen to the material carefully. Sometimes one can say, without directly referring to the "Godly" experience, "I wonder if your mother used to say..." or "I wonder if your father used to say..." (whatever it was that God said).

Often a patient who would resent a direct challenge will immediately accept the statement as true, sometimes adding, "But how did you know?" even though they had just finished describing "God's" statement. After such parallels have been explored several times, it is sometimes possible to point out and get acceptance to the notion that people occasionally impute to God things their mother or father said to them when they were young.

If the voice of God is challenged, it should only be because it has said something so clearly destructive that you cannot wait, like, "Kill yourself!" You can say that you don't believe God is destructive, and therefore the voice is not God.

When the issues are dealt with consciously, hallucinations sometimes simply disappear. In other cases, hallucinations gradually change from being indistinguishable from reality, to being distinct but equally real, to being less real, to eventually merging with and becoming a part of ordinary thought processes.

In general, dealing with hallucinations gets across to the patient the power of psychotherapy, that the problems become the means of solution. Difficulties, rather than being dead ends or catastrophes, become the building blocks from which the patient can learn and grow. It is the difference between learning from your problems that everything is hopeless and that you are bad or worthless, and learning from your mistakes something about why you make mistakes and what difficulties might arise again, and what might be done to change them. Eventually, the patient realizes this is not a view of therapy, but a general view of life, and one which, unfortunately, our culture rarely teaches.

NOTE

1. If you are tempted to use such a semi-magical technique, you should be uncomfortable with it, and allow the patient to see you realistically when they can tolerate it. John Rosen's (Rosen, 1964; Brody, 1959) mistake was that he so much enjoyed the omnipotent role that he could not abandon it.

REFERENCES

Breheny, L. (1990). The phenomena of hearing voices: Results of a survey. Unpublished manuscript, Nottingham Polytechnic, Applied Social Sciences, Nottingham, England.

Bleuler, E. (1950). Dementia praecox, or the group of the schizophrenias. New York: International Universities Press.

Brody, M.W. (1959). Observations on "direct analysis." New York: Vantage Press.

Ferenczi, S. (1953). To whom does one relate one's dream? Further contributions to the theory and technique of psychoanalysis (p. 349). New York, Basic Books.

French, T.M. (1954). The integration of behavior: Volume II, the integrative process in dreams. Chicago: University of Chicago Press.

———— & Alexander, F. (1941). Psychogenic factors in bronchial asthma. Psychosomatic Medicine Monographs. Washington, DC: National Research Council.

Karon, B.P. (1958). Some clinical notes on the significance of the number four. Psychiatric Quarterly, 32, 281-288.

———— & VandenBos, G.R. (1981). Psychotherapy of schizophrenia: The treatment of choice. New York: Aronson.

Modrow, J. (1992). How to become a schizophrenic: The case against biological psychiatry. Everett, WA: Apollyon Press.

Rosen, J. (1964). Psychoanalysis, direct and indirect. Doylestown, PA: Doylestown Foundation. Sterba, R. (1987). The collected papers. Croton-on-Hudson, NY: North River Press.

CHAPTER 7
The Oedipus Complex in a Case of Deteriorated Schizophrenia

Jack Rosberg and Bertram P. Karon

The existence in psychotic patients of classical oedipal problems as described by Freud is unmistakable. The authors feel that any observer who comes in close contact over a prolonged period of time with psychotics cannot fail to see evidence of such fantasies. However, the meaning, as we see it, of such fantasies seems to be somewhat different from the classical interpretation and more in keeping with Freud's 1931 statement, in a different context, that ". . . it seems that we shall have to retract the universality of the dictum that the Oedipus complex is the nucleus of neurosis . . ." (1, p. 253).The significances which we have found in psychotic patients for such fantasies were most clearly presented to us by an apparently deteriorated and almost unreachable patient. The patient had a long history of slowly developing problems. He had been sent to school after school for disturbed children, each school eventually finding him too difficult to handle and sending him on to a school for the more severely disturbed. Eventually, he entered a conventional outpatient analysis at the age of 17. After a short period, his analyst gave up, saying he was psychotic. He was sent to a psychiatric institution, where he was unsuccessfully treated by standard procedures, including electric shock and insulin treatments. After physical therapies had proved unsuccessful, psychological therapies, including several psychoanalytic ap-proaches, were attempted at several different institutions. These also failed to remit the psychosis.

At this point, the authors, whose own approach to the treatment of psychotics is a modification of direct analysis, began treatment. The patient, a young man of muscular build, was approximately 26 years old at the time. At this point he showed little responsiveness to his environment and had lost all control over his bodily functions. It was necessary in the treatment milieu to care for him in every respect—feed him, clothe him, bathe him, care for all his physical needs. This was complicated by the fact that the patient was given to periodic outbursts of violence. These were accompanied by a relative improvement in contact to the point where he would utter one or two intelligible words. The most frequent of these were "room," "dear," "drink, drink," "the work," and "get out."

There were marked signs of physiological disfunction. The patient's hands were generally cold, his fingernails blue, and his skin showed goose pimples even in the hottest weather. His digestive processes were sluggish as evidenced by the odor of decaying food which emanated from his mouth, due not to a mouth but a stomach condition. It will be noted that all of the physiological disturbances manifested by the patient are components of the normal terror syndrome—vasoconstriction, slowed digestive processes, and lack of control over excretory functions. With respect to the last, however, he would at times manifest an extreme control over his bowels, with no movement occurring for weeks at a time.

Interestingly enough, in his bursts of aggression, he might lash out with equal vehemence at the people in the treatment milieu, at thin air, or even at himself. This was a considerable problem inasmuch as his physical strength had enabled him to break the jaws of two attendants at one institution.

The nights were fraught with terror for this patient; his sleep was light and the people who cared for him were awakened nightly by his terror-stricken screams, which were apparently in response to his hallucinations.

Because of the patient's strength and potential violence, it was necessary to keep him in restraints a good deal of the time.

At the time the authors began working with the patient, the junior author spent eight continuous hours with him, During this period, nothing the patient did or said was intelligible to the therapist; nothing the therapist said seemed to have the slightest impact. As a last resort, the therapist sat the patient in front of a TV set, hoping that the screen would hold the patient's attention, but it did not. The therapist sat down next to the patient, placed his arm around the patient's shoulders and said, "What a nice baby you are." The therapist hoped that the physical contact might reach the patient at some preverbal level. He continued this for a half hour. The patient showed little apparent awareness of even this contact.

In all future sessions, the two authors worked together. This had several advantages. Physical restraints could be discarded without danger to the therapists; the patient could be induced to move around, which seemed to "loosen" the psychosis; the emotional intensity of the therapy session could be maintained at a fairly high pitch for longer periods of time (by alternating therapists), and the therapist not working at the moment with the patient could pick up cues that were missed by the therapist who was intensely involved with him. Moreover, it is of prime significance that what restraint and control were necessary were imposed directly by the therapists and not by artificial restraints. The import of this will be discussed later in some detail.

It might be argued on the basis of classical techniques that the use of two therapists would lessen the therapeutic relationship by "diluting" the transference. The original object relationship, it might be pointed out, consisted of one person the mother. However, it is our experience with psychotics that the needs of the patient for mothering are so intense that he readily forms a transference to several people. Moreover, it is questionable what meaning can be assigned to the concept of "diluting" the transference unless a therapeutically usable transference exists. In this patient, although transference needs were present, they were therapeutically unusable because of his massive psychotic defenses. It was only by the combined efforts of both therapists that these massive defenses were penetrated and a workable transference established.

Incidentally, the apparently apathetic, deteriorated, unresponsive appearance of such patients is at least in part an active defense, It is a successful defense insofar as it exhausts any therapist who attempts to breach it. But by the continued persistent efforts of two therapists who alternated in a continued long-term high-pressure session, this patient's apparently almost insuperable defenses began to give way.

Each day the therapists devoted several hours to intensive continued work with the patient. A single question based on his fragmentary utterances, such as "What happened in the room?" might be repeated to the patient innumerable times day after day until the patient seemed totire and respond. The lack of mechanical restraint and the willingness of the therapists to deal with the patient's aggression directly gave him a feeling both of freedom and of security. He had the assurance that nothing he could do could place him in jeopardy, that he could always depend on the therapists to control those urges in himself of which he was afraid. That this control would be exerted directly by the therapists enhanced the personal relationship and helped to build the therapists into the omnipotent benevolent parent figures which the sick patient typically has never had but which he wishes for so desperately.

The first meaningful material which emerged from this patient (after about a week of such therapy) did not deal directly with the oedipal fantasies, but with a homosexual episode. In response to the question, "What made you crazy?" the patient finally said he was sick because of what he and his brother did. On further questioning, he stated that they had performed fellatio upon each other. The patient then became angry with no apparent cause. The senior author asked him why he was mad at his brother. The patient responded saying that his brother had performed fellatio upon him first (that is, the brother taking the oral role and the patient taking the genital role), instead of letting the patient take the oral role first.

On the following day, the first oedipal fantasy appeared. One of the words which the patient had from time to time muttered aloud was "the room." Again and again the therapists had repeated the question, "What happened in the room?" Finally, the patient responded that he had seen "them making love, being affectionate, knowing each other." In response to further questioning, he said that he was "in the room. The door was stuck." He couldn't get out, and he was scared. When asked who was on top, the man or the woman, the patient said, "The woman."

[And which one did you wish was dead, the one on the top or the one on the bottom?] The one on the bottom.

Here we see a classical primal scene with oedipal feelings expressed, whether it be reality or fantasy. The child sees the mother and father having intercourse, and he wishes the father were dead.

On the following day we explored this material further. The active defense of the apparent inability to concentrate was demonstrated by the fact that the patient would talk coherently until the threatening material was approached and then he would get dreamy and fragmentary. He finally admitted that he had been in the room and had watched them have intercourse.

[Who were they?] The big. [The big who?] The parents. [Who was on top?] The lovely wife. [Who was on the bottom?] The patient would not answer this question. After repeated interrogation, the patient muttered something about "the brother," but was unwilling to elucidate.

Tiring of this tack, the therapist returned to asking what happened in the room, and when the patient said he saw them having intercourse, the therapist asked him how he felt about that.

I have to give them a shot. [Both of them?] One of them. [Which one?] The lovely wife.

He then drifted oh'. The therapist brought him back again and again to the room situation. On one of these occasions he was asked how he felt and he said, "Western."

[What does that mean?] The cow.

Again he became incoherent. After several more attempts by the therapist to bring him back to the room situation, the patient suddenly said, "Ouch." He seemed to be holding his testicles with his right hand, which was in his pocket. He then said he wanted his mother to play with it, but she might hurt it.

[Did they say they'd cut them off?] Yes.

He was then asked who it was that said they would cut off his testicles, and he replied, "She."

[Did your mother say she would do it?] She didn't mean it.

Here we may note that the castration threat seems to come from the mother and not the father. This is typical of castration fears as we have encountered them in psychotics.

The pattern was much more clearly demonstrated in a later therapy session. After describing an incestuous fantasy concerning his sister, who he said resembled his mother, the patient was plied with classical interpretations. For half an hour or more, the senior author (to test the theory) at-tempted to get the patient to react to interpretations that his incestuous wishes led to a fear of castration by the father. These repeated and intensive interpretations produced no sign of anxiety or of recognition. Finally, after an unsuccessful leading question, the therapists allowed the patient an opening for describing the mother as the castrator.

[If your father had a knife, what would he do to you for incest?] I'm not sure.

The junior author interrupted at this point and asked whether it was his mother or his father who would take the knife to him for having intercourse with his sister.

My mother. (What would she do to you?) Cut it off. [Cut what off?]

The patient said that it was his penis that would be cut off. It was possible at this point for the therapists to gain insight into the dynamics of this fantasy by pursuing their line of inquiry. They asked the patient why his mother would cut off his penis for incest.

So that she could get a platter regularly.

The patient was asked whether he meant that his mother could use his penis "to feed her whenever she wanted." "That's right, so that she could get a platter all the time."

Thus, the patient told us that the reason he felt that his mother would castrate him was not as punishment for incest, but because she wished to appropriate a source of food.

Intercourse is viewed by the patient as a feeding experience with the penis doing the feeding and the vagina being a mouth (which makes accountable the patient's earlier use of the word "cow" in the primal scene).

Penises, he said, go into vaginas, and "a penis is like a breast. Breasts give milk."

The patient told of another incident in which his sister had "dropped her pants" and showed him her vagina. He said she was trying to seduce him because, "she wanted me to feed her. She was like my mother."

One of the most effective questions employed by the therapists proved to be, "What's the worst thing that ever happened to you?"

On one occasion when this question was asked, the patient responded by saying that his mother had taken "it" off and "put it in the drawer."

[What?] Her bathing suit.

The patient said that she had sat down on "the desk" and spread her legs and showed him her vagina and that he was scared. "She was always taking things away from me." He continued that he was afraid "she wanted me to feed her" and he couldn't. The patient was asked whether this was an "illusion" or reality, and, after some hesitation, the patient replied: "I think it really happened once."

On another occasion in response to the inquiry, "What's the worst thing that ever happened to you?" the patient replied:

It hurts in the stomach. [What hurts?] Being hollowed out.

It was clear at this point that the basic problem was one of being fed, filled up, as opposed to having to feed, to give up one's products, to be hollowed out. A demand is felt from the mother that he feed (have intercourse with) her, which conflicts with his own never fulfilled need to be fed, He characterized vaginas as being "sadistic," and once described his mother's vagina as being "like a food chopper."

His reaction is shown in the therapy session in which the therapists brought up the subject of intercourse. The patient was asked whether he preferred having intercourse with an anus or a vagina. He said he preferred anal intercourse. He was then asked whether he preferred intercourse with a man's anus or a woman's anus. He said he preferred a man's anus,

(Why?] Because you can get a drink. (From what?] From the penis, the patient said.

IWhere?] (After a pause) In the arm.

This reply puzzled the therapists. Eventually, the therapists got the idea that he meant a magic vagina which he formed with his fingers while he talked. When he was asked if this was the case, the patient said that it was. The therapists decided to put this to a further test at a later time, which they did by having the senior author form a circle with his fingers and ask the patient:

(What is this?) A zero.

The patient was asked whether it was a vagina, and he replied that it was not. The therapist then made the opening long and narrow, and again asked the patient whether it was a vagina. When the patient again said it was not a vagina, the therapist asked him to make it into a vagina. The patient reached out and reshaped the therapist's fingers until they were a replica of his own hand.

This wish to have a vagina, which was manifested by the magic vagina on his hand, came out clearly at another time when the patient said that he envied his sister. When asked why he envied his sister he replied that he envied her because she had a vagina. When asked why he envied her vagina he said, "Because it is beautiful and the old guy likes it,"

On another occasion when he said that he wanted a vagina, he was asked why he wanted it and replied, "So that I can get my groceries through it."

His wish for a vagina implied a wish for castration; not only would he have another "mouth" to be fed through, but the possibility of his being called upon to act as a feeder would be eliminated, or, as he stated, no one could make him urinate in their mouths.

His visual hallucinations consisted of innumerable repetitions of two themes. The first of these consisted of bis mother or sister making such "seductive" and terrifying demands that he "feed her." The second consisted of a series of related "room" fantasies. These "room" fantasies were related by the patient in response to the question, "What happened in the room?"

By far the most frequent answer related to the primal scene, which was apparently also the most frequent hallucination. The patient described this primal scene in detail in a therapy session, saying that they (his parents) were standing up and that his mother was bending over (more ferarum), He demonstrated the position. He said that he saw his father's penis go in but he didn't see it come out, and "I felt bad."

In a later therapy session, he commented on the primal scene, "I want to go home, but they don't want me."

At times when the patient was asked, "What happened in the room?" he would describe other scenes. In each of them, however, there were two people in the room. Sometimes they were his mother and stranger having intercourse; sometimes they were his father and a stranger having homosexual intercourse; sometimes they were his father and his brother having homosexual intercourse; once it was his mother and his brother without specifying their activities. Although the most frequent event referred to was the mother and father having intercourse, the most disturbing was the session during which he said that the two people in the room were his mother and sister. During this session, the therapists had asked him insistently again and again, "What happened in the room?"

The patient was at first mute, then as the questioning continued unabated, got very angry. He rose from the chair in which he was sitting., but since each of the therapists held one of his arms he was unable to throw a punch. He nevertheless kicked out in front of him (luckily, neither therapist was directly in front of him) with sufficient force to split the table that was in the therapy room. When this burst of violence produced no effect on the therapists (who simply held his arms and repeated the question), the patient sat down and began to cry. The therapists repeated their question, "Who was in the room?" and the patient sobbed that his oldest sister was in the room on the bed with his mother. In the further elucidation of this, the patient explained that his mother was feeding his sister. As the patient talked, it became clear that, inasmuch as he viewed intercourse—both heterosexual and homosexual—as a feeding situation, all of the "room" fantasies, including the primal scene, dealt with a single theme: Two people are in the room, including at least one from whom I expect food. Someone else is being fed and I am not wanted.

In summary, a severely regressed case of schizophrenia produced classical oedipal material, including a classical primal scene, during the process of a developing therapeutic relationship. Upon further elucidation, the material seemed to show dynamics which differ somewhat from the classical interpretations of the oedipal situation.

The patient interprets intercourse as an oral situation, equating the vagina with the mouth and the penis with the breast. His own needs to be fed and mothered were not met by the mother; rather he sees her as making demands on him to "feed" her. Thus incest is seen as a feeding situation whereby he is forced to feed his mother against his will. Her demands seem so all-engulfing as to swallow up the penis itself, i.e., the mother and not the father is seen as the castrator. But underlying the castration fear is not only these insistently felt demands from the mother but, also, the wish to be castrated so that such demands can no longer be made. In place of the organ through which he can be drained, he wishes for a vagina through which he can be fed. Such a wish means turning from females to males for "feeding/' The primal scenes seem to have been experienced as the mother's devouring needs being met by the father, and neither of them caring about the needs of the child.

REFERENCE

Freud, S. Female sexuality. Collected Papers. Vol. V London: Hogarth, 1950.

CHAPTER 8
The Fear of Understanding Schizophrenia and the Avoidance of the Acutely Disturbed Student
Bertram P. Karon, Phd

Although it is generally believed that a treatment that is more effective than its alternatives will be used, psychological treatments for schizophrenic and other psychotic reactions have been avoided despite the evidence of their effectiveness from the time of "moral treatment" to the present. Less effective (or even destructive) treatments have been seized upon, in part because they do not require understanding patients. Understanding them means facing facts about ourselves, our families, and our society that we do not want to know, or, in the case of repressed feelings and experiences, do not want to know again. This reluctance to understand is particularly tragic in the case of the acutely disturbed college student, whose crisis may lead either to reorganization at a higher level of functioning and growth or to a wasted life. The central role of terror in producing symptoms and the genesis and handling of symptoms, including delusions and hallucinations, are briefly discussed.

My first course in clinical methods in psychology, taught by Dr S. Roy Heath, included studying a paid student volunteer for a year. Dr Heath, who had been an undergraduate at the same university, was concerned about the lack of adequate mental health services. He saw himself as a pioneer in the treatment of the relatively "normal" college student, who, as all of you know, benefits so much from even limited help. He made himself available, without charge, to as many as 100 students a year.

The student I studied was unusual. He was a senior, an officer in an undergraduate club who later graduated with honors and pursued a career in a creative field. What was most unusual about him was that, as a sophomore, he had had a psychotic break. Instead of being told to leave, which was usual at that school, he had been treated by Dr Heath with psychotherapy.

Not everyone was happy with Dr Heath's work. The undergraduates dedicated the yearbook to him as the man who had contributed most to their undergraduate education, the graduate students admired him, the faculty of psychology unanimously voted to promote him, and the administration fired him. When pressed, they stated that it was not true that he had been fired for doing psychotherapy with students, but it was a good thing he was gone, because psychotherapy makes people dependent. Fortunately, he was later able to fill a constructive role at the University of Pittsburgh.

Shortly after her chronically ill father died, a sexually anxious freshman woman at a small college, while walking at night with an equally anxious date, was threatened by him with rape. Terrified, she ran. Although they were some distance from any building, nothing happened, but she was terrified. She began to hallucinate, which she did not tell anyone about, nor did she tell about the threatened rape. But she was obviously disturbed, and she was told to leave school. After each of several suicide attempts, she was hospitalized.

Supposedly "totally uncommunicative" (which usually means no one has tried to communicate with the patient), she was scheduled for shock treatment (ECT).

After published information about ECT was called to her mother's attention, the mother withdrew permission and brought her to me for evaluation. After the third interview, she was discharged from the hospital. At the end of 18 sessions (when I went on sabbatical), she was earning her own living, sharing an apartment with young people her own age, and making arrangements to attend a community college. Once the school year started, however, she sought out further treatment and was seen once per week for a year at the MSU psychological clinic. She dropped out of school voluntarily and took a secretarial course to become self-sufficient. Eventually, she married and then completed her education. Five years later, both her marriage and her education were successful.

The lives of these two students could easily have been wasted.

The Early Treatment Era
and Lessons About the Human Condition

It is ordinarily believed that if a treatment is more helpful than its alternatives, it will be used. Yet an early psychologically based treatment for schizophrenics and other psychotics—"moral treatment"—was tried, found to be successful at the end of the eighteenth and the beginning of the nineteenth centuries, then abandoned.'

In our time, psychological treatment modalities for schizophrenia (including acute psychotic reactions) are not fashionable; not because they are not helpful, but because they make the professionals who become therapists, as well as the public at large, so uncomfortable. It is usual to attribute this discomfort to the fact that these patients are so different from the rest of us, but the truth is just the opposite. What makes both professionals and the general public uncomfortable is not their difference from us, but their lack of difference. We do not want to know what they have to teach us about the human condition, including ourselves.

In the 1930s, Harry Stack Sullivan and Frieda Fromm-Reichmann consistently helped schizophrenics. The treatment was arduous, but patients improved; and the two psychiatrists described their psychoanalytic treatment in their papers and books.[23] The novel *I Never Promised You a Rose Garden*[4] described that early treatment. Yet many professionals act as if psychotherapy with schizophrenics and other psychotics is something of which no one has heard.

For the past 30 years, I have treated schizophrenic patients, among other people, using psychotherapy. Whenever, in the course of this treatment, something about a schizophrenic has come to light, it has always illuminated the human condition in general; and whatever psychoanalysis or psychology has learned about the general human condition has illuminated schizophrenia as well and is helpful in its treatment.

To understand schizophrenics is to perceive painful facts about the human condition that we would rather not know, or, more frightening, is to be reminded of painful facts we once knew and repressed.

Even the sociological data about schizophrenia remind us of unpleasant realities. Thus, the dramatic increase in schizophrenia among people of low socioeconomic status, which cannot be accounted for by downward drift, suggests, and psychotherapeutic experience makes vivid, the physical and psychological pain, the humiliation, and the physical danger associated with being very poor in our society—an association those of us who are not very poor do not like to perceive or remember. The increase in incidence of schizophrenia among those who are the victims of prejudice and discrimination means that, in psychotherapy, the crude and subtle implications of prejudice and discrimination will be confronted. The fact that the long-term prognosis for schizophrenics is better in non-literate cultures reminds us of the relative lack of kindness in our civilization.

Many schizophrenics have talked about incest, sexual abuse, and physical abuse; but it has been dismissed as the ravings of lunatics. Freud reported that the incest memories, specifically of conversion hysterics, were revealed more often, during psychoanalysis, to be fantasies rather than real events, although in many cases they were undoubtedly real. Psychology, psychiatry, and psychoanalysis falsely generalized that all such memories of patients were fantasies because it was believed that incest was a rare event.

Therapists and researchers who worked with schizophrenics (eg, Lidz[5]), however, reported that the incest material of those patients more often related to real events, as did their memories of child abuse. The ugly realities of child abuse, sexual and physical, and of incest in our society are only now apparent to the rest of psychology and psychiatry. It is now known, for example, that one out of six, and perhaps one out of three, women have been sexually abused.

Psychotherapeutic work with schizophrenics revealed the wish to be one's own mother, which, consciously or unconsciously, underlies many symptoms. Kestenberg,[6] on the basis of her observation and treatment of children, reported that at the age of 2, nearly every child goes through a stage where he or she wants to be a mother. Girls want to be a mother to a little girl, and boys want to be a mother to a little boy, so it is clear whose mother they want to be.

In order to help a postpartum schizophrenic, it was necessary to learn (in her psychotherapy) about the fantasy that anything that filled the body was food. But Michel-Hutmacher reported that normal children under the age of 7 regularly reported that belief. One schizophrenic patient revealed clearly, and other schizophrenic patients confirmed, the existence of a terrifying fantasy of having the inside of your body emptied out and drained, a terror originated in early infancy and augmented or diminished by later experiences. This fantasy takes various symptomatic forms, including, in some male patients, that of a fear of being emptied or drained through the penis. This is often experienced as more frightening than castration, leading some patients to attempt to cut off their penises as the lesser evil. One should consider this fantasy when an acute psychotic reaction occurs in a male student after sexual intercourse. Knowledge of the "draining" fantasy allows one also to recognize the subtle evidence of the fantasy that occurs in some relatively normal men whose impotence is derived from this fear and, consequently, to help these impotent patients.

But what happens when a therapist talks to a schizophrenic, even an acutely schizophrenic college student? The therapist gets uncomfortable, feels depressed, feels angry because the patient doesn't react the way the therapist wants him or her to react; the patient often does not show the therapist respect. What the therapist knows doesn't seem to work. In addition, the therapist feels scared and isn't sure why. Despite their personal therapy and professional training, mental health professionals don't like to experience those feelings any more than anyone else does. It is not an accident that the most illuminating discussions of negative countertransference have come from therapists who have worked with schizophrenics (eg, Searles[10]).

One of the reasons for these uncomfortable feelings when one talks to schizophrenic people is that these are their feelings. One of the great mistakes about schizophrenia, a mistake that even Bleuler," who originated the term, made, is to assume that, because they look as if they have no feeling, they have no feelings. In reality, they have very intense feelings, but primarily the feeling is fear; in fact, it is terror. Human beings are not easily able to tolerate chronic, massive terror. The chronic terror masks weaker feelings. Nonetheless, the schizophrenic also frequently experiences, chronically or intermittently, anger, hopelessness, loneliness, and/ or humiliation.

All of the symptoms of schizophrenia may be understood as being manifestations of, triggered by, or defenses against the chronic terror. Knowing that the acutely disturbed student is a terrified human being makes effective treatment possible.

The Modern Treatment Era

If it is believed that schizophrenics have no affect, then it becomes a puzzle why the major tranquilizers and similar medications, which are well known to diminish affect greatly, should be helpful. But once the centrality of terror in schizophrenia is understood, their utility makes sense. All the medications that are of some use to schizophrenics are medications that, among other things, damp down the affect system and, therefore, diminish the fear.

It was a public relations coup to relabel major tranquilizers as "antipsychotic" medication, implying that they are as specific and effective for psychosis as vitamin C is for scurvy. Unfortunately, there is no "antipsychotic" medication in that sense.

Someone living at half affect has some handicaps in adjusting to life. For example, in most big cities such as Detroit, gangs of teenage hoodlums prey on medicated patients who are unable to be alert and self-defensive. The patient load keeps decreasing because the patients tend to die of the effects of multiple muggings.

We don't want to know about schizophrenia because we do not want to feel terror at that intensity. All of us have the potential for schizophrenic symptoms; the only differences seem to lie in the quantity and quality of the necessary stress.

In World War II, the word schizophreniform psychosis was used to describe patients who looked just like schizophrenics in every way, but "couldn't" be because the patients got better. One battlefield situation that apparently provoked these schizophreniform reactions in every soldier was very simple—an infan-tryman was under fire. He dug a hole and, because the enemy was trying to kill him, he got into it as soon as it was barely big enough. The enemy kept shooting at him, and he had no place to go without being killed. He urinated on himself, and he defecated on himself. When his rations were gone, he did not eat and did not drink. If this lasted for 3 or more consecutive days, every soldier who survived looked like a classic schizophrenic when the shooting stopped. But if he had been a reasonably healthy person before this trauma, security and rest almost always led to a spontaneous recovery. In those days they "knew" schizophrenics never got better; therefore, it could not really be schizophrenia, hence the diagnosis of a schizophreniform reaction. Yet the key to understanding schizophrenic reactions lay in those observations.

The myths of the lack of meaning, the irrelevance of understanding, and the incurability of schizophrenic symptoms are still with us.

Deikman and Whitaker[12] instituted a regimen of almost purely psychological treatment on an "experimental" ward of a psychiatric hospital. Despite dire warnings that their failure to medicate was malpractice, their ward program resulted in decreased need for rehospitalization, and there were no suicides, suicide attempts, or elopements. A comparison ward that was more fully staffed, had "expert" pharmacology practiced, and sent its more disturbed patients to a long-term state hospital nonetheless had three suicides in the same period. The experiment was discontinued and never imitated, despite its success.

Among the problems with the Diagnostic and Statistical Manual of Mental Diseases (DSM III) is its rationalization of bad treatment and preservation of the myth of the incurability of schizophrenia. The very same symptom picture is diagnosed as "brief reactive psychosis," "schizophreniform psychosis," or "schizophrenia," solely on the basis of whether the patient recovers in less than six weeks, more than six weeks but less than six months, or more than six months. The only real difference, however, may be the adequacy of treatment.

In the 1950s, as senior clinical psychologist at a reformatory for male adolescents, I instituted a policy of psychotherapy for all psychotic reactions. Patients received daily sessions without medication for 5 days before state hospital transfer was considered. Psychotherapy was continued, at a minimum, of once per week. During a 6-month period, no state hospital transfers for reason of psychosis were necessary. The usual procedure before and after that 6-month period was to transfer psychotic patients to the state hospital; the usual length of stay (in the 1950s) was approximately 2 years before they were returned to the reformatory. But DSM III makes that comparison seem irrelevant. In the same reformatory, only "brief reactive psychoses" occurred during the 6 months when the psychotherapy was available, whereas before and after, the state hospital treated true "schizophrenics" from the same population.

The acutely disturbed student will generally be a "brief reactive psychosis" if adequately treated; throughout this paper, schizophrenia is used as a generic term in describing the issues that will help therapists achieve as rapid, real, and lasting a recovery as possible. One can be sure that the acutely disturbed student is terrified, and, if one listens, one will eventually discover what it is that has the meaning, consciously or unconsciously, of imminent annihilation.

A treatment for schizophrenics with a discharge rate of 80% as either recovered or improved would be valued today. That was achieved in 1800 (Bockoven[1]), but it took the French Revolution to give Phillip Pinel his opportunity to initiate "moral treatment." It was soon tried in the United States, in England, and elsewhere. At the height of "moral treatment" in the first part of the nineteenth century, the recovery rate for first admissions was around 70%. In the same hospitals, the recovery rate dropped to 20% to 30% by the end of the nineteenth century, when moral treatment was abandoned. (Critics using more stringent criteria and all admissions claim the true recovery rates were 45% to 48%, but the same stringent criteria yield only 10% to 15% after its abandonment.) Of course, the early figures included an unknown proportion of manic-depressives with a better prognosis without medication and an unknown proportion of persons with syphilitic and other organic psychoses who could not recover.

Meanwhile, psychiatry was congratulating itself on how scientific it was and how much progress had been made; that patients no longer recovered was not noticed.

What, then, was "moral treatment"? Treatment principles were very simple and should be achievable today. First of all, no cruelty was permitted. Physical force was permitted only to keep a patient from hurting himself or another person, but not for punishment, not for "negative reinforcement," not for anything else. Harassment, ridicule, and humiliation were banned. Hippocrates' principle that if you do not know how to help the patient, at least do nothing that will be harmful to the patient, was taken seriously. Second, an accurate case history was kept. It might reveal something about the particular patient and possibly even about similar disorders. Third, the treatment called for understanding the patient as an individual human being; work and social relationships were encouraged as part of normal life.

Contrast this with the experience of a schizophrenic person, even a college student, seeing a mental health professional today. He or she is likely to be told something that approximates, "You have this genetic physiological disorder that is absolutely incurable and that you are going to have to live with for the rest of your life. With the very best treatment (by which I mean medication) you might be barely tolerable to other human beings. Now what can I do for you?" That does not reassure the patient, and it is false.

Although there are other reasons why professionals believe each part of that statement, it also serves to rationalize not having to understand the patient.

There has never been a lack of treatments that do more harm than good. They have in common that they do not require understanding the human condition.

This makes intelligible the fact that Freud, whose work, despite errors, revolutionized psychology and psychiatry and laid the basis for much of our modern understanding of man and most modern psychotherapies by bringing to light troubling aspects of the human condition, never was awarded a Nobel Prize. Such an award was presented to Moniz, the pioneer of pre-frontal lobotomy, an operation that is now illegal in many countries and is rarely practiced in the remainder because of its destructive effects.

What did the lobotomy do? It allowed one to treat these people without having to understand them at all. It got them so they would not bother anyone.

Electric shock treatment is still practiced despite clear evidence that it produces brain damage.[13,14] (This is disputed, of course, by some advocates of ECT.[15-17] Examination of the original studies, however, readily reveals that they are not cited accurately in these sources.) It accelerates spontaneous recovery but makes the probability of relapse much greater and leaves permanent side effects. Why is it used? Because the doctor has been trained to believe he should use it, because he knows no other way of treating the patient, but also because he does not have to understand the patient at all. He or she does not have to relate to the patient but can feel like an authority who is effective without having to feel the pain of either the patient's disorder or its treatment. In my experience, when psychiatrists who have given shock treatments have become patients, the first thing they have done was beg not to be shocked; and the more people they have shocked themselves, the stronger they have begged.

Problems with Somatic Treatment and Explanation

The predominant treatment that does not require understanding today is medication, which does reduce negative affect and its consequences. The patients' behavior improves, and they become more compliant. That sometimes is very helpful because other people are often scared of schizophrenics. If the hospital staff is scared, they tend to be cruel. When people on the outside are scared, they tend to be cruel. Cruelty, in general, makes schizophrenic people more schizophrenic.

But there is a problem with psychiatric medication. The syndrome tardive dyskinesia, which refers to certain involuntary movements of the tongue and mouth and is clearly caused by brain damage, occurs in at least 30% of patients who are chronically maintained on currently used, so-called antipsychotic medication.[18] There is accumulated evidence for tardive psychosis, that is, that the physiological changes in the brain as a result of continued medication lead to a psychotic reaction when the medication is withdrawn, due not to the original disorder, but to these changes in the brain.

One of the most troubling books in recent years is Breggin's[19] review of the literature on brain-damaging effects of psychiatric medication. These facts are troubling because the mental health system now relies almost entirely on medication and is inadvertently creating a population of brain-damaged people. Not only are the patients given medication, but they are told they must take the medication for the rest of their lives. There are professionals who think psychotherapy with schizophrenics is finding out why they do not take their medication. Yet if the patients are good patients and continue to take their medication in heavy doses or for long periods of time, at least 30% of them are going to be brain damaged.

The only thing that is keeping us from doing more damage is that patients sometimes lie. Luckily, the medication is unpleasant. Men are often made impotent by it, women often cannot enjoy sex either, and the feeling of not having feelings is unpleasant. Some studies suggest that 60% of patients who are believed to be taking maintenance medication lie about it. Patients lie because they are afraid they will be hospitalized or forced to take their medication if they tell anyone the truth.

Medication has been so popular and advertised so well that the current generation of psychiatrists has been trained almost exclusively to treat patients by means of medication and has neglected training in psychotherapy. Unfortunately, the medications do not live up to their advertisements. As this is being learned, some psychiatrists are going back to shock treatments, which are more hazardous to the brain. The use of shock treatments with acutely disturbed college students, although it does occur, is a practice that is hard to defend scientifically.

Fear Of Understanding Schizophrenia

Sometimes it is argued that research shows that psychotherapy is not helpful to schizophrenic patients. The Michigan State Psychotherapy Project[20] made a blind evaluation of schizophrenic patients who were randomly assigned to an average of 70 sessions of psychoanalytic psychotherapy per patient, to medication, or a combination of the two. The study found that psychotherapy alone, or accompanied by initial medication that was withdrawn as the patient could tolerate living without it, led to earlier discharge from the hospital, kept the patients out of the hospital, and improved their thought disorders more than medication. The patients lived a more human life in a variety of ways. Because of the hospitalization and, particularly, re-hospitalization findings, psychotherapy was less expensive to provide in the long run, saving nearly half the treatment costs in a 4-year period.

Unfortunately, decision makers are not interested in saving money over 4 years or more. In that time, there will be a different political administration, a different dean, a different head of the hospital or the particular department of the insurance company. The decision makers want to save money in this 6 months, and this is unfortunate.

One early controlled study showed that a modified Rogerian

approach was helpful to schizophrenics,[21] especially if the therapist was warm, genuine, and empathic, and if the patient was "experiencing." Another controlled study showed that a carefully executed behavioral approach was more helpful than medication.[22] These psychological approaches were cost effective; but psychological approaches are always based on attempts to understand the patient.

It should be noted that in all three studies, careful attention was paid to whether the treatment was carried out appropriately. In the Michigan study, for example, the experienced therapists chosen had over 10 years of experience in treating schizophrenics with psychoanalytic therapy, were knowledgeable about treating black and lower socioeconomic patients (the majority of the patients), and were considered by their colleagues to be effective. The inexperienced therapists wanted to learn how to do this kind of therapy, valued their supervisors, were paid for their time, and were given careful training and supervision.

The Michigan study was different in these respects from the most widely cited controlled studies in this country, those of May[23] and Crinspoon et al,[24] which found that psychotherapy was not as effective as medication. Understandably, a drug company widely distributed free copies of May's book. Although those studies had many methodological flaws, the most important was that they involved so-called psychotherapists and supervisors who had never treated a schizophrenic patient by psychotherapy before. They either had little training in any psychotherapy or had training in treating a different kind of patient with a different kind of therapy (a psychoanalyst experienced only in treating upper-middle-class neurotic outpatients on a couch, for example).

If the therapist does not know how to do therapy, it is true that medication works better than psychotherapy. If the teaching of bicycle riding were carried out the same way, using only teachers who had never ridden a bicycle themselves, it would be concluded that human beings clearly cannot be taught to ride bicycles.

Luckily, the real world is very consistent. A Swedish study by Sjostrom and Sandin[25] compared patients who had received therapy from an experienced therapist and found that it was much better than medication alone.

The McLean[26] study is apt to be cited as evidence that psychotherapy is not helpful, yet the only findings were that supportive therapy was more helpful than insight therapy in enabling schizophrenic patients to return to work. Even that was doubtful—only one fourth of the patients stayed in treatment and were assessed, there was no control group on medication only, and all "psychotherapy" patients were maintained on continuing medication, which may have accounted for the lack of cooperation by the patients.[27] More recently, it has been found that whether patients benefited from either treatment was primarily a function of whether they formed a therapeutic alliance with the doctor.

It is not true, however, that a therapist who is inexperienced with schizophrenics specifically cannot be very helpful, because it is more important to know about human beings than about so-called schizophrenics. In my experience, such therapists are always good therapists—kind, not rigid in technique, neither withdrawn nor hostile. This is especially true with the acutely disturbed college student who is a much better prospect for psychotherapy than the poor, uneducated, chronic patients of the Michigan study.

So desperate have professionals been not to have to listen and understand that nearly every physical system in the body has been claimed to be the cause of schizophrenia (cf, Beliak's reviews of the literature, published every 10 years[28 31]). The claims have never been replicated, and they have never lasted more than 5 years.

Thus, for example, a few years ago the excess dopamine receptors theory was popularized: It was discovered that there were too many receptors for dopamine, a neurotransmitter, in the brains of schizophrenics. According to this theory, the excess dopamine receptors led to neural excitations' being conducted in the wrong directions. Further, it was said, "antipsychotic" medications block dopamine receptors, thus "proving" that this must be the cause.

These findings, however, were on medicated patients. Several years elapsed before brains of schizophrenics who had not been medicated were examined. Unmedicated schizophrenics were not found to have excess dopamine receptors. Continued medication that blocks dopamine receptors apparently leads the body to grow more receptors in an attempt to adapt.

This finding lends support to the concept of "tardive psychosis," that is, psychotic reactions on withdrawal of medication that are due, not to the return of symptoms, but to the brain changes resulting from the medication. After all, excess dopamine receptors were considered sufficient to explain psychosis before it was learned that they were a consequence of medication.

A viral cause has been "discovered" independently in Italy and in

England (different viruses), which did not replicate elsewhere. Most recently, Torrey[32 34] has put forth with enthusiasm a viral theory, although admitting there is no clear evidence for it.

One hospital in Michigan, my favorite example, "discovers" the physical cause of schizophrenia every 4 years. The discovery always gets national publicity in the mass media; people who should know better always take it seriously, but the finding is never replicated elsewhere. The news of lack of replication is carried on an inner page of the newspaper in small print, whereas the original "discovery" is usually printed on page one because of the desperation to find a simple answer that does not require understanding.

The genetic findings, too, are much more impressive in secondary sources than in the original research. For example, if the mothers of children who were adopted away at an early age were schizophrenic, there was a higher rate of schizophrenia among the children than if their mothers were not schizophrenic. It should be noted that these were not experiments; the researchers simply looked up records. A typical finding was that 10% of the children became schizophrenic if the biological mother was schizophrenic, and 0% of the adopted children did so if the biological mother was not schizophrenic. In one classic experiment, Wender and associates[35] examined the foster parents. In cases where the adopted child who later became schizophrenic was born of a schizophrenic mother, the study found that the foster parents were more disturbed than adoptive parents whose child was born of a mother who was not schizophrenic. From this they concluded, strangely, that the psychological disturbance of the foster parents could not have caused the difference in the rate of schizophrenia in the offspring because the foster parents were not diagnosed as schizophrenic. Wender et al also administered psychological tests—the Rorschach, Thematic Apperception Test (TAT), the Minnesota Multiphasic Personality Inventory (MMPI), and the Word Association Test—to the foster parents and reported finding no differences.

Parents of schizophrenics have never been reported to be different on the Word Association Test or the MMPI, but Wynne and Singer[36] described a pattern of interaction they termed "communication deviance," which they found in family observations of parents of schizophrenics and could score from the Rorschach and the TAT.

Wender et al's research assistants scored the Rorschachs and TATS of the foster parents; "communication deviance" did not differentiate the two groups of foster parents. They then sent the intermixed Rorschachs to

Margaret Singer, who scored them blindly. All 20 of the Rorschachs that she scored as being like those of parents of schizophrenic children were in the group that had adopted children who became schizophrenic from biological mothers who were schizophrenic. None of the 20 Rorschachs of the group that had adopted children who were not schizophrenic from normal mothers were scored as showing "communication deviance." Remarkably, she had correctly identified every adoptive parent whose adopted child became schizophrenic, with no false positives and no false negatives.[37] Wender and associates did not send her the TATs, but published their original findings, reporting no psychological test differences. That is what gets cited in the literature. Their data actually suggest that there is a tendency for adopted-away children of schizophrenics to be placed with more disturbing adoptive parents.

Those geneticists who claim evidence for the genetic factor admit that it accounts for only 10% of the variance. It is not surprising that Wender was one of the researchers who claimed to have demonstrated that the crime of breaking and entering is genetic.

Tienari et al[3a] have replicated Singer's finding that adopted-away offspring of schizophrenic parents become schizophrenic only if the foster parents manifest communication deviance.

Clinical experience leads one to be skeptical of genetic factors. Of course, hospital records and superficial examination often make the disorder seem uncaused. But if one dares to listen carefully, the disorder always makes sense and seems inevitable in terms of the life as experienced.

Kraepelin[39] taught the field that schizophrenia was a chronic disorder, that it might have remissions, but that the outlook was poor in the long run. This was a typical course. But only hospitalized patients were followed. Ciompi[40] has published 40-year follow-up data, beginning in 1900, for patients in Switzerland. He found that less than half of them ended up in the hospital in the long run, and something like 20% to 30% were fully recovered. Manfred Bleuler, the son of Eugen Bleuler, who originated the term schizophrenia, has published similar results.[41]

Harding[42] has investigated 25-year follow-ups of deinstitutionalized patients in Vermont. The figures were almost identical with Ciompi's Swiss data, as are the results from other American studies.[43] Using DSM-III diagnoses does not alter the findings. This is a very robust finding. Harding has pointed out that, although many of the professionals who have encouraged patients to take their medication have been well meaning, it appears that the continuing medication may prevent the 20% to 30% full recovery from ever occurring.

Thus, the pessimism about the future that treatment personnel feel and communicate to even acutely disturbed individuals is unjustified.

Symptoms of the Human Condition

Let us consider what can be learned about the human condition from the most bizarre symptoms of schizophrenia. Take the catatonic stupor, the man or woman who sits in the corner and doesn't move. These persons are either absolutely rigid or may be waxily flexible; they may stay in one position for hours or for days.

Fromm-Reichmann[3] reported long ago that catatonic patients see and hear everything that is going on around them, even though they do not react. They look as if they are in a stupor, but they are not. They feel that they will die if they move. Fromm-Reichmann understood this because the patients told her so when they finally came out of the stupor.

Some years ago, Ratner[44] investigated animals in a state that used to be called animal hypnosis. If one turns an animal upside down and presses it, it becomes rigid or waxily flexible. Rabbits, lions, tigers, alligators, 70 species of birds, fish, octopuses, in fact, just about every species of animal, fish, bird, and insect tested show this response. The major exceptions are pet dogs and cats and laboratory rats in a laboratory where they had been handled gently every day. Although this is sometimes referred to as animal hypnosis, it is not actual hypnosis—there is no verbal induction, and the animals do not obey commands. But the animal will not move, even if great pain is inflicted. After the passage of time, the animals unpredictably come into rapid, violent motion.

Classical conditioning experiments, pairing two stimuli while the animal is rigid, lead to learning that can be demonstrated after the animal comes out of the state, so it is fully conscious of external stimuli. In fact, this state is identical with the catatonic stupor.

Ratner discovered its meaning. Most animals are prey for some predator. Every species has a species-specific sequence of behaviors when it is under attack by a predator—sham death, cries of distress to warn the others in the group, etc. The last stage for every species seems to be this state of rigidity. Most predators, if they are not hungry, will kill their prey and save it for later. Some predators will not even attack something that does not move, but most predators will. When the animal goes into this catatonic-like state, most predators act as if they think it is dead. In an experiment with ferrets and frogs, a ferret, for example, ate the eye out of one frog in this state, and the frog did not flinch. The ferret crunched up the foreleg of another frog in its teeth, and the frog did not flinch either. In this experiment with ferrets and frogs, 70% of the frogs survived. According to Ratner, if even 30% survive to one mating, the effect on evolution is massive.

So the catatonic stupor is a life and species preservative strategy that is built into just about all living animals, including college students. The biological evidence is consistent with the clinical evidence from somebody like Frieda Fromm-Reichmann3 who actually listened to her patients. That needs to be said because there are many "experts" on schizophrenia who have never listened to any of their patients for more than half an hour.

We do not want to know that you and I would go catatonic if we were terrified enough. Nor do we want to know what it feels like to be that terrified. But you can reassure the catatonic patient that you will not allow anyone to kill him or her, that it is safe, and that you are on their side; and you can reiterate this message for as many sessions as necessary, knowing that the patient can hear you.

As with the catatonic stupor, every other schizophrenic symptom is a universal human potentiality. Take hallucinations, the most dramatic symptom of all. Schizophrenic patients, as well as professionals, like to say that nobody understands hallucinations. But hallucinations are entirely understandable in terms of Freud's[45][47] theories of dreams, with a few additions. Today, the concept of the collective unconscious seems scientifically untenable; it was based on the then-accepted biological theory of the inheritance of acquired characteristics, which is no longer acceptable to biologists. There is no evidence of universal symbols; there are only symbols that are frequently used with a given meaning. There are, however, always people who will use any symbol with an entirely different meaning.

Unlike most people, schizophrenics hallucinate while they are wide awake. Everyone hallucinates when asleep. Dreams may take any sensory modality, but the predominant experience is visual. Schizophrenics also may hallucinate in any sensory modality, but the predominant modality is auditory. Whatever other hallucinations they have, they almost always hear voices. That is different from toxic psychoses, where the hallucinations are primarily visual.

Why auditory hallucinations? Because, basically, schizophrenia is an interpersonal disorder. If someone is blind, he or she is more physically incapacitated than someone who is deaf. In terms of the probability of emotional disorders, however, someone who is deaf is more likely to have emotional problems resulting from it because the deafness cuts the individual off from people.

Is the capacity to hallucinate while wide awake restricted to schizophrenics? Not at all. It is well known that starving people start seeing food. It is a human capacity that is activated when the motivation is strong enough; luckily, most of us will never be desperate enough to have to hallucinate. A trivial example illustrates the meaning of hallucinations. In the middle of a therapy session, a disturbed college student asked, "What's that bell?"

"I didn't hear a bell."

"Well, I did."

"It may well be. There are a lot of funny noises in this building. I work here all the time and maybe, like a lighthouse keeper, I just don't pay attention to them anymore. What did the bell sound like?"

"It sounded like a telephone bell, only very loud."

"That's surprising. A telephone bell I would have heard. What comes to mind when you think of a telephone bell?"

"Trying to get through to somebody."

"I think I know what's happening. I've been talking about what I thought was important, but you know I'm off somewhere; and you wish I would get through to you and talk about what is really going on here."

Then the patient smiled. She was too intimidated to tell the therapist he did not understand and to ask why he was talking about irrelevancies when there were some things that were important. The most she could do was wish that somehow he would get through to her; and even that was too frightening to deal with consciously, so she had to have it come through in disguise, as a hallucination.

As mentioned above, attempts to understand delusions would have led to considering incest, sexual abuse of children, and physical abuse of children as serious problems in our society. What else do we not want to know?

There are four bases for delusions in college students, as in other patients. The most important source of delusional material is Freud's concept of transference, reliving feelings, fantasies, and experiences from the past with no awareness that it is the past. Of course, Freud thought schizophrenics did not form a transference, the "libido" (conceptualized as limited in quantity) was turned on to the self and not available for transference. He was mistaken because he did not talk to schizophrenics. According to people who knew him, Freud said schizophrenic patients scared him. He certainly had enough work to do without schizophrenic patients. But even Freud's inferences are unlikely to be accurate unless they are based on clinical observations.

Freud originally thought of transference as a phenomenon occurring only in psychoanalysis, as the chief resistance, which, by understanding, he was able to transform into its most potent therapeutic tool. Ferenczi[48] first pointed out, and Freud accepted, that transference, like other resistances, was a defense used to cope in ordinary life. What was unique about transference in therapy was not its occurrence, but that it was studied.

The transference reactions of normals and neurotics, however, are sufficiently subtle and realistic that one need not be upset by being reminded of how pervasively we recreate and re-experience our past. But schizophrenics, if listened to, are not subtle in their transference.

Nor are the specific contents of their transference matters of which most of us wish to be reminded. It is not pleasant to be reminded of the varieties of misery that are inflicted on children in our society. Even more troubling than the awareness of obviously hurtful or neglectful treatment of children is the insight that parents of admirable character, with the very best of intentions, may harm their children, either because their hurtful interactions are unconscious[49,50] or because the parents are misinformed about the consequences of their actions.

The most famous example of this is Schreber,[51,52] a judge in Germany, a paranoid schizophrenic who, after he was declared sane, wrote a book exposing the plot against him. Freud read the book[53] and had some important insights[54] but missed the point that much of the delusional system was based on the transference of real childhood experiences.

Schreber claimed that God put metal bands around his head and his chest and tightened them "lovingly" until it hurt. Further, God wanted to castrate him and make him a woman.

Schreber's father was a world-famous pediatrician who wrote books on how to raise children. His advice included advocating that "bad habits," by which he meant masturbation, should be punished immediately and then will disappear by the age of 4 and never recur, with no bad aftereffects. He knew because he had done this with both of his sons. One committed suicide and the other became the most famous paranoid schizophrenic ever. The father used anti-masturbation devices with spikes that penetrated the child's penis if he had an erection.

The father also believed that exercise and posture were very important for children. To improve their posture, he invented chairs, tables, and beds with rods and metal rings that went around the head and around the chest to make the child sit up straight or lie absolutely straight. He said he used them "lovingly." We would probably consider them torture devices today.

What God did in Schreber's delusions was what Schreber's real father actually did to Schreber as a child. What psychiatrist would even consider the possibility that a world-famous pediatrician could have done such terrible things? But remember, his father was not intending to torture Schreber; his father thought this was good for the child.

To use a more contemporary example, a college aged young woman alarmed the hospital staff by repeatedly cutting and burning herself. When asked about her religion, she said, "I was raised a Catholic."

"Oh, you were raised a Catholic, but you're not now."

"Actually, I'm a Satanist."

"Why don't you tell me about it."

"I used to feel I had to save people. I had to save all the people in Beirut."

"That's a marvelous image. Beirut, that's a marvelous image. You know who the people in Beirut are, don't you?"

She started to say yes, and then she said, "Well, no."

"What a marvelous image. What's Beirut? Beirut is a city where people are killing each other, and then they declare peace. But when you look, they are killing each other. And then they find out why they are killing each other, and then deal with those problems and solve them, but they are killing each other. Then they have a truce, and then they are still killing each other. What a marvelous image; your family must have been like that."

She became very interested at that point. "Satan says that if I hurt myself, he'll keep me with him. That's what he says."

She was very scared. She described Satan's voice and his appearance.

153

She described his face in considerable detail. When asked whether she knew anybody who looked like that, she thought and said, "Yes; he doesn't look like it now, but he used to."

"Who?"

"My father."

Indeed, according to later information from the family, it turns out her father used to beat her mother, and her mother eventually left the house. One can understand a little girl's belief that pain is the price of not being abandoned.

That hallucination disappeared. All one had to do was to ask the patient to describe her experience and ask what it could possibly mean.

The second source of delusions was described by Freud[54] on the basis of insights derived from his reading of Schreber's book. As is widely cited, Freud derived many paranoid delusions from the fear of homosexuality as different ways of contradicting the implicit guilt-producing feelings (for a man), "I love him." Thus, I do not love him, I love me—megalomania; I do not love him, I love her—erotomania; I do not love him (using projection), she loves him—delusional jealousy; I do not love him (using projection), he loves me—the delusional threat of being endangered by homosexuals; I do not love him (using reaction formation), I hate him—irrational hatred; or, most common, I do not love him (using reaction formation), I hate him, but I cannot hate him for no reason, so (using projection) he hates me, that is why I hate him, and if I hate him, obviously I do not love him—delusional feeling of persecution.

Secondary sources, however, almost never mention one part of Freud's insight that is most meaningful and essential for therapeutic effectiveness. In the language of libido theory, Freud said that the patient with schizo-phrenia feels withdrawn from emotional relatedness to everybody. Consequently, he wants to be able to relate to someone again. But we know that, in growing up, it is usual to feel comfortable in relating closely to peers of the same sex before becoming comfortable with the opposite sex. People of the same sex are more like us than those of the opposite sex. When one feels withdrawn from everybody, there is a strong urge to get close to people of the same sex. Unfortunately, the patient's conscience, and often many other people, interpret this self-curative tendency as "homosexuality." But is this different from the normal adolescent and post-adolescent who is having trouble with the opposite sex? Time spent with friends of the same sex leads to becoming more comfortable with people and with the opposite sex. This is the normal developmental sequence. With normal and neurotic college students, the fear of homosexuality leads to withdrawing from friends of the same sex, and that makes relating to the other sex even more difficult. Hence, the generally useful advice to those having trouble with the opposite sex is that more time spent with same-sex friends will make relating to the opposite sex easier.

Even the specific dynamics of paranoid feelings as defenses are mirrored in the dynamics of some similar feelings in people who are not schizophrenics.

It is usually helpful to let schizophrenic patients, including acutely disturbed students, with symptoms based on the fear of homosexuality know that their fear of being homosexual is unfounded (if, as is usually the case, it is unfounded), that they are simply lonely, that their loneliness is normal, and that we all need friends of both sexes.

Unless they have had a meaningful and benign homosexual relationship, schizophrenics are not helped by reassurances concerning the increased acceptability of homosexuality, but they always feel understood when their therapist talks of loneliness.

The third basis for delusions is that some families actually teach strange ideas. The study of schizophrenic patients[3] reveals how human beings depend on their families to teach them the categories of thought and the meaning of those categories. Children (and adults) assume that other people use concepts in the same way, unless confronted with understandable contradictions. For example, if a person believes "I love you" includes in its meaning "I hurt you, physically assault you, occasionally even try to kill you," that person is unlikely ever to be able to relate closely to another in a loving relationship.

It has been noted that families with disturbed children have a tendency to discourage the use of people outside the family as sources of information and corrective identification. Patients from very disturbing families, who do not become schizophrenic, are inevitably found to have remedied the defects in their nuclear families with relationships outside the nuclear family. This is a normal mechanism. Nobody ever had a perfect mother or father. Most children (and adults) use people outside the family to correct any problems in their family.

When parents interfere with this mechanism, any problem in the family is enormously magnified in its destructive impact. The parents, of course, do not do this to be hurtful; they are unaware that it has any harmful consequences. Indeed, they may even believe that it is good for the child.

Parents who discourage extra-familial identifications are spared the normal discomfort of having their values and beliefs challenged by their children. But these challenges, whether or not communicated overtly, par-tially shield the child from the impact of the inevitable parental mistakes. College is an ideal place for corrective experiences and identifications, first with the therapist and then with other students and faculty.

The last basis for delusions is the general human need for a more or less systematic explanation of our world. Most people share similar systematic understandings. One who believes the world is flat is normal if the year is 1400 and is suspect if the year is 1990. The belief is the same; it is the relationship to others' beliefs that makes it normal or suspect. In our pluralistic modern era, one is not considered mentally ill if there is an obvious basis for a different understanding. Thus, a fundamentalist usually does not think that those of us who take evolution seriously are mentally ill; he understands that such people take biology, geology, and physics seriously but do not realize the "truth" that God created fossils as fossils.

Schizophrenic people have had strange experiences. In part, the symptoms are strange experiences by ordinary standards. In addition, their lives often include unusual real events. Therefore, their systematic explanations of their world seem strange. But they demonstrate a need to be as realistic as their anxieties permit. Insofar as discrepancies between their understanding and reality become apparent to them, and as dynamic balances change, the patients continually revise their understanding.

The more intelligent patients are more apt to develop a systematic understanding that is adequate enough to obviate the need for more deteriorated symptoms and, hence, to be diagnosed as paranoid or paranoid schizophrenic. The less intelligent are less likely to develop as functionally adequate a "paranoid system."

Because the paranoid system is not an abnormal process but a normal process used to cope with unusual problems, it is possible for a nonfrightened, non-humiliating therapist to share the patient's systematic understanding, respectfully call attention to inconsistencies, and helpfully supplement the patient's understanding with the therapist's knowledge of the world, other people, and more important, the workings of the human mind.

Although more detailed descriptions of appropriate therapeutic techniques useful with acutely disturbed students are outside the scope of this article, they may be found in Karon[55] and Karon and VandenBos[20].

A Final Example

The best description of what it feels like to be schizophrenic came, not from a college student, but from a catatonic man, a high school dropout, for whom it took eight weeks of psychotherapy (without medication) to get out of the hospital and back to work. One of his symptoms was bowing. When asked why he bowed, he said,

"I don't bow."

"Yes, you do."

"No, I don't bow."

"Wait a minute. You do this." The therapist bowed. "This is bowing; you bow."

"No, I don't bow."

"But you do this."

"That's not bowing."

"What is it?"

"It's balancing."

"What are you balancing?"

"Emotions."

"What emotions?"

"Fear and loneliness."

That is, when he was lonely, he wanted to get close to people, so he leaned forward. When he got close to people, he got scared and had to pull away, so he straightened up. But then he was lonely again.

Balancing between fear and loneliness is the best description of what it feels like to be schizophrenic at any age, but that is what the rest of us do not want to understand.

REFERENCES

Bockoven, J.S. Moral Treatment in Community Mental Flealth. New York, Springer, 1972.

Sullivan, H.S. Schizophrenia as a Human Process. New York, Norton, 1953.

Fromm-Reichmann, F. Principles of Intensive Psychotherapy. Chicago, University of Chicago Press, 1950.

Greenberg, J.I. Never Promised You a Rose Garden. New York, Holt, Rinehart, & Winston, 1964.

Lidz T. The Origin and Treatment of Schizophrenic Disorders. New York, Basic Books, 1973.

Kestenberg, J. Children and Parents: Psychoanalytic Studies in Development. New York, Aronson, 1975.

Rosberg, J., Karon, B.P. A direct analytic contribution to the understanding of post-partum psychoses. Psychiatr Q 1959 April;33(2):296-304.

Michel-Hutmacher, R. Das Korperinnere in der Vorstellung der Kinder. Schweizerische Zeitschrift fuer Psychologie understanding ihre Anwendungen 1955;14(1):1-26.

Rosberg, J., Karon B.P. The Oedipus complex in an apparently deteriorated case of schizophrenia. I Abnorm Soc Psychol 1958 March;57(2):221-225.

Searles H.F. Collected Papers on Schizophrenia and Related Subjects. New York, International Universities Press, 1965.

Bleuler, E., Dementia Praecox, or the Group of the Schizophrenias, Zinkin J (trans). New York, International Universities Press, 1950.

Deikman A.J., Whitaker, L.C. Humanizing a psychiatric ward: Changing from drugs to psychotherapy. Psychother: Theory Res Pract 1979 Summer;16(2):202-214.

Breggin, P.R. Electro-shock: Its Brain-disabling Effects. New York, Springer, 1979.

Morgan R.F. Electric Shock. Toronto, IPI Publishing, 1985.

Kalinowsky L.B., Hippius H. Pharmacological, Convulsive, and Other Somatic Treatments in Psychiatry. New York, Grune & Stratton, 1972.

Fink M. EST and other somatic therapies for schizophrenia. In Beliak L (ed). Disorders of the Schizophrenic Syndrome. New York, Basic

Books, 1979, pp 353-363.

Task Force Report: Electroconvulsive Therapy. Washington, American Psychiatric Association, 1978.

Task Force Report: Tardive Dyskinesia. Washington, American Psychiatric Association, 1980.

Breggin, P.R. Psychiatric Drugs: Hazards to the Brain. New York, Springer, 1983.

Karon, B.P., VandenBos G.R. Psychotherapy of Schizophrenia: The Treatment of Choice. New York, Aronson, 1981.

Rogers, C.R., Gendlin, E.T., Keisler, D.J., Truax, C.B. The Therapeutic Relationship and Its Impact. A Study of Psychotherapy with Schizophrenics. Madison, Wl, University of Wisconsin Press, 1967.

Paul, G.L., Lentz, R.J. Psychosocial Treatment of Chronic Mental Patients: Milieu vs. Social Learning Programs. Cambridge, MA, Harvard University Press, 1977.

May, P.R.A. Treatment of Schizophrenia: A Comparative Study of Five Treatment Methods. New York, Science House, 1968.

Grinspoon, L., Ewalt. J.R., Shader, R.I. Schizophrenia, Pharmacotherapy, and Psychotherapy. Baltimore, Williams & Wilkins, 1972.

Sjostrom, R., Sandin, B. Effects of psychotherapy in schizophrenia—A retrospective study. Paper presented at the First European Conference of Psychotherapy Research, Trier, Federal Republic of Germany, Sept 1981. Psychiatric Research Center, Utleraker Hospital S-750, 17 Uppsala, Sweden.

Gunderson, J.G., Frank, A.F., Katz, H.M., Vannicelli, M.L., Frosch, J.P., Knapp, P.H. Effects of psychotherapy in schizophrenia. Schizophr Bull 1984; 10(4): 564-598.

Karon, B.P. The fear of reducing medication and where have all the patients gone? Schizophr Bull 1984; 10(4): 613-617.

Beliak, L., Dementia Praecox. New York, Grune & Stratton, 1984.

———, Schizophrenia. Plainfield, NJ, Logos, 1958.

——— & Loeb L. The Schizophrenic Syndrome. New York, Grune & Stratton, 1969.

——— Disorders of the Schizophrenic Syndrome. New York, Basic Books, 1979.

Torrey, E.F. Schizophrenia: An interview with E. Fuller Torrey. Public

Citizen Health Research Group Health Letter 1985 Apriljl(4):2-4.

———— & Kaufmann, C.A. Schizophrenia and neuroviruses. In Nasrallah HA, Weinberger DR (eds). The Neurology of Schizophrenia. Amsterdam, Elsevier, 1986, pp 377-396.

———— Schizophrenia and Civilization. New York, Aronson, 1980.

Wender, P.H., Rosenthal D, Zahn T, Kety S. The psychiatric adjustment of the adopting parents of schizophrenics. Am I Psychiatry 1971;112(8):1013-1018.

Wynne, L.C., Singer, M. Thought disorder and family relations of schizophrenics. II: A classification of forms of thinking. Arch Gen Psychiatry 1963 August;9(2): 199-206.

————, Singer, M., Touhey, M. Communication of the adoptive parents of schizophrenics. In Jorstad J, Ugelstad E (eds). Schizophrenia 75. Oslo, University of Oslo Press, 1976, pp 413-451.

Tienari, P., Sorri, A., Lahti, I., et al. The Finnish adoptive study of schizophrenia, Yale I Biol Med 1985;58(3):227-237.

Kraepelin, E., Dementia Praecox, Barclay, R.M. (trans). Edinburgh, ES Livingston, 1919.

Ciompi, L. Catamnesic long-term study on the course of life and aging of schizophrenics. Schizophr Bull 1985;6(4): 606-617.

Bleuler, M. The Schizophrenic Disorders: Long Term Patient and Family Studies. New Haven: Yale University Press, 1978.

Harding, C.M., Brooks, G.W., Ashikaga, T. Aging and social functioning in once-chronic schizophrenic patients 22-62 years after first admission: The Vermont story. In Hudgins G, Miller M. Schizophrenia and Aging. New York, Guilford Press, 1987.

————, Zubin, J., Strauss, J.S. Chronicity in schizophrenia: Fact, partial fact, or artifact? Hosp Community Psychiatry 1987 May;38(5):477-486.

Ratner, S.G., Karon, B.P., VandenBos GR, Denny MR. The adaptive significance of the catatonic stupor in humans and animals from an evolutionary perspective. Acad Psychol Bull 1981 Jurie;3(2):273-279.

Freud, S. The Interpretation of Dreams. New York, Macmillan, 1950.

———— A General Introduction to Psychoanalysis. New York, Liveright, 1935.

———— New Introductory Lectures on Psychoanalysis. New York,

Norton, 1933.

Ferenczi, S. Introjection and transference. Sex in Psychoanalysis. New York, Brunner/Mazel, 1950, pp 35-93.

Karon, B.P. A clinical note on the significance of an "oral" trauma. / Abn Soc Psychol 1960;61 (3):480-481.

Meyer, R.G., Karon B.P. The schizophrenogenic mother concept and the TAT. Psychiatry 1967 May;30(2):173-179.

Niederland, W.G. Schreber: Father and son. Psychoanal Q 1959 Apri I ;28(2): 151 -169.

——— Schreber's father, j Am Psychoanal Assoc 1960;8(3):492-499.

Freud, S. Psychoanalytic notes upon an autobiographical account of a case of paranoia (dementia paranoides). Complete Psychological Works, vol 12. London, Hogarth Press, 1958, pp 1-82.

Schreber, D.P. Memoirs of My Recent Nervous Illness. London, Dawson, 1955.

Karon, B.P. The treatment of acute schizophrenic reactions in private practice. Br I Psychother 1987;4(2):135-140. assistance.

CHAPTER 9
Recurrent Psychotic Depression Is Treatable by Psychoanalytic Therapy Without Medication
Bertram P. Karon, Ph.D.

In most of my papers and in my book (Karon & VandenBos, 1981) I have repeatedly made the point that schizophrenic patients are treatable by psychoanalytic therapy, that psychoanalytic therapy without medication is the treatment that is most effective, and that medication may be used as a temporary adjunct but it should be withdrawn as rapidly as the patient can tolerate. As we found in my Detroit project, with randomized assignment and blind evaluations, even 70 sessions of psychoanalytic therapy, as compared to medication properly used, led to a much greater improvement in the thought disorder.and a more human life in a variety of ways, and consequently a much lower rate of re-hospitalization. But the effectiveness of psychoanalytic therapy for deeply disturbed human beings is not confined to schizophrenics. As Michael Teixeira has written in his classic paper on the treatment of manic-depressive disorders by psychoanalytic therapy (Teixeira, 1992) similar approaches to psychoanalytic therapy are similarly effective with these patients as well. And again, patients are more likely to make optimal progress without the use of medication, or with temporary medication which is withdrawn as rapidly as the patient can tolerate.

Every diagnostic category consists of a highly varied group of people. Among others, Harry Stack Sullivan and Karl Menninger emphasized how poorly diagnostic categories characterize patients. Luckily, psychoanalysts treat people, not symptoms. For depressed patients, as with anyone, the conscious and unconscious fantasies underlying any symptom always result from the interaction of their actual life experiences with pre-existing fantasies so that their whole life history from early infancy onward is relevant. The defense mechanism of isolation is an almost invariable defense of severely depressed patients. If you ask a depressed patient what was going on in their life just before the depression started, they will say, "Nothing." If you persist, they will typically say, "Nothing important.." If you persist, that you want to know the unimportant things that were going on, they will tell you things which would depress anyone, but which they do not connect with their feelings.

Unfortunately, it not fashionable these days to get an accurate case history. After I had presented a Grand Rounds at a major Department of Psychiatry recently, one of a group of advanced residents said with a puzzled look, as if it were a new idea, "I guess what you are talking about might be called historicity. If we knew the patient's history, what they're talking about would make sense."

Just because a patient calls him or herself depressed, or professionals have diagnosed the patient as depressed, does not mean you know what the affective experience of the patient really is. As Henry Krystal has pointed out (personal communication), one should always try to find out what is the actual affect. It may be sadness, terror, self-disgust, shame, guilt, anger, undifferentiated negative affect, or no feeling at all, to name some of the possibilities. Every depressive has moments (or long periods) of terror, just as every schizophrenic endures periods of depression even when getting better. Psychotic depressives often have no feelings at all, and when they begin to feel sad and/or weep they are usually improving. One way of understanding this process is that the lack of feeling is repression in order to avoid unbearable pain, and the re-experiencing of sadness in bearable quantities is frequently a part of the process of recovery.

Severely depressed patients are geniuses at convincing you that their lives are hopeless and the therapy is of no value, but unconsciously they desperately hope that they will not convince you. A clear statement that you do not share their pessimism is very helpful. While other determinants of depression are more fashionable, the role of anger should not be neglected.

One of the mistakes of Psychology, Psychiatry, and even Psychoanalysis was the puritanical belief that feelings are irrational. But Rappaport, a long time ago, said there were no thoughts without feelings, and Tomkins pointed out that emotions are a central part of rational thinking. If we are happy something good has happened, if we are depressed, there is something to be depressed about, if we are angry, something is hurting us, if we are frightened, there is something to be scared of. If it is not in consciousness, then it is unconscious, and if it is not in the present, it is in the past, and. something in the present symbolizes it.

I remember discussing this with Viggo Jensen early in my career. I said that he had treated many more depressives than I had, but every endogenous depression I had ever treated had very good reasons for being depressed. He said, "Don't you know what an endogenous depression is? That's a very severe depression in someone whom you haven't talked to long enough to find out why they are depressed."

Thus, I was recently referred a woman in her 70's, diagnosed with an endogenous depression, who was hospitalized for the second time within a year. She had been treated with medication during both hospitalizations and the intervening period. The medication was accompanied by some kind of counseling when she was not in the hospital, but the so-called therapist acted as if the medication was the real treatment and the patient felt she had learned nothing from the counseling. During my first interview with the patient, as well as my first interview with the patient's grown-up daughter, and my telephone conversation with the referring professional (a friend of the family who was concerned about the adequacy of the treatment), the same fact was disclosed. The patient's husband of 50 years had died. The patient held together for a month, and then fell apart, and was hospitalized. When I mentioned on the phone to the ward chief (who is also a faculty member at our Department of Psychiatry) that this was a mistake even Kraepelin would not have made, there was a pause, and a puzzled voice said, "He's not a recent psychiatrist, is he?"

I arranged for her to begin psychoanalytic therapy with me after discharge and her medications (they had her on three) to be withdrawn in a medically responsible way. Later, her daughter, impatient with psychoanalytic therapy, thought she should be treated with medication. The daughter had her tested by a psychologist who suggested that the daughter was right and that she should see a psychiatrist and be treated with medication.

The daughter said that she hoped I would tell her mother to comply with the recommendation. I told the daughter that the psychologist's husband was a psychiatrist who had once bragged to me that he had treated 700 patients simultaneously. "That is not the kind of psychiatrist your mother needs."

I reminded the patient that she had already tried medication and it had probably helped at first, and then did not seem to help. "You're wrong," she said. "The medication did not help at all." I then suggested that if she saw a psychiatrist, she should see a competent one, and recommended a medical psychoanalyst I trusted. The patient reminded me that I had already mentioned that name as a reasonable alternative if she were unhappy with me, or preferred a medical professional, but that she was not interested in a psychiatrist.

"Yes, I guess you have seen a number of psychiatrists before you saw me."

She said, "I saw them. But they never saw me." Patients often say it more clearly than we do.

The patient's face was a block of wood when we started; it is now affectively alive, and appropriately emotional and spontaneous. There is much she is still not doing, but she confessed she is wasting a lot of time. Every Saturday she is now listening to the full Metropolitan Opera broadcasts and it is glorious. (She has always liked classical music, before she was depressed.) The first one she listened to was Carmen.

I remarked that the first time I saw Carmen performed, it was not music, it was magic.

"I guess, " she said, " there's no one who does not like Carmen."

 She has been listening ever since. She has a way to go, but that is not a part of a depressed way of life.

Unfortunately, there is a professional zeitgeist that suggests that depressive affect does not have meaning, and is not related to the life history. A chronically depressed man, who had been treated for 20 years by a series of psychiatrists, some of whom were psychoanalysts, was referred to treatment. All of his previous treatments involved medication, usually accompanied by psychotherapy. Given his long history of treatment, I informed him that he should be seen three times a week and that the treatment would probably take two or three years. He said I have friends who are physicians who work for an HMO and I know that no one needs to be seen more than once a week and no one needs to be seen for more than 20 sessions and you are just trying to run a bill on me.

I suggested I would see him once a week for 20 weeks, and we would do what we could. After 10 weeks, as I always do when there is a time limit, I pointed out that we only had 10 more sessions. He got mad at me for being such a son of a bitch that I would not see him more than 20 sessions. I said that if he felt that strongly we did not have to stop at 20 sessions. In later sessions he then got furious at me because I would not see him more than once a week. I said that if he felt that strongly, I could see him more than once a week. He later got angry because I would not see him more than twice a week. I said that if he felt that strongly, I could see him three times a week. The treatment lasted three years. At the end this man who had been in treatment for 20 years said that no professional before me had ever related his depressions to the way his mother and his father had related to him. "I guess they helped. I limped through life getting along, sort of. But I don't think I was ever really in therapy until now."

Anti-depressant medication has been over-sold. They are more effective than placebos, but the difference seems to be surprisingly small (Hirsch et al)., They are particularly ineffective with children and adolescents, a fact which has been hidden until England banned the use of all but one with children and adolescents, and that one must have a warning on the label that it is not recommended for children and adolescents. The ban is not merely because they are ineffective but because they dramatically increase suicide and homicide. Luckily, most people even on antidepressants will not commit suicide. An even smaller group will commit murder. But the rates are increased and the manufacturers have withheld this information from physicians. That is why I prefer not to have patients medicated. I tell patients I will never ask you to give up anything you need. However, the odds are that you will eventually get off medication if you are in treatment with me. If they ask for information, I will summarize what I know about the current research data, and suggest readily available sources., like Breggin and Cohen's Your Drug May be Your Problem, where the known side effects, and the known withdrawal effects of most currently used psychiatric medications are accurately summarized as well as advice, drawn from the general literature in pharmacology, on how best to safely withdraw from a medication, both in terms of general advice and of specific medications. The research literature suggests that several types of psychotherapy are as effective for depression as medication, adding medication to psychotherapy does not increase effectiveness, but does increase the relapse rate. You are not likely to have heard this because most Continuing Medical Education seminars are prepared and the lecturers hired by pharmaceutical manufacturers. Whether the patient is a new patient or a patient already in treatment, I will always summarize the research literature as I know it at least once to explain why I do not recommend medication. Further, they have a right to accurate information which they probably do not have. However, patients, especially doctors and nurses, have taught me that, after the first time, patients bring up the issue of medication at a later time as a resistance, knowing that I tend to give a little lecture on the subject. I have learned to point out that patients know I do this, and therefore bring it up when there is something else important that they do not wish to talk about.

If a depressed patient is a new patient, not yet on medication (which is rare these days) I will tell them that some professionals would treat them only with medication, some with both medication and psychotherapy, and some professionals would treat them as I do, because I think it is best, with psychoanalytic therapy.

If they would like to be treated with medication, I would be glad to refer them to Dr. A, who reads the literature, and will give them the right medication at the right dosage and check for side effects. If they want a combination, I would be glad to refer them to Dr. B who also reads the literature and will give them the right medication at the right dosage and check for side effects, but he also talks to his patients. And if they want to work hard, they should stay here and work with me. I say the same thing to patients working with me, who ask about being put on medication. In either case, they ask, "Won't you work with me if I go on medication?'

"No. But I'll be here after you try it. You can come back, if you want to." They typically get mad at me, but stay in treatment.

Not sleeping is an issue which frequently comes up with depressed patients. They try to panic the therapist. But Alfred Adler, many years ago, pointed out that people do not need to sleep, they need to rest. Rest includes a reasonable amount of tossing and turning; no one is absolutely still even when asleep. Eight hours of rest while wide awake is as good as five hours of the deepest soundest sleep. It is an extremely boring way to spend a night, but you can function the next day.

For any patient with a sleep problem, including depressives, you first give this advice. If the patient can do it, they will discover it works. Frequently, the sleep problem goes away, but if it does not they can still function. About two thirds of patients can make use of this advice.

For those who say that it does not work or who cannot even try it, the next step is to give an Adlerian interpretation. Using the example of the student who cannot sleep the night before an exam, Adler suggests neurotics create a distance between themselves and their life, by creating an unconscious alibi in advance: how can anyone expect me to pass when I did not even get a good night's sleep. And if I do well, think how much better I would have done if I had a night's sleep. Like a good neurotic you are perfect no matter what happens, but like a good neurotic you are more likely to fail in the real world. After explaining this, you ask the patient," What do you need an alibi for failing at?"

Such an Adlerian interpretation will help approximately two-thirds of those who were not helped by advice. The one patient in nine that neither of these procedures help requires that their dynamics be investigated individually.

Suicide is always a troubling concern. Depressives are no more likely to commit suicide than schizophrenics, but it is a troubling concern in any event. Hopelessness is a necessary but not sufficient cause for suicide. No one kills themselves if they have a strong hope of getting something important by staying alive.

There are only three theories of suicide that I find worth being concerned with. The first is the idea that suicide is an attempt to get even with someone else . As the folk-culture puts it, I'll eat me some worms and then I'll die and then they'll be sorry." Every child has thought this, and anything every child has thought is in the unconscious of every adult. This leads to the idea that, on the one hand, you must create hope by the relationship with you. It's not that you can solve everything today, but most of the things that people commit suicide over are solvable. Secondly, you should tell them that many people commit suicide to get even with someone else, and it's stupid because it means that the other person is a lot more important than you are, if you are willing to hurt yourself a lot to hurt them a little. Besides it is surprising how quickly spouses, and ex-lovers, and even parents get over it. (As you probably know the one set of people who do not get over it are the children of suicides. I don't usually describe that to patients unless they have young children they seem to care about.)

The second view is the rescue fantasy, originally described by Jensen and Petty. Their view was that the suicide really does not want to die, that he or she projects their superego into someone else, and asks them implicitly "Do I deserve to die?" That is why suicides almost always tell someone else, and that person does nothing to save them, the message is "You deserve to die." From this standpoint, the one thing a therapist should not do is do nothing. The therapist should indicate by words or actions that you don't think the patient deserves to die.

The third view is that the suicide has internalized a parent whom they felt wanted them dead.

The Thematic Apperception Test (TAT) can be useful when you are not sure about suicide. The dangerous protocol consists of stories in which the hero of the same age and sex and under similar circumstances as the patient commits suicide. Symbolic suicides and suicidal thoughts do not predict suicide. The TAT may suggest the specific circumstances under which the patient may or may not be suicidal.

When in doubt always ask the patient whether they are thinking of killing themselves. Most dangerous is a matter of fact statement that they intend to kill themselves in a realistic manner. Fantastic techniques are not generally dangerous. Patients who are agitated and afraid are not as dangerous as those who are matter of fact.

It is well known that some seriously depressed patients kill themselves when it looks like they are getting better. The usual explanation is that they did not have enough energy before, but George Atwood pointed out that is not what is going on. Some patients decide to solve their problems by killing themselves. They then seem to be improving and then carry out their solution.

Deeply depressed patients who are improving show increased insight into why they are depressed. They also talk more about the future. If you ask them about suicide, they will discuss it.

Patients who appear to be getting better because they are going to kill themselves seem to be getting better but have no more insight into why they were depressed. They don't talk more about the future because they don't have any. If you raise the subject of suicide, they either will not talk about it, or will unemotionally tell you they are going to kill themselves.

These three indices will tell you whether the patient is genuinely getting better or whether you need to take effective action.

Hispanic patients who are hospitalized or in jails have a high risk of suicide. The family is typically more important in every day functioning than for Anglos or for African-Americans, and jail or hospitalization interferes with the relationship with the family. If there is a further impairment of the relationship with their family, like the family moving out of town, they are likely to become suicidal. However, if watched for 24 hours, the crisis is usually over.

Having someone with a suicidal patient is in general very helpful. But it is most helpful to deal with the issues. SSRI antidepressants are not useful for suicidal patients; some patients who are not suicidal become suicidal on SSRI's. Healey's research found that 10% of normal volunteers who had never been in treatment or clinically depressed became suicidal on SSRI's

With almost any kind of patient, the more frequently the patient is seen the easier it is for both patient and therapist. The one exception I can think of was a psychotic depressive woman who had been hospitalized several times, given ECT the first time, but it was discontinued because of spinal damage. This time she saw me instead of going to the hospital. One of her daughters had taken my undergraduate class in Personality from a Psychoanalytic Perspective and wanted her mother to get first rate treatment.

Instead of going to the hospital, she stayed at her parents' house, which was 50 miles away. They could only bring her in once a week. In this case that was lucky. She was so irritating that I usually was very angry at her by the end of each hour. A week later I had forgotten my irritation, and she had a kind an accepting therapist for almost all of the hour. I might not have been able to do that, especially early in therapy, if I had seen her more frequently.

As she improved, I discussed her return to her own home with her husband. I pointed out to her husband as well as to the patient that her husband knew how to take care of the house and their five children without her, as he had whenever she was hospitalized, or now when she was living with her parents. I suggested that he continue to run the house as if she were not there when she first moved back. Expect nothing from her at first, and she would take over functioning and helping at her own pace as she could.

When she moved back, I tried to help her avoid likely mistakes in parenting. In one session I talked about the normality of masturbation and how she must not punish her children but let them know that it is impolite to masturbate in front of other people. Not sick, not bad, just impolite in front of other people. Of course, she was angry at me.

She started the next hour by saying, "I do that." I did not know what she was talking about, so I asked her. She said, "I do that. I masturbate. I do that because I'm crazy."

"No," I said, " You do that because you're human. You don't enjoy it, because you're crazy." She got mad at me and insisted , and I repeated my view. If I had agreed with her puritanical statement, I would have made her insanity necessary to cope with her guilt over masturbation.

She stopped masturbating after a year of treatment because sex with her husband was so much better. "It's like we just got married."

Very often depressed people, even when their judgment is poor, try to control the other people in their family. She would not allow her husband to make decisions about his job, the car, insurance, or an accident settlement. It is one of my principles, that I tell patients, that the person in the family who knows the most about something should be the one who makes the decision about that matter. She stopped trying to control him about these matters and others where he clearly knew more than she did. He grew, making better decisions about his job and other matters. She was impressed and she liked him more. She became a pleasant person toward the end of therapy, which was only a year or two, at which time she was taking care of her home and children. She was also working for the first time at a part time job as a school aid.

Finally, I will discuss a man in his 60's who suffered from recurrent severe and sometimes psychotic depressions and "spontaneous" panic attacks. In his depression there was also a terror dimension, because he was afraid he might die. If he died, he would go to Hell. Hell is a lake of burning fire in which you burn forever. He deserved to burn forever because he had committed "the unpardonable sin." The unpardonable sin, he believed, was masturbation. He knew about the lake of burning fire and about masturbation because he had been told these things by his Fundamentalist minister and by his mother.

His father also had a low opinion of him, but that did not matter since his father did not go to church, and therefore his opinion did not matter. But his mother also had a low opinion of him, and her opinion mattered.

The patient had been "cured" of his depression in his twenties by insulin coma treatment, and consequently was re-hospitalized nearly every year for the rest of his life. Despite this, he had managed to have a successful career as an executive by lying to his employers, and telling them he had gone into the hospital for physical disorders. He had been treated for both his depressions and panic attacks primarily by medications, which helped a little. His daughter's fiancée was a graduate student in Clinical Psychology doing his internship in Boston at Massachusetts General Hospital. He asked Gerry Borofsky, then Chief Psychologist, about his prospective father-in-law's problems. Gerry said, "If I had serious problems and lived near East Lansing, there's someone at Michigan State I would try to see," and suggested me. Just before seeing me, the patient had been treated by a well-respected faculty member of our Department of Psychiatry who told him that with the best of modern treatment, by which that psychiatrist meant medication, they could decrease his pain and misery by 20%.

When the patient told me this, I asked, "Is that good enough for you?"

"What choice do I have?"

Classically, I said, "Well, you do have a choice. I can't guarantee that I can help you. All I can say is that people with similar problems have been helped. What I can guarantee you is it's going to take time, it's going to be hard work, it's going to be painful, and it's going to be expensive. But if it is successful, you won't be 20% better. You'll be better."

We then discussed fees, and I lowered my fee so that he could afford three times a week. He took a week to think about it, and then began treatment. This was my first patient over the age of 60, and I discovered that when an older patient decides to come into analysis they work hard, and make good use of the time. As he described it later, "You were right. It's taking a lot of my time, it's expensive, and it's certainly painful." The patient's analysis took 3 years.

In an early session he described his treatment with insulin comas when he was hospitalized in his twenties. I told him that it was very unpleasant. He said that it wasn't. I suggested I would read him a description of insulin coma treatment from a textbook. He said that wasn't necessary, because he was scared now, and didn't need any more evidence. Then I said, "There's something to be learned here. If you can repress the memory of this very unpleasant experience, then it is likely that there are other unpleasant experiences you can also repress and have no memory of."

Within a couple of weeks he was able to use the couch. As I always do, I told the patient that I would never ask him to give up anything that helped, but the odds were that if he continued to talk to me eventually he would be off all medication. He and I agreed that he would stop all medications immediately, and begin real treatment.

As I have described in a previous paper (Karon, 1990), while neither he nor his previous psychiatrists had found any precipitant to his "spontaneous" panic attacks, 18 to 24 months into the treatment I noticed his "spontaneous" panic attacks seemed to occur whenever he made a presentation to executives on the same level as he, but not when presenting to superiors or inferiors. He also had a "spontaneous" panic attack when he was feeling good. This became especially problematic when his depression began lifting, and he began to have increasing and intolerable panic attacks as a result of feeling good, which fits the rubric of a negative therapeutic reaction. It was not hard to make a reasonable clinical guess as to who executives on the same level might represent. He at first angrily rejected my interpretation that maybe his brothers envied him.

"I wonder if your brothers envied you."

"No. We got along fine. There was no envy between us."

"Sometimes brothers do envy each other."

But later in the same hour, he suddenly said, "I told you about the hanging, didn't I?"

"No."

"I must have."

"I might forget some details, but if you had ever told me you had been hanged, I'm not likely to forget it."

"Well, when I was 5 years old, my older brother and I were playing Cowboys and Indians, and he lynched me." He went on to say that his brother had tied a rope to a tree branch, had the patient stand on a box, put the rope around his neck, and then kicked the box out from under him. He was hanged until he was unconscious, and his mother had to cut him down.

"You must have been panicked, terrified."

"Oh, no, no."

He was told it was a biological reflex, that whenever we cannot breathe, we go into a panic.

"Oh, no, there was no anxiety."

"Yes, there was. You have the panic now without the memory, and the memory without the panic."

He still denied it, but then remembered other situations in which he could not breathe, and in those other situations he had gone into a panic. He then remembered another incident with his brother, a year later. He remembered his brother telling him he was Batman, giving him an umbrella, and getting him to jump off the roof of a three-story building. Luckily, children are rugged, and he was not seriously injured. But that was not his brother's fault.

"Tell me," I asked, "Were you having fun?"

"Yes, of course. You know, he never used to let me play with him. But he let me play with him those two times, and I was really enjoying it."

"And now whenever you feel good, or whenever you make a presentation to someone who represents your brother, you feel like your brother is going to kill you."

"Oh, he wouldn't do a thing like that!'

"But he tried twice."

The patient said, "Oh, no, he wouldn't do a thing like that" and I had to remind him of what he had just said. This seemed to resolve not only his negative therapeutic reaction, but all of his "spontaneous" panic attacks.

I felt I had done brilliant work. I was proud of myself. But two weeks later I received a phone call from him saying he could not keep his appointment. He was very angry because he had had another panic attack and one leg was now paralyzed.

I wondered whether at his age this could be a stroke, and tried to think of a good neurologist to recommend. However, when he came in, he informed me that he had already made an appointment with a neurologist. He expected me to be angry at him, as his parents would have been, for challenging my judgment. He was startled when I said, "Very good. This could be caused by emotional factors or it could be caused by neurological ones. You are seeing me to check out the emotional factors and a good neurologist to check out the neurological possibilities. I can't imagine anything more rational."

He had chosen his neurologist well. The neurologist checked him over very carefully and concluded that the paralysis was not neurological in origin. The patient was furious at his competent neurologist. He then told me that something like this had happened once before when he was a teenager. His leg had been paralyzed and he had been bedridden. The doctors never did find out what caused it, but it got better in a couple of months.

I asked what was going on in his life at that time. Like a typical depressive, he said, "Nothing."

"Something must have been going on. You were alive."

"No. Nothing."

"Something must have been going on."

"Nothing important."

"Tell me the unimportant things."

"The only thing I can remember from around that time was that a cousin came to visit us. (They lived on a farm.). He spent the day with my older brother, and I tried to tag along. Eventually, they started to walk into town. I started to follow them. My brother turned around and said 'If you take one more step, I'll kill you.'"

"Would you believe he had such a mean expression on his face that I believed him."

"Of course, you believed him. He had already tried to kill you twice."

"My brother wouldn't do a thing like that!"

I then reminded him again of what he had so recently told me. Then I pointed out that his unconscious was trying to protect him. His brother had said, "If you take one more step, I'll kill you," and his unconscious prevented him from taking one more step. He began to have some movement in his leg after that session and it fully remitted fairly quickly, and, with some working through, his "spontaneous"panic attacks permanently remitted. I wondered why the symptom of a paralyzed leg had recurred at this time. It seemed as if there was a part of him that wanted to understand what it was all about.

The patient had been raised as a Fundamentalist. His mother's father had been a minister in the same Fundamentalist church, a self-taught man who had written several books and preached and was very strict. Indeed, he said his grandfather was considered practically a saint by the religious community.

His first wife belonged to the same Fundamentalist group. From his description, she seemed very unpleasant and very much like his mother. However, she told him and their grown-up children that he was a sinner who would go to Hell for divorcing her. He believed her, and avoided his children because he believed they would never forgive him for having gotten a divorce. From his description his second wife seemed like a very nice person and an extraordinary improvement. She was a Methodist, and they both now went to a Methodist church. He said the people at the Methodist church were very nice, but "it doesn't feel much like religion."

In the course of the analysis I suggested that his children were much more likely to be concerned about working out their own sexual lives than they were about his. He contacted them with trepidation and discovered they liked him and were glad he reached out to them. Much to his surprise he also discovered that they liked his second wife when they met her, thought she was a nice person, and thought that he had been very sensible to divorce their mother and had been very sensible in his choice of a second wife.

When he talked about the unpardonable crime, his hand twitched at his side. His father had been a depressed man, who did not think the patient was worthwhile or of much value and "bad-mouthed" him frequently. But the patient knew his father was not a good person, because he did not go to church. His mother was the good one because she always went to church. She taught the patient all about God. She used to whip him with a switch for misbehavior. He was not mad at her for that, because he knew that she only punished him for his own good. He was told to go cut a switch which she then used to whip him, and if he had not cut a thick enough switch, he would get extra strokes. She would do this with all the children, but she beat him, the youngest, the most. She often beat him for offenses he had not committed. His brothers and sister often blamed him for what they had done, and he would get beaten, but she also beat him for offenses he had not committed, even without anyone blaming him. He resented that a little bit. It didn't seem fair. But mostly he knew she punished him for his own good.

Sometimes she would whip him until the blood ran. He did not blame his mother for that, however. As children and adolescents she and her sister had been punished by his grandfather by being stripped to the waist, tied to a tree, and whipped them until the blood ran from their backs. What he received was nothing compared to their beatings. And, after all, his grandfather was a saint.

At first I accepted his statements, but eventually said I did not consider a man who got his sexual kicks by stripping his daughters to the waist and whipping them much of a saint. This made the patient very angry. He said, of course, his grandfather did not enjoy it, and there was nothing sexual about it. But then, he noted, I seemed to have a dirty mind.

His mother used to frequently show him a picture of her sister. The sister had burned to death when the two of them were teen-agers, and the picture was of the horribly burned corpse of the aunt in her coffin. He said the picture was horrible. The sister had been ironing in the basement with an old-fashioned iron that had gasoline in it. The sister had spilled gasoline on herself and her clothes. The gasoline caught fire and killed her. His mother from time to time showed him the gruesome picture and told him the story.

I suggested, "I wonder if your mother thought she was responsible in some way. Sometimes sisters are angry at each other, or siblings are. If they are, and something bad happens, they think they are responsible."

He remembered more details. His mother told him that she had been with her sister when her sister died. The two girls were ironing the laundry in the basement with the old-fashioned irons that had gasoline in them, when the accident occurred. He began to wonder if she used to show that picture to his brothers and sisters the way she would show it to him. He concluded that, as a matter of fact, he did not remember her showing the picture and telling the story repeatedly to them, but only showing it to him repeatedly.

"I wonder if she showed the picture to the other kids. I think she did, but not like she did with me. She always showed it to me."

Then I said she treated him as if he were the bad part of her. As if you deserved to burn to death for what she did." After all, spending eternity burning in a lake of fire would be the appropriate punishment for burning someone to death.

To check his memory, he asked his own sister if their mother used to show the picture to her, and, as he had remembered in treatment, their mother had not. But he learned more about the death of their aunt from his sister, who had obtained an old newspaper clipping,

It seems that the two girls (his mother and her sister) were ironing in the basement. They were quarreling as teenage sisters sometimes do. But no quarreling was allowed in the saint's house. So he came downstairs, and the sister was so terrified of her saintly father that she backed into the iron, spilled the gasoline on herself, and burned to death. There even had been a police investigation at the time to see if his grandfather was not in some way responsible for his daughter's death, but they finally concluded that he was not.

It became increasingly clear to the patient that his mother had indeed treated him as if he were the bad part of her and that is why he deserved to burn forever, for having burned her sister to death. Obviously, his mother could not allow herself to get angry at her saintly father. Instead of feeling – which would have been appropriate – that her father had caused the death of her sister with his terrorizing tactics, she blamed herself. But then instead of blaming herself, she had blamed the patient. That is why she had punished him and that is why she had encouraged the fear of eternal burning for his sins.

The "unforgivable crime," he eventually discovered, for him was feeling angry at his mother and wanting to punish her. He unconsciously wanted to beat his mother the way she beat him. That is why his hand twitched.

The analysis was a success. He was able to enjoy his marriage, his children, and his life. He was able to work more comfortably and plan for the transition to retirement.

REFERENCES

Karon, B.P. (1990). The specific determinants of a negative therapeutic reaction. Psychoanalysis and Psychotherapy, 8, 137-144.

———— & VandenBos, G.R. (1981). Psychotherapy of Schizophrenia: The Treatment of Choice. New York: Jason Aronson.

Teixeira, M.A. (1992). Psychoanalytic theory and therapy in the treatment of manic-depressive disorders. Psychoanalysis and Psychotherapy, 11, 81-95.

CHAPTER 10
On Being Abducted by Aliens
Bertram P. Karon, PhD

Abstract

Many people have reported memories of having been abducted by aliens. A female patient reported a frightening dream wherein she was kidnapped by giant aliens whose way of thinking and behavior she could not understand even though she tried. Her associations led to her parents and the other adults with whom she lived as a child. This provides a possible meaning of dreams and screen memories of being at the mercy of inscrutable aliens.

There are many reports of individuals who recall being kidnapped by aliens. Some of these memories are reported by people who have never been near a mental health professional, but some are reported by patients or by individuals who are submitting themselves for examination. Sometimes the memories are clearly recalled consciously, sometimes they are recalled in therapy, and sometimes they are remembered only under hypnosis or sodium pentothal.

Most mental health professionals find these accounts improbable. But from time to time, we hear about improbable events that turn out to be true. Indeed, in our culture, belief in the existence of aliens is real for many people. Even in the 1930s, Orson Welles's broadcast of H. G. Wells's "The Invasion From Mars" was taken seriously by a surprisingly large number of Americans. We also hear about improbable events that turn out not to be true in their literal sense.

Harvard University psychiatrist John Mack (1994) has become the center of controversy because he is convinced that the accounts of abduction by aliens that he has investigated are true. It is always possible that such events have occurred.

As honest professionals, we cannot dismiss them as impossible, just as highly improbable. We can investigate with the patient their possible meaning and whether they did or did not occur.

A dream of a female patient in psychoanalysis would seem to shed light on the meaning of many of these memories.

I was captured by aliens. I was in their space ship. They were huge. I was terrified. I did not know what they were trying to do. I kept trying to figure out how they thought what they were doing. But I couldn't. They were aliens. I was scared.

The patient's associations to the big aliens who controlled her and whom she could not understand led easily to the adults in her childhood home. These adults indeed seemed to be motivated by forces that would be inscrutable to a child—forces that adults seemed to wish to be inscrutable.

But of course flat situation is common. All children live in a world of giants whose motives and behavior are hard to comprehend. Nonetheless, the giants are in charge, and they can do what they want. It is often scary and confusing. It is, therefore, not unlikely that many people have had such dreams. It is also not uncommon for people to remember past dreams as if they had occurred and only later, by incongruities, figure out that no such thing had occurred in waking life. It is also not uncommon, though more rare, to have memories of events that never occured which are based on unconscious memories of dilemmas that were experienced and/or fantasied and that are symbolically expressed—that is, one type of screen memory.

Such dreams, memories of dreams, or screen memories based on this common childhood dilemma would account for the existence of alien abduction memories. But it must be admitted that the existence of a logical, realistic, highly probable alternative explanation of these memories does not rule out the possibility that some of these experience:; might be true.

REFERENCE

Mack, J.E. (1994). Abduction: Human encounters with aliens. New York; Scribner's.

CHAPTER 11
Treating The Severely Disturbed Patient In Private Practice Without The Luxury of Long Term Hospitalization
Bertram P. Karon, Ph.D.

There have always been more severely disturbed patients in every diagnostic category, including schizophrenia, outside hospitals than in them. But at this time in the United States the hospital as a long term facility in which patients could be observed, regressions and exacerbations could occur without harm to the patient, alternatives explored, and growth occur over a long period, are gone. Of course, such benign hospitals were always a rarity. It has been known since the 1600's that 80% of even very severe depressions recover within two years without special treatment if kept in a safe place until the recovery occurred. But as I was told in the '50's by a training analyst in Philadelphia. "In the old days everyone knew that depressions always got better, but you can't get a hospital now to keep a patient and not do anything until they get better." He was on the staff of the most psychoanalytic hospital in Philadelphia, where I was doing a post-doc, a hospital where all the psychiatric residents were candidates at one of the two psychoanalytic institutes and most of the medical staff were analysts, but almost all the inpatients and 50 outpatients were shocked every Monday, Wednesday, and Friday. Most of the analysts on the staff had shock practices as well. When I asked about this anomaly, I was told, "It depends what you mean by psychoanalysis."

We mean the treatment of the classic syndromes four or five days a week on a couch. What do you do with patients who have something else wrong with them or who can't afford it. Either you don't treat them, or you shock them. We shock them. We think it's kinder." When the psychiatric residents discovered that I knew a lot about treating difficult patients and my advice helped, they began to consult me until an edict came down forbidding the clinical staff and the research staff from having coffee breaks or lunch in the same room. That hospital temporarily soured me on psychoanalysis.

Most of my career I have been lucky enough to practice in a town where none of the hospitals would have cooperated with me and I had to learn how not to use them. At the time I did not know that my patients benefitted. Psychiatrists, except for the better trained psychoanalysts, generally did not get along with psychologists in the 60's.

By the time I had psychiatric colleagues in Lansing who trusted me, I found my patients did not need hospitalization.

For all severely disturbed patients, including schizophrenics, the treatment of choice is psychoanalysis or psychoanalytic therapy, which is best defined as much like psychoanalysis as the defenses of the patient, the time available, and the skill of the therapist permit. As Charles Brenner succinctly put it, "The differences between neurotic, borderline, and psychotic are sick, sicker, sickest, but the mechanisms are the same."

The dichotomy between supportive therapy and expressive therapy is an artificial one. You provide as much support as the patient's defenses require. You always give information that you have that would be helpful to the patient if you are not sure the patient knows it. Then you and the patient can analyze why they cannot make use of what they know to help themselves. Borderline and psychotic patients need structure. Ambiguity scares them. The blank screen inevitably becomes a monster.

Change is produced in psychoanalytic therapy by insight and by internalization of the therapist. Two important ideas are: first, it is absolutely necessary for a therapist to be confused; and second, it is not "accurate empathy" which cures patients but it is our attempt at accurate empathy (whether or not we are successful) which cures patients.

It is almost universally accepted that empathy characterizes good therapists. Among psychoanalysts, Kohut (1977) most emphasized empathy as a centrally curative part of psychoanalysis; he also said failures of empathy in a basically empathic relationship were necessary for the process of cure. These failures helped the patient realize that analysis was not an adequate substitute for life.

And yet he was partially wrong. As part of my graduate class in the Psychotherapy of Psychosis twice a week I would treat a patient whom I did not know. Most graduate students have been taught that severely disturbed people do not get better with psychotherapy; inevitably, however, the students would observe that despite my mistakes the patients talked about the things described in my and other psychoanalytic papers, and the patients would greatly improve in front of them.

The late Norman Kagan, as part of his research, videotaped an initial segment of one such psychotherapy session with a 17 year old ambulatory schizophrenic, who was also alcoholic. Kagan immediately replayed the videotape with the patient, stopping it frequently, and asking the patient what was going at that moment.

The thought processes of the patient were extremely complex and the patient described them in detail. Then Kagan asked: "Do you think Karon understands this?

"Of course he does," said the patient.

But the truth was that I did not understand. I understood as best I could the fragments that the patient had told me, but he had only revealed fragments of his conscious thought processes and I had no idea of the complexity of his thoughts and of most of what was going on.

What the patient was responding to as my understanding him was not my correct understanding of him, but my attempt to correctly understand him. I have since realized this is very general.

We may or may not be capable of correctly understanding our patients, but we are capable of doing our damnedest to try to understand them. That is usually what they perceive and are responding to when they say and feel we understand them.

When in life do we have a bright concerned person really trying hard to understand us, no matter how confusing, terrifying, or obscure our life might be, or how much our defenses slow the process? Never—except in good therapy.

Of course, sometimes we do succeed at understanding. As the late Richard Sterba used to say to patients: "All I have to offer you is understanding, but that is really a great deal."

Nonetheless, there is no way for an analyst to escape being confused. Early in my career, I was often intimidated by professionals who seemed always to understand exactly what was going on with their patients. But their patients did not seem to benefit very much, and sometimes did very badly with such certainty.

The confused analyst is not only able to learn by not excluding possibilities, but provides a model for the patient; that being confused is tolerable. As I sometimes say to patients who complain that analytic therapy is confusing: "Good. You are not sick because you are confused. You are sick because you are certain of things which are not true."

Valuing confusion does not mean valuing arbitrariness, or the narrative point of view, which, in its most extreme form, holds that any consistent narrative which the patient and the therapist accept is equally good, that objective truth is irrelevant, and unobtainable anyway. I strongly disagree. The patient has lived a life and wants to know what it was. It is frequently possible to reconstruct it. When I have reconstructed it wrongly, even when it was accepted by the patient, it was never helpful.

But when all the material fell into place, and the patient improved, the reconstruction turned out to be true. In many cases, it has been possible to validate from external sources, such as family, the truth of such helpful reconstructions of the repressed past.

It may be, of course, that you cannot reconstruct the past. But even an uncertain past is bearable if you can share that uncertainty with an acceptant and tolerant other, and continue to think about it. I had one patient, in a second analysis, who had pretty clear evidence of sexual abuse except who sexually abused her. After years of work, we concluded that she probably did not know who was sexually abusing her at the time of the trauma, and therefore all that we could reconstruct was the horror enhanced by the uncertainty.

Central to change is the internalization of the therapist. The therapist is internalized into the superego so that the patient treats him or herself the way the therapist would, as opposed to the way the parents did. The therapist is internalized into the ego as a model for the self. The therapy relationship is internalized as a model for what a human relationship might be like. Sometimes therapists worry that the patient will internalize their defects. But, like an adolescent, the patient will eventually discard what is not useful. Further, therapists value patients who keep growing, who are different from them, and who can do better than they can; unlike the parents of most patients—who are often more like the father of Oedipus or the mother of Snow White.

Once internalization is taken seriously, it becomes obvious why it is important that the analyst be tolerant of the human condition. It is especially important for the analyst to be kind, so that the patient dares to be kind to him or herself, and even to others. The Stockholm Outcome of Psychotherapy and Psychoanalysis Project (Sandell, Blomberg, Lazar, Carlsson, Schubert, and Broberg, 1997) recently found that psychoanalysis and psychoanalytic therapy were very helpful, were more helpful than alternative treatments, and that psychoanalysis was more helpful than psychoanalytic psychotherapy; if you spend more time, you get more done. They found that psychoanalysts tended to have the same general values about psychotherapy which were different from non-psychoanalytic therapists. But on one dimension, analysts differed from each other: the importance of being neutral versus the importance of being kind. When doing psychoanalysis, analysts with both views were equally helpful. But when doing psychoanalytic therapy, defined as once or twice per week treatment, those analysts who stressed neutrality were far less helpful. When seeing patients intensively, patients come to accurately know even neutral? analysts. But when doing psychotherapy, a neutral analyst can succeed in being "neutral" which may be perceived by the patient as rejection.

The good analyst is stubborn. There is a part of you that just does not want to give up, no matter what it looks like. Rudolf Ekstein once described the ideal therapist for a psychotic child as "someone who knows as much as possible scientifically combined with an absolutely irrational belief that, no matter what, this child is going to make it." It's not a bad prescription for any analyst.

Indeed, the analyst must not only retain hope, but create hope in the patient. The patient has no reason to be hopeful, and depends on the therapist to create and maintain hope, while often consciously trying to prove how hopeless is the world and worthless is the therapy. For all patients in the United States today the prime delivery system for mental health care is the psychoanalyst or psychoanalytic therapist in private practice. Schizophrenics, paranoids, and psychotic depressives are a small part of most practices. That is not a bad idea; I think it is optimal to have a varied practice—it is more interesting and the challenges are different. Of course, the basic problems are the same with all of us, but the defenses, difficulties, and therapeutic challenges differ. Right now my practice goes from overtly psychotic individuals to high level unusually well functioning individuals with areas of misery. That makes it easier to help all of them.

On the other hand, borderline and character disorders are very common, if not nearly universal, although they differ greatly in severity. Letting your colleagues know that you will take difficult patients is a good way to build a practice.

Obviously, patients who are so violent that they cannot be endured in an ordinary office must be seen in a hospital setting if it is available. But the majority of the severely disturbed are not dangerously violent. In general, the most violent individuals are character disorders with a substance abuse problem. This does not mean that you cannot treat a patient with a violence problem, as long as it does not intrude on the therapy.

Thus, a Vietnam veteran with a 100% disability who was supposedly uncooperative with treatment was referred. I asked, as I always do, in a first session," What seems to be the trouble, how can I help?" I always take the answer very seriously.

He said, " I hurt people, and I don't want to." (It turned out later that he beat people up, even stabbed, or shot them.)

"That sounds like a real problem, and I want to help you. But I have to tell you that sooner or later, you're going to feel like busting me."

"I'd never do that."

"Yes, you will. Everybody who talks to me, feels like busting me sooner or later. But you've got to tell me about it and not do it, and we will always learn something valuable."

And he relaxed. I had told him what to do. And we had a therapeutic relationship beginning. Both he and I agreed that hurting people was the most important problem. But if I had told him his problem was "paranoid schizophrenia", or if I insisted he would be helped by always taking his medication, I would have the same uncooperative patient others described.

Even though I told him that I did not care whether he took his medications and that, even though I would never ask him to give up anything that helps him, the odds were that he would be off medication in the long run if he worked with me, he did not believe me. It was not until the sixth week that he told me had not taken any medication for over six months before seeing me.

Every diagnostic category consists of a highly varied group of people. Luckily, psychoanalysts treat people, not symptoms. Schizophrenics have in common that their current life as given meaning by their conscious and unconscious phantasies presents them with the terror of annihilation with which they cope by means of defenses we consider psychotic, such as hallucinations, delusions, thought disorders as well as neurotic like symptoms and various kinds of acting out. As with anyone, the conscious and unconscious fantasies always result from the interaction of their actual life experiences with pre-existing fantasies so that their whole life history from early infancy is relevant.

Severely depressed patients are geniuses at convincing you that their lives are hopeless and the therapy of no value. But unconsciously they desperately hope that they will not convince you. A clear statement that you do not share their pessimism is very helpful. While other determinants of depressions are more fashionable, the role of anger should not be neglected.

Isolation is an almost invariable defense used by depressed patients. In the words of Viggo Jensen, "an endogenous depression is a very seriously depressed individual whom you haven't talked to long enough to find out why they are depressed. If you ask a depressed patient what was going on in their life just before the depression started, they will say, "Nothing." If you persist that they were alive something must have been going on, they will typically say "Nothing important." If you persist, that you want to know the unimportant things that were going on, they will tell you things that would depress anyone, but which they do not connect with their feelings.

This is an instance of the fact that feelings always make sense and are an essential part of rational thinking. Once you take the unconscious into account, not only are there are no endogenous depressions there are also no spontaneous anxiety attacks. If you are depressed, there is something to be depressed about, if your are anxious, there is something to be scared of, if you are angry there is always something hurting you. If it is not conscious it is unconscious. If it is not in the present, it is in the past and something in the present symbolizes it.

The literature abounds with the wrong questions. Should the therapist be a man or a woman, should the therapist be active or passive, should the therapist be a psychologist, psychiatrist, or social worker? All are the wrong questions. The therapist should know about the human condition in general and about psychotherapy, should want to help the patient, and know or be willing to learn about psychosis. That does not seem much to ask but it is not the experience of most severely disturbed patients.

The first thing we do for a schizophrenic or other severely disturbed patient, and do over and over again, is not run screaming from the room. No matter how awful what the patient is saying or doing or making us feel, whether we understand or not, we do not run screaming from the room. The moment you have decided you will stay there, you are already being helpful to the patient. The patient is overwhelmed. The patient is terrified; it is useless to the patient if the therapist is equally terrified of the human condition.

The therapist must listen, ask relevant questions, offer help. There is no therapy for any patient without a therapeutic alliance. You, the therapist, create it by telling the patient that you have something to offer and that you want to offer it. The patient does not know, but you do, that psychoanalytic therapy can be helpful, that he or she is not doomed to a lifetime of suffering, that all of his or her symptoms make perfectly good sense once you take unconscious processes and the patient's specific life history into account, and that patients like him or her regularly get better with hard work and an adequate therapist. The analyst must educate the patient and thus infuse realistic hope.

The patient also does not know that you want to help. The more severely disturbed the patient the less helpful his or her parents were likely to have been; unlike the neurotic, the typical preformed parental transference will not be of gratifying dependency. Moreover there will usually be transferences from previous professionals who did not want to help or were misinformed, and who consequently misinformed the patient or were hurtful in other ways. To form a therapeutic alliance with the patient you have to take the patient's point of view and help him by being a strong helpful protective object, someone who is dependable. Pick up any indication of or veiled allusion to a negative transference and interpret it immediately, but not as if it were a crime. "I wonder if it annoys you when I.." "It would only be human to be annoyed when it seems as if I.." The patient will usually deny negative feelings, but the fact that you have put them into words makes them less dangerous.

The question, "What seems to be the trouble, how can I help you?" will elicit a relevant answer from more than half of even the most deeply disturbed patients. If the patient tells you what his problem is, help the patient with that problem. Do not define the problem as something else. Especially do not define the problem as "You are schizophrenic" or "You are paranoid" or "You are bipolar" or " You are borderline." That is of use to insurance companies, hospital record keepers, and to people who have to look up their treatment in the Merck Manual. It is of no help to the patient and is experienced as either an insult or a sentence of doom. Of course, if a patient asks you if they are schizophrenic, you ask them what they mean by it. "If by schizophrenic, you mean a genetic, physiological incurable disease, you are not schizophrenic. If by schizophrenic, you mean a very sick human being, whose sickness consists of being scared to death, and the things he has to do to cope with it, then some people would call you a schizophrenic." If they tell you they have a "chemical imbalance, ask them what they mean by it. You can tell them that all feelings and thoughts are complex chemical and electrical events in the body, there is no magic, but their disorder is not caused by a chemical problem but their life history, although all feelings, including depression, are chemical events, and that the ads on TV are grossly distorted biochemistry. So, by the way, are the genetic data reported in many textbooks. Further, you can go into the details, if they are interested.

It may be helpful to illustrate how you ought to respond in the first and early sessions, by using a common complaint, being unable to sleep. First, you give them advice, that is, that human beings don't really need sleep, they need rest. If you lie reasonable quietly but wide awake for eight hours with normal amounts of agitation and restlessness, it is as good as five hours of the deepest, soundest sleep. It is a boring way to spend the night but you will be able to function the next day. For two thirds of patients, this advice is sufficient.

If it doesn't work, most will be helped by an Adlerian interpretation (Adler 1914, 1912), namely, that the lack of sleep is a way of preparing in advance an unconscious alibi for what they will not be able to do or will fail at the next day. (That explains why when they learn they can function without sleeping, he sleep disturbance itself usually disappears.) Only if that does not work, must you investigate the individual dynamics. Thus, any therapist can help patients with their sleep disorder and usually easily and quickly. Of course, if a patient seems to have the symptoms of sleep apnea, and wants to try a sleep disorder evaluation, they should be encouraged as long as they go about it and use what they learn rationally.

This raises the general question of what do you interpret and when. There are very complete guidelines in the literature that make sense. But do not read more than one authority because they don't agree. Thus, for example, if a patient is very anxious, Melanie Klein says you have not interpreted deeply enough quickly enough. For the same situation, Anna Freud says you have interpreted too deeply too quickly. Part of this is semantic—for Melanie Klein oral interpretations are deep and oedipal are shallow, for Anna Freud, oral interpretations are shallow and Oedipal are deep. But nontheless there is a fundamental disagreement.

The only rule that I have found to work is a terrible one —you interpret what you think the patient can make use of at this time. There are times when a deep interpretation early makes sense of something the patient is struggling with and is very helpful. With another patient the same interpretation would make no sense at all.

Freud's dictum that you should generally interpret from the surface is a good one. You should exhaust the most plausible common sense explanations before expecting the patient to take seriously a deeper interpretation. Whatever you interpret should be done tactfully, "It would be only human to feel..", "Anyone would feel." Most children feel..." Almost anything can be interpreted from the side of the defense.." I wonder if you are afraid you might feel, be, or do something.." Patients hear every interpretation as an accusation, almost always implicitly adding "and you shouldn't" to anything we say about them. We have to try to phrase our interpretations so they cannot easily be distorted into condemnations. "I wonder if.." is always a good beginning indicating it is alright to reject anything you say—psychoanalytic therapy is not a power struggle, and an interpretation is a calling attention to something the patient is both trying not to notice as well as trying to understand.

If in the first session a severely disturbed patient tells you they have a sexual disturbance, help them with that. If they tell you they don't get along with their wife, husband, lover, child, or boss, then help them with that. Always take the patient's views seriously. Stay with the patient's complaints.

If the patient does not give you a clear problem with which you can help them, you can always be sure, if he is a schizophrenic, that he is afraid of dying; thus it is almost always helpful in the first or second session to say, "I will not let anyone kill you." This reassurance seems strange, but the real danger is intrapsychic, and who but a therapist can solve that problem.

Of course, if a patient directly tells you they are afraid of being killed, ask what makes him think so. Don't deal with it as intrapsychic unless you are sure that it is. Even paranoids are sometimes in real danger.

An ambulatory schizophrenic told me he felt a large corporation, and in particular, his foreman, was going to kill him for discovering some illegal activity. (His father had been a foreman for the same company.) Only after exploring his recollections carefully could one say," You probably have discovered illegal activity, and they were angry at you, and they did harass you. But unlike the company that apparently killed Karen Silkwood, this company has a history of harassing people but it has made large financial settlements to people when it would have been cheaper to kill them. So it doesn't seem likely that they will kill people to save money. Anyway, the illegal matter would only have involved a fine and is unprovable now." The patient agreed, and then could consider the idea that "Your parents made you feel like they wanted to get rid of you, which is death to a kid. Whenever there is ambiguity, you fill it in from your past, making bad situations unbearable."

This leads us to the treatment of delusions. If you think the patient is delusional, ask him or her to tell you about it in as much detail as possible, and sort through the experience and beliefs the way you would sort through your own world view. Do not attack or humiliate the patient or prematurely call it delusional.

You never know that something is delusional because it is improbable. If you don't know whether something is inaccurate, tell the patient that you don't know. If you think something is improbable, then tell the patient you think it is improbable.

You cannot interpret or solve what is not a problem for the patient. If you investigate a delusion from the patient's point of view, he will discover the inconsistencies or even that it is delusional. Then your interpretations will solve a problem for him by making it meaningful.

A patient described out of body experiences and said, in the first session, "You don't believe me." I said, "I find it improbable, but I wasn't there and you were. Tell me about it." That was sufficient.

Months later, when he described rising to the moon which looked like a smiling face, I said, "I have an idea, but it's not your way of understanding it."

"What is it?"

"It's not your way of understanding it."

"Cut that out. What is it?"

"It seemed like a baby being lifted.."and he finished "in his mother's arms to her face" and excitedly began to reinterpret his experiences. But that was only possible because I let him explore his understandings first.

Delusions have four major sources. The most important is transference, the re-experiencing in the world at large of unbearable childhood experiences; and this should be the hypothesis of first resort.

I was asked by her parents to interview an 18 year old girl who had been hospitalized for years and who still hallucinated and who cut and burned herself. The ward chief said we have tried everything, and listed the 18 medications they had tried.

When asked about her religion, she said "I was raised a Catholic."

"You were raised a Catholic, but you're not now."

"Actually, I'm a Satanist."

I started to go on, until I realized she had something important. "Tell me about it."

"I used to feel I had to save all the people in Beirut." (There was then continuing violence in Lebanon).

"You know who the people in Beirut are."

She started to say yes, and then realized she didn't, and said no.

"Beirut. What a marvelous image. People are killing each other. Then they declare peace. But they keep killing each other. Then they have a truce and talk about heir problems. But they keep killing each other. Then they have another truce. But they keep killing each other. What a marvelous image. Your family must have been like that."

She got very interested. "Satan says that if I hurt myself he will never get rid of me. She described Satan's face so carefully I could practically see it.

"Do you know anyone who looks like that?"

She looked puzzled and then said, "Yes. He doesn't look like that now, but he used to. My father."

After that interview the hallucination of Satan disappeared.

Afterwards, the parents, who were both currently in therapy, told me that the father used to beat the mother, who eventually left the household while the patient was young. Is it any surprise that a little girl would conclude that pain was the price of not being abandoned?

I was able to make some further recommendations, including telling her she needed practice in talking about anger, so instead of expressing anger by not talking to her current therapist, instead tell him every stupid and destructive thing he had ever done, and that she should never worry about being angry at a therapist, because they can take it, and if they can't, they shouldn't be doing therapy. To the hospital I recommended psychotherapy with a woman therapist, since the most helpful person in her life had been her grandmother, which led to her eventual recovery.

The second source is the denial of, projection of, and reaction formation against homosexuality, based on the misinterpretation of the longing to be close to someone of the same sex as homosexuality, which Freud (1911) so aptly described in the case of Schreber. The secondary sources cite everything except what is important and therapeutically useful in Freud's description, namely the schizophrenic's withdrawal from everyone and the consequent loneliness underlying this longing to be close to someone of the same sex. It is useful to tell the patient, "You are not homosexual, but you are lonely, and we all need friends of both sexes." Paranoid patients are not reassured by statements about the increased acceptability of homosexuality, but they always respond and feel understood when their therapist talks about loneliness. Of course, one does not discourage gay relationships if they are healthy, any more than one would with any other kind of patients. It was Hedda Bolgar who first taught me that whether a patient is gay or straight is too important a decision for a therapist to make; we must only help our patients understand themselves and make their own choices. For very disturbed patients any human relationship, gay or straight, is a movement toward health, but they tend to find not very good relationships first, and we must help them work through and improve their relationships. It sometimes helps to inform patients, when a relationship fails, that almost everyone goes through several relationships before they find one that is good enough, and that bad relationships are stages of growth, and if you try to make it better and learn from it, the next one will be better, and so on.

The third source of delusions is strange beliefs actually taught in the family. Everyone depends on their family to teach them the meaning of concepts and assumes that people outside the family use concepts in the same way. People with strange concepts do not usually discover it except in therapy. As one patient said, "You don"t care about me, because you never hit me or kick me, and you will not let me hit you or kick you."

"You're right, I will never hit you or kick you, and if you hit or kick me, the therapy's over. But if you want to hit a therapist, I have some colleagues I would be glad to refer you to. "

The fourth source is the attempt to make sense out of a world where one' s real life experiences as well as one' s symptomatic experiences are different from what other people have experienced.

The patient is trying to make the best sense he or she can out of his or her world. Be on their side in this as in everything else.

I often say of a delusion, "That is a brilliant explanation."

The patient is usually startled, "Then you think it's true." "No, but that' s because I know some things about the human mind you don't know yet, and I'll be glad to tell you about them if you are interested. But given what you do know, that is a brilliant explanation."

All of us have a more or less systematic explanation of our world and our selves. Since their experiences are more bizarre their explanations seem bizarre but they are no more so than are necessary. Since systematic delusions are not a pathological process, but a normal process dealing with pathological problems a non-frightened, non-humiliating analyst can listen carefully, point out contradictions, and suggest alternate explanations that fit better, based on your knowledge of the world, other people, and, most of all, how the human mind operates.

Hallucinations have exactly the same structure as dreams. They should be listened to carefully. If possible get the patient to associate to the material. Failing that, the content of the hallucination together with your knowledge of the patient's life, of the human condition in general, and of symbolism should enable you to interpret it. The interpretation should be phrased in a way which, far from humiliating the patient, gives him or her useful information. As long as you deal with hallucinatory and delusional material seriously from the patient's standpoint and use it to help the patient learn more about themselves and their lives, you are reducing anxiety and creating and maintaining a workable alliance; and the therapy can progress to a satisfactory conclusion.

The first week of therapy should consist of five sessions per week if possible. The sessions need not be more than half an hour if time is at a premium. The severely disturbed patient needs to form a very strong bond with the therapist. With almost any kind of patient the more frequently the patient is seen, the easier it is for both patient and therapist. The one exception I can think of was a psychotic depressive woman who had been hospitalized several times, given ECT the first time but it was discontinued because of spinal damage. This time she saw me instead of going to the hospital. This time she went to her parents' house. Her husband was told that he knew how to take care of the house and their five children, and that when she came home to continue to run the house as if she were not there, and she would take over as she could. Her parents lived 50 miles away. They could only bring her in once a week. But she was so irritating that i was usually very angry at her by the end of each hour. A week later I had forgotten my irritation and she had a kind and accepting therapist for almost all the hour. I might not have been able to do that if I saw her more frequently. Trying to help her avoid likely parenting mistakes, in one session I talked to her about the normality of masturbation and how she must not punish her children but let them know that it is impolite to masturbate in front of other people. Of course, she was angry at me. She started the next hour by saying."! do that." I did not know what she was talking about so I asked her. She said, "I masturbate. I do that because I'm crazy."

"No, you do that because you're human. You don't enjoy it because you're crazy." She got mad at me and insisted, and I repeated my view. If I had agreed with her puritanical statement, I would have made her insanity necessary to cope with her guilt over masturbation. She stopped masturbating after a year of treatment because sex with her husband was much better. "It's like we just got married."

Very often depressed people, even when their judgement is poor, try to control the other people in the family. She would not allow her husband to make decisions about his job, the car, insurance, or an accident settlement. It is one of my principles that the person in the family who knows the most about something should be the one who makes the decision about that matter. She stopped trying to control him and he grew, making better decisions about his job and other matters. She was impressed and she liked him more. She became a pleasant person toward the end of therapy which was only about a year or two, at which time she was taking care of her home and children. She also was working for the first time at a part time job as a school aid.

For severely disturbed patients, just talking is a helpful process. Some years ago a therapist treating a borderline patient consulted me about the fear that the patient might have a psychotic break. I suggested strongly that the therapist just keep the patient talking. The therapist took me literally, more literally than I intended. She kept the patient talking for 12 hours until the patient came out of the psychotic state and was then able to continue psychoanalytic therapy to a successful conclusion. I do not recommend such heroic efforts to people routinely; nonetheless, they are helpful.

Even though the patient may talk, you will not understand everything the patient says. In some cases you will not understand most of what the patient says. That is because the patient does not intend you to understand. The patients do not tell you everything they understand because they are afraid it will be used to hurt them. They will even hold back the fact that you are helping them in many cases. That is because what they have to transfer from childhood is awful, often including the experience that revealing something about oneself has been used to hurt them. This was best described by the mother of a 6-year old schizophrenic, who was successfully treated as an outpatient, with twice a week individual sessions for the child and each parent. When I asked her about using some form of discipline other than hitting, she said, "You don't understand. He never tells us what he likes. If we knew what he likes, we'd take it away from him of course. But he never lets us know what he likes."

In my experience, no one ever goes psychotic or has severe problems whose life history would not produce similar symptoms in me or anyone else. By this I mean the real life history, and not the life history recorded in hospital records by people who do not want to know how bad that life really was. Unfortunately, it is not fashionable these days to get an accurate case history. One of group of psychiatric residents said with a puzzled look, as if it were a new idea, after I had presented a grand rounds at a major department of Psychiatry, "I guess what you're talking about might be called historicity. If we knew the patient's history, what they're talking about would make sense."

Nonetheless, John Read (Read, Perry, Moskowitz, & Connolly, 2001) has shown that even using ordinary hospital records severely disturbed patients have an unusual frequency of severe traumas in their childhood.

The relatives of psychotics, particularly the spouse and parents, are often your best allies. This may seem strange because so many of the therapeutic issues have to do with hurtful experiences concerning their relatives, but typically the psychologically destructive experiences of parents have derived from those unconscious defenses of the parent which I have described as "Pathogenesis" (Meyer & Karon, 1967; Karon & Widener, 1994). The parent is not a criminal and is not to blame any more than a patient is for hallucinating. The parents had no conscious knowledge or control of these defenses, and in most cases are very decent people who would never consciously hurt their child. Often they will go to great lengths to help their child become a whole, functioning, and growing human being. On the other hand, I would not treat a severely disturbed child unless both parents (if the child is living with both parents) are also seen in therapy.

The parents, spouse, other relatives and friends will often provide a place for the patient while being treated. For most patients hospitals provide nothing special other than a place to live. Relatives may find it very difficult to tolerate a psychotic individual if they think they are going to have to live with a psychotic forever. But you can assure them that most psychotic individuals in therapy will not be psychotic if they are seen intensively. The Michigan State Psychotherapy Project (Karon & VandenBos, 1981) found that with five days per week therapy without medication most schizophrenics were capable of living independently outside the hospital in less than eight weeks even though those patients were not acute, but chronic psychotic individuals. If the patient is truly acute, that is, has developed psychotic symptoms of a blatant sort within a few days of being seen by the therapist, you can usually have the patient out of the grossly psychotic state within a week or two. It is therefore reasonable to ask parents or spouses if they could live with the patient as a psychotic for six or eight weeks. In most cases they are quite willing to do that.

One of the resources that is most valuable to the outpatient therapist of the severely disturbed is the telephone. Patients should be given your home telephone number and allowed to call. Very rarely will schizophrenic patients abuse this privilege. In almost all cases patients will hesitate to call, but it is extremely reassuring to them to know that the therapist can be reached by telephone. I find it helpful to have a telephone by the side of the bed so that if patients call me at night, I do not even have to get out of bed to talk to them. The few patients (usually depressives) who abuse the privilege can be handled by asking simply "Why are you calling?" and insisting on an answer. For those who need to call, the answer is obvious. By making a phone call to you, a patient can often avoid a psychotic break or come out of one, or avoid committing suicide. With the real assurance they derive from knowing that their therapist is only a phone call away, patients often manage without help very difficult situations that they would otherwise be unable to manage. I had one ambulatory schizophrenic who made many phone calls each day, until I realized that she had been in Alcoholics Anonymous for years and thought she was being good by making many phone calls. I had to tell her I had a different value system, that I was available for emergencies, but that I did not enjoy phone calls, and weaned her from them gradually.

For depressives who call to torment you, I have found it useful to use a Fairbairn-like interpretation that they are trying to get me to reject them so that they can prove that even a therapist can't stand them, so how can they blame their parents?

Up to this point I have not discussed use of medication. That is because I prefer to work with patients without medication. One of the findings of the Michigan State Psychotherapy Research Project was that the adjunctive use of medication made behavioral control and discharge from the hospital easier to obtain, but slowed down the improvement in the thought disorder, that is, it slowed the fundamental changes in the underlying process. If the patient, the therapist, and the setting can tolerate it, the patient will improve faster without medication. If the patient or the setting or the therapist needs medication, then medication may be used. But it should be withdrawn as rapidly as the patient can tolerate it. It should always be seen, and the patient should be told this, as a temporary expedient to make things more bearable, but which does not cure anything. The drug companies, by calling major tranquilizers "antipsychotic medication", imply that they are specific treatments for psychosis, which they are not. All medications which help schizophrenics massively interfere with the affect system and consequently decrease the terror. The problem is that when you decrease the affect, you are also diminishing one of the things which change people during psychotherapy.

More important, however, are the frightening findings reported in Peter Breggin's summaries (1983) of the available evidence on neurological damage due to antipsychotic medication and the major antidepressants. It has become clear that they are damaging to their neurological health. We are creating a population of brain-damaged people. Therefore, if medication is used, it should be a short-term adjunct to be withdrawn as soon as the patient can tolerate it. Breggin & Cohen's book, *Your Drug May Be Your Problem* is a good summary of the known side-effects. But more importantly the known withdrawal effects of most currently used psychiatric medications, as well as advice on how best to withdraw, both in general and for specific medications.

Robert Whitaker's book, *Mad In America,* describes the World Health Organization studies showing two and five year positive outcome in schizophrenia is twice as common in countries that can't afford to medicate as in countries where almost all patients are medicated, and chronic bad outcomes are twice as common in countries where patients are medicated, and this is not due to differences in medications or social factors.

Neither antidepressant nor anti-anxiety medications are necessary, nor is psychotherapy enhanced. They both habituate, and have withdrawal effects which have to be coped with. Relapse rates are higher if adjunctive anti-depressant medication is used.

Patients who do not eat can be force fed in a hospital, or to use an old psychiatric trick, given a shot of sodium amytal or pentathol, during which they will improve temporarily to the point where they can be fed a meal, but will then relapse. However, such heroic measures are not necessary. It takes about 30 days to starve to death, so you have time to solve the problem. In most cases, if you have the session at meal time you can deal with the problem. See them once a day. You should be served the same meal as the patient, or if you are in a cafeteria, choose from the same selection as the patient. Talk about not eating and its possible meanings while you eat. Most analysts think of meals as pleasant social situations, most patients do not. Tell the patient your food, drink, or milk is not poisoned. Let them play James Bond games with you in which they switch cups or plates with you to make sure they are not going to be poisoned. You can tell them that the feelings that they are going to be poisoned are based on the fact that their mother got angry at them when she fed them. After all, poison is simply something that you eat, and you get hurt afterwards. If mother is angry when she feeds you, a baby reacts like it's being hit with a sledgehammer. But my food isn't poisoned. Let them talk about any of their unpleasant associations to eating or being fed. Usually it only takes a few sessions at meals before patients begin to eat.

Murder is a problem that understandably concerns analysts. Rarely is it a real problem. But the danger is a real concern and homicidal or nearly homicidal actions should be dealt with quickly. Having treated some real murderers I found that they are always people who cannot stand conscious anger. Either they become aware of anger and act on it immediately, or more commonly never feel angry at all. Treatment should be aimed at helping them feel angry and wanting to kill, but not do it because it's stupid. It would ruin their lives.

Bob McKie, one of my students, studied a group of murderers and found that my clinical observations were general. They could not tolerate conscious anger. They had a model of violence in childhood, and tended to have trouble with all affects. They were less likely to be physically aggressive than others of their social group, but if they did get violent, they were more likely to be lethal—use a gun or knife rather than hit someone.

Robert Litton after hearing me describe the treatment of a multiple murderer who could not tolerate anger, said that the Nazis, when they were recruiting murderers for the annihilation camps, did not choose sadists but found that guards who had no feelings made the most efficient murderers.

The TAT is very helpful. The most dangerous protocols are those in which there is no anger or aggression. Characters who feel angry indicate a measure of safety. Next most dangerous is stories in which a character of the same age and sex as the patient and under similar circumstances commits murder.

The TAT can be useful in not only indicating degree of danger but the circumstances under which the patient might become dangerous. It also is useful in predicting non-lethal violence. The best descriptions of the conscious meanings of non-lethal violence is Hans Toch's book, *Violent Men*, a study of violent criminals and violent police officers, who were very similar.

Suicide is the next most troubling concern. Hopelessness is a necessary but not a sufficient cause for suicide. No one kills themself if they have a strong hope of getting something important to them.

There are only three theories of suicide that I find worth being concerned with. The first is the idea that suicide is an attempt to get even with someone else. As the folk-culture puts it, "I'll eat me some worms and then I'll die and then they'll be sorry." Every child has thought this, and anything every child has thought consciously is in the unconscious of every adult. This leads to the view that on the one hand you have to create hope by the relationship with you. It's not that you can solve everything today, but most of the things people commit suicide over are solvable. Secondly, you should tell them that many people commit suicide to get even with someone else, and it's stupid, because it means the other person is a lot more important than you, if you're willing to hurt yourself a lot to hurt them a little. Besides it's amazing how quickly parents, spouses, and ex-lovers get over it. (As you probably know the one set of people who do not get over it are the children of suicides, I don't usually describe that to patients, unless they have young children they seem to care about.)

The second view is the rescue fantasy, originally described by Jensen and Petty. Their view was that the suicide really doesn't want to die, that he or she projects their superego into someone else, and asks them implicitly "Do I deserve to die?" That is why suicides almost always tell someone else, and if that person does nothing to save them, then the message is "You deserve to die." From this standpoint, the one thing a therapist should not do is nothing. The therapist should indicate by words or actions that you don't think the patient deserves to die.

The third view is that the suicide has internalized a parent who they thought wanted them dead.

Again, the TAT can be useful when you are not sure. The dangerous protocol are stories in which the hero of the same age and sex and under similar circumstances as the patient commits suicide. Symbolic suicides and suicidal thoughts in the stories do not predict suicide. The TAT again may suggest the specific circumstances under which the patient may or may not be suicidal.

When in doubt always ask the patient whether they are thinking of killing themselves. Most dangerous is a matter of fact statement that they intend to kill themselves in a realistic manner. Fantastic techniques are not generally dangerous. Patients who are agitated and afraid are not as dangerous as those who are matter of fact.

It is well known that some seriously depressed patients kill themselves when it looks like they are getting better. The usual explanation is that they didn't have enough energy, but George Atwood pointed out that isn't what is going on. Some patients decide to solve their problems by killing themselves. They then seem to be improving and then carry out their solution.

Deeply depressed patients who are improving show increased insight into why they are depressed. They also talk more about the future. If you ask them about suicide, they will discuss it.

Patients who appear to be getting better because they are going to kill themselves, seem to be getting better but have no more insight into why they were depressed. They don't talk more about the future because they don't have any. If you raise the subject of suicide, they wither will not talk about it, or will unemotionally tell you they are going to kill themselves.

These three indices will tell you whether the patients genuinely getting better or whether you need to take effective action.

SSRI anti-depressants are not useful for suicidal patients; some patients who are not suicidal become suicidal on SSRI's. Healey's research found that 10% of normal volunteers who had never been in treatment or had a clinical depression developed acute suicidal ideation on SSRI's.

Hispanic patients who are hospitalized or in jail have a high risk of suicide. The family is more important in everyday functioning than for Anglos or African-Americans, and jail or hospital interferes with this; if there is a further impairment in the relationship with their family, like the family moving out of town, they are likely to become suicidal. However, if watched for 24 hours, the crisis is usually over.

Having someone with a suicidal patient of course is very helpful. But it is most helpful to deal with the issues.

Some of the difficulties in dealing with economically poor patients are two countertransference problems. There are after all only two types of analysts—those who have never been poor and those who once were poor but by hard work and deferring gratification have become not poor. Those who have never been poor are often appalled at the lives of their patients and feel guilty because they have never suffered the way their patients have and they feel could not have managed. But what do we do to people who make us feel guilty? We get rid of them. Those who have become not poor by hard work and deferring gratification see in the patient their bad self — what they would have been like if they did not work hard and defer gratification. And what do we do with our bad self? We get rid of it.

Frequently we do not know how to survive and cope in the patient's world. But the patients know a lot about that. People are like a nation fighting a battle on many fronts. If we help them with the problems we know about, they frequently are able to win other battles on their own.

It is sometimes helpful to tell them about the differences in social classes in the US. They are just as interested as we were. Then when they want to change and be middle class, because our society is cruel to the poor. But they discover they can't even though they want to, and then we can help them deal with their problems in changing.

It is important not to arbitrarily impose middle class solutions when they don't fit. Thus, in some social groups physical violence may be the best solution; to avoid, it might place your patient in real danger. You must consider the patient's solutions in the light of what the patient knows about their world.

Prejudice and racism are real problems. Members of any ethnic group both have a wish to be ethnic and a wish not to be ethnic. Only analysts understand that both wishes are healthy, and that conscious compromises are the ones work best.

The feelings of every prejudiced against group, whether ethnic, or gender, has a three layered structure. The first is the problem out there in society, and the patients need to know about it and to feel angry at it, and to take whatever realistic actions they can to cope.

But below that is another level. The problem is not just out there. The prejudiced against patient has internalized the prejudice into his or her own thoughts. Sometimes patient can talk about the outside problem but not notice their own bias against people like themselves.

Below that is still another layer. That they did not learn the prejudice directly form the outside world but from the people closest to them. Usually African-Americans know that being Black is bad by they time they are three years old. Particularly hurtful, and usually not understood by white therapists, is finding that your mother prefers a lighter skinned sibling. And girls are hurt more by their mother's prejudice against girls than by their father's, because she is a woman herself and must be therefore be right. (Of course, mothers are more important for most children than fathers for good or bad).

There is an old paper by LeMaurice Gardner on the resistances and countertransference problems of the white patient with a Black therapist, a Black patient with a white therapist, and a Black patient with a Black therapist, which is still useful. I find it helpful to let African-American patients know that it is reasonable for them to be angry at me for having a white face since there have been lots of people with white faces who have made trouble for them.

Sexism is important. Penis envy as an innate envy of the penis makes no sense. But there is lots of evidence of envy of the prerogatives of men in our society, particularly if your mother prefers boys to girls, symbolized in dreams and symptoms as envy of the penis. Similarly, envy of their mothers or their mother's preference for girls over boys is expressed by men in dreams and symptoms as breast or vagina envy. As Irene Fast so aptly put it, "All a child wants is everything. When they find there is something they cannot have or cannot do, they don't like it. "

In dealing with alcohol, it is important to pay attention to what the alcoholic does when drunk. In our society alcohol is often a 100 proof alibi. No one does anything drunk they do not want to do when sober.

One of the satisfactions of most drugs including something as mild as pot is the illusion of being in a close relationship with the people one is with when taking the drug, without the difficulty of forming a real relationship. That it is an illusion eventually becomes clear.

It was Hedda Bolgar who first suggested to me that the Odyssey was a good metaphor for analysis. It is a scary journey of self-discovery which is bearable because the analyst is there.

We help patients think about their lives and their contradictory feelings. We allow them to discover their own complexity, and that their feelings are a necessary part of rational thinking. What they cannot remember or think about is important; what is unconscious does not change, but has the most control. What they can think about, they can control. With our help, they reconstruct their lives and their traumas including their fantasies, and they learn the defenses they use. They learn about transference and its ubiquity; and they learn to use their transferences as sources of information. Indeed, they learn to use all of their problems as sources of information that will make their lives better.

You will quickly discover if you have not already done so, that if you have the courage to stay there, to listen, to hear the patient's terror without being equally terrified, to hear the patient's depression without being equally depressed, to try to make sense out of what seems meaningless, to help the patient relate his or her conscious experience of pain to what is unconscious, what seemed to make no sense now makes good sense in terms of their life history. The severely disturbed patient will not only improve in a way that will startle and impress you, but in many cases will go on to live a life which you or I would be happy to live, and that for us is the criterion of successful psychoanalytic treatment.

REFERENCES

Adler, A. (1968). Nervous insomnia. In The Practice and Theory of Individual Psychology. (Ed. A. Adler), pp. 163-171. Totowa, New Jersey:Littlefield, Adams. (Original work published 1914).

——— (1968). Individual psychological conclusions on sleep disturbances. In The Practice and Theory of Individual Psychology. (Ed. A. Adler), pp. 163-171. Totowa, New Jersey: Littlefield, Adams. (Original work published 1912).

Breggin, P.A. (1983). Psychiatric Drugs: Hazards to the Brain. New York: Springer.

Freud, S. (1911). Psychoanalytic notes upon an autobiographical account of a case of paranoia (Dementia paranoides). In Collected Papers, 3, pp. 316-367.

Karon, B.P., & VandenBos, G.R. (1981). Psychotherapy of Schizophrenia:TheTreatment of Choice. New York: Aronson.

——— & Widener, A.J. (1994). Is there really a schizophrenogenic parent? Psychoanalytic Psychology, 11, 47-61.

Meyer, R.G., & Karon, B.P. (1967). The schizophrenogenic mother concept and the TAT. Psychiatry. 30, 173-179.

Read, J., Perry, B.D., Moskowitz, A., & Connolly, J. (2001). The contribution of early traumatic events to schizophrenia in some patients:Atraumatogenic neurodevelopmental model. Psychiatry, 64, 319-345.

CHAPTER 12
A Direct Analytic Contribution To The
Understanding of Postpartum Psychosis

by Jack Rosberg, M.A., and Bertram P. Karon, Ph.D.

Approximately nine per cent of all psychotic reactions in women develop in connection with pregnancy, according to Pasquarelli's review of the literature. Despite the physiological changes associated with pregnancy, he finds that "nearly all writers have agreed that psychological factors are of prime importance in the etiology of puerperal mental disorders." Unfortunately, there is no such agreement as to the nature of these psychological factors. As Pasquarelli points out in a footnote, "The discussion of psychoanalytic concepts... is unfortunately brief because of a lack of specifically pertinent literature[1]."

Physical discomfort, the meaning attached to being a mother, and sexual guilt are mentioned in Boyd's description of the psychological roots of puerperal disorders[2]. The physical discomforts that he lists include pains and sleeplessness during pregnancy, exertion during the delivery, and exhaustion following it. According to Boyd, being a mother may mean the end of carefree youth, may mean being irrevocably tied to a husband who is disliked, and/or may mean having to compete for the husband's love (sibling rivalry). In discussing sexual guilt, he states that when such feelings are strong (especially when incestuous fantasies are involved), pregnancy may be seen as the punishment for sexual activities. Frigidity as an indicator of susceptibility to psychosis is mentioned by Boyd; Pasquarelli, on the other hand, doubts its prognostic value in view of its high incidence in the general population.

Pasquarelli mentions, as etiological factors, the anxious expectation of delivery as a great physical ordeal, leading to mutilation or death, and the factor of economic insecurity as indicated by the increased incidence of pregnancy disorders during the depression of the 1930's.

Both Boyd and Pasquarelli state in general terms that psychotic reactions are determined by the previous personalities of the patients and that one must be careful to distinguish cases where a previous psychosis is merely complicated by the pregnancy from those in which the pregnancy is a major etiological factor.

These discussions seem somewhat unsatisfactory. In the first place, most of the problems which are mentioned are such as to reach their maximum intensity before—not after—the childbirth; yet only 15 per cent of the psychotic reactions to pregnancy occur before delivery. Thus the great majority of pregnancy psychoses remain inadequately explained.

Moreover, the factors mentioned are more likely to lead to gradually increasing anxiety and guilt reactions than to an acute psychotic break. Davidson[3] reported that patients in whom psychoses developed during pregnancy did indeed show gradually increasing mood swings, insomnia, headache, and mild anxiety. But he found a considerably different picture in postpartum cases: sudden onset, mostly with excitement, which was sometimes precipitated by the patient's return from the hospital. Again, one can find no adequate explanation in the literature.

Finally, the discussions of psychological factors by the writers surveyed seem superficial. Although fantasies are mentioned (incest, sibling rivalry), they are not thoroughly explored.

Fortunately, direct analysis, Rosen's method of psychoanalytic treatment of psychosis,[4] provides an ideal technique for the investigation of underlying fantasies, because of the intensity and depth of therapy necessary with psychotics. In the course of the direct analysis of a schizophrenic woman, a postpartum case, certain fantasies were discovered which, the writers believe, shed new light on the postpartum psychoses.

The patient, a woman in her thirties, had been unsuccessfully treated in several institutions. Her treatments included both insulin and electric shock therapies.

At the time the direct analysis began, she was extremely aggressive, so much so that she was kept in restraint in bed during the first part of the therapy. Far from objecting, she preferred this treatment "because getting up makes me dizzy" (i.e., makes her lose control). At that time the patient was grossly overweight (approximately 55 pounds more than her normal figure). Most of this weight had been gained in the latter part of her institutionalization before the beginning of the direct analysis.

The reason for her illness, she said, was that "my husband made me pregnant." Pregnancy, she referred to, as "going through the mill." "The mill is responsible for my illness." At other times, she would deny any relationship between intercourse, pregnancy, and children; she would then say that children came by an arrangement "with the state." During the "pregnancy" she was nauseated but never vomited, according to her account.

As the analysis progressed, it became clear that her husband had, in many ways, replaced her mother in her emotional life. Their relationship to her might best be described as dominating dependence, whereby the mother, and later the husband, dominated her so that she would gratify their own dependency needs. Her mother had forced the patient to assume the mothering role to the patient's own siblings, and finally to the mother herself, on innumerable occasions. The transfer of this attitude to the husband is exemplified by the patient's description of the role of the ideal wife: "A good wife calls her husband at his place of business at least six times a day to make sure that things are going well and that she's available in case anything comes up. Also, she tells him what to eat, and how much to eat, and also when to change his underwear and his outside apparel. If she doesn't do this, she can't be considered a good wife."

This replacement of the mother by the husband was most graphically demonstrated when the patient was finally able to face the fact that her feelings of guilt about sex were derived from her mother. She then identified the voice she heard saying "Shame, shame," whenever she masturbated, as that of her mother. At this point her mother's voice disappeared, only to be replaced by her husband's voice saying, "Hermit."

"Hermit" was a word of reproach used by her husband to her during their courtship when she seemed uninterested in getting married. She said that she did not know what he meant by it, and asked people for many years thereafter what the word meant, since her husband would not tell her.

The change in the hallucinatory reproach not only mirrored the earlier temporal replacement of mother by husband, but also reflected a change from guilt about sex per se as opposed to sex in which she did not gratify the demands of the husband (mother).

The reverse process, replacing the husband with the mother, was shown during the periods when she attributed pregnancy and children to "the state." The state, it turned out, represented the impersonal controlling mother. This same impersonal controlling mother was represented in her delusions by the cathedral of Notre Dame, with herself as the cathedral's hunchback whose only security lay within the structure's impersonal confines.

Sexual relations were described by her as "the woman sucks with the vagina or mouth" (fellatio). She sometimes referred to her vagina as a "vagina-mouth." "A woman has two mouths: an oral mouth and a vagina-mouth." She insisted that she had "on doctor's advice" had intercourse "Russian style," that is she had put the testicles as well as the penis in her vagina. No matter how much she got she could never get filled. She referred to the testicles as "the two T's" which also seemed to mean teats. Semen, she said, was like milk. After intercourse she was full of "semen and milk."

"Being through the mill," her expression for pregnancy, referred to the "mill" where flour was made; flour was white like semen and milk. Pregnancy, she said, was being "filled up with semen and blood and milk." The swelling had the significance of becoming "more and more full." "It's the only time I was completely full." In other words, a pregnancy represented the final solution to the oral problems of her life. These may be summarized as having to give (be a mother) instead of receiving (mothered) which is the need of every child. The husband (who replaced the mother) was at last giving, instead of taking, during intercourse. But he could never give enough. When, however, she had actually been pregnant, this signified, on the level of fantasy, that she was getting "fuller and fuller" of milk. The satisfaction she longed for was at hand; but just when she was satisfied, the child would be born, and she would be empty again. During the period in her psychosis in which she had gained the excess weight, she had eaten prodigiously and was so fat "that I couldn't move." She said she had been trying to fill the emptiness, but she had never been satisfied.

"When I went to school, I was hungry. My mother wouldn't feed me. So when my husband badgered me to marry him I accepted, thinking he would provide me with the things I needed, food and a home. When it turned out that he couldn't I became pathological. The mill, or pregnancy as you called it, also did this and I got lockjaw." When the therapist interpreted the lockjaw as punishment for wanting to suck the penis or paternal breast, the patient got very angry, and denied the interpretation, saying it was "a movie version." She added that the therapist was "as draining" as her mother, husband, and sisters, who, she said, made constant demands upon her. If only she could avoid these relationships and rest, she could "fill up again."

A good deal of the delusional material dealt with scars. She felt that she had scars all over her body, including her face. Almost all of these were hallucinatory. One scar which did exist, and which she talked about considerably, was a scar in the vaginal region caused by childbirth. The hallucinatory scars on her face seemed related to a sense of shame. In addition, these scars, with the other hallucinatory scars, were proliferated representations of the vaginal scar, which she felt was very ugly. When she said that this scar was "growing," she was asked if she felt the vagina was growing. She said yes, and indicated that she felt the vagina itself was very ugly, like the scar.

The "ugliness of the vagina" was related to her feelings of guilt about her sex (about being female), which, upon analysis, seemed to be predicated upon two fantasies: First, her mother needed a man and it was wrong, therefore, to be a woman; second, it was wrong for her to want so badly to be fed by the mother-husband as to have a second mouth—the vagina-mouth.

Thus, when the oral catastrophe of childbirth had befallen her, the earlier explanations for her mother's mistreatment of her were reactivated to explain the fantasied loss (that is, the loss of all the "food" that had been filling her).

The attempt at a psychotic solution to this oral problem may be seen in her description of her "two mothers, the person on the outside who calls herself mother and the mother inside of me that is warm, loving, and affectionate." Was it any wonder, then, that she should cling so tenaciously to a psychosis which included the inside mother, when recognizing the external mother seemed the only alternative!

To recapitulate the fantasy connected with childbirth: Being pregnant signified being filled with milk—the final solution to all the patient's deep oral problems—and the childbirth represented a catastrophic loss of this gratification. The prevalence as a severe oral trauma, of such fantasies of childbirth seems likely, because of their potency in precipitating psychotic reactions; the preponderance of oral content has long been reported in the literature on psychosis[5].

Moreover, Seidenberg and Harris[6] have noted the relative absence of nausea and vomiting before delivery in women who later developed postpartum psychoses, as in the ease discussed here. This may be understood when one considers vomiting as representing an undoing of the pregnancy in oral symbolic terms (Grace and Graham[7]). The woman heading for a postpartum psychosis has no wish to undo the pregnancy, it is the delivery which is the trauma. The observation that the return from the hospital is often the precipitating factor becomes understandable, inasmuch as the hospital represents a temporary gratification of oral dependency needs. The problem becomes acute when the patient is deprived of even this gratification.

At this point several objections may be raised to the implication that such fantasies as are discussed here form the basic factor in postpartum disorders: (1) That this is, after all, a single ease; 2) that the case is that of a severe schizophrenic, whereas postpartum psychoses more frequently show manic-depressive than schizophrenic symptoms; and (3) that such fantasies might be present in previously pathological individuals but certainly not in normal persons or even in neurotics.

As to the first objection, a single case thoroughly understood is of far more scientific value than any number of cases superficially presented. And the other objections are based on the assumption that the fantasy pattern suggested here is special and limited—where the fact is that evidence can be cited pointing to the existence of this fantasy both in normal and pathological individuals. Further, there is value in setting forth a hypothesis, even when the initial clues are few, for only when a hypothesis exists, as a guiding thread in the scientific literature, can further empirical data be assembled.

Such fantasies as those under discussion operate largely on an unconscious level. But the unconscious can be unearthed, and the existence or nonexistence of specific fantasies can be determined through the direct analysis of psychotics and the conventional psychoanalysis of neurotics.

Interestingly enough, analysts (for example, Silverberg[8] and Klein[9]) have reported dreams and fantasy productions of neurotics which are highly suggestive in terms of the present postpartum hypothesis. They report material which indicates that intercourse was viewed as being fed at the breast. It is a short step from such a view of intercourse to viewing pregnancy as being filled with milk.

Moreover, Michel-Hutmacher[10] reported that in response to the question of what they believed was inside their bodies, children up to the age of seven said that the body was a bag filled with food. From seven to nine anatomical details began to appear, but, only around the age of 10, were correct answers given. Apparently then, the notion that anything which fills the body is food not only can be found in normals, but is present in consciousness up to the age of seven.

Finally, consideration of a case of postpartum neurosis reported in the literature will serve to eliminate the possibility that this fantasy is peculiar to schizophrenic reactions. The case was reported by Freud in 1893, when he was just beginning his discoveries. He treated the patient by means of suggestive hypnosis which was, surprisingly enough, successful. The patient, a young and normal-appearing woman, happily married and mother of one child, found herself repeating, with her second baby, certain extraordinary difficulties she had had with her first one. These had to do with her inability to nurse. As long as she tried to nurse her newborn baby, she was unable to eat, vomited, became agitated when food was brought to her bedside, and was reduced to a state of extreme depression and exhaustion. Her family doctors brought in Freud, and he tried hypnosis. The very first night he gave ordinary reassurances and commands: "Do not be afraid. You will make an excellent nurse and the baby will thrive. Your stomach is perfectly quiet, your appetite is excellent, you are looking forward to your next meal, ..." and so on. This worked temporarily, but at noon of the following day all the mother's symptoms had returned. That night Freud hypnotized her again and this time "acted with greater energy and confidence. I told the patient that five minutes after my departure she would break out against her family with some acrimony: what had happened to her dinner! did they mean to let her starve, how could she feed the baby if she had nothing to eat herself? and so on." (Italics the present writers'.)

Note that this second suggestion was markedly different in character from the first. The first hypnotic suggestion had consisted merely of directions to suppress symptomatology, and its effects were temporary. The second suggestion was closer to an interpretation: The patient was directed to express oral needs rather than to suppress symptoms. Surprisingly enough, this peculiar character of the second suggestion, which, the writers believe, accounts for its effectiveness, is nowhere discussed by Freud.

From then on, the mother had no trouble. "Her husband thought it rather queer, however, that after my departure the evening before she had clamored violently for food and had remonstrated with her mother in a way quite unlike herself. But since then, he added, everything had gone all right."

The symptoms returned with a third child, but again were relieved by Freud. Unfortunately, he was not concerned explicitly with psychosexual development at that time and so has left no hint as to whether the same kind of interpretive suggestion was responsible for the second "cure."

Freud[11]—in 1893—then confines his theoretical discussion to a consideration of the hysterias in general in terms of the operation of an "antithetic idea" which he says is inhibited, dissociated, and "often" unconscious, and which puts "itself into effect through the agency of the somatic innervations" despite the conscious intentions of the patient.

"I therefore consider that I am justified in describing my patient as an hysterique d'occasion since she was able, as a result of fortuitous cause, to produce a complex of symptoms so supremely characteristic of hysteria. It may be assumed that in this instance the fortuitous cause was the patients excited state before the first confinement or her exhaustion after it. A first confinement is, after all, the greatest shock to which the female organism is subject, and as a result of it a woman will as a rule produce any neurotic symptoms that may be latent in her disposition."

From the vantage point of 1956, one may believe that Freud's 1893 discussion can be expanded to include the rather important description of the "antithetic idea" in terms of the later development of Freudian theory and of the present writers' own investigations. The remarkable effectiveness of the direct suggestion would seem to be due to its interpretive character. This interpretive suggestion consisted of directions to act out the oral problems which the writers have reconstructed in their own schizophrenic patient. When Freud's patient was able to comply, the symptoms disappeared.

Summary

The deficiencies in our present knowledge of postpartum psychosis seem to be due to the inadequate consideration which has been given to the fantasy structures which underlie the traumatic impact of childbirth.

Through the direct analysis of a schizophrenic woman with a postpartum psychosis, certain fantasies came to light which shed new light on the problem. Pregnancy had the significance to her of the final gratification of unresolved oral fantasies. The patient felt the increase in girth as caused by the body's filling up with semen, which was equated with milk. The delivery was then viewed as a sudden catastrophic loss of this gratification.

Such unconscious fantasies seem to account for many of the unexplained characteristics of postpartum disorders.

REFERENCES

Pasquarelli, B.: Psychotic reactions to pregnancy. In: Manic-Depressive Psychosis and Allied Conditions. L. Beliak, editor. Pp. 206-219. Grune & Stratton. New York. 1952.

Boyd, D.A.: Mental disorders associated with childbearing. Am. J. Obst. Gynec., 43:148-163, 335-349, 1942.

Davidson, G.M.: Concerning schizophrenic and manic-depressive psychosis associated with pregnancy and childbirth. Am. J. Psychiat., 92: 1331-1346, 1936.

Rosen, J.N.: Direct Analysis. Grune & Stratton. New York. 1953.

Fenichel, O.: The Psycho-Analytic Theory of Neurosis. Norton. New York. 1945.

Seidenberg, R., and Harris, L.: Prenatal symptoms in postpartum psychotic reactions. Psychiat. Quart., 23:715-719, 1949.

Grace, W.J., and Graham, D.T.: Relationship of specific attitudes and emotions to certain bodily states. Psychosom. Med., XIV: 243-251, 1952.

Silverberg, W.V.: Childhood Experience and Personal Destiny. Springer. New York. 1952.

Klein, Melanie: Contributions to Psycho-Analysis, 1921-1945. Hogarth. London. 1948.

Miehel-Hutmacher, Rosalie: Das Korperinnere in der Vorstellung der Kinder. Schweiz. Z. Psychol. Anwend., 14:1-26, 1955. Freud, S.: A case of successful treatment by hypnotism. Collected Papers. Vol. V. Hogarth. London

CHAPTER 13
Medication and/or Psychotherapy with Schizophrenics: Which Part of the Elephant have you Touched?

Bertam P. Karon, Ph.D. and Gary R. VandenBos, Ph.D.

The question of the relative effectiveness of psychotherapy, medication, and combined medication and psychotherapy as treatments for schizophrenic patients is a difficult and important matter. Inasmuch as clinical observation alone has not proved decisive, controlled studies have been undertaken. Unfortunately, their results also conflict. Since no study is without flaw, and since there are many specifications of relevant conditions which may vary (e.g., type of psychotherapy, situation in which the treatment is carried out, training and motivation of therapists, types of medication, dosage level, patient population, criteria of improvement), it is useful to specify the specific differing conditions under which differing results have been obtained.

It has been argued (May & Tuma, 1970a) that inconsistencies in the literature merely reflect gross inadequacies in design, particularly in those studies (such as ours) whose conclusions, at first glance, seem at odds with one's own experience or assumptions. It is our contention that careful scrutiny of the current research does not reveal "gross inadequacies" in some, and perfection in others, but differing conditions under which meaningfully different results occur which are consistent not only with each other, but with clinical experience. This article will attempt to articulate some of the more striking differences in conditions between two major studies of the treatment of schizophrenics which produced meaningfully different findings.

The most frequently cited study in which medication was judged to be superior to psychotherapy for schizophrenics is that of May (1968); the findings are presented as demonstrating that medication was primarily responsible for patient change and that psychotherapy made no appreciable difference. Our study (Karon & VandenBos, 1972) had quite contrary findings. We found that twenty months of psychoanalytic psychotherapy with schizophrenics led to greater long-term change in the thought disorder, better over-all adjustment, and shorter over-all hospitalization than medication alone. Moreover, the experience and the personality of the psychotherapist were relevant to outcome, and medication used adjunctively with psychotherapy facilitated behavioral control (and hence discharge) but somewhat slowed change in the

217

thought disorder as compared to psychotherapy alone.

May's study involved assigning patients to five kinds of treatment (milieu—sometimes referred to by May as "no treatment'", ECT, medication, psychotherapy, and medication plus psychotherapy). Each therapist was required to treat patients under all five modalities. The therapists were primarily psychiatric residents, supervised by more experienced professionals. Patients were chosen from "the middle third' of severity prognosis. Patients were evaluated before treatment began and on the day of discharge. Treatment after discharge could be obtained but was not routinely offered. Although follow-up data have been collected, we have not seen any published analyses thereof.

Our study involved assigning patients to three treatments (medication, psychotherapy, and psychotherapy plus medication). Within the two psychotherapy groups, patients were assigned to either inexperienced therapists or experienced therapists (who also supervised the inexperienced therapists). Patients were evaluated pre-treatment and at six, twelve, and twenty months. A follow-up of hospitalization in the two years after treatment has also been carried out.

Unfortunately, Drs. May and Tuma, to whom we made available our data, published two reviews of our methodology which were in some cases factually inaccurate, and in others misleading May & Tuma, 1970a; May & Tuma, 1970b). At that time, only two brief notes (Karon & O'Grady, 1969; Karon & VandenBos, 1970) had appeared which did not provide sufficient data and information to judge the conditions of our study.

First of all, our data do not contradict, but supplement the findings of May (1968), and indeed earlier studies. If our project had included only therapists who were inexperienced at doing psychotherapy with schizophrenic patients (as is typical in research on psychotherapy with schizophrenics) and had terminated after only six months of treatment (also typical in such research), it would have been concluded that psychotherapy made no difference and only medication made an appreciable difference. (However, even at that time, the patients of the experienced therapists clearly showed greater improvement than the comparison group, particularly with respect to the thought disorder.)

That medication, particularly the phenothiazines, is of value was not challenged. We assumed that the evidence is clear that medication is of some value (Shapiro, 1971), and that the findings of May could be accepted in this respect. Indeed, patients in our study receiving phenothiazines as primary treatment clearly improved over their own pretreatment conditions. We did not feel it necessary to replicate that part of their study in which no treatment (medication or psychotherapy) was utilized. It was only the way in which psychotherapy was made available to the patients and the tangentially relevant way that it was evaluated, that necessitated further investigation. Our study did not have a control group in the sense of a "no treatment" group, rather we utilized a comparison group receiving medication and minimal support (that is treatment as provided by good large-scale programs).

Our study can be seen as an elaboration and specification of the differential results achieved with differing conditions of treatment. We have no doubt that if we replicated their exact conditions of treatment and criteria, difficult as that might be, we would replicate their findings. Let us examine some of the differential conditions between the two studies:

1: *Experience of Therapists.* Experience as used here refers specifically to experience in doing psychotherapy with schizophrenics. May used psychotherapists inexperienced in doing psychotherapy with schizophrenics, except as supervisors. Karon and VandenBos used both experienced and inexperienced psychotherapists; both experienced therapists had over ten years of such relevant experience. May and Tuma (1970a) believe that experience in treating physical disorders is highly relevant, even for the psychotherapists; we feel that even experience in the psychoanalysis of neurotics is only partially relevant.

2: *Therapist Knowledge of Patient Population.* Knowledge of the characteristics and consequent specific resistances of people of a given socio-economic, ethnic, and sub-cultural background is at least as important as knowledge of the specific psychopathology being treated; the two supervisors in our study were better acquainted with poor and with Black patients than are most psychotherapists. One supervisor (Thomas Tierney, M.D.) had completed his residency in that hospital with that patient population and had continued to be available to the hospital and this patient population over a ten year period. Not only was he familiar with these patients, but he had a real commitment to understanding and helping such patients, a point which cannot be overemphasized since poor patients are not typically "popular" with professionals. After the completion of the clinical phase of our study, he became director of resident training. The other supervisor had earlier investigated the effects of discrimination on Blacks (Karon, 1958) and had worked with lower class individuals and with Black patients to a considerable extent. It is not clear how familiar the supervisors of psychotherapy in' the May study were with patients of the socioeconomic and sub-cultural background of the patients, even though these patients were not so low in the socio-economic hierarchy as were our patients.

3: *Training of Therapists.* May (1968) is inexplicit about the kind and amount of psychotherapy training. Apparently, it consisted of supervisory hours on project patients in addition to that training usual in their residency. It is not clear how much experience the supervisors in general and in the treatment of schizophrenic patients of that socioeconomic class, with or without medication. Even the difference between doing psychotherapy with medication as an integral adjunct, as opposed to doing psychotherapy without medication, raises different technical considerations which require considerable experience to master. One does not ordinarily teach very well what one does not know.

In our study, in addition to didactic material, the inexperienced therapists watched, through closed circuit TV, the experienced therapist work with two patients before themselves beginning to work with project patients, and the inexperienced therapists' sessions, particularly the early ones, were watched by the supervisor and the other inexperienced therapists in that treatment group, and discussed. In the later phases of the study more conventional supervision sessions were held. It is our belief that learning a complex skill is difficult, and in the early phases a great deal of attention must be paid to training. One cannot learn by osmosis or fiat. A striking difference exists between the studies in the amount of systematic attention paid to training.

4: It is a well-intended' but confounding control for the same therapist to practice more than one treatment, controlling personality structure, but ignoring motivation. One does not ordinarily practice well a treatment one does not believe in, as compared to a treatment one values. A better control is to have each treatment practiced by therapists who believe in it, as in our study. Indeed, our student therapists chose their supervisor as someone whose training they valued. That is not to say that personality differences are unimportant, or that it would not be of value to study the determinants of treatment preference among therapists. Again, the extra difficulty and time invested in learning psychotherapy well was recognized in our study by paying the student therapists for their additional trouble. The importance of motivation, modeling behavior, and expectation of patient improvement far out-weigh in importance any possible hindering effect on student performance of the student-supervisor role relationship, a consideration about which May and Tuma

(1970a, 1970b) seem to be overly concerned. That is, they seem to be afraid that the student therapist, without relevant training, will better know how to treat their patients than their supposed instructors, and that our design might obscure this effect. One might well wonder why this is such an important consideration, as to outweigh arranging for careful training and appropriate motivation of the students.

5: *Continuity of Treatment.* Both studies have problems with the continuity of treatment. May (1968) interrupted psychotherapy on day of discharge from the hospital, and did not routinely provide follow-up psychotherapy with either the same or different therapists. Medication, however, was maintained after discharge. Termination of psychotherapy, coupled with discharge from the hospital, is a traumatic period. Most of his conclusions, however, are based on evaluations made during this period of trauma for the psychotherapy group.

Our study maintained continuity of psychotherapy, and even of psychotherapist, up to one year of hospitalization or up to 20 months of total treatment. The same psychotherapist had the patient both as an in-patient and as an out-patient. While many hospitals do not follow such procedures, any reasonable theoretical rationale for psychotherapy readily yields the importance of the continuity of relationship (transference) in the treatment.

May and Tuma (1970a, 1970b) rightly point out the discontinuity in our study: patients who were on medication (hospital comparisons) and did not respond quickly were, as is the usual procedure at DPI, transferred to a State hospital. Treatment was maintained, but not in the same buildings or with the same physicians. We did not feel that continuity of relationship was as integral to drug therapy as to psychotherapy. Medication, of course, was continued in both hospitals and on an out-patient basis as is usual. This procedure was followed because of what seemed to be the most appropriate control group: patients treated in the "usual" way.

While transfer to the second hospital might be seen as second-rate treatment (and May and Tuma assume this to be the case), the fact is that, aside from the lack of a staff capable of intensive psychotherapy, the second hospital is better equipped with auxiliary services. While the patient-to-doctor ratio is higher at the State hospital than DPI (but still small enough for adequate drug treatment), all other services are, in fact, better staffed. (The staffing of DPI was designed for two week stays, and fully developed auxiliary services did not seem as imperative.) But the availability of the psychotherapist made retention in DPI necessary if psychotherapy were to continue on an in-patient basis. Thus, psychotherapy patients (both groups A & B, with and without medication) were relatively deprived in the availability of auxiliary services. That such a transfer did not work to the marked detriment of the patient seems to be reflected in the fact that our comparison group (medication only) did not spend any more time in the hospital during the first year of treatment than did the medication only group in May's study; our worst group in terms of hospitalization spent no more time in the hospital than his best group, despite the fact that data from the two studies suggest that our patients were sicker.

6: *Number of Cases.* There is no question that May has a much greater sample, 228, or some sub-set, depending on which comparison or publication we cite. Our own study consists of a total of 36 original patients, one of whom died within the first month of treatment.

His larger sample permits subtle differences to be statistically significant, while the small sample in our study permits only striking differences to be statistically significant.

On the other hand, it was possible for us to be more careful in gathering data on the patients, including more careful, detailed, and more rigorously blind outcome evaluations, to obtain greater quality control, so to speak, on the psychotherapy being studied, and to obtain data on every patient at 20 months after the initiation of the study. Since many of the characteristics of the patient population became clear only after repeated follow-ups, we suspect that less careful work, as is unfortunately necessary with a large sample, would be more misleading (e.g., it was only after considerable work that we observed that patients in a public hospital, and their families, routinely lie about previous hospitalization, alcoholism, and drug abuse since they obtain better treatment if they do not disclose this information).

Accuracy of inference from a sample is obviously affected not only by the number of cases, but even more by any systematic (planned or unintentional) bias in selecting these cases. The infamous Literary Digest poll included thousands of cases.

7: *Patient Population and Selection.* In both studies, the patients were drawn from a public hospital and considered clearly schizophrenic on clinical examination. Nonetheless, there were striking differences in demographic characteristics, as well as severity of pathology. Our patients were primarily lower class, poor, and Black. May (1968) managed to select in an "unbiased" manner an unusual set of patients.

He described his "average" patient as high school educated, with above average IQ, employed predominantly as a skilled laborer (or as a housewife); in other words, the patients are at least lower-middle class. By contrast, our "average" patient was a high school dropout, with below average IQ, and employed as an unskilled laborer (or receiving public assistance). The sociological data have been unequivocal that the typical schizophrenic population is predominantly poor and lower class. For example, Hollingshead and Redlich (1958) reported schizophrenics as twelve times more frequent among admissions from the lowest socio-economic class (on a five class basis) than in the highest. Aside from the proportion being Black, which will vary with geographic and urban location, the demographic characteristics of our patients are consistent with those reported of schizophrenics treated at public hositals in the U.S., while May's patients seem to have been, at least inadvertently, subject to some kind of economic screening. Possibly, this is the result of May intentionally choosing as a treatment population of the "middle third" in severity (i.e., neither the very sick nor the relatively well). It is not clear why this should exclude the poor so effectively.

An additional screening on the basis of severity of symptoms occurs in the May study even though it is never described as such. He analyzed data only in terms of patients who took both the pre-test and post-test, thus excluding the sicker patients. It is a practically easier, but hardly comprehensive, procedure of investigation that leads to conclusions applicable only to those patients well enough and cooperative enough to take elaborate testing before treatment. We strongly felt no such limitation makes sense. Our own sample is biased toward the severest cases, since these are the cases where the diagnosis was the most clear-cut.

May and Tuma (1970a) suggest that three patients in our study have dubious diagnoses and should have been excluded from the data. Of the three to which they presumably refer, two are excluded. One patient died of a pulmonary embolism in the first month of treatment and is necessarily excluded from the data, but would appropriately have been excluded later on the basis of the subsequently available background information (drug addiction, alcoholism, lengthy hospitalization under a different name as well as imprisonment, and ECT).

The second patient was a man whose clinical material, psychological evaluations, and EEG progressively more clearly suggested diffuse brain involvement. It was only after the third evaluation (12 months) that the patient and his family developed sufficient trust to reveal his history of taking large dosages of benzedrine, dexedrine, barbiturates, and nutmeg daily for years; he was excluded from the data beginning with the twelve month data.

The third patient, a female, was eventually diagnosed as multiple sclerosis as well as schizophrenic. This patient had been cleared by both the neurology and internal medicine services before being chosen for the study as clearly schizophrenic. It was only after psychotherapy had progressively changed her thought disorder, reality-testing, and ability to relate to others, while the motor symptoms did not change and progressively worsened, that the diagnosis of multiple sclerosis was possible. The fact that the two sets of symptoms followed independent courses led us to include her in all data analyses as properly schizophrenic as well as motorically impaired on a neurological basis.

May and Tuma argue that all three (and not just two) patients should have been excluded; such analyses have been run, and they do not materially affect the conclusions. (It was necessary, at the 20 month evaluation, to eliminate one more case because of hospital staff interference with the treatment; analyses including and excluding this patient were run, and do not materially differ).

8: *Randomization.* Both studies attempted randomization. In our study, suitable patients were selected in sets of three, and randomly assigned to the three groups; hospital comparison, psychotherapy without medication, and psychotherapy with medication. Patient selection and assignment was done in the same manner throughout, by research personnel not involved in treatment or supervision. Assignment between experienced and inexperienced therapists and among inexperienced therapists was on a rotation basis. Supervisors did not select which patient they would work with. Since we believe that psychotherapy has to be learned, it seemed necessary that the cases chosen in the first weeks be assigned to the supervisors, so that their work could be observed by the inexperienced therapists, via closed circuit TV, and discussed. Because of the schedules and commitment of the inexperienced therapists it was necessary that they begin to be assigned by the third "set" of patients. Hence the supervisors treated the psychotherapy patients selected in the first two sets and in the last two sets of patients chronologically. Any differences in patient characteristics reflect possible week-to-week fluctuation in admissions (although they were well within the bounds to be expected from random variation).

The May study also attempted random assignment of patients to treatments and therapists. Like our study, assignment to treatment groups was random, but assignment to therapists was not. Seventeen per cent of the psychotherapy patients were on a random basis assigned to therapists with less than six months of residency. This was a disqualifying condition for his study, and the cases were re-assigned to other therapists. Both studies used random assignment to treatment groups, but not to individual therapists.

9: *Statistical Procedures.* Both studies use analyses of variance and co-variance. May relied primarily on analysis of variance, since he reported no great difference in his data between the use of analyses of variance and analyses of co-variance (leaving out patients too sick to take the tests initially).

We use analysis of co-variance to correct for possibly relevant background variables in our study, after a multiple regression procedure determined which of the many possibly relevant background variables need to be taken into account. May and Tuma's objection to our procedures do not impress us with their statistical sophistication. In recent years, the severe limitations of co-variance analysis (Campbell, 1970) have become clear; however, our data meet these most recent stringent standards. Matching, difference scores, and analysis of variance are subject to more serious errors and regression effects as Campbell, among others, has made clear. Moreover, the F-test, as used here, is not invalidated by minor violations of normality assumptions, particularly where the small sample size will permit only large effects to be significant. We rely on analysis of co-variance because we felt it is most appropriate for our situation.

Interestingly enough, analysis of variance yields essentially the same results with our data. There is only one finding that is seriously affected by the co-variance procedure, namely that the corrections for sex and initial Porteus Maze performance lead to the conclusion that hospital stay is shorter for inexperienced psychotherapists using medication than for their supervisor in the first 20 months. None of our other conclusions are. affected, nor are our long term (2 year after end of treatment follow-up) hospitalization data.

Many of May's procedures are questionable for regression effects, and for possibly biased selection of sub-sets of the data. Comparisons are made for sub-sets of as few as 2/3 of the cases. His procedures seem to exclude the sicker patients (who would not take some tests) from his analysis of his already selected "middle third". In addition, his procedure of "winsorizing (deleting those patients) doing most well and badly in each group), when all data are used, leads to ignoring 20 cases in his data when "winsorizing" once, and 40 cases when "winsorizing" twice.

Since the particular sub-set of patients used by May varies almost with each test of significance, it would be necessary for the analyses to be rigorous to check each time that the distributions of the samples actually used are within the limits of random variation on relevant back-ground characteristics. There is no evidence such tests of significance were routinely carried out.

Moreover, when May utilizes analyses of co-variance, it is an unusual way (Forsythe, et. ai, 1973). Regression coefficients are determined only from 44 "control" patients, which means that fewer coefficients will be found to be statistically significant than if the total sample were used, and a new "stopping rule" was devised for his study which justifies stopping earlier, i.e., taking into account fewer co-variates than more conventional procedures. Thus his procedures must result in the conclusion that fewer background characteristics need to be taken into account, and that taking these into account is less important and makes less difference than more traditional statistical procedures.

The point is not that May was a bad scientist, but that ideal data analyses do not exist; our analysis is as careful, rigorous, and controlled as any in the literature, and more careful than May's despite the fact that his residual sample is considerably larger than our total sample.

10: *Untestable patients.* May's (1968) procedure of deleting from analysis data obtained from patients too sick to take the tests before treatment, as well as those too sick after treatment, is simple and straightforward. However, it introduces the problem of studying a biased sample of schizophrenic patients, as we have discussed earlier.

May and Tuma (1970a, 1970b) erroneously state that we uniformly assigned untestable patients an arbitrary theoretically determined score on two of the intellectual criteria, and that this could account for some of our findings. The assignment of theoretically determined scores was done only for the initial (pre-treatment) data, solely for the purpose of establishing regression coefficients for the analysis of covariance, and statistical criteria were used to examine whether the regression coefficients so determined were, in fact, appropriate. If not, a correction was estimated from the data. Thus, we could, and did, check statistically as to whether or not such a procedure would lead to an artifact, and could correct its effects. Theoretically determined values were not assigned to patients who were untestable in any of the periodic outcome evaluations, since such a use would introduce a possible distortion whose existence could not be established and removed statistically. However, it is important to note that in the final 20-month evaluation all patients took all of the intellectual tests.

In discussing our procedure for statistically introducing the fact that the patients were untestable into the regression equations, May and Tuma (1970a, 1970b), in addition to misrepresenting the statistical procedures, make the surprising statement that we confuse motivation of the patient with his intellectual deficit, as if the deficient performance on intellectual tests by schizophrenic patients were ever an accurate reflection of intellectual ability, free of motivational problems. In fact, it should be obvious that we are using the change in performance on the intellectual tests not as a measure of the patient's true intellectual ability, but as a measure of the change in motivational state and emotional adjustment.

Our procedures included all the data. The alternative would have been not to examine the regressions or not to take them into account, or to delete sick patients from the study, hardly appropriate procedures, although employed all too often.

11: *Time of evaluation.* May (1968) bases most of his conclusions on the evaluation of the patients on the day of discharge from the hospital, whether that be one month after treatment begins or twelve; he (1970b) professes not to understand our procedure, namely our patients were evaluated at fixed intervals after the inception of treatment, irrespective of whether they were in or out of the hospital, were cooperating with or resisting the treatment. Our intervals were 6 months, 12 months, 20 months (end of the treatment phase) and 44 months. This would seem to be a logical treatment evaluation. Day of discharge, besides being a highly variable time interval, is a traumatic time for patients receiving psychotherapy if, as in the May study, the therapeutic relationship is terminated at that time, particularly if the relationship were meaningful.

12: *"Blindness" of Evaluations.* In our study, each evaluation was carried out by personnel not otherwise connected with treatment, and to whom the treatment group was not disclosed. Since a good clinical status interview is not likely to leave the interviewer "blind," these interviews were recorded on tape, and references to treatment deleted from the tapes before being rated "blindly" with regard to clinical status using the following criteria: ability to take care of self, ability to work, sexual adjustment, social adjustment, absence of hallucinations and delusions, degree of freedom from anxiety and depression, amount of affect, variety and spontaneity of affect, satisfaction with life and self, achievement of capabilities, and benign versus malignant effect on others. Discharge was not entirely "blind" but determined by ward chiefs, who were not biased in favor of the study being done by an "outside" and "non-medical" psychotherapist. May (1968) used primarily criteria which are likely to be "contaminated" by knowledge of the patient's treatment and the value system of the evaluators, e.g.. discharge, ward behavior, and therapist reports. His "independent" team of psychoanalysts making ratings relied heavily on narrative accounts of the patient prepared by personnel (nurses, therapists, and social workers) fully cognizant of the treatment the patient received, in addition to their own interviews. It is not clear whether the psychological tests were given and evaluated "blindly".

13: *Drug Dosage*. Both studies permitted psychiatrists familiar with this patient population to adjust medication and dosage level for each patient individually, in terms of their judgment of the optimal dosage for the patient at that time. Both studies did not hold medication at a fixed arbitrary level, but allowed it to vary in accordance with good clinical practice.

In the May study medication is reported only in terms of average total dosage (medication alone: males, 4.02 gms Stelazine, females, 3.19 gms; medication and psychotherapy; males 3.71 gms., females 2.2 gms) and maximum daily dosage (medication alone: 20-120 mg; medication and psychotherapy: 4-120 mg).

Our study has been criticized by May and Tuma (1970a 1970b) for lack of dosage information. The dosage level in our study has not been reported in detail, because full medication records would require more space than journal publication would permit. Dosage levels typically were approximately 400 mg of thorazine daily, varying at different times from a low of 100 mg to a high of 1400 mg daily.

It was noted that three patients in the non-medication group received medication upon the demand of the ward staff as an alternative to mechanical restraints. However, two of these cases do not appear in the final data. Medication for these patients was rare and typically for very brief periods of time (in no case more than two weeks during twenty months of treatment) and in response to the distress of the ward staff. Our willingness to cooperate with the ward staff when their tolerance had reached its limit enabled them to cooperate with us in tolerating the additional trouble of non-medicated patients in general. However, one of these medicated patients had to be deleted from the study because of evidence of organic pathology as mentioned earlier. One had to be deleted because of staff interference with the treatment (of which the medication turned out to be the least). Deleting the last (the third) patient would only increase the apparent effectiveness of psychotherapy; again, we chose the conservative approach of including him.

Summing Up

No study is perfect (in this, we are in agreement with May and Tuma, 1970a); moreover, no two studies are identical. We take exception to the approach of simply discarding apparently conflicting data. A more fruitful approach is carefully to examine the contrasting conditions which give rise to these seemingly contradictory results. Such an examination leads us to the generalizations that medication is clearly helpful, and that psychotherapy, when reasonable care is taken in its implementation and in the training of the therapists, leads to even more benefits-particularly in the reduction of the thought disorder and in the long term consequences of that reduction on one's way of life, and hence on hospitalization in the long run.

The basis, from our data, for these conclusions about the additional positive change in the thought disorder from psychotherapy (with or without medication) and its long term consequences becomes clear from Table 1, which summarizes the data on thought disorder (Visual-Verbal Test [Drasgow & Feldman, 1951]), from the evaluation at the end of the treatment phase (20 months), hospitalization during the treatment phase, hospitalization during a two year follow-up, and total hospitalization. (Hospitalization data are not corrected for background variables, since May and Tuma take exception to the procedure of correcting. Our statistical analysis indicates that the use of co-variates is necessary for the 20-month data, but not for the follow-up data. However, even in the 20-month data the corrections affect only the comparison between the supervisor and inexperienced therapists using medication adjunctively. No other conclusion is affected.) Even though we do not feel that May used a particularly sensitive measure of the schizophrenic thought disorder, he, too, reports (although without extensive discussion) an additional improvement in the thought disorder for patients receiving psychotherapy (in addition to medication) as compared to medication alone. (Long term follow-up data from May's study have not yet come to our attention.) Only with respect to psychotherapy alone (where our patients showed the greatest improvement in the thought disorder) and in the importance attached by the investigators to change in the thought disorder do the studies disagree, for reasons which we have discussed. But the well-known prognostic centrality (Bleuler, 1950) of the thought disorder has been re-affirmed in recent psychiatric research (Cancro, 1968, 1969), as well as our own data.

CHAPTER 14
Recovery of An "Incurable" Schizophrenic
Bertram P. Karon, Ph.D.

Abstract

A schizophrenic was evaluated by all his psychiatrists as "incurable" after several years of unsuccessful outpatient and two months of inpatient treatment, both with medications. Electro-convulsive therapy (ECT) was strongly but pessimistically recommended. He was not eating, not sleeping, and continuously hallucinating. He began outpatient psychoanalytic therapy. All medications were stopped. After three days he began eating. After four months he began working at an intellectually demanding job. After two years he could be assured that he would never be psychotic again under normal stresses. But that was not good enough for him. He kept raising new issues: problems in living, difficulties writing his first book, psychosomatic problems, problems in enjoying ordinary pleasures, marital problems, undoing problems he had caused his son. The total treatment took 14 years. More than 20 years after the completion of treatment the patient sent a note indicating his continued professional accomplishments and thanking the therapist for "giving me my life back."

1. Case Context And Method

Many mental health professionals do not know that any person diagnosed as schizophrenic ever got better with psychotherapy. In 1963 a graduate student in experimental psychology asked about a friend of his, a young faculty member in another department, who was hospitalized as schizophrenic. The graduate student had heard me give a colloquium on treating persons with schizophrenia with psychoanalytic therapy and wanted to know if there was any hope for his friend. I said he needed psychoanalytic therapy, and that, if he received it, he would probably get better, and that under no conditions to permit electro-convulsive treatment (ECT), a treatment this patient's family was considering.

"Can his wife call you?" asked the graduate student.

"Of course."

The wife called me and told me that he had seen someone in New York for therapy and medication for several years and when he came to Michigan he received medication and psychotherapy on an outpatient basis for roughly a year from a psychiatrist with a very good local reputation. The patient had deteriorated, and the medication increased until he was finally hospitalized. Despite increased and combined medications, he had continued to deteriorate even more, and the patient's wife was told he was an "incurable schizophrenic" by both his outpatient psychiatrist and by a consensus of the inpatient psychiatric staff. His only hope, she was told, was electro-convulsive therapy, which probably would not cure him, but it was the only hope he had. The patient's wife, on my advice, withdrew her permission for electro-convulsive therapy, which was scheduled for the next morning. I asked colleagues about the hospital and was told that it was one which emphasized ECT. Also on my advice, she withdrew him from the hospital, despite the staff's objections. She was told that she was killing him by not permitting ECT. They refused to tell her what medications he was on, but when she had him leave the hospital anyway, they relented and told her what medications he was on. She brought him to my office immediately upon discharge. He was not eating, he was not sleeping, he had trouble standing, and he was continuously hallucinating. We began psychotherapy immediately, and later continued while the client lived at home. The patient was not violent, but he was scared. During the first month or two, his wife and friends took turns staying with him. After that it was not necessary.

At that time I did not have a cooperating hospital. Relations between psychologists and psychiatrists were so bad that less than two years before I started working with this patient, the County Medical Society had declared that it was unethical for a physician to refer a patient to a psychologist.

The therapy was carried out in an out-patient office, except for a few at an all-night restaurant described below, with his wife accompanying him to the office during the early part of the therapy when he was not yet able to drive, but not participating after the first hour. As is my usual practice, she also had one confidential hour with me, and the right to call me at any time thereafter, but our conversations after that first hour were always to be described to the patient.

The patient, too, had the right to telephone me at any time. If he did not reach me, he was to phone an hour later. If that did not reach me, phone an hour later. He was to continue until he reached me. He was told that even if it was two in the morning, he knew that I had been home less than an hour, so he was not disturbing me. It is very reassuring for a patient to know they can reach their therapist by phone if necessary, and very few patients abuse that privilege. In his case it helped him pull out of very disturbing experiences.

It is, of course, difficult to remember the details of each session. In my experience, much of every session makes no sense to me, or is repetitive; and what I remember is when things coalesce and become clear. But every therapy hour is full of detail and confusion and repetitiveness, whose feel does not come through in concise case summaries.

The therapist must create a therapeutic alliance by becoming unequivocally helpful, tolerating incoherence, tolerating not understanding, and being realistically optimistic. The patient is usually surprised that you expect them to get better, with hard work. They do not believe you, because most of them have been told by professionals that they have a genetic disease whose biological defect is known and which is incurable. With the best of modern treatment, by which the professionals mean medication, they can be tolerable to other people most of the time. In other words the aim of treatment is to help them become tolerable invalids.

But these premises are wrong. The genetic evidence is very weak. There are no replicated physiological findings except for those which occur in anyone suffering terror and those which have been demonstrated to be the result of the medications (and/or ECT).

The therapist must give a feeling of strength in the sense that you are willing and able to deal with anything and go anywhere the patient needs to go, no matter how scary. If you know things that will help the patient with the patient's current concerns (not yours), you let them know. The patient is often surprised that you have anything to offer that actually helps, that you care about what they are afraid of, and that you listen carefully and take seriously what they say. Unlike working with neurotics, the therapist for a psychotic must avoid being ambiguous. Ambiguity is experienced by the patient as the therapist being a monster, because the ambiguity is filled by the patient with negative transferences. As with any person transference experiences always seem like realistic perceptions. It helps to sit where the patient can see you, and to try to be helpful, not neutral. It is also helpful to talk freely if you have something to say that you think might be helpful to the patient at that moment.

Typically, psychotic patients do not trust you. You cannot expect a psychotic patient to tell you everything they understand. They are afraid that anything they tell you might be used to hurt them. That is why it is essential to tolerate not understanding as well as to try to be unambiguously helpful.

Psychoanalytic ideas often suggest meaning in the midst of the chaos, which often gives the therapist a helpful first approximation, but one with large gaps and places where it seems to contradict itself. Then we can listen around the gaps and contradictions. The therapist deals with what he or she can understand, corrects his own misunderstandings, pays careful attention to what is going on, with the certainty that eventually it will all make sense, and when it does, the patient will get better. Even grossly incoherent patients will sometimes say important things clearly in the midst of their incoherent verbalizations, which they do not expect the therapist to notice or take seriously. (The unconscious meaning of this is probably the patient's wish that the therapist will treat it as nonsense, so that the patient does not have to deal with the anxiety of thinking about it seriously, or the patient's wish that the therapist will confirm earlier experiences with a parent or previous professional, or both, that neither the patient's real feelings nor their observations of bad things should be taken seriously.) As you deal with those fragments that make sense, more and more of what the patient says makes more sense. Of course, this is easier if you have seen similar patients get better with psychotherapy, or have a supervisor who has seen patients get better with therapy. The patient, of course, does not have any reason to be optimistic or to trust the therapist.

Following Freud's advice on technique, I do not use process notes. I do make some notes in the first session and once in a while if I think it will be helpful. Freud felt that taking notes after the hour was better than taking notes during the hour, because you do not listen as carefully when you take notes. Not taking notes at all is even better, because your thoughts tend to stick to your notes, and you are not as sensitive to new material. Of course, if there was something complicated that you were concerned you might forget, Freud recommended that you write it down. None of his technical recommendations were ever rigid. (He made a point of saying his technical recommendations were "recommendations" which usually help, but which you will change if they don't help, rather than "rules," which are things you always do.)

A reviewer of this paper asked why did I not use medication. In this case one did not have to be theoretical. Medication had been tried and found wanting. That is why his treating psychiatrists were insisting on ECT. However, my clinical experience as well as the findings of my later research (Karon & VandenBos, 1981) indicated that the optimal treatment was psychoanalytic therapy with a competent therapist without medication if the therapist, the patient, and the setting (e.g., hospital, family, etc.) can tolerate it. Temporary medication, withdrawn as rapidly as the patient can tolerate, is the next best option accompanying psychoanalytic therapy is the next best option.

Two University Deans contacted me about the patient during the early months of his treatment. One wanted to know whether there was anything the Dean might do to help. I suggested he call the patient, ask him that question, and take seriously anything the patient said.

The other, Dean of his College, wanted to know when the patient might be ready to go back to work. I told the Dean I would think about it, and get back to him. When I told the patient about the conversation (as I did with any conversation about him with anyone) and asked him, he said, "Not next term. Maybe the term after." I then called the Dean and said, "In my best clinical judgment, he won't be ready to go to work next term, but probably the term after."

In the first hour when I asked the patient what he wanted help with, he said, "I don't want to have this scared feeling, can't hold up straight. I don't know what it means, to have tension in the head. I don't want to have to hang around my wife's apron strings. I can't leave her by a foot. I don't want to be nauseating when my wife steps out of the room." (I made a note of this initial statement, which is why I can recall it verbatim.)

At some time in the first session, as I often do with patients who are feeling terrified, I said I would not kill him or let anyone else kill him. This is based on an observation by Bruno Bettelheim (in a 1954 colloquium at Princeton University) that every first psychotic episode is accompanied by an acute conscious fear of dying. In fact, most schizophrenics are consciously aware of such a fear. This patient neither acted as if that were very helpful nor as if it were strange. Probably he did not believe me, but he did not say so.

2. The Client

Mr. X was from a middle-class family and had considered himself lucky to have such good parents, particularly such a good mother. However, even before this first psychotic break at the age of 31, he could not remember his childhood before the second year of high school, although he had never considered that to be abnormal.

Mr. X. was raised as a Jew, but was not religious as an adult. He had a brother three years older than he. His father had been given a course of ECT treatment for depression some years earlier, and had not held a job since. His mother still worked. Neither one of his parents had gone to college, but both he and his brother had. His brother was in business for himself. The patient had gone to a more reputable college than his brother and had earned a Ph.D. Shortly thereafter, the patient's problems seemed to get worse and worse.

3. Guiding Conception With Research and Clinical Experience Support

Schizophrenia is a chronic terror syndrome. All of the symptoms of schizophrenia may be understood as manifestations of terror or defenses against terror. I have never treated a schizophrenic patient whose life history, as experienced by the patient, would not have driven me psychotic, and with the same symptoms.

When the patient's life as given meaning by his or her conscious and unconscious fantasies seems to mean that they are about to be annihilated, they go psychotic. Fantasies are formed on the basis of real experiences and pre-existing fantasies, so that all of life, from early infancy onward, is relevant. Usually something happens early which changes subsequent fantasies, which change how subsequent events are experienced, which again change the fantasies, and so on.

All of us have the potential for schizophrenic symptoms if life becomes bad enough. Luckily, most of us will never have to develop psychotic symptoms. While there are adult experiences that are sufficiently horrible to produce schizophrenic symptoms in basically healthy people, most people who become schizophrenic have had a series of subtle and unsubtle bad experiences which have made them vulnerable.

Early in my career I was taught to dismiss schizophrenic patients' unusual or unusually severe experiences as psychotic delusions. But my clinical experience is that the severe traumas, even seemingly improbable ones, are usually true. Sometimes the initial description is distorted (if not completely repressed). But even distorted memories are related to the real problems. As they are discussed in therapy, they becomes more accurate. Patients who recover repressed or distorted memories almost always try to check on their accuracy, if it is possible and safe to do so. In my experience when the details become consistent, and consistent with the other material, and the patient improves, the reconstruction is almost always confirmed as accurate, if information is available from reliable outside sources such as family members or newspaper reports.

People with schizophrenia are highly varied, aside from their symptoms. Their life histories and specific traumas are equally varied. There are patients whose traumas have nothing to do with their parents. But for most patients as for most people, their relationships with their parents are complexly related to their strengths and weaknesses. There are obviously abusive and hurtful parents, but they are a minority. Most parents of schizophrenic patients are good people who would not consciously do anything to harm their child. Often they will go to great lengths to attempt to get help for their child. Sometimes they do hurtful things because they mistakenly believed that their hurtful actions were good for their child. Unfortunately, to understand traumatic parenting completely, it is also necessary to take into account unconscious processes (Karon & Widener, 1994; Karon, in press). Many parents of schizophrenics suffer from unconscious problems, based on their own life history, which can be measured from the Thematic Apperception Test, and which have been shown in a series of studies to make their children vulnerable. They are not culpable, any more than their children are for hallucinating, or anyone else is for any other unconsciously caused symptom. Unfortunately, unconscious problems cannot be changed until they are thought about consciously.

The thought disorder (the inability to think rationally when you want to) in persons with schizophrenia varies with the degree of conscious terror and with the adequacy of the patient's defenses at a given time. There is no general schizophrenic language, but each patient has a language that the therapist must learn. The apparently weak affect, in schizophrenic patients, is usually a chronic terror state in which lesser affect are blanched out by terror. Apparently inappropriate affects are usually socially inappropriate, but not inappropriate to the patient's inner life.

Catatonic symptoms are simply a specific chronic terror state. According to Fromm-Reichmann (1947), the patients see and hear everything that is going on, but feel as if they will die if they move. Ratner's biological research (Ratner, Karon, VandenBos,& Denny, 1981) showed that the catatonic state has developed in evolution as the last stage of defense of a prey in the clutch of a predator. In that state, while fully conscious, the animal does not seem to react to even intense pain, and the predator acts as if the animal is already dead.

Hallucinations are waking dreams, understandable and treatable using Freud's theory of dreams, with minor modifications.

Delusions have four primary bases:

1) Transference to the world at large.

2) Defense against pseudo-homosexual anxieties, as described by Freud.

3) Peculiar concepts or meanings to concepts taught within a specific family.

4) The need to have a more or less systematic understanding of our selves and our world, even if we have strange experiences. (Patients have strange experiences, both because of their symptoms but also frequently because of unusual real experiences.)

The therapist must help the patient create a livable world. As in any therapy creating a therapeutic alliance is essential; but with psychotic patients it is more difficult and it forms a more persistent part of the therapist's work.

The severity of the symptoms generally means there are more bad things to transfer, and hence the transference to the therapist will tend to be negative. When there is ambiguity, and sometimes even when there is not, the therapist may be perceived as hostile, dangerous, shaming, belittling, and/or conspiring against the patient. This makes the therapeutic alliance harder to create and maintain. The therapist should try to be unambiguously helpful; the blank screen will inevitably become a monster. Frequently the patients do not communicate even what they already understand, because they do not trust you. It is important to tolerate not understanding; the moment you decide you will not abandon the patient just because you do not understand or the material is painful or the patient is hostile, you are already being helpful.

As in any therapy, what changes the patient is the internalization of the therapist as well as the insights gained. The patient internalizes the therapist into the superego, so that the patient treats him or herself in the kindly, rational way the therapist would instead of the rigid, punitive way that most patients treat themselves (based on their early identifications). The patient internalizes the therapist into the ego as a model for how a human being might be, discarding those quirks of the therapist which are not useful. The patient internalizes the therapy relationship as a model of what a human relationship might be. The process of internalization is central to effective therapy, particularly with psychotic patients, but it goes on without explicit attention as an automatic part of the patient-therapist interaction.

The therapist must repeatedly distinguish between thoughts and feelings versus actions. All thoughts and feelings are permissible; and actions can best be controlled if the patient dares to allow him or herself freedom of feeling and of thought.

The role of insight is the same as in any psychoanalytic therapy: making the unconscious conscious, changing the defenses in part by awareness, making the connection between the past and the present. Understanding the transference is central. The more severely disturbed the patient, the more obvious the transference reaction. Schizophrenics are constantly trying to solve their problems, but they are too frightened to deal with the real problems directly; they deal with symbols. Only when the symbolic act (or symptom) and the original traumatic experience are reconnected in consciousness can the person overcome it.

When in doubt material is related by the therapist as probably concerning the mother because mothers are more important for both good and bad effects for most children than anyone else. And in early childhood, mothers seem so powerful that every experience is believed by the child to be her fault, whether or not that is objectively true.

Belief in a defect in the infant which has to be lived with rather than understood may be a way of trying to help parents not feel guilty about the possibility that they made hurtful mistakes in raising their children.

Of course, belief in a defect in the infant may be a psychoanalytically phrased justification for medication. But clinical experience as well as the research evidence is that while psychoanalytic therapy accompanied by medication may often be the fastest way to improve behavioral control, faster than either medication or therapy alone, there is a price to be paid. Psychoanalytic therapy is much more effective than medication in the long run, and the most striking advantage is the improvement in the thought disorder, the ability to think logically when you want to. But continued accompanying medication decreases the improvement in the thought disorder. When we discovered this, we thought this was probably due to the fact that all antipsychotic medications decrease emotions, including terror, which is probably the basis of their therapeutic effect. But affects within the therapy hour are also one of the curative factors in psychotherapy (not the only one, of course). Since then, however, there has been increasing evidence that antipsychotic medications are also neurotoxic (e.g., Jackson, 2005).

4. Assessment Of The Client's Problems, Goals, Strengths, and History

At the beginning of treatment, the patient was psychotic and largely incoherent, and he had no memory of anything before high school, even before his psychotic break. The material about his history emerged during the therapy sessions.

The question has been raised whether the patient was not really a manic-depressive (or severe bi-polar) rather than schizophrenic. At the time of treatment, the diagnosis was not an issue, because his outpatient psychiatrist, the psychiatrists who examined him in the hospital, and a consensus of the psychiatrists on the hospital staff had all diagnosed him as schizophrenic, with no disagreements. Similarly, he fits the current clinical criteria, *DSM-IV-TR* (American Psychiatric Association, 2000) for schizophrenia rather than bi-polar disorders. From my clinical perspective, the patient was clearly schizophrenic: his material was primarily related to terror, not to depression nor to manic symptoms.

It is interesting that when a patient diagnosed as schizophrenic recovers with good psychotherapy, many professionals raise the issue of whether the patient was not really a manic-depressive, probably because manic-depressives are known sometimes to have spontaneous recoveries. In my experience, some of those same professionals would nonetheless warn a manic-depressive against undergoing psychotherapy and warn that patient that they are doomed unless they take medication for life. That the patient got better with psychotherapy without medication would then still have been an important finding. But this patient was schizophrenic.

5. Formulation And Treatment Plan

An explicit case formulation was never a part of the treatment. A good therapist deals with what the patient brings up and where the patient is at that time.

The beauty of psychoanalytic therapy is its flexibility. At each stage, indeed in each session, the therapist deals with what seem most important at that moment, and can flexibly follow the patient into problems of any sort as they arise in the treatment.

The patient was a severely schizophrenic individual with hallucinations and delusions who nonetheless had achieved a Ph.D level of education, a good work history, and a marriage before breaking down. He had been held together by the fantasy that if only he were good enough, then his parents would accept him. When that did not happen, his defenses unraveled. But even this was not clear to me until well into the treatment.

6A. Course Of Therapy

I immediately stopped all medications and started intensive psychoanalytic treatment – 7 days the first week; 6, the second; a 5-day-a-week schedule for several months; then a four-session-per-week regimen; and eventually, a regular 3-day-a-week schedule came to be our routine. After the third year, he was seen on a once per week basis. His wife and friends of the family took turns being with him for the first 2 months of treatment. Since not eating can kill you in 30 days, the treatment started with that symptom. The second session was at 7:00 a.m. at an all-night restaurant, the kind that looks like the men's room on the subway – all white tiles.

He said, "I can't go in there. They'll think I'm crazy."

"No," I responded, "They'll think you're drunk."

"I'll throw up."

"Do you think you're the first drunk who threw up here tonight?"

I discussed food, the fear of poisoning, and its possible origins while I ate. Most important is that his mother may have resented feeding him and, therefore, felt angry whenever she fed him, which hurts a child (Karon, 1960). This was interpreted symbolically: poison, after all, is simply something you eat and you get hurt afterwards. For a baby, an angry mother is like being hit with a sledge hammer. The patient reported nausea while watching me eat. But by the second restaurant session, he took some coffee for himself. Then coffee and toast at the third session. Finally, he ate breakfast, but he objected, "I'm paying for therapy and all I do is watch you eat. I've got a right to be listened to!" At that point, we returned to the office for more traditional treatment.

I allow family members, like spouses or parents, one confidential session; any other sessions, if they wish, or contacts would be discussed with the patient. I also make myself available to spouses or parents for advice. In my initial talks with his wife, she told me they had met when they were both on Fulbright scholarships to Paris. They began living together. I got the impression of two very anxious young people clinging to each other. She said he was the most interesting man she ever met.

She had finished a Masters degree but stopped her education and was not currently working. She had grown up in the South and was, and felt she ought to be, a stay-at-home wife who was taking care of their five-year-old son. She did mention that their son was an accident.

The patient had first taken a job at a prestigious small college, but socializing with the members of his department and other faculty and administrators seemed to be a required part of the job, and he found it uncomfortable. Taking a job at a larger research university seemed to them as if they would have more choice about their private lives and more privacy. Nonetheless, things did not go well. I suggested that since he was incapacitated, she needed to resume working. This advice was helpful: she actually resented not working, but did not say so at the time because this was the early 1960's, and she felt obliged to be a traditional wife and mother. Nonetheless, she got a job teaching high school and eventually finished a Ph.D. and became a successful faculty member and assistant dean at the same research university. (It should be noted that she did go into psychoanalytic therapy herself before accomplishing these career moves.)

The details of the patient's life emerged in therapy, at first in fragments, later coherently. He described meeting his wife on the Fulbright in Paris. She was very bright and very attractive, but she was not Jewish. He had been told by someone she was "wild," but he did not know whether to believe it or not, and this still troubled him in the early years of the analysis. His mother literally told him, like the apocryphal Jewish mother stories, that he did not have to worry about the wedding because she would not be there. She would commit suicide. Right up to the day of the wedding, he was terrified that she would carry out her threat.

His previous experiences with women were not good. He both felt that he ought to be sexually active and attractive and, at the same time, any interest in sexuality or sexual activity was bad. He was intensely guilty about masturbating, feeling as many disturbed people do, that his body and his penis really did not belong to him. I told him that his parents were wrong, that his penis and his body belonged to him and that he had a right to enjoy them; his penis did not belong to his mother but to him.

The year before he went to Paris, he had been seeing a woman seriously and they took a trip to Mexico together. She met another man on the trip and had sex with the new man in the room next to his in the motel where he could hear them. This was repeated on several nights. He described his feelings of humiliation and, with my help, rage.

At the beginning of treatment, he could not read, which is a serious problem for an academic, which needed to be helped before he could consider going back to work. Taking seriously the analytic writers who relate reading inhibition to a defense against learning about sexual matters (e.g., Fenichel, 1945), when he raised this issue, I decided to give him advice. "Don't try to read professional writings or even good literature. Forget about it for now. I want you to buy a copy of Playboy and try to read it, and we'll talk about your difficulties."

It turned out he had never read Playboy, and all his life had always read only what was highly thought of. He protested my lousy taste and how awful the magazine was. I insisted he try to read it and talk about his difficulties, without explaining my choice of material. Within a few sessions, he was able to read it, while protesting all the while that it was a terrible, "pandering" magazine. While throughout the therapy, I always emphasize the importance of being able to think about anything, what seemed to make a difference was having an authority figure tell him to read sexy material, and being able to continually denounce it, and denounce my poor taste in suggesting it, and talk about the sexual ideas that came to mind. I, of course, talked about the normality of sexual curiosity and interest. After being able to read one issue, he discovered he could read ordinary books and his professional reading without trouble.

As we worked, he recalled more of his childhood. His mother, whom he idealized, used to dress him in white clothes when he was around five years old and send him out to play and then punish him for getting dirty. He felt that was all right because it was his fault. Of course, any parent knows that if you put a little boy in all white clothes in a hermetically sealed room, he would still manage to get dirty in half an hour or less. I pointed out how his mother set him up for this, that any child would get dirty, and that she probably enjoyed punishing him. He got mad at me, as most patients do when you make uncharitable comments about their parents. They often defend their parents by admitting defects that they earlier denied but which are less derogatory than your suggestions; at which point, I usually tell them they are right and I am wrong, unless they leave out something that is not speculation, but facts that they already know.

Although the patient and his family were Jewish, they lived in an Italian neighborhood in New York City. His mother, ostensibly for his safety, told him to go out and play, but not to play with those Italian kids because they are very dangerous. Of course, in an Italian neighborhood in New York City all the kids are Italian, and this advice prevented him from having friends.

All his life, he had wanted his parents' approval, and made extraordinary efforts to gain it, but nothing was enough. His parents continually cut him and his brother down. His older brother was a businessman, and when they talked to his brother, the parents talked about how brilliant the patient was and, when the patient published, what he had published. When his parents talked to the patient, they only talked about how much money his brother made and how little he did. Of course, his parents were neither brilliant nor wealthy, but they could always make their sons feel inadequate instead of feeling inadequate themselves. It was necessary to point out that both he and his brother were unusually bright and competent, but that time is limited and there is not time enough to do everything. If you decide to become a businessman, you are not going to write or get a PhD, if you become an academic you will write and get a PhD, but you're not going to make a lot of money. There just isn't time to do everything, but to do either one is an achievement.

This is particularly relevant because his psychotic break came when he finished his Ph.D. He had the fantasy that this would finally earn him the love and respect of his parents. He started teaching while completing his dissertation. When he finally finished, he was given a promotion, a raise, and tenure. He had finally done it. He called his parents to tell them the good news. They did not react. His father only asked him how much he was making. He told them he was getting a raise. Their response was that they were telling people he made more than that already.

From that point, his defenses unraveled until he was finally psychotic. Medication could not replace the triumph through acceptance that never would be.

7. Therapy Monitoring and Use of Feedback Information

Obviously, the improvement in his symptoms was the most relevant feedback that we were on the right track.

Thus, for example, one of his initial terrifying hallucinations was burning in hell. This was not a verbal or abstract thought, nor a fear of eventual punishment. It was a horrible apparently real experience.

The friend who had first referred him for treatment asked me if he had ever talked about the scar on his hand and suggested I ask him about it. When I asked the patient whether he had a scar on his hand, he told me that he did, and there was a story his mother told about the scar. According to her, they were in a store when he was a five. She saw him with a toy in his hand, and asked him where he had gotten it. He said a lady had given it to him. She asked the lady, who had not given it to him. His mother made him put it back and apologize to the lady. Then she took him by the hand, walked him home (four or five blocks), up the stairs to the third floor to their apartment, turned on a gas burner, and held his hand in the burner to teach him not to steal. The burn left a permanent scar. However, he maintained that it had no effect on him because he could not remember it.

I told him that I had a different opinion, that what you cannot remember has the most profound effect on you. I added further: "Most of us can only imagine what it would be like to burn in Hell. But you've actually been there."

Even correct interpretations do not always lead to dramatic improvement. This one did. His hallucination of burning in Hell disappeared after that session.

Early in his treatment, as he began to improve, he began to interact with people again. However, at a social gathering a physician told him that he was killing himself by seeing a psychologist, and that he should stop immediately and see a psychiatrist if he wanted to get any help at all. This set him back abruptly. His symptoms got considerably worse, and we had to spend weeks to work through the meaning of this encounter and the feelings of inevitable doom it produced, relating it not only to the present situation and the physician's lack of knowledge, but to the bad advice his mother regularly gave him, and that he needed to learn to trust his own experience, especially his own experience with people outside the family. Interestingly enough, a year later that physician developed a psychotic depression and called for help to a psychoanalytic psychiatrist in New York, who then referred the physician to the Chair of Psychiatry at the best medical school in the state, who then made a referral to a psychologist in the local area. The Chair said that he did not like referring to psychologists, but this one had done her internship in his department and was a remarkable therapist and the only professional in our local area he would trust. This psychologist, who for personal reasons was at that time confining her practice to evaluations, in turn referred the physician to me. The physician recovered with therapy. I resisted with difficulty the temptation to tell the physician how destructive that conversation had been to my patient, or even to mention that I knew of that conversation.

(Of course, I did not mention the physician's symptoms or treatment to the patient.)

When it was time for the patient to go back to work, six months after he began treatment, it was possible to schedule an appointment just before his first class. Needless to say he was scared, but we talked about it. We then walked to his class, and I waited outside the classroom until it was over. He said, "It was OK," and I left and saw him at his next appointment the next day.

Several months later he reported that his colleagues said to him, "You're not still seeing that guy, are you? You're the healthiest guy in this department."

"You know how sick I am."

"Yes, I know how sick you are, but they may be right anyway."

Even though he never kept his hospitalization or diagnosis or psychoanalytic treatment a secret, he has been offered the chairmanship of his department several times in the ensuing years. He turned it down each time because he would rather be a scholar than an administrator. He also has had an extremely helpful effect on students. "You don't have to suffer like that," he has told students with problems. "There are competent people out there who can help you. I know. I really know. I was schizophrenic. And if I can get help, you can get help."

They do not believe he was ever schizophrenic, but he assures them that he really was, and "If I could get help, you can get help."

6B. Course Of Therapy (Continued)
The Move Towards Traditional Psychoanalytic Psychotherapy With Broadening Interests

A year after treatment began, I could say to him: "Anyone can go crazy under enough stress, but under the stresses of ordinary life, you will never be psychotic again." He said, "This is better than I have ever been, better than what I used to call normality, but if you think this is good enough for me, you're crazy."

The treatment process then became more traditional. We moved to a couch and I sat behind him when it seemed more useful. (The relevant criteria are when the therapist and the patient believe that greater ambiguity and more dramatic transferences would be more likely to lead to useful material, rather than leading to less useful material, or even to re-traumatizing the patient.) In his third year, the patient startled me by saying, "I have a book to write and I can't. Is that something that you can help me with?" Somewhat dubiously, I said, "People do go into analysis for writer's block." We spent most of a year on it, and he wrote that book. He has written several since. Others in his field have told me, however, that his professional reputation is based on that first book, now considered a classic in his field. Obviously it was well worth a year's analytic work. He knew that, even if I did not.

In his pre-psychotic period, he had never eaten a meal without nausea. When eating in a restaurant he would ask his wife, "Is it safe to eat this?" But he made progress. After years of treatment, he returned from a professional meeting in San Francisco to tell me how good the food was. He gave me the name of several restaurants.

"They're not like the places you recommend. You have to spend money there. But the food is magnificent."

He returned from a trip to France and recounted with tears in his eyes, "I can't tell you what French cooking is like. There is nothing like it in the United States." I knew we had made a lot of progress.

He reported with guilt his getting cable TV just so he could watch professional football. Both he and his son would watch together.

He showed even more guilt when he got a kitten and reported liking it. His parents disapproved of any animals in the house. They said animals were dirty and no reasonable person would let a dog or a cat live with them. Remember, he thought his parents were reasonable. But his wife wanted a cat, and with misgivings he went along with her, only to discover as almost all pet owners do, that their lives are better. It was with great shame that he reported that, when his cat fell from a tree and broke its leg, he paid a $40 (in the 1960s) veterinarian fee to get its injuries attended to. "Of course you did; he is your friend," I said. His parents of course would have disapproved.

This patient saw me for 14 years, although it was on a once-per-week basis after the third year. He kept raising new issues.

He went through psychosomatic problems. At one point his upper lip became swollen for no apparent reason. He described a horrible hallucinatory experience that had occurred even this late in therapy. He didn't know what it was. Something big and white. He couldn't see it clearly. Then it was close, it felt good, it was in his mouth. But then he couldn't breathe. It was awful. He couldn't get loose or breath. It did stop, but it didn't feel like it would. I had to interpret the obvious: This was his mother's breast which felt good, but almost smothered him.

She didn't seem to know enough to make sure he could breathe. It felt like she nearly killed him and might the next time. The hallucination disappeared. And the lip swelling disappeared shortly afterwards. Now by hindsight we might think of it as a summary of his relation with his mother, but I did not think of it that way at the time.

He had a heart attack. I visited him in the hospital. He wanted to know if his heart attack was emotional in origin. I talked to his cardiologist and his internist. When I visited the hospital, the nurses asked me if I would meet with them to talk about how they should relate to heart patients because they weren't getting help. I agreed, and we met in a group, where primarily they shared with each other what they knew and their experiences of such patients. They knew more than I did, but seemed to need permission to take what they knew seriously.

I told the patient I would like his permission to get a consult with a medical psychoanalyst who would know more about heart attacks than I did. "That sounds like a good idea. What the hell do you know about heart attacks?" My consultant suggested that I encourage the patient to find out everything he could about the physical factors, and that we should review the possible emotional factors thoroughly, and we might figure it out, or we might never be sure. I relayed the advice to the patient and we reviewed everything, but we never did become sure. He reviewed all the physical factors as well, took an active attitude towards his treatment and rehabilitation, and did not become a cardiac neurotic. He did come in angry several times when he asked his physicians why they were not doing the proper tests, according to his reading, and they agreed that he was right. "I'm no doctor, why should I be telling them what to do. They should know." But his realistic anger and his ability to act intelligently on his own behalf was helpful. Interestingly enough, he has not had a second attack.

As a child, he had taken piano lessons and, as usual, worked his heart out to gain his parents' approval and eventually developed some skill at classical piano. His brother had not done well, so the teacher decided to not try to teach him much but instead taught him a couple of popular tunes. Ready for appreciation of his hard work and the skill that the piano teacher seemed to find, the patient played for his parents, only to discover that his parents did not like classical music, but they were interested in his brother's popular piano tunes. This was just another example of hard work, apparent success, and what seemed to him to be subsequent failure, that is, realistic success which was not appreciated by his parents, so it failed to win him the approval he so desperately wanted.

In therapy, he decided to take piano lessons.

"My wife isn't interested, and my kid doesn't like it, but I like it. I'm not going to bother them, I'll do it where they can't hear it, but I like it, and I am going to do it."

Eventually, he developed an interest in opera. "I know it's the lowest form of classical music, but I like it." This eventually led him to an interest in the local opera society. For years, he helped them by giving several free lectures around town before each opera presentation, with the help of a singer and pianist. He has helped create an appreciative audience for the opera guild productions.

Later, he began offering a general education course on opera at the University, which students very much liked. It was, of course, a labor of love, and undergraduate students tell me that they learned more about psychoanalysis in his discussions of the stories of operas than in their psychology courses. And he made both psychoanalysis and opera sound fascinating to them.

The Treatment of His Wife and Marital Problems

The patient also had marital problems.

I could leave her. There are bright, attractive, interesting women out there, but it would devastate her. When I needed her, she saved my life. The doctors said, "Shock him." My family said, "Shock him." People in your department said, "Shock him," but she had the courage to defy them and see that I got real treatment. And I just can't do that to her.

But as we talked about his marital problems, he finally had the courage to tell her that when they made love, he felt like a rapist. She then said, "I never told you this. I was once raped." A trusted relative had set her up on a blind date with an older man who took her to a secluded place and raped her.

The patient said to me that he wanted her to get therapy, and that she wanted therapy. "I want her to get good therapy, and I do not trust the professionals in this town. Will you please see her." We discussed whether that would be upsetting to him, but he insisted that it would not be, and he would feel better knowing she was getting competent help.

I agreed to see her, and she told me more. Not only was she raped once, but when her mother tried to arrange an abortion, the obstetrician/gynecologist told her he would abort her if she had sex with him on the obstetric table. Her mother and the nurse were on the other side of the office door. Terrified, she agreed, and when he finished, he called her a whore and said he would never do anything as unethical as abortion. This second rape was more traumatic than the first. She eventually got an abortion. Years later, she heard that the obstetrician who performed the abortion safely and for a reasonable fee was jailed for a later abortion.

Despite my patient's urgings, it became clear that my seeing his wife was causing problems in the treatment for both of them. His treatment was slowing down. Material about being treated for someone else's benefit kept coming up, but discussion of it did not seem to help. I sought consultation, which helped me undo my mistake. I referred her to the nearest analyst of any competence, 40 miles away. She was sad and angry at me for that decision, but we talked about it, and she followed through and got real help. Her husband also got angry at me, but it was clear that afterwards both treatments were much better.

She developed breast cancer, and had one breast removed. Because the hospital would not trouble the cancer surgeon on the weekend, when she developed a pulmonary infection postoperatively they did not treat it with antibiotics for three days, and she still suffers from complications to her breathing.

He said the surgery and her lack of breast did not bother him. But he got interested in another woman. His wife learned of it, and luckily was still in therapy. He said she told him that maybe he was working through something, but she would give him three months. If it wasn't over by then, their marriage was. While initially angered, he began to bring up material indicating that the scars and absent breast were horrible and scared him, and his associations led to his own fear of castration, that is, literal fantasies of being mutilated and castrated. Long before the three months were up, he had given up his interest in the other woman, because he realized how much he really liked and admired his wife.

When she got her Ph.D., she was hired by the University. She became interested in methods of teaching and taught well. He talked about being guilty because he was not a good teacher, because he did not live up to her views on what a good teacher does. Of course, he was an excellent teacher, but he needed me to point out that there are many ways of teaching, that his wife knew one, which worked very well for her, but that he was also a good teacher, and there was no reason to change or to have to do things her way. Of course, the transference from his mother had to be pointed out.

The Final Years: Work on His Relationship With His Son

He described his need for the last two years of treatment: "I have a teenaged son. When he was a kid, he had a psychotic father. That was a hell of a thing to do to a kid. And I need help in undoing the harm I did him."

He and his son shared an interest in spectator sports -football and basketball. While he had been anything but athletic in his younger years, he had often shared a fantasy with me of wishing he could be a professional football player, a defensive lineman -Alex Karras – who, in addition to being a very funny man, was a very good football player. He was disappointed with his son, who refused to go out for high school football as a freshman, and he felt that the son would be a weakling like him. The son was neither tall enough nor agile enough for basketball to be an issue. The same medical analyst who had helped me with dealing with his heart attacks pointed out to me that high school football was a medical risk and his son was being rational and he should support his son's decision. It was helpful to him to think about it that way.

His son was having academic problems, despite having two parents who were college professors. As we talked, it became clear that the patient was terrified that his son would have the same problems in life he had. To save his son, he withdrew and did not share most of his life and thoughts with his son. He did not allow the son to identify with him, for fear of his son going through the hell he had gone through. He had to become aware of this fearful withdrawal from his son and to learn to not hold back, but to share all the good things in life that he knew about and enjoyed. The boy straightened out, went on to college, earned a Masters degree and had a successful career. When his son had a child, the patient was afraid his son would not be able to relate to the child, but both he and his wife were delighted to discover how well their child was relating to his infant son, their grandson.

8. Concluding Evaluation Of The Therapy's Process and Outcome

The patient is now internationally renowned in his field. He is an outstanding scholar and teacher, as well as a good husband and father. His therapy did not make him a bright man or a kind man, but it did keep his brightness and kindness from being destroyed. It did allow him to feel safe, perceive and think realistically and creatively, and use his intelligence and kindness to make his own and other people's lives more interesting.

A few years ago (more than 20 years after the completion of treatment) the patient sent me a copy of a magazine article about a prestigious award that he had received with a note saying that he had never properly thanked me for giving him back a life. Remembering the role of his parents never acknowledging his achievements had in producing his problems, I wrote back that, "From time to time I have heard from people in your field about your accomplishments and from your students about your teaching, and it has always been a source of satisfaction that I was available when you needed me."

REFERENCES

American Psychiatric Association (2000). Diagnostic and Statistical Manual of Mental Disorders, Fourth Edition, Text Revision. Washington, DC: American Psychiatric Association.

Breggin, P.R., & Cohen, D. (1999). Your Drug May Be Your Problem. Cambridge, MA: Perseus.

Deikman, A.J., & Whitaker, L.C. (1979). Humanizing a psychiatric ward: Changing from drugs to psychotherapy. Psychotherapy: Theory, Research, and Practice, 16, 204-214.

Dorman, D. (2003). Dante's Cure. New York: Other Press.

Fenichel, O. (1945). The Psychoanalytic Theory of Neurosis. New York: Norton.

Fromm-Reichmann, F. (1947). Transference problems in schizophrenia. In S. S. Tomkins (Ed.), Contemporary Psychopathology (pp. 371-380). Cambridge, MA: Harvard University Press.

Greenberg, J. (1964). I Never Promised You a Rose Garden. New York: Holt, Rinehart, and Winston.

ISPS-US (2006). Web site of the United States Chapter of the International Society for the Psychological Treatments of Schizophrenia and Other Psychoses: http://www.isps-us.org/

Jackson, G.E. (2005). Rethinking psychiatric drugs: A guide for informed consent. Bloomington, IN: AuthorHouse.

Joseph, J. (2004). Schizophrenia and heredity: why the emperor has no genes. In J. Read, L. R. Mosher, & R. P. Bentall (Eds.), Models of Madness: Psychological, Social, and Biological Approaches to Schizophrenia (pp. 67-84). Hove and New York: Brunner-Routledge.

Karon, B.P. (1960). A clinical note on the significance of an "oral" trauma. Journal of Abnormal and Social Psychology, 61, 480-491.

―――― (1994). Effective Psychoanalytic Therapy of Schizophrenia and Other Severe Disorders (videotape and supporting written material). The APA Psychotherapy Videotape Series. Washington, D.C.: American Psychological Association.

―――― (2003). The tragedy of schizophrenia without psychotherapy. The Journal of the American Academy of Psychoanalysis and Dynamic Psychiatry, 31, 89-118.

―――― (2005). Recurrent psychotic depression is treatable by psychoanalytic therapy without medication. Ethical Human Psychology and Psychiatry, 6, 45-56.

―――― & VandenBos, G.R. (1972). The consequences of psychotherapy for schizophrenic patients. Psychotherapy: Theory, Research & Practice, 9, 111-119.

―――― (in press). Karon's Pathogenesis Index. In S. R. Jenkins (Ed.), Empirically Validated Scoring Scales for the Thematic Apperception Test.

―――― & VandenBos, G.R. (1981). Psychotherapy of Schizophrenia: The Treatment of Choice. New York: Aronson. (Blue Ridge Summit, PA: Rowman & Littlefield Edition).

―――― & Widener, A.J. (1994). Is there really a schizophrenogenic parent? Psychoanalytic Psychology, 11, 47-61.

Ratner, S.G., Karon, B.P., VandenBos, G.R., & Denny, M.R. (1981). The adaptive significance of the catatonic stupor in humans and animals from an evolutionary perspective. Academic Psychology Bulletin, 3, 273-279.

Read, J., Goodman, L., Morrison, A.P., Ross, C.A., & Aderhold, V. (2004). Childhood trauma, loss, and stress. In J. Read, L.R. Mosher, & R.P. Bentall (Eds.), Models of Madness: Psychological, Social, and Biological Approaches to Schizophrenia (pp. 223-252). Hove and New York: Brunner-Routledge.

――――, Mosher, L.R., & Bentall, R. P. (Eds.). (2004). Models of Madness: Psychological, Social, and Biological Approaches to Schizophrenia. Hove and New York: Brunner-Routledge.

―――― & Ross, C.A. (2003). Psychological trauma and psychosis: Another reason why people diagnosed schizophrenic must be offered psychological therapies. The Journal of the American Academy of Psychoanalysis and Dynamic Psychiatry, 31, 247-268.

————, Seymour, F., & Mosher, L.R. (2004). Unhappy families. In J. Read, L.R. Mosher, & R.P. Bentall (Eds.), Models of Madness: Psychological, Social, and Biological Approaches to Schizophrenia (pp. 253-268). Hove and New York: Brunner-Routledge.

Silver, A.S., & Larsen, T.K. (eds.) (2003). Special Issue: The Schizophrenic Person and the Benefits of the Psychotherapies – Seeking a PORT in the Storm. The Journal of the American Academy of Psychoanalysis and Dynamic Psychiatry, 31(1).

Strean, H.S., & Freeman, L. (1990). The Severed Soul. New York: St. Martin's Press.

Teixeira, M. (1992). Psychoanalytic theory and therapy in the treatment of manic-depressive disorders. Psychoanalysis and Psychotherapy, 11, 81-96.

Whitaker, R. (2002). Mad in America. Cambridge, MA: Perseus.

Section 2:
ESSAYS ON PSYCHOANALYSIS AND PSYCHOTHERAPY

CHAPTER 15
Techniques of Primitive Witchcraft in Modern Psychotherpy
Edward S. and Bertram P. Karon

It is one of the conceits of western man that only his culture is rational. But the apparent irrationality of so-called "primitive" tribes is often more a function of a lack of understanding on the part of the observer than of a real increase in irrationality over western society. As Malinowski (1945: 41-51) pointed out, every culture includes an empirical body of knowledge and techniques necessary for subsistance, and this knowledge is never confused with magic. If a society did not have such a body of knowledge, it could not have survived. However, in every society there are problems for which there seems to be no answer. To meet the psychological need for an answer to the unanswerable, as for example, the problem of death, man evolves magical and religious beliefs. What is often not recognized is that these magical beliefs may, themselves, have a perfectly empirical base; that is, they work. Although the members of a primitive society may not know why they work, those magical techniques which produce the desired effects will be reserved, and those which are ineffective will not be retained.

To western man this seems like a contradiction. How can magic be based on empiricism? Yet even in western society if we go back to the time when magic was widespresd, we will find that it had an empirical basis.

For example, in the writings of Paracelsus (Pachter, 1951) we find that magic consists of finding the immutable laws by which the universe operates. Although we would disagree with his conclusions about the nature of demons or even their existence, we would disagree very little with his manner of arriving at these conclusions; for this turns out to be quite simply whether or not they predict events which, in fact, occur and whether or not his attempts to utilize supernatural forces produce results he desires.

From the early days of psychoanalysis, it has been recognized that there is a functional kinship between the psychoanalyst in modern society and the witchdoctor in primitive society, that is, that the psychoanalyst performs the same function — psychotherapy — for modern society that the witchdoctor performs for primitive society.

In western society the most highly developed technique of psychotherapy is, of course, psychoanalysis. The classical technique was devised by Freud (1950) in dealing with conversion hysterias. With only slight modifications it proved to be applicable to anxiety hysterias and obsessive-compulsive neuroses as well. Although the theory of psychoanalysis has far ranging implications, as a therapeutic technique it becomes less and less effective as the patient's symptoms diverge from these classical syndromes. Freud (1950), himself, was very careful again and again to stress the limited range of problems for which it had proved effective.

None-the-less, the attempt to deal with other pathologies has been spurred on by the insights which psychoanalytic theory provides. In general, these other syndromes have yielded to therapeutic efforts only when supplementary techniques have been devised to surmount those obstacles on which classical techniques have foundered. Psychosis, especially schizophrenic psychosis, has proved to be one of those pathologies most recalcitrant to therapy whether that therapy be physical or psychological. The core of the therapeutic problem, according to Freud (1950), was the inability of the patient to form a transference, that is, a strong emotional relationship with the therapist. Fromm-Reichmann (1943: 371-380, 1950) demonstrated that a transference could be established with such patients; but she and her co-workers have found the transference in such cases to be fragile and to require a long period of patient work before it gained sufficient strength. More recently, alternative psychoanalytically-based psychotherapies are in the process of being developed. The junior author, whose approach to the therapy of psychosis is a modification of one of these, Direct Analysis by Rosen (1953), has found in certain situations that the transference could be established quickly and therapeutic progress gained through the use of certain techniques which have a psychoanalytic rationale, but which turn out upon examination to be identical in form with what any good witchdoctor would have done.

For example, a male paranoid schizophrenic, age 32, after 16 years of institutionalization arrived at an institution where the junior author was to work with him. The patient continuously made magic gestures to protect himself. Shortly after he arrived, he went into a state of catatonic-like rigidity when his magic gestures were interfered with. When the therapist tried to talk to him he suddenly ran to the farthest corner of the room. The therapist followed him, and he ran away again. He repeated this a couple of times and finally screamed, "Don't hit me! Don't hit me! Don't hit me!"

The therapist who was taken by surprise , reacted spontaneously, "I won't hit you. I promise you I won't hit you."

"I know you won't, but him." The patient pointed his finger at empty space. The therapist whirled and began arguing with "him".

"You! Get out of here or I'll kill you. If you hurt him you'll have to deal with me and I'll kill you!"

The therapist went through the motions of arguing and threatening, all the while keeping one eye on the patient. When the patient relaxed the therapist turned toward him and said, "You see, he's gone."

The patient agreed and was ready to talk about his problems to the therapist who he now thought would protect him. He could face the omnipotent malevolent figures of his schizophrenic world now that he had an omnipotent benevolent figure (from the psychoanalytic standpoint, an omnipotent benevolent parent-figure) in the form of the therapist. With this security he could afford to neglect his own magical defenses and try to understand his sickness. To use the patient's words, "They (the people of his fantasies) said there wasn't any real world, that I didn't have to pay any attention to anything in the outside world. But they lied to me because they're afraid of you. When you talk, they run away." The only difficulty in the therapy which was engendered by the use of this technique was that occasionally the patient would complain that he didn't understand why the therapist would insist on analyzing hallucinations when "you can get rid of them the easy way."

The parallel between this technique and the regular practice of witchdoctors becomes even more evident in the following case.

This is the case of a chronic catatonic patient who was given to intermittent periods of extreme violence. The patient, a muscular man in his twenties, lay writhing in restraints in bed, screaming continuously in terror. He had been screaming for hours according to the people who were taking care of him despite all efforts to calm or reassure him. The therapist tried to find out what the problem was. "What's the matter, son?"

The patient gasped, "Ghosts," and then continued screaming.

The therapist turned his back on the patient and commanded, "Listen ghosts! Listen to me! Leave this boy alone. You may come into the room, but you may not harm him tonight or I will kill you, myself. If you harm this boy I will destroy you. I will kill you! You may come into the room, but you must not harm this boy or I will kill you, myself!"

The screaming had ceased. The patient lay there quietly sleeping.

Here we see that what was said is practically identical with witchdoctor's incantations as they are transcribed from various parts of the world.

Both of these patients were institutionalized psychotics. However, the use of the witchcraft-like techniques in therapy is not limited to such cases. Whenever a patient believes in magic and includes in his complaints the feeling that he is under some magical attack it is useful, and in fact indicated, to deal with the magic in quasi-magical terms.

A 53 year old married woman was brought to the out-patient clinic by one her sons. Her complaint was that she was being killed by a voodoo spell that had been cast upon her. She believed there was a snake coiled around one of the lamps in her home, and she would sweep all rubble under that lamp as an offering. Although the initial examination revealed quite clearly that she was an ambulatory psychotic who was actively hallucinating, the senior author felt that the case could be adequately treated on an out-patient basis. His prognosis was confirmed by the subsequent progress of the patient.

The patient had been surrounded in her childhood with people who believed in voodoo, and her own interest had only been whetted by the fact that her father had strictly forbidden any mention of voodoo in his home. As an adult she had for some years numbered among her friends a woman who was a voodoo witchdoctor. Her psychotic symptoms seemed to have been precipitated by the simultaneous occurrence of her menopause, the marriage of three of her children, and her husband becoming so ill that he could no longer help support the family. She had interfered in her oldest daughter's marriage, but the dissolution of the union had not reinstated the patient's former position of dominance with respect to the daughter.

It was the in-laws of this daughter whom the patient felt had placed the hex upon her. She, at first, had complained that those possessions which her daughter had left with her were hexed. When the family ignored these complaints, she became more violent and bathed herself in urine and insisted that the daughter must do the same in order to avoid the voodoo. Since the patient was of considerable physical strength, the family became frightened and brought her for therapy.

In the early sessions when the patient mentioned the voodoo attack, the therapist told her flatly that his magic was superior to other types of magic, "White magic is always stronger than black magic. The healer, from Jesus on, always wins over the destroyer. If this were not so, we would all be dead." The patient was able to accept this. With the security of the therapist's protection, the patient could now face the true meaning of her symptoms. For example, it was now possible for the therapist to say to her in the presence of her family, "Do not bathe your daughter in urine unless you wish to harm her." As mentioned before, this patient, whose symptoms were far more severe than those which are usually treated on an out-patient basis, progressed to a complete remission under psychotherapy.

Even with neurotics, situations may arise where the use of so-called witchcraft is indicated.

An 18 year old, unmarried girl, a freshman coed at a teacher's college, was referred to the senior author. Her symptom consisted of a single, fixed, obsession; namely, that her stepmother would have her destroyed by magic before the end of the school year. She had been born and reared in a superstitious part of Northern Nebraska, and despite her high intelligence, had absorbed the local belief that death was inevitable once a real witch-woman had so predicted. The underlying basis for her death fear proved in the analysis to be a death wish directed against the step-mother for taking the place with the father that she wished for herself. Before psychoanalytic therapy in the conventional fashion was possible, it was necessary to give this girl a sense of security.

But with a neurotic one cannot simply say, "I am a magician more powerful than those who oppose you". The neurotic will see through any such statement as having been concocted by a therapist who does not take her complaint seriously. Instead, it is necessary to allow the patient to come to this conclusion without being told directly.

When the patient raised the problem of witchcraft, she expected the therapist to be dubious. Instead, she was greeted by the statement, "I can't very well poke fun at witchcraft or magic. No one from my town ever can". In response to the patient's query the therapist, who was in fact from Massachusetts, told her that his home town was Salem. In view of the connotations of Salem, the therapist felt that no further reference need be made, except for a casual statement that there are superior and inferior witches, and inferior witches can be destroyed.

The patient's associations showed clearly that, as expected, she had jumped to the conclusion that the therapist was, indeed, a witch of superior force who could protect her against any magical attack. This conclusion gave her the security to face a psychoanalytic exploration of her difficulties.

Thus we see that two different therapists working in western society, and faced with the problem of devising techniques for dealing with situations where classical techniques were inadequate, found themselves employing procedures which proved to be effective and which, upon subsequent analysis, were revealed as being essentially the same as those employed by primitive witch doctors. This suggests the pragmatic validity of primitive practices which may account for the similarities in magical practices occurring in unrelated cultures. The differences between our procedures and those of the witchdoctor may be summarized as follows: first, of course, we do not believe the words we use literally, but explain their effectiveness in terms of western psychoanalytic theory, whereas, the witchdoctor presumably believes in what he is saying in a more direct fashion; secondly, this for us is not the end of therapy, but is a means of developing a transference and giving the patient sufficient security so that he can utilize ordinary psychoanalytic and psychotherapeutic techniques for gaining insight into his problem.

Any remission of symptoms, no matter how complete, if produced by a therapy which does not lead to increased insight would be termed by analysts a transference cure. Certainly, the authors would place the cures of the witchdoctor in this category. But when we are tempted to sneer from the vantage point of enlightened western civilization, that these are transference and not "real" cures, we recall that Glover (1955: 37) reports that here in western civilization transference cures occasionally occur which are as lasting and effective from the patient's standpoint as what we would call "real" cures. This in no way alters the major weakness of such a "cure". In the transference cure the prime faith and reliance is entirely upon the analyst instead of the self. Circumstances may arise that cause injury to that faith. If the patient's major reliance is in himself and his faith in himself is shaken, the counselor, or possibly another counselor, would be able to restore it. In other words, so long as the entire burden is not placed upon a god-like figure, whatever reliance is placed can be more easily retained over the years.

Yet sometimes we are tempted to wonder whether if we knew as much about producing transference cures as does the witchdoctor, we might not then have the solution to the now insolvable problem of what to do with the great mass of people who need help and who will never get it because of the lack of adequately trained therapists in our society.

Summary

The irrationality of "primitive" tribes is often more a function of the observer's inability to understand than of a real increase in irrationality over Western society. Every culture includes practitioners of psychotherapy. Modifications are still being evolved to deal with problems which are unresponsive to conventional approaches. Techniques similar to those employed by primitive witchdoctors produced therapeutic progress for two institutionalized psychotics, an ambulatory psychotic, and a phobic neurotic, when conventional techniques proved inapplicable or ineffective. The techniques, their aims, and limitations in psychoanalytic therapy are discussed.

REFERENCES

Freud, S.: On psychotherapy. Collected papers, vol. I, pp. 249-263 (Hogarth and the Institute of Psychoanalysis, London 1950a). — On the history of the psychoanalytic movement. Collected papers, vol. I, pp. 287-359 (Hogarth and Institute of Psychoanalysis, London 1950b). — Psychoanalytic notes upon an autobiographical account of a case of paranoia (dementia paranoides). Collected papers, vol. Ill, pp. 372-390 (Hogarth and the Institute of Psychoanalysis, London 1950c). — On narcism: an introduction. Collected papers, vol. IV, pp. 30-59 (Hogarth and the Institute of Psychoanalysis, London 195 od).

Fromm-Reichmann, Frieda: Transference problems in schizophrenics. In S.S. Tomkins (ed.). Contemporary psychopathology, pp. 371-380 (Harvard Press, Cambridge, Mass. 1943). — Principles of intensive psychotherapy (University of Chicago, Chicago 1950).

Glover, E.: The technique of psychoanalysis, p. 37 (Balliere, Tindall & Cox, London 1955).

Malinowski, B.: The functional theory of culture. The dynamics of culture change, pp. 41-51 (Yale, New Haven 1945).

Metraux, A.: Voodoo in Haiti, chapts. III-V (Oxford University Press, London 1959)-

Pachter, H.M.: Magic into science (Schuman, New York 1951).

Rosen, J.N.: Direct analysis (Grune & Stratton, New York 1953).

Sigerist, H.E.: A History of medicine, vol. 1, pp. 377-492 (Oxford University Press, London 1951).

CHAPTER 16
Analyzability or the Ability to Analyze?

BERTRAM P. KARON, Ph.D.

How is it possible to analyze? It used to be traditional for psychoanalytic institutes to have a course in analyzability. While many institutes today do not have such a course, others still do. Even in many of the institutes that do not have such a course, the question is still considered seriously, but often inadequately. The question is usually formulated in terms of there being certain patients who are analyzable and certain patients who are not analyzable. In essence, the question is whether the patient is good enough to be analyzed; that is, whether the patient has a high level of ego functioning and object relations, which will make a therapeutic alliance easy to achieve, and a full transference neurosis easy to develop, easily tolerated, and easily resolved. A great deal of thought has gone into what aspects of ego functioning are most relevant and how best to measure them. On the other hand, history shows how vain this search is.

It is the wrong question. The right question is, What needs to be done to make this person an analyzable patient?

The problem of the analyzable patient is not just a problem for institutes and training. Today we hear analysts decrying the absence of suitable patients. You cannot make a living as a psychoanalyst; there are just too many psychoanalysts and not enough psychoanalytic patients. And if, by "suitable patient," you mean someone who does not have serious problems, has no serious ego deficits or characterological problems, makes no phone calls, has no emergencies or unexpected crises, comes in four or five times a week, and pays a large fee, indeed there may very well be few analyzable patients.

But if a suitable patient is someone who is hurting badly and is willing to work because he or she is desperate, who may have to be seen on a sliding scale, who has crises and provides challenges, then there are patients, and they are interesting, treatable patients.

In the 1950s, it was traditional in many institutes, perhaps in most, to rule out all borderlines as unanalyzable; it was believed you could precipitate a psychotic break by uncovering, and if you precipitated a psychotic break, there was nothing you could do. Yet, today, it is not unusual to hear that the borderline patient represents the domain where psychoanalysis is uniquely effective, even from professionals who prefer to treat their patients with medication or makeshift therapies.

Of course, even by the 1950s, Karl Abraham had treated manic-depressives in Berlin; Editha Sterba had successfully treated two autistic children in Vienna; Sullivan and Fromm-Reichmann and their students had analyzed schizophrenics; and the Kleinians, with different theory and technique, had treated both schizophrenics and manic-depressives successfully. Bettelheim, Ekstein, and Anthony had already separately written about pioneering work with psychotic children. Aichhom had worked with delinquents. The list goes on: Lidz, Boyer, Giovacchini, Benedetti, Rosenfeld, Eissler, Tustin, and many others. One can argue that the diagnoses were wrong, but our careful reading of the published case histories indicates that their patients fully meet the DSM-IV (*American Psychiatric Association,* 1994) diagnostic criteria. (This does not preclude the possibility that there may be primarily organic syndromes that also meet the diagnostic criteria, as is claimed for autism, or the possibility that neurotoxic medication or ECT may produce organic syndromes.) There was a growing body of exciting literature dealing with difficult patients that all analysts knew, but of whom most analysts seemed afraid. Unfortunately, in a day when drug companies attempt to intimidate psychoanalysts with advertising, often presented as continuing education, the fact that diffi-cult patients have frequently been treated successfully by psychoanalysis and psychoanalytic therapy is surprisingly not known. Thus, Willick (2001), despite being a psychoanalyst, seems not to know that any schizophrenic ever was successfully treated by psychoanalytic therapy, and certainly not without medication, when he argues, in similar fashion, that ADHD, obsessive-compulsive disorders, borderline, and character disorders are biological disorders best treated by medication and chides his colleagues for not agreeing with him.

Among those who derided psychoanalysis in the past, the analyzable patient was referred to snidely as the YAVIS-patient (that is, young, attractive, verbal, intelligent, and successful). A myth developed that only such people were treated by psychoanalysts. The equally hostile current phrase is "the worried well." Of course, this was never the truth. Fre-quently, only the patient and the analyst knew the hell in which the patient lived before analysis. Nor should anyone else know. Nonetheless, the kernel of truth in these criticisms lay in the search for the "analyzable" patient. In the words of Reuben Fine (1990), "It is clear that among analysts, a considerable caution has arisen concerning which patients are analyzable and which are not. This caution suggests that the image of 'analyzability' has become an ideal fiction that few patients can live up to" (p. 506). Obviously, Fine did not agree with such limitations.

On the other hand, there are more optimistic recent discussions, like Ehrenberg (1992) and Rothstein (1995), which are more in keeping with my experience. They argue persuasively for the analyst doing what is necessary to enable the patient to become analyzable.

Fenichel's (1945) criteria of analyzability, originally formulated for psychoanalytic institutes, is used as a basis for organizing this discussion. Although antiquated, his criteria are more sensible than many, because he explicitly stated that there were frequent examples of their being wrong.

Age between sixteen and forty, although he noted successes younger and older did occur. Of course, even then child analysis was fully accepted as real, but he obviously felt that the technique was so different that it warranted a separate discussion. One of Freud's most serious mistakes (which Fenichel apparently accepted) was the notion that patients over forty were not analyzable. Most of us today regularly work with patients in their fifties and sixties, and Riess (1992) reported working successfully psychoanalytically with patients into their eighties and nineties.

Feeblemindedness is a contraindication, although he noted that pseudo-feeblemindedness may disappear in analysis, and that some truly feebleminded patients may nonetheless benefit from analytic therapy. Sarason (1968) has reported analytic therapy being very helpful for people with low IQ's whose IQ does not change, but whose life adjustment typically does, although analysts and thera-pists find them uninteresting, which is not the same as untreatable.

Unfavorable life situations. Here, Fenichel is different from Freud, as quoted by Rollo May (personal communication), who said he would still analyze because "it is better to go down in a fair fight with destiny than to be a neurotic." Of course, all of us know that what may seem like unalterably bad circumstances may be changeable when the patient becomes more effective.

Triviality. Some symptoms are not worth the trouble.

Disturbances of speech (although he mentions cases where the analysis was carried out in writing temporarily).

Secondary gains that make the symptoms too valuable to lose. Certainly this is still a valid concern. He here includes, however, the fears artists have of losing their creativity. He suggests that more artists have been helped to overcome blocks to productivity than have had their art interfered with. I have worked with three artists and one writer, and their art played no role in their analyses—it was the one area of their lives that was least problematic. They did not want nor need help with their art. Almost everything else in their lives was a disaster. Luckily for them, this analyst knows so little about art that it would not have been possible to intelligently intrude in their work. Nonetheless, their colleagues felt their art improved after analysis.

The one instance where an artist asked about art was a chronic paranoid schizophrenic artist who explicitly asked about the connection between "shitting and painting" after being in a phase where he could only paint in browns and blacks. After our discussion of feces as gifts to his mother, and the disillusioning discovery that she really did not like them, and the substitution of smearing brown and black substances on canvas, he was able to paint in color and never asked another psychodynamic question about painting.

Urgency. It may be felt that relief is urgently required and that analytic technique is too slow. Of course, one deals with an emergency in the way most likely to succeed. Hospitalization is a resource. Medication, if you believe it is the best way to handle a crisis, is a resource. Medication can be helpful in a crisis. Medication can also be helpful to temporarily stabilize the patient so therapy can begin, but if so used it should be withdrawn as quickly as the patient can tolerate (Karon & VandenBos, 1981). Medications have been oversold, are not nearly as effective as the manufacturers say, have more side-effects (including possible neurotoxicity of antipsychotics) than the manufacturers say, habituate, and have serious withdrawal effects (Breggin & Cohen, 1999). Moreover, they frequently represent the analyst's wish for relief from having to think about the meaning of difficult patients, or the analyst's wish for omnipotence, or the need to devalue the analyst's abilities (from the analyst's childhood), or the wish to increase one's income (medicating patients is more lucrative than analyzing, e.g., Moran, 1993) or ingratiate oneself with biologically oriented colleagues.

Some analysts today are afraid of being sued for not medicating, not realizing there is a literature of successful treatment without medication. The Chestnut Lodge case is usually cited as if it set a legal precedent (an impression the drug companies have tried to foster). A physician who had been referred to Chestnut Lodge because previous medication had not helped him was treated without medication. He was unhappy with his treatment, signed himself out of the hospital, claimed that antidepressant medication subsequently helped him, and sued the hospital for not medicating him. The hospital settled the claim out of court. But the case never came to trial, and out-of-court settlements do not set legal precedents (Stone, 1990). The empirical data on the limited effectiveness of antidepressant medication is summarized in Antonuccio, Danton, DeNelsky, Greenberg, and Gordon (1999) and the empirical data on the limited effectiveness of mood-stabilizing medication is presented by Gitlin, Swendsen, Heller, and Hammen (1995). Breggin and Cohen (1999) include good advice for minimizing legal risks when helping patients withdraw from medication.

ECT is not a helpful resource (Breggin, 1998; Morgan, 1999). The worst parody of the criteria of analyzability came from a senior staff psychologist of what was often described as the most psychoanalytic hospital in Philadelphia in the 1950s. In this hospital, where all the psychiatric residents were psychoanalytic candidates and most of the psychiatric staff were analysts, almost all the in-patients and fifty outpatients were shocked every Monday, Wednesday, and Friday. Common in Philadelphia at that time were psychiatrists who were analysts for prestige with a shock practice for income. It depends, I was told, on what you mean by psychoanalysis. They meant the treatment of the classical syndromes four or five times a week on a couch. What do you do with people who have something else wrong with them or who can't afford it? Either you don't treat them or you shock them. "We shock them. We think it's kinder."

At a recent meeting, a psychoanalyst discussed obsessively the parameter of being more active and kindly to a patient who was anxious, but mentioned putting the patient on medication as if it were a trivial decision that did not have transference and countertransference implications incidentally, it has been reported that now 30% of training cases at one prestigious psychoanalytic institute are on medication. It is interesting that recovery in training cases at that institute has been reported to have dropped from 69% before 1987 to 39% from 1988 to 1992 (Glick, Eagle, Luber & Roose, 1996). It might be argued that this is the result of choosing more difficult training cases, which require medication and still do not do well. More likely, the use of medication slows down the process of underlying change with psychoanalysis, because all psychiatric medications interfere with affective responses; affective responses during the analytic hour, and learning to pay attention to them, are essential parts of the analytic process of therapy (Karon & VandenBos, 1981).

It was a training analyst at that institute who described, in an out-of-town colloquium on sexual addictions, treating an attractive young woman who was a gym instructor who slept with a different man each day. She would not lie on the couch, and this analyst could not figure out why. One day she came in and said she was ready for the couch. She was wearing a miniskirt and the top buttons of her blouse were unbuttoned, exposing her breasts. She crossed her legs, and she was wearing no underwear.

If this were my patient, I would have asked her if she had seen the movie, Basic Instinct. If, as was most likely, she said yes, I would have said, "I wonder if you are afraid you might kill me?" Other psychoanalytic colleagues have told me they would have asked her if she were afraid she might be a lesbian, or most tactfully, if there was something that she did not want me to find out about? Any of these questions might have furthered a psychoanalytic exploration. But this psychoanalytic "expert" did none of these. He explained that he did not have sex with her (as if that were even an issue) and that he put her on Prozac. (The audience, but not the expert, noticed the similarity to her mother putting her on Ritalin to quiet her down.) When a member of the audience asked if he helped her get off Prozac, he said, "I find I can't stop Prozac," and most of the audience uncharitably concluded he was speaking of himself.

There are, however, emergency psychotherapeutic interactions for crisis situations. One can argue that they are psychoanalytic therapy, not psychoanalysis. The important thing is to do what is necessary to deal with the crisis, whether it is suicide, homicide, or some other serious issue (e.g., Karon & VandenBos, 1981, pp. 231-320). But political considerations have clouded the issues.

In the early days of psychoanalysis, Freud and the other psychoanalysts did whatever they thought was necessary for their patients' good. When the phrase "psychoanalytic therapy" was used, it referred to psychoanalysis as therapy. But in the 1940s, the work of Alexander and French (1946) and their co-workers, in attempting to speed up psychoanalysis to make it more widely available, stirred up a hornet's nest of political strife. Psychoanalytic institutes split over whether these ideas should be considered a part of psychoanalysis, instead of simply asking of each idea whether it was good or bad, and what the advantages and disadvantages were of each technical procedure. It became important politically to prove that one was practicing "psychoanalysis" and not "psychoanalytic therapy." In the words of a psychoanalytic candidate in the 1950s, now a well-known analyst, "In our institute we practice psychoanalysis just exactly the way Freud did. As a matter of fact, I don't know what Freud was doing, Freud wasn't practicing analysis." To know that Freud would be too creative to be acceptable may have been accurate, but to be proud of it (as opposed to disagreeing with specific ideas) was bizarre.

Sharp distinctions between psychoanalysis and psychoanalytic therapy are problematic, as is what Eissler has termed "parameter phobia," a disorder of inadequate analysts. Preferable is the definition used by many analysts that psychoanalytic therapy is as much like psychoanalysis as the defenses of the patient, the time available, and the skill of the therapist permit.

When I was first supervised by Richard Sterba, I expected this egoanalyst and student of Freud's to object to my active intervention in a case. I had been treating the patient for several months before beginning the supervision. I recounted how, in the third week of analysis, the patient casually mentioned for the first time that her husband beat her approximately once a week. He was a very athletic man, who was probably a borderline disorder with poor impulse control, despite a successful professional career. She said that she left him early in their marriage after a beating, but his father had said to her that she really did not know much about men. She agreed that she did not. He then proceeded to tell her that men are just like that and that she should accept it. She told him that she did not know that, and went back to her husband and stayed with him for the many years of their marriage.

As is usually the case with abused wives, it was the analyst rather than the patient who considered it a serious problem. I asked for more details. It became clear that he hit her under two circumstances. One, he told her he had done something wrong; she agreed with him and told him how wrong he was, and he hit her. Two, there was an issue between them, and she took the women's-magazine view that they should talk it out until they agreed. Eventually, to stop the conversation, he hit her.

I pointed out the two situations and gave her direct advice. I told her that when her husband says he has done something wrong, he is not asking for moral instruction. In fact, she was not even giving him useful information, because he had already told her he had done something wrong. Instead of his feeling guilty, she became his punisher. No one likes to be punished, and then he hit her. When he told her he had done something wrong, all she had to do was listen. That is all he wanted, and that is all she needs to do.

Secondly, she was told that when she and her husband disagree, they did not have to agree about anything. She did not have to tell him she did not agree, if she did not think it was safe to do so. If she thought it was safe, she should tell him she disagreed, because she would feel better.

But when she had told him once, she should stop. She had given him the useful information. She was told that no one ever changes his or her mind in an argument. If he likes you, he will take it into account when he has a chance to think about it. But immediately he will only defend his view, and eventually hit her to stop the conversation. She was told to say it once and stop.

After this one session, she was never hit again. She said that he did not hit her any more, but that she knew how to make him hit her, and that she felt like doing it. That, she was told, was why she needed analysis. (In fact, as was revealed in the analysis, she had had a mother who only held her when she was hitting her.) Her husband later said that all the fun had gone out of their marriage. Eventually, they divorced, and she went on to a much better second husband.

Naively, I expected this classical Viennese ego-analyst, teaching me ego analysis, to object to my activity. Surprisingly, he smiled approvingly. He well understood and approved of my feeling that first you keep your patient alive. Nor did I then understand that the rigid "blank screen" technique was a parody of the human psychoanalytic technique as it was practiced in Vienna. Finally, the most important issue and the most difficult to assess is the lack of a reasonable and cooperative ego. This is still the most important issue. Although it does relate to the probable course and difficulties, however, it should not be the criterion of analyzability.

The best criterion is the response of the patient during the early stages of analysis. Freud's dictum that every analysis should start with a trial analysis is still a good one, with the understanding that if things do not work out, the analyst will help the patient find someone more helpful. As I explain it, "Even a motivated patient and a competent analyst may not work well with each other. If the treatment isn't helpful, I will help you find someone else who will help. You never owe your therapy to a therapist, you only owe it to yourself." Rarely is that an issue, but it is usually important for the patient not to feel trapped. The only decision I require of patients after an initial interview is whether to come back one more time, and after a second interview whether to come back a third time, although I usually tell them what I think they need by the second interview. After the third interview they need to make a decision about a trial of therapy. Equally important to not making patients feel trapped is not making them feel on trial, not making them feel that you may decide they are not good enough. With that meaning, the trial analysis itself becomes a trauma. It is my experience that the best prognosticator is the feeling of the analyst that he or she can help this person, irrespective of all other aspects of the case.

Freud himself said any investigation that took seriously the concepts of the unconscious, repression, resistance, and transference was psychoanalysis, even if it differed from him in every other respect (which, of course, it would not, if it took these concepts seriously). Some analysts cite Freud as requiring the Oedipus complex to be the central issue for it to be analysis, not noticing he had written by 1931 that we must abandon the concept of the Oedipus complex as the nuclear complex of the neuroses, or redefine it to include all relations of the child to both parents (Freud, 1931, p. 226).

Luckily, the culture of psychoanalysis has changed. Largely as the result of Kernberg and Kohut in the United States, it is now fashionable to treat borderlines and other character disorders. (Kernberg makes the distinction "psychoanalytic therapy" rather than "psychoanalysis" for the technical procedures he recommends for borderlines. But not all analysts would agree with that distinction, nor would they agree specifically with all of his technical recommendations. But they appreciate his role in keeping open the option of psychoanalytic treatments for these patients, even if they disagree on specific technical issues.) Fairbairn was publishing his ideas in the 1930s, but only in the 1980s and 1990s have the ideas of Fairbairn and Guntrip become fashionable in the United States, including the way they routinely consider the issues involved with difficult patients. Charles Brenner (personal communication) has said it most succinctly: "The difference between neurotic, borderline, and psychotic is simply sick, sicker, sickest, but the mechanisms are the same." (Here some analysts, like Kemberg, would argue that this is an oversimplification and that borderlines are characterized by the use of certain defenses different from neurotic and psychotic defenses. This is a reasonable dialogue, but there is no defense used by specific diagnostic categories that is not used in general; there is simply a difference in frequency of utilization.)

Meanwhile, patients with simple, delimited neurotic symptoms have become scarce. One candidate at a good institute in California said, when she finished her training, that if a real neurotic ever came in, she would treat the patient for nothing, because she would like once to treat a real neurotic.

The more serious the problems, the more likely the patient is to be willing to make the commitment of time, effort, and resources that analysis requires. In my experience, the usual psychoanalytic patient today has had three to five attempts at treatment before applying for analysis, some of which were so destructive it is hard to believe anyone would call them "treatment."

Change is produced in psychoanalysis and psychoanalytic therapy by insight and by various aspects of the analytic relationship itself, especially the internalization of the therapist and of the relationship, about which I have more to say. In the early days, the emphasis was entirely on insight, "to make the unconscious conscious," and obviously this is still central to our efforts. Therefore it seemed like the only curative activity was interpretation, and only interpretative activity was analysis. A kind of political correctness grew up, in which analysts only talked about their interpretations, made fine-grained obsessive distinctions as to which comments were truly interpretations, as opposed to other categories of speech, decided that only transference interpretations were mutative (e.g., Strachey, 1934), were careful to prove they did not do anything other than interpret, became guilty about ordinary human kindness, and frequently lied about what they actually did with their patients in order to maintain the apparent "purity" of their work.

Let me present two important ideas that are probably new to you, at least in your reading, but will probably resonate with your experience as an analyst. They are particularly helpful to the analyst in working with borderline and psychotic patients, but they are also helpful in working with neurotics. First, it is absolutely essential for an analyst to be confused; second, it is not "accurate empathy" that cures patients, but it is our attempt at accurate empathy (whether or not we are successful) that cures patients.

It is almost universally accepted that empathy characterizes good analysts. Among psychoanalysts, Kohut (1977) most emphasized empathy as a centrally curative part of psychoanalysis, as part of remedying the deficits in development that led to ego defects; he also said failures of empathy in a basically empathic relationship were necessary for the process of cure. These failures helped the patient realize that analysis was not an adequate substitute for life.

And yet he was partially wrong. As part of my graduate class in the psychotherapy of psychosis, twice a week I would treat a patient whom I did not know. Most graduate students in clinical psychology have been taught that severely disturbed people do not get better with psychoanalytic psychotherapy; inevitably, however, the students would observe that despite my mistakes, the patients talked about the strange things described in my and other psychoanalytic papers, and the patients would greatly improve in front of them.

The late Norman Kagan, as part of his research, videotaped an initial segment of one such psychotherapy session with a seventeen-year-old ambulatory schizophrenic, who was also alcoholic. Kagan immediately replayed the videotape with the patient, stopping it frequently, and asking the patient what was going on at that moment.

The thought processes of the patient were extremely complex, and the patient described them in detail. Then Kagan asked the patient whether he thought I understood what the patient had described.

"Of course he does," said the patient with certainty.

But the truth was that I did not understand. I understood as best I could the fragments that the patient had told me, but he had only revealed fragments of his conscious thought processes, and I had no idea of the complexity of his thoughts and of most of what was going on.

What the patient was responding to as my understanding him was not my correct understanding of him, but my attempt to correctly understand him. I have since realized this is very general. We may or may not be capable of correctly understanding our patients, but we are capable of doing our damnedest to try and understand them. That is usually what they perceive and are responding to when they say and feel we understand them.

When in life do we have a bright, concerned person really trying hard to understand us, no matter how confusing, terrifying, or obscure our life might be, or how much our defenses slow the process? Never—except in good analysis.

Of course, sometimes we do succeed at understanding. As the late Richard Sterba used to say to patients: "All I have to offer you is understanding, but that is really a great deal."

Nonetheless, there is no way for an analyst to escape being confused. Early in my career, I was often intimidated by analysts and other professionals who seemed always to understand exactly what was going on with their patients. But their patients did not seem to benefit very much, and sometimes did very badly with such certainty.

Adding to our confusion is a defense more often used by schizophrenic and severely disturbed patients: not to communicate clearly what they know consciously, even not communicating that the therapist is being helpful, for fear that it will be used against them in some way.

The confused analyst is not only able to learn by not excluding possibilities, but provides a model for the patient—that being confused is tolerable. As I sometimes say to patients who complain that analysis is confusing, "Good. You are not sick because you are confused. You are sick because you are certain of things that are not true."

Valuing confusion does not mean valuing arbitrariness, or the narrative point of view, which, in its most extreme form, holds that any consistent narrative the patient and the analyst accept is equally good, that objective truth is irrelevant, and is unobtainable anyway. I strongly disagree. The patient has lived a life and wants to know what it was. It is frequently possible to reconstruct it. When I have reconstructed it wrongly, even when it was accepted by the patient, it was never helpful. But when all the material fell into place, and the patient improved, the reconstruction turned out to be true. In many cases, it has been possible to validate from external sources, such as family, the truth of such helpful reconstructions of the repressed past. Patients almost always attempt to determine the accuracy of their reconstructions, if it is possible and safe to do so.

A supposedly incurable schizophrenic repeatedly hallucinated burning in Hell. When asked about the scar on his hand, he said there was a story his mother told. When he was five years old, his mother and he were in a store and she asked him where he had gotten the toy in his hand. He said the lady gave it to him. She asked the lady, who had not given it to him. She made him put it back, and she made him apologize to the lady. She then took him by the hand and walked home (five blocks). They went upstairs (third floor). She turned on the gas burner, and held his hand in it to teach him not to steal. It left a scar. But he said it had no effect on him, because he did not remember it.

I told him I had a different view, that what you cannot remember has the most effect on you. Most of us can only imagine burning in Hell, but he had actually been there.

Insights sometimes, but not always, lead to immediate dramatic change; this one did. His hallucinations of burning in hell ceased permanently.

It may be, of course, that you cannot reconstruct the past. But even an uncertain past is bearable if you can share that uncertainty with an acceptant and tolerant other, and continue to think about it.

Central to change is the internalization of the therapist. The therapist is internalized into the superego so that the patient treats himself or herself the way the therapist would, as opposed to the way the parents did (Strachey, 1934). (Of course we recognize that one of the problems with the classical structural theory is that patients frequently have multiple superegos based on the internalization of different people.) The therapist is internalized into the ego as a model for the self. The therapy relationship is internalized as a model for what a human relationship might be like. Sometimes analysts worry that the patient will internalize his or her defects. But, like an adolescent, the patient will eventually discard what is not useful. Further, analysts value patients who keep growing, who are different from them, and who can do better than they can, unlike the parents of most patients, who are more like the father of Oedipus or the mother of Snow White.

Once internalization is taken seriously as a therapeutic process, it becomes obvious why it is important that the analyst be tolerant of the human condition. It is especially important for the analyst to be kind, so that the patient dares to be kind to himself or herself, and even to others. The Stockholm Outcome of Psychotherapy and Psychoanalysis Project (Sandell et al., 1997, 2000) recently found that psychoanalysis and psychoanalytic therapy were very helpful, were more helpful than alternative treatments, and that psychoanalysis (three or more sessions per week) was more helpful than psychoanalytic psychotherapy (one or two weekly sessions). If you spend more time, you get more done. After termination, patients who received psychoanalytic therapy maintained their gains, but patients who received psychoanalysis actually continued to grow. Sandell and colleagues also found that psychoanalysts tended to have the same general values about psychotherapy, which were different from non-psychoanalytic therapists. But on one dimension, analysts differed from each other: the importance of being neutral versus the importance of being kind. When doing psychoanalysis, analysts with both views were equally helpful. But when doing psychoanalytic therapy, those analysts who stressed neutrality were far less helpful. Most analysts are kind people. When seeing patients intensively, the patients usually come to know even "neutral" analysts accurately. But when doing psychotherapy, a neutral analyst can succeed in being "neutral," which may be perceived by the patient as rejection. The more regressed, ego-fragmented, or reality-distorting the patient is, the more it is important for the reality of the analyst's kindness to be obvious.

The good analyst is stubborn. There is a part of you that just does not want to give up, no matter what it looks like. The more difficult the defense, the more stubborn the analyst. We persevere, sometimes innovate, sometimes seek consultations, always rethink. When we seem to have made a mistake, we ask how did this happen. Patients often ask us why we put up with them at their worst, why we did not just get rid of them. The extraordinary patience of Frieda Fromm-Reichmann was evident from her writings (e.g., Fromm-Reichmann, 1939). A graduate student treating a borderline patient twice a week had been supervised for a year by a Kohutian. The treatment was sensible, but there was no apparent change. The student changed supervisors, hoping that my way of working would be more helpful. Six months later, there was still no apparent change. After eighteen months of total treatment, however, the patient began to change. It was pointed out to him that this was a valuable learning experience; the patient was not changing because of his interventions that month, but because of eighteen months of very good work, whose effect was now beginning to appear. This experience would help him the next time he had a patient who did not seem to respond for a long time.

Rudolf Ekstein once described the ideal therapist for a psychotic child as "someone who knows as much as possible scientifically (i.e., psychoanalytically) combined with an absolutely irrational belief that, no matter what, this child is going to make it." It's not a bad prescription for any analyst. Indeed, the analyst must not only retain hope, but create hope in the patient. The patient has no reason to be hopeful, and depends on the analyst to create and maintain hope, while often consciously trying to prove how hopeless is the world and how worthless the analysis.

We help patients think about their lives and their contradictory feelings. We allow them to discover their own complexity, and that their feelings are a necessary part of rational thinking. What they cannot remember or think about is important; what is unconscious does not change, but has the most control. What they can think about, they can control. With our help, they reconstruct their lives and their traumas, including their fantasies, and they learn the defenses they use. They learn about transference and its ubiquity, and they learn to use their transferences as sources of information. Indeed, they learn to use all of their problems as sources of information that will make their lives better.

In dealing with the more difficult patient, it is important to do what is necessary to cope with crises. You must present as much structure as the patient's defenses demand. You must keep the patient's terror and acting out within tolerable bounds. Specific technical suggestions can be found in *Psychotherapy of Schizophrenia* (Karon & VandenBos, 1981). They are useful not only with schizophrenics, but also with borderlines and other difficult patients.

It was Hedda Bolgar who first suggested to me that the Odyssey is a good metaphor for analysis. It is a scary journey of self-discovery that is bearable because the analyst is there.

Psychotic patients are often the most dramatic examples. A patient, termed "incurably schizophrenic" by a consensus of the psychiatric staff of a private hospital, was brought to my office (over the staffs objections) after his wife, on my advice, refused to permit electroconvulsive therapy and withdrew him from the hospital. The psychiatric staff told her she was killing him. He was not eating, he was not sleeping, and he was continually hallucinating.

He was from a middle-class family and had considered himself lucky to have had such good parents, particularly such a good mother. Even before his psychotic break, however, he could not remember his childhood before the second year of high school; he did not think this was abnormal.

I immediately stopped all medications and started real treatment—seven days the first week, six the second, and so on, until a regular three-day-a-week schedule. His wife and friends of the family took turns babysitting with him for the first month or two.

Inasmuch as not eating will kill you in thirty days, I did what is recommended in Karon & VandenBos (1981). The second session was at 7:00 a.m. at an all-night restaurant. He said he could not go in there because they would think he was crazy. He was told that they would think he was drunk.

He objected that he would vomit. He was told it was unlikely that he would be the first drunk to throw up there that night. We went in and I ate and we talked about eating. Four days later he was eating and we moved back to my office.

Six months later he was working at an intellectually demanding job. A year later I told him that anyone can go crazy under enough stress, but under the normal stresses of everyday life, he would never be psychotic again.

He said that this was better than he had ever been, better than what he used to call normality, but if I thought living like this was good enough for him, I was crazy.

The process eventually became more classical looking. We moved to a couch and my sitting behind him when it seemed more useful. Patients usually get angry at that change. They often point out that I used to tell them what to do, and demand to know why I will no longer do that.

"Your judgment used to be terrible. You needed someone to tell you what to do. Now your judgment is as good as mine, and sometimes better. It would be silly for me to tell you what to do." Patients typically get angry but keep growing.

He saw me for fourteen years. He kept raising the stakes. In his third year, he startled me by saying that he had a book to write and he could not. He wanted to know if that was something I could help him with.

Somewhat dubiously, I told him that people do go into analysis for writer's block. We spent most of a year on it, and he wrote that book. He has written several since. Others in his field have told me that his professional reputation is based on that first book, now considered a classic in his field. Obviously it was well worth a year's analytic work. He knew that, even if I did not.

In his pre-psychotic period, he had never eaten a meal without nausea. During treatment after a trip to France he recounted, with tears in his eyes, that he could not tell me what French cooking is like. "There's nothing like it in the United States."

We went through psychosomatic problems, and then marital problems. He said he could leave his wife, that it would be easy, that there were bright, attractive, interesting women out there, but it would devastate her. He said that when he needed her, she had saved his life. The doctors said shock him, his family said shock him, people in my department (psychology) said shock him, but she had the courage to defy them and see that he got real treatment. And he just could not do that to her, that is, leave her.

He described his need for the last two years of treatment in terms of dealing with his teenage son. He said that when his son was a child, he had a psychotic father, and that was "a hell of a thing to do to a kid." He felt he needed help in undoing the harm he had done his son. Indeed, because of his fear of his son identifying with him too much and repeating his agony, he was still withholding the healthy parts of himself and discouraging his son's healthy identification with him. He was able to discover this and change.

He is now internationally renowned in his field, as well as having a good marriage and being a good father. He recently sent me a magazine article about a prestigious award he received for his scholarship. His therapy did not make him a bright man nor a kind man, but it did keep his brightness and kindness from being destroyed. It did allow him to feel safe, perceive and think realistically and creatively, and use his intelligence and kindness to make his own and other people's lives more interesting. That is psychoanalysis.

But difficult cases are not just suitable for experienced analysts. As an advanced candidate, Pat Marciniak (1997) described treating a patient who had been on five or more simultaneous medications for eight years after a suicide attempt. He had been diagnosed as manic-depressive, borderline schizophrenic, and paranoid, by the medicating psychiatrist. At no time had psychotherapy been suggested. He was unable to work, but was informed by his psychiatrist that she did not want to continue to treat him. When she discovered he had been referred for, and was receiving psychoanalytic treatment from, a social worker, however, she called him to tell him it was dangerous, to stop, and to double his medication dosages. Luckily, Marciniak had already arranged for him to see a rational medicating psychiatrist, who not only approved of psychoanalysis but was himself a candidate at another institute. This psychiatrist helped him by prescribing more rationally, tapering and changing the medications appropriately, and when the patient requested it, helping him stop the medication entirely.

While there were serious physical withdrawal effects, the patient's ability to think clearly greatly improved when he stopped the medication while continuing his analysis. The anti-therapeutic intervention of his previous psychiatrist precipitated a crisis, but it was resolved when it was related to his guilt about no longer conforming to his mother's values.

When he started treatment three times a week, he said that he feared a race not; he had acquired an assault rifle and 4000 rounds of ammunition. He hated almost all of the men he worked with and had been fantasizing killing fourteen of them and then himself. He felt they hated him. He experienced wide mood swings, sometimes was extremely physically aggressive, talked cruelly and grandiosely, and sometimes secluded himself in a basement bedroom, refusing to talk to anyone. He sometimes slept with a loaded handgun on his chest and rifles nearby. He also reported washing his hands twenty or more times a day.

After eight months of treatment, the patient decided he was ready to go back to work. The first day on the job the other men teased him cruelly about being sick, and he described being enraged and humiliated. He called Marciniak that evening, swearing he would go to work in the morning armed, shoot as many as possible, and then shoot himself. He was in excruciating emotional pain, panicked and enraged. Marciniak dealt with the emergency by talking to him for two hours that evening. He was exhausted, but refused to change his plans for 8:00 a.m. the next morning.

Marciniak tried to talk to her analytic supervisor, who was out of town, but did talk to another supervising analyst in our group,1 who was helpful, but basically allowed the trainee to use her excellent clinical judgment. Marciniak met with the patient early in the morning for a session before work. By the time the hour was over, he agreed these men were not worth dying for, and that as long as he was alive there was the possibility things would get better. He agreed to go home and not go to work. Marciniak described him as being "exhausted from rage and lack of sleep" and herself as "exhausted from sheer fear."

It was at this point the patient decided to stop medication, and both homicidal and suicidal crises have ceased since then. He has also described a dramatic clearing of his ability to think. There were severe physical symptoms connected with the discontinuation of Xanax, but they were handled medically. The patient, however, understandably resented the emergency room physician's offer to prescribe more Xanax "to make things easier."

With understandable anxiety, the candidate had weathered the crisis and got the patient not to go back to work until he could do so without murdering anyone. The analysis eventually enabled him to go back to work, and then move to a better job (with great difficulty and guilt). Needless to say, his relations with his wife and child also improved enormously. The changes were slow, the treatment was intense and difficult, and the improvement real. The transference bases of his terror, shame, and hatred were examined.

The treatment continued with difficulty, but now his problem was not murder or suicide, but vocational success or failure, marital success or failure, and the ability to come to therapy when things were going badly. He was still an extremely difficult "unanalyzable" patient by many standards, but the work that had been done was magnificent, and he continued the hard work for several years. Although he interrupted his analysis before achieving all the vocational goals his analyst would have liked, he was working stably, responsibly, and without undue anxiety at a job that provided well for his wife and child, was relating well to them, enjoyed a good deal of his life, and was not psychotic or violent or involved in illegal activities.

REFERENCES

Alexander, F. & French, T.M. (1946), Psychoanalytic Therapy. New York: Ronald Press.

American Psychiatric Association (1994), Diagnostic and Statistical Manual of Mental Disorders, 4th ed. Washington, DC: Author.

Antonuccio, D. O., Danton, W. G., DeNelsky, G.Y., Greenberg, R.P. & Gordon, J.S. (1999), Raising questions about antidepressants. Psychotherapy and Psychosomatics, 68: 3-14.

Breggin, P.R. (1998), Electroshock: Scientific, ethical and political issues. International Journal of Risk and Safety in Medicine, 11:5-40.

——— & Cohen, D. (1999), Your Drug May Be Your Problem. Reading, MA: Perseus Books.

Ehrenberg, D.B. (1992), On the question of analyzability. Contemporary Psychoanalysis, 28:16-31.

Fenichel, O. (1945), The Psychoanalytic Theory of Neurosis. New York: Norton.

Fine, R. (1990), The History of Psychoanalysis. Northvale, NJ: Jason Aronson.

Freud, S. (1931), Female sexuality. Standard Edition, 21:225-243.

Fromm-Reichmann, F. (1939), Transference problems in schizophrenics. Psychoanalytic Quarterly, 8:412-426.

Gitlin, M.J., Swendsen, J., Heller, T.L. & Hammen, C. (1995), Relapse and impairment in bipolar disorder. American Journal of Psychiatry, 152:1635-1640.

Glick, R., Eagle, P., Luber, B. & Roose, S. (1996), The fate of training cases. International Journal of Psycho-Analysis, 77:803-812.

Karon, B.P. & VandenBos, G.R. (1981), Psychotherapy of Schizophrenia: The Treatment of Choice. New York: Aronson.

Kohut, H. (1977), The Restoration of the Self New York: International Universities Press.

Marciniak, P.M. (1997), Facets of kindness: Grappling with self-deception in the analytic hour. Unpublished manuscript.

Moran, M. (1993), Payment calculations under health care reform indicate need for diverse practice. Psychiatric News, 4:Aug. 6.

Morgan, R.F., ed. (1999), Electroshock: The Case Against. Mangilao,

Guam: Morgan Foundation Publishers.

Riess, B.F. (1992), Some thoughts and material on age-related psychoanalysis of the aged. Special Issue: Psychoanalysis of the Mid-life and Older Patient. Psychoanalysis & Psychotherapy, 10:17-32.

Rothstein, A. (1995), Psychoanalytic Technique and the Creation of Analytic Patients. Madison, CT: International Universities Press.

Sarason, S. (1968), Psychological Problems in Mental Deficiency. New York: Harper & Row.

Sandell, R., Blomberg, J., Lazar, A., Carlsson, J., Schubert, J. & Broberg, J. (1997), Findings of the Stockholm Outcome of Psychotherapy and Psychoanalysis study. Panel at the annual meeting of the Society for Psychotherapy Research, Geilo, Norway.

——— Blomberg, J., Lazar, A., Carlsson, J., Broberg, J. & Schubert, J. (2000), Variety of long-term outcome among patients in psychoanalysis and long-term psychotherapy: A review of findings in the Stockholm Outcome of Psychoanalysis and Psychotherapy Project (STOPP). International Journal of Psycho-Analysis, 81:921-942.

Stone, A.A. (1990), Law, science, and psychiatric malpractice: A response to Klerman's indictment of psychoanalytic psychiatry. American Journal of Psychiatry, 147:419-427.

Strachey, J. (1934), The nature of the therapeutic action of psychoanalysis. International Journal of Psycho-Analysis, 15:127-157.

Willick, M. S. (2001), Psychoanalysis and schizophrenia: A cautionary tale. Journal of the American Psychoanalytic Association, 49:27-56.

CHAPTER 17
Internalizing the Tolerant, Kind, Confused, and Stubborn Therapist and Insight

Bertram P. Karon

Change is produced in psychoanalytic therapy by insight and by internalization of the therapist. Deep-seated change refers to changes in thinking, feeling, and functioning that are permanentor at least long lasting and which seem highly improbable without therapy, and ideally lead to continued growth.

The two most important ideas in this article are: first, it is absolutely necessary for a therapist to be confused; and second, it is not "accurate empathy" which cures patients but it is our attempt at accurate empathy (whether or not we are successful) which cures patients.

It is almost universally accepted that empathy characterizes good therapists. Carl Rogers (e.g., 1958) found it to be one of the three therapist conditions for being helpful. Among psychoanalysts, Kohut (1977) most emphasized empathy as a centrally curative part of psychoanalysis; he also said failures of empathy in a basically empathic relationship were necessary for the process of cure. These failures helped the patient realize that analysis was not an adequate substitute for life.

And yet these theorists were partially wrong. As part of my graduate class in the Psychotherapy of Psychosis, twice a week I would treat a patient whom I did not know. Most graduate students have been taught that severely disturbed people do not get better with psychotherapy; inevitably, however, the students would observe that, despite my mistakes, the patients talked about the things described in my and other psychoanalytic papers, and the patients would greatly improve in front of them.

The late Norman Kagan, as part of his research, videotaped an initial segment of one such psychotherapy session with a 17 year old ambulatory schizophrenic, who was also alcoholic. Kagan immediately replayed the videotape with the patient, stopping it frequently, and asking the patient what was going on at that moment.

The thought processes of the patient were extremely complex and the patient described them in detail. Then Kagan asked: "Do you think Karon understands this?"

"Of course he does," said the patient.

285

But the truth was that I did not understand. I understood as best I could the fragments that the patient had told me, but he had only revealed fragments of his conscious thought processes and I had no idea of the complexity of his thoughts and of most of what was going on.

What the patient was responding to as my understanding him was not my correct understanding of him, but my attempt to correctly understand him. I have since realized this is very general.

We may or may not be capable of correctly understanding our patients, but we are capable of doing our damnedest to try to understand them. That is usually what they perceive and are responding to when they say and feel we understand them.

When in life do we have a bright concerned person really trying hard to understand us, no matter how confusing, terrifying, or obscure effect on you. Most of us can only imagine burning in hell, but you have actually been there."

Insights sometimes, but not always, lead to immediate dramatic change: this one did. His hallucinations of burning in hell ceased permanently.

It may be, of course, that you cannot reconstruct the past. But even an uncertain past is bearable if you can share that uncertainty with an acceptant and tolerant other, and continue to think about it. I had one patient, in a second analysis, who had pretty clear evidence of sexual abuse except who sexually abused her. After years of work, we concluded that she probably did not know who was sexually abusing her at the time of the trauma, and therefore all that we could reconstruct was the horror enhanced by the uncertainty.

Central to change is the internalization of the therapist. The therapist is internalized into the super-ego so that the patient treats him or herself the way the therapist would, as opposed to the way the parents did. The therapist is internalized into the ego as a model for the self. The therapy relationship is internalized as a model for what a human relationship might be like. Sometimes therapists worry that the patient will internalize their defects. But, like an adolescent, the patient will eventually discard what is not useful. Further, therapists value patients who keep growing, who are different from them, and who can do better than they can; unlike the parents of most patients-who are often more like the father of Oedipus or the mother of Snow White.

Once internalization is taken seriously, it becomes obvious why it is important that the therapist be tolerant of the human condition. It is especially important for the therapist to be kind, so that the patient dares to be kind to him or herself, and even to others. The Stockholm Outcome of Psychotherapy and Psychoanalysis Project (Sandell, Blomberg, Lazar, Carlsson, Schubert, and Broberg, 1997) recently found that psychoanalysis and psychoanalytic therapy were very helpful, were more helpful than alternative treatments, and that psychoanalysis was more helpful than psychoanalytic psychotherapy: if you spend more time, you get more done. They found that psychoanalysts tended to have the same general values about psychotherapy which were different from non-psychoanalytic therapists. But on one dimension, analysts differed from each other: the importance of being neutral versus the importance of being kind. When doing psychoanalysis, analysts with both views were equally helpful.

I immediately stopped all medications and started real treatment seven days the first week, six the second, and so on, until a regular three day a week schedule was achieved.

Four days later he was eating. Six months later he was working at an intellectually demanding job. A year later I could say to him: "Anyone can go crazy under enough stress, but under the normal stresses of everyday life, you will never be psychotic again."

He said, "This is better than I've ever been, better than what 1 used to call normality, but if you think living like this is good enough for me, you're crazy."

He saw me for 14 years. He kept raising the stakes. In his third year, he startled me by saying, "I have a book to write and I can't. Is that something you can help me with?" We spent most of a year on it, and he wrote that book. He has written several since. Others in his field have told me that his professional reputation is based on that first book, now considered a classic.

In his pre-psychotic period, he had never eaten a meal without nausea. During treatment after a trip to France, he recounted with tears in his eyes, "I can't tell you what French cooking is like. There's nothing like it in the United States."

We went through psychosomatic problems, and then marital problems:

"I could leave her. It would be easy. There are bright, attractive interesting women out there, but it would devastate her. When I needed her, she saved my life. The doctors said shock him, my family said shock him, people in your department said shock him, but she had the courage to defy them and see that I got real treatment. And I just can't do that to her."

He described his need for the last two years of treatment: "I have a teenage son. When he was a kid, he had a psychotic father, and that was a hell of a thing to do to a kid. And I need help in undoing the harm I did him."

He is now internationally renowned in his field. He recently sent me a magazine article about a prestigious award he received for his scholarship. His therapy did not make him a bright man nor a kind man, but it did keep his brightness and kindness from being destroyed. It did allow him to feel safe, perceive and think realistically and creatively, and use his intelligence and kindness to make his own and other people lives more interesting. That is deep-seated change.

CHAPTER 18
A Type of Transference Based on Identification With an Abusing Parent

Bertram P. Karon, Ph.D.

"Come and get your money." The patient held a check in one hand and a knife in her other hand.

"I don't need money that badly."

"What's the matter? Are you chicken?"

"I don't enjoy fighting with patients. If you want to fight, I will be glad to refer you to someone else."

The patient, an ambulatory schizophrenic who had been in therapy for a couple of years, eventually stabbed the chair she was sitting on, and was immediately and profusely apologetic.

"Better the chair than me."

That comment seemed to be totally incomprehensible to the patient. When I insisted that if the patient attacked me, the therapy would be terminated and she would have to find another therapist, she accused me of being selfish, uncaring, and cruel.

During the next session, her menacing behavior ceased, but, nevertheless, she brought along the knife and played with it. Finally, I said: "You are going to have to stop bringing that knife here. Frankly, all I am doing is watching that knife, and I'm really not hearing a word you're saying. If you insist on bringing the knife, there's no point in our talking, and you're going to have to find another therapist."

The patient again accused me, "How can you be so heartless and cruel!" (However, when I finished work that evening, I found the knife lying on the front seat of my car.)

A man in his late 20s, a borderline patient, desperately needed therapy; he was unable to hold a job or take course work or keep his wife from leaving him; he admitted, as well, that he could not live without his wife. A familiar pattern developed; after our session would begin, he would first describe his desperation and ask for help. Then he would abruptly stop talking. When I would query his behavior, he would say nothing. Sometimes he would say in a weak voice: "I'm tired. I'm tired." He apparently was unwilling to be cooperative so as to further the therapy process.

Both of these vignettes are examples of a type of transference which is very common, particularly with borderline and schizophrenic patients, but not at all infrequent with neurotic patients as well. It usually occurs when the therapist is absolutely exasperated with the patient, when the patient is making us uncomfortable, and when we're not exactly sure of its significance.

It is not that the patient is treating us as if we were the patient's mother or father. The first patient would never have threatened either parent with violence. The second patient could never have said: "I'm tired," and expect that to be accepted by either parent.

Rather, they are reenacting emotionally laden experiences from the past, but they are in the role of the parent and place the therapist in the role that they actually played.

Thus, the first patient was convinced that her mother literally tried to kill her as a child; indeed, both her mother and father had made attempts on each other's lives. While apparently not valuing her, or each other, they valued money, property, and the furniture highly. She reenacted all of this in the therapy session with the use of the knife. She also accused me of being selfish and uncaring because I would not permit her either to kick or hit me and insisted that, if she did, I would terminate our professional relationship. "Would you really abandon me? How could you do that?" These recriminations had been addressed to her by her mother not only when the patient was a child, but even through her adolescence and 20s, when her mother continued to physically assault her. Even when she was middle-aged, her mother still acted irrationally about financial matters, and threatened her when she attempted to collect money owed her.

The second patient's mother was prone to repeated episodes of severe depression and when the young boy was in need of her help, simply did not respond, as is so often the case with a depressed parent, or told him: "I'm tired." Instead of helping him, she let him know that she expected him to help her, but she would not tell him precisely what he should do.

It must be emphasized that this is not a conscious maneuver on the part of the patient. The patient simply relives emotionally laden experiences which they either cannot remember directly or cannot relate to their current life circumstance. It is only when the therapist acts as if something unusual, something worth paying attention to, has occurred, that the patient seems to take this interaction as being strange, unusual, or worth analyzing.

The interpretation of this kind of transference furthers both patient insight and the therapeutic process. "I wonder if your mother (or father) did this," or "Your mother (or father) must have done this to you," or "Someone must have done to you what you are doing now. Who could it have been?" Obviously, the phraseology should be whatever is most likely to be acceptable to the patient and least likely to be considered an accusation. (Of course, one should never be vague, but describe specifically what you believe is being relived.)

As therapists we are so accustomed to always asking ourselves which figure from the past we are in the patient's drama, that frequently we do not recognize this reversal of the usual roles, and hence find the interaction puzzling. When we consider the possibility that the patient is acting like his or her parent, very often a puzzling session not only becomes less puzzling, but in fact becomes useful. This is particularly important since these usually are the sessions in which the therapist is very uncomfortable, just as the patient was very uncomfortable in childhood.

As is well-known, transference is not something that occurs uniquely during the psychotherapeutic or psychoanalytic session. Ferenczi, in his paper, "Introjection and Transference" (1909/1950), first pointed out that transference does occur, indeed, in life in general, but that in psychoanalysis (or in psychoanalytic therapy) it is studied. So, too, this kind of transference is not restricted to the therapeutic interaction, but is manifested in the patient's everyday life. The first patient, while she did not actually attack people, indicated how often she would like to, and considered that if she were really healthy and if therapy were really successful, then she would, thereby becoming her idealized adult mother. The patient who did nothing under stress to the therapist also reenacted this painful segment of his life with his wife and other people, which underlay part of the difficulties he encountered in his marriage and in his work. Dr. Richard Sterba (personal communication) pointed out that this is, of course, identification with the aggressor. Anna Freud (1936/1966) described identification with the aggressor as it occurs in psychoanalytic therapy, emphasizing its use as a defense against experiencing unpleasant affects and unacceptable impulses.

However, in the psychotherapeutic situation, the interaction is not merely identification with the aggressor in order to experience actively what one has experienced passively, nor simply the attempt to relive the trauma and somehow to master it, nor resistance. In therapy, the patient enacts this kind of transference, reliving what the parent did to the patient by doing it to the therapist, though with a specific unconscious motive — the hope that the therapist will not be devastated by this sequence of interaction, which would be the patient's reaction. This explains why we are always uncomfortable when this occurs during therapy sessions. These patients are always repeating events which made them uncomfortable. If we can tolerate these repetitions and not be devastated by them, it serves a useful therapeutic purpose; the patients learn that one can be subjected to this kind of unreasonable pressure and not be devastated. They frequently internalize the coping mechanisms that they see the therapist using and are then able to use that in their own lives if they are still being subjected to these kinds of pressures. The first patient was still being verbally abused and threatened with violence by her aged mother. After we relived this traumatic interaction, and I had set limits and interpreted it, she was able to reject her mother's actions and accusations as inappropriate and to set limits on her mother's bizarre reactions.

Or course this process has to be interpreted properly in terms of its earlier genetic basis in order for the patient to derive therapeutic benefit from the interaction. However, understanding that this is a form of transference, allows us to continue therapy with particularly troublesome and irritating patients whom otherwise we might find unable to tolerate.

REFERENCES

Ferenczi, S. (1950). lntrojection and transference. Sex in psychoanalysis: Collected papers (Vol. 1). New York: Basic Books, 35-93. (Original work published 1909)

Freud, A. (1966). Identification with the aggressor. The ego and the mechanisms of defense (Chap. 9). New York: International Universities Press, 109-121. (Original work published 1936)

CHAPTER 19
The Specific Determinants of a
Negative Therapeutic Reaction
Bertram P. Karon, Ph.D.

The negative therapeutic reaction, where a patient who seemingly should get better, gets worse, is usually attributed to such factors as unconscious masochism, guilt, the wish for punishment, and envy of the psychoanalyst. Such explanations rarely lead to therapeutic resolution and distract from specific antecedents. A man suffering lifelong recurring psychotic depressions entered psychoanalysis. Whenever he started to feel better about himself on the basis of analytic work he had a severe panic reaction "for no reason." The "negative therapeutic reaction" was due to unconscious fantasies connected with attempts by a brother to kill him in childhood. He had been feeling good, "having fun," just before each game turned nearly lethal. The negative therapeutic reaction was first described by Freud (1918) in connection with the Wolf Man:

> Every time something had been conclusively cleared up, he attempted to contradict the effect for a short while by an aggravation of the symptom which had been cleared up. It is quite the rule, as we know, for children to treat prohibitions in the same kind of way. When they've been rebuked for something (for instance, because they are making an unbearable din), they repeat it just once more after the prohibition before stopping it. In this way they gain the point of apparently stopping of their own accord and of disobeying the prohibition. (p. 69)

It should not be noteworthy, but it is noteworthy in the light of later writers, that there is nothing condemnatory in the way Freud understands what the patient is doing. It is not that the patient is defying him; rather, it is this patient's way of trying to maintain independence. Later, Freud (1923) described the negative therapeutic reaction in a more general way:

> There are certain people who behave in a quite peculiar fashion during the work of analysis. When one speaks hopefully to them or expresses satisfaction with the progress of the treatment, they show signs of discontent and their condition invariably becomes worse. One begins by regarding this as defiance and as an attempt to prove their superiority to the physician, but later one comes to take a deeper and juster view. One becomes convinced, not only that such people cannot endure any praise or appreciation, but that they react inversely to the progress of the

treatment. Every partial solution that ought to result, and in other people does result, in an improvement or a temporary suspension of symptoms produces in them for the time being an exacerbation of their illness; they get worse during the treatment instead of getting better. They exhibit what is known as a "negative therapeutic reaction." (p. 49)

This suggests that Freud, like all of us, may have had countertransference reactions in which the resistances were felt as personal affronts, but that he recovered his objectivity (presumably by understanding) and was able to arrive at a more psychoanalytic understanding, it is to be hoped, like the rest of us. Later still, in the *New Introductory Lectures,* Freud (1933) described:

People in whom this unconscious sense of guilt is excessively strong, betray themselves in analytic treatment by the negative therapeutic reaction which is so disagreeable from the prognostic point of view. When one has given them the solution of a symptom, which should normally be followed by at least its temporary disappearance, what they produce instead is a momentary exacerbation of the symptom and of the illness. It is often enough to praise them for their behaviour in the treatment or to say a few hopeful words about the progress of the analysis in order to bring about an unmistakable worsening of their condition.. . you will see in this behavior a manifestation of the unconscious sense. of guilt for which being ill with its suffering and impediments is just what is wanted, (pp. 109-110).

Finally, Freud (1937) added:

One portion of this force has been recognized by us, undoubtedly with justice, as the sense of guilt and need for punishment, and has been localized by us in the ego's relation to the super-ego. But this is only the portion of it which is, as it were, psychically bound by the superego and thus becomes recognizable; other quotas of the same force, whether bound or free, may be at work in other, unspecified places.

If we take into consideration the total picture made up of the phenomena of masochism immanent in so many people, the negative therapeutic reaction and the sense of guilt found in so many neurotics, we shall no longer be able to adhere to the belief that mental events are exclusively governed by the desire for pleasure. These phenomena are unmistakable indications of the presence of a power in mental life which we call the instinct of aggression or of destruction according to its aim, and which we trace back to the original death instinct of living matter.

Patients do sometimes say, "I don't deserve any better," in explaining such a pattern when they become aware of it. The usual explanations to be found in the later psychoanalytic literature are not very different from Freud. Explanations of the negative therapeutic reaction include unconscious masochism, an unconscious sense of guilt and the need to be punished, envy of the analyst and the wish to make the analyst fail, the need to keep from separating from the analyst, and the need to put the analyst down instead of the patient having been put down, because those are the only two possibilities in the patient's internalized model of an enduring relationship (cf. the summary in Thoma & Kachele, 1987, pp. 120-123).

All of these explanations are interesting, but they tend to be abstract. An explanation like "unconscious masochism" does not usually further the treatment, and often hinders further understanding. Explanations like "envy of the analyst" are ready-made rationalizations for countertransference, justifying wanting to punish the patient. The easiest and most devastating way to punish a patient, of course, is to stop listening.

The more abstract our psychoanalytic understanding, the more it is suspect. Always people are made sick by very specific fantasies, conflicts, and experiences, and the more specific our understanding of a symptom, the better. Therefore it is worth reviewing a case history of a man who demonstrated a clear negative therapeutic reaction and the specific basis for it that came to light.

The patient was approximately 60 years of age when I first saw him. He suffered recurring severe depressions for which he had been hospitalized repeatedly. He had been "cured" in his early 20s by insulin coma treatment and therefore continued to suffer from severe depressions nearly once a year for the rest of his life.

Despite this, he had managed to achieve a position of some importance as an executive. I was puzzled as to how he managed to keep his repeated hospitalizations from ruining his career. It was very simple. He told his employers that he was going into the hospital for a physical condition and did not reveal, sensibly enough, the nature of his disorder.

His latest depression was treated by a psychiatrist who told him that with the best of modern treatment, they could reduce his pain and misery by 20%. The best of modern treatment, of course, was medication. Luckily, a friend of one of his children, a psychologist in another state, suggested he contact me, and so this man made an appointment, and we reviewed his depressions and their treatments.

When he said that with the best of modem treatment his pain and misery could be decreased by 20%, I asked, "Is that good enough for you?"

"What choice do I have?"

Classically I said, "Well, you do have a choice. I can't guarantee that I can help you. All I can say is that people with similar problems have been helped. What I can guarantee is iit's going to take time, it's going to be hard work, it's going to be painful, and it's going to be expensive. But if it is successful, you won't be 20% better, you'll be better."

Then we discussed fees, and I reduced my fee so he could afford to come in three times a week. The patient took a week to think about it, and then began treatment on a three times per week basis, and worked very hard at it. Within a couple of weeks he was able to use the couch. As he described it later, "You were right. Itt's taking a lot of my time, it's expensive, and it's certainly painful."

In addition to his intense depressions, he also suffered panic attacks periodically. Since he did not know why he was panicked, these had been diagnosed as "spontaneous" panic attacks by his psychiatrists. In his depression there was also a terror dimension, because he was afraid that he might die.

He had been raised as a Fundamentalist. If he died, he would go Hell. Hell is a lake of burning fire in which you burn forever. He deserved to burn forever, because he had committed "the unpardonable sin," which he thought was masturbation. He knew about the lake of burning fire and about masturbation because he had been told these things by his minister as well as by his mother. His mother's father had been a minister in this same Fundamentalist church, a self-taught man who had written books and preached and was very strict.

The patient also felt very guilty because he had gotten a divorce from an extremely unpleasant first wife, who was very much like his mother, and married a much kinder and more pleasant second wife. That was a horrible crime, he felt (and his first wife still insisted). He felt his grown-up children could never forgive him for his divorce, and it was only during the analysis that he discovered that his children liked him as a person and even liked his second wife.

When he first talked about his insulin coma treatment, I told him that it was very unpleasant. He said that it wasn't. I suggested that I would read him a description of insulin coma treatment from a textbook. He said that wasn't necessary. When I started to go into the next room to get a book, he stopped me and said it wasn't necessary, because he was scared now, and didn't need any more evidence. Then I said, "There's something to be learned here. If you can repress the memory of this very unpleasant experience, then it is likely that there are other unpleasant experiences you can also repress and have no memory of."

His father had been a depressed man, who did not think the patient was worthwhile or of much value and "bad-mouthed" him frequently. But the patient knew his father was not a good person, because he did not go to church. His mother, on the other hand, was a good person, because she went to church regularly. She taught the patient all about God. She punished the patient, but he was not mad at her for that, because he knew she only punished him for his own good. Of course, she punished him more than the other children—and sometimes punished him when he hadn't done anything. His brothers would sometimes blame him for what they had done. Then she would punish him. He resented that a little bit. That didn't seem fair. But mostly he knew that she punished him for his own good.

She used to punish him by having him go cut a switch, and she would then whip him with it. If it wasn't thick enough, he would get extra strokes. She would whip him sometimes until the blood ran. But he didn't mind that, because she only did it for his own good. Anyway, he said, maybe it seems a little severe, but, you know, it's a lot less severe than what she suffered. Her father, who is a saint, used to punish his two daughters by always whipping them until the blood ran when he finished. He would have his daughters strip to the waist and tie them to a tree and then whip them. So by comparison she was really being kinder. And after all, his grandfather really was a saint.

At first I accepted this description, but later told him that I didn't think that a man who got his sexual kicks by stripping his daughters to the waist and beating them was particularly saintly by my standards. This made the patient very angry at me. It never occurred to him that his grandfather could have enjoyed doing that or that there was anything sexual about it. But then, he noted, I seemed to have a dirty mind.

His mother did something rather peculiar with him also. Her sister had died when the two of them were teenagers. The sister had burned to death. She had been ironing with one of those old-fashioned irons that have gasoline or kerosene in them and had spilled the gasoline on herself and caught fire and burned to death. A picture had been taken of her burned corpse in the coffin. His mother used to tell the story to the patient from time to time and show him the gruesome picture of

297

her burned sister. As he described that, I said to him, "I wonder if your mother thought she was responsible in some way. Sometimes sisters are angry at each other, or siblings are. If they are and something bad happens, they think they are responsible."

Then he remembered a few more details. His mother was with her sister when the accident occurred; they were ironing together. He began to wonder if she used to show that picture to his brothers and sister the way she would show it to him. He concluded that, as a matter of fact, he did not remember her showing the picture and telling the story repeatedly to them, but only showing it to him repeatedly.   Then I said that she treated him as if he were the bad part of her, "As if you deserved to burn to death for what she did." After all, spending eternity burning in a lake of fire would be the appropriate punishment for burning someone to death.

To check his memory, he asked his own sister if their mother used to show the picture to her, and, as he had remembered in treatment, the mother had not. But he learned more about the death of their aunt from his sister, who had obtained an old newspaper clipping.

It seems that the two girls (his mother and her sister) were ironing in the basement, and they were quarreling as teenage sisters sometimes do. But no quarreling was permitted in this saint's house. So he came downstairs, and the sister was so terrified of her saintly father that she backed into the iron, spilled the gasoline on herself, and burned to death. There even had been a police investigation at the time to see if the grandfather was not in some way responsible for his daughter's death, but they finally concluded he was not.

It became increasingly clear to the patient that his mother had indeed treated him as if he were the bad part of her and that is why he deserved to burn forever, for having burned her sister to death. Obviously, his mother could not allow herself to get angry at her saintly father. Instead of feeling—which would have been appropriate—that her father had caused the death of her sister with his terrorizing tactics, she blamed herself. But then instead of blaming herself, she had blamed the patient. That is why she had punished him and that is why she had encouraged the fear of eternal burning for his sins. (The "unforgivable crime," he eventually discovered, for him was feeling angry at his mother, and wanting to punish her.)

These reconstructions did help his depression. Bit by bit his associations would lead to increased feelings and memories, and together we were able to put together what was going on. He would get outside information, and the pieces would fit together, confirming our reconstructions. His depression began to lessen. But whenever he started to feel better, he would say, "I feel good. It's not me." And he would get very panicky.

Thus, he would have terrible panic attacks whenever he started to feel not depressed. This seemed like a massive negative therapeutic reaction. During these panic attacks he did not know of what he was afraid. He would report that he was not afraid of anything, he was just afraid. He accepted the psychiatric diagnosis of "spontaneous panic attacks" and insisted they were biological and genetic, just as he had been told by psychiatrists.

Patients who have "spontaneous" panic attacks obviously use denial and isolation as defenses. In my experience, denial and isolation are also essential parts of the depressive reaction. Depressives always tell you, "Nothing happened before I got depressed"—as do patients suffering "spontaneous" panic attacks. If you examine what was going on in their experience, there is always something that one would expect to frighten the patient (or depress the patient, in the case of "meaningless" depression). For this patient, it seemed to me that there were two conditions under which he had spontaneous panic attacks, although he had not noticed the regularity, or connected these conditions with his panic. One was when he gave a presentation in front of other executives on the same level, and the other was when he was feeling good. Thus, whenever his depression lifted in therapy, he had a panic attack.

When I finally noticed (18 months to 2 years into the treatment) that he had a "spontaneous" panic attack whenever he had to make a presentation to executives on the same level, but not when presenting to superiors or inferiors, I pointed this out and inquired whether his brothers were envious of him. He told me that was never a problem. I reminded him of his older brother turning him in to their mother for things he had not done. He said his brother was just trying to get out of trouble, "We got along fine. There was no envy between us."

Later in the same hour, however, he suddenly said, "I told you about the hanging, didn't I?"

"No."

"I must have."

"I might forget some details. But if you had told me about being hanged, I'm not likely to forget about it."

"Well, when I was 5 years old, my brother and I were playing Cowboys and Indians, and he lynched me. He put me on a box, and he threw a rope around a tree branch and tied it and put it around my neck, and then kicked the box out from under me. My mother had to cut me down. I was unconscious." "You must have been panicked, terrified."

"Oh, no, no."

"Yes you were. Biologically, if you cannot breathe, you go into a panic. That is a biological mechanism."

"Oh, no, there was no anxiety."

"Yes, there was. You have the panic now without the memory, and the memory without the panic."

He still denied it, but then he remembered other situations where he could not breathe. He recalled that in those other situations he had gone into a panic. That made him wonder.

Then he remembered that about a year after the hanging, his brother had got him to go to the roof of a three-story building and had told him that he could be like Batman. The brother gave the patient an umbrella and told him to jump off. He did. Luckily, children are rugged. He did not get killed, or even badly injured. But that was clearly no thanks to the brother. The brother obviously had tried to kill him. No wonder facing executives on the same level caused a panic attack.

"Tell me," I asked, "were you having fun?"

"Yes, of course. You know, he never used to let me play with him. But he let me play with him those two times, and I was really enjoying it."

"And now whenever you feel good, you feel like your brother is going to kill you."

"Oh, he wouldn't do a thing like that."

I said, "But he tried twice."

The patient said, "Oh, no," and I had to remind him of what he had just told me.

In the next session, when I referred to the fear of his brother that he had uncovered, the patient again denied that his brother could possibly attempt to kill him, or that he was afraid of his brother, until he was reminded of these two events in his life that he had described. He began to realize that his brother had not always been kind or friendly to him even as an adult, a fact which he had hitherto avoided. After those two sessions the panic attacks stopped.

He no longer demonstrated a negative therapeutic reaction. He was feeling pretty good.

As his therapist I too was feeling pretty good. I had found out the basis of his negative therapeutic reaction and resolved it, as well as his spontaneous panic attacks in general.

Our shared euphoria lasted for about 2 weeks. I received a very angry phone call from the patient. He had had a panic attack at work, and his left leg was paralyzed. He had to cancel his session, of course. With a man of this age, obviously one has to consider the possibility that he had a stroke, and I began to consider to which neurologist I should refer him.

After a few days he called to make an appointment. In the hour he described his panic attack and physical symptom. Then, shamefacedly, he mentioned that he had made an appointment with a neurologist. He expected me to be very angry at him, as his omnipotent-acting parents would have been, for recognizing the realistic limits of my competence. I complimented him on his good judgment, noting that his paralysis might be psychological or it might be neurological. I could not imagine anything more rational than taking steps to check both of these out. He was uncomfortable that I was not angry with him.

The patient had chosen a good neurologist, who checked him carefully, and informed the patient that the paralysis was not a neurological problem. Predictably, the patient was furious at the neurologist.

But in the therapy he did remember that once before in his life he had a similar symptom. When he was about 16, he had a panic attack. Afterwards his left leg was paralyzed, and he had been in bed for about a month and a half. They never did find out what caused it. Eventually, it got better. I asked him what was going on in his life about that time. He said, "Nothing, nothing important."

"Yes, but what can you remember. Tell me anyway."

"Well, I can't remember anything from that year. The only thing I can remember is something trivial. I remember a cousin came to visit. He was around with us, with my older brother, and I was sort of tagging along. Then they started to go off into town, and I started to follow them. My brother turned around and said to me, 'If you take one more step, I'll kill you.' And you know how silly I was, he had such a mean look on his face, I believed him."

"Of course, you believed him, because he had tried twice already."

"Oh, no, my brother wouldn't do a thing like that."

Some days our function is that of external memory. I reminded him of the two attempts his brother had made to kill him. "Of course, you believed him. And your unconscious was preserving your life. He said, 'I'll kill you if you take one more step.' So your unconscious prevented you from taking one more step. You stayed alive."

His paralysis disappeared, and he continued the analysis. Although it never became certain why the paralysis recurred at that time, it seemed likely that at some level he wished to understand what had happened to him earlier.

This patient's negative therapeutic reaction was resolved when the specific meaning of that symptom was uncovered and understood, in the same way other symptoms are resolved by understanding. The specific meaning of this patient's negative therapeutic reaction was not derivable from previous literature, nor was it closely related to the usual generalized explanations.

It is axiomatic that the more general and abstract an understanding of a symptom, the less helpful it is. This is true of all symptoms, including negative therapeutic reactions. Abstract explanations available in our literature may distract us from listening carefully to the specific details of our patients, and we may not hear the specific details. Ferenczi's (1919) paper on the utility of the phrase "for example" made clear the importance of specific details, and of not being satisfied with the patient's abstractions or generalizations. But we must not be distracted by our own abstractions either.

REFERENCES

Ferenczi, S. (1919) On the technique of psychoanalysis. III. 'For example' in analysis. In The selected papers of Sandor Ferenczi, Vol. II. Further contributions to the theory and technique of psychoanalysis, (pp. 184-186) New York: Basic Books, 1953.

Freud, S. (1918). From the history of an infantile neurosis. Standard Edition, 17, 1-122.

———— (1923). The ego and the id. Standard Edition, 19,1-66.

———— (1933). New introductory lectures on psychoanalysis. Standard Edition, 22, 1-182. Freud, S. (1937) Analysis terminable and interminable. Standard Edition, 23, 209-254.

Thoma, H., & Kachele, H. (1987). Psychoanalytic practice. Berlin: Springer-Verlag.

CHAPTER 20
Discussion of "Preventive Therapy for High-Risk Mothers and Children"

Eva Gochman, Ph.D.
Bertram P. Karon, Ph.D.

Infancy is a period of great importance and of great vulnerability. Fantasies formed during earliest infancy become the bases for apprehending later experiences, and for the development of succeeding fantasies, both conscious and unconscious. Inevitably, the events of infancy have profound and far-reaching consequences for the development of the personality and of psychic structure. While there are disputes about the roles of preoedipal factors in the development of neurotic symptoms among the various schools of psychoanalysis, there is no disagreement among theorists that the experiences of infancy and early childhood are crucial in creating vulnerability to later psychosis. Both schizophrenic and manic-depressive psychoses can be traced to such early bases for vulnerability.

Even those non-analytic theorists who stress the role of hereditary factors admit that what is inherited is at most a greater vulnerability, which only results in psychosis under conditions of environmental stress appropriate to the pathology (the so-called diathesis-stress model).

In the Scandinavian adoption studies, supposedly genetically "tainted" individuals did not become schizophrenic unless their adoptive parents manifested "communication deviance" (Lidz, 1973, p. 66).

Thus, effective preventive efforts are clearly possible. But prevention is a concept honored by more lip-service than effective efforts. The work of Dr. Gochman and her associates is reminiscent of that of Fraiberg, Adelson, and Shapiro (1975), who intervened in the mother-infant dyad of mothers with "failure to thrive" infants. Such mothers are unable to make use of good advice, and the infant's survival is problematic. Fraiberg, Adelson, Shapiro and their co-workers entered the home and helped the mother consciously to relate traumas of her own early infancy to her current difficulties with her own infant. These interventions, which were very brief, literally saved the lives of the infants. The mothers were able to mother appropriately and make use of relevant advice and professional help. The effectiveness of these interventions demonstrates the power and specificity of early infantile traumas. But interest in following up that project and making similar services widely available has waned in recent years.

One is also reminded of the little-noted fact that the primary control group in Rene Spitz's (1965) classic study of the overwhelmingly destructive effects of maternal deprivation was a group of mothers in a reformatory whose IQ averaged about 80. These mothers attended their own infants, with the benign supervision of a nurse. At the end of the first year, the infants seemed above average in IQ, as measured by the Hetzer-Wolf baby test, suggesting that such intervention can be highly effective. (Without special intervention, infants from intact families, where the parents were slightly below average in IQ, were slightly below average in IQ at the end of the first year, and if the parents were above average in IQ, the infants tended to be above average at the end of the first year, so that these modest gains, and the disastrous drop in the IQs of the maternally deprived infants, could not be attributed to the effects of time or of some function of initial IQ.)

With respect to the prevention of schizophrenia, there have been two previous notable leads. Manfred Bleuler (1971), in view of the greater vulnerability of the offspring of schizophrenics, told schizophrenic patients he treated that their children would need brief counseling with him at some time. He reported that with the availability of such counseling, these offsprings of treated schizophrenics showed no greater vulnerability to schizophrenia than the general public.

Perhaps the most important breakthrough in the prevention of schizophrenia was the finding that the rate of schizophrenia drastically increases as one descends the scale of socioeconomic status (i.e., the Yale 5-class index). While attempts have been made to dismiss such findings as the result of "downward drift," it is clear that the findings hold for status of family-of-origin and are related to the process of coping with the severe stresses of low socioeconomic status in the United States (Hollingshead & Redlich, 1958; Roger & Hollingshead, 1965; Srole et al., 1978). Indeed, it became clear that making the conditions of life less destructive for the poorest segment of the population would do more to decrease the real rate of schizophrenia (not just the rate of diagnosis or of hospitalization) than all the efforts of mental health professionals. Unfortunately, the political trend in the last few years has been to make life tougher for the poor.

Studies of family characteristics have been promising, particularly Lidz's (1973) description of skewed and schismatic families, Singer and Wynne's (1965) description of "communication deviance," characteristic of families whose children tend to become schizophrenic, and Vaughn and Leffs (1976) puritanically named "expressed emotionality" (actually a measure of intrusive hostility, and not emotionality in any general sense), characteristic of families whose schizophrenic members return to the hospital quickly. But family interventions based on these findings have been aimed at preventing the family from interfering with the recovery of an already schizophrenic member rather than preventing schizophrenia in the first place.

In general, the psychological pressures from parents which produce schizophrenia are not identical with schizophrenic pathology. On the basis of the reconstructions from psychoanalytic therapy with schizophrenics and their parents as well as observations of their interactions, it is possible to describe an unconscious defense, "pathogenesis," characteristic of parents of schizophrenics (i.e., the tendency unconsciously to act in terms of one's own needs and/ or ignore the conflicting needs of the child, when there is a conflict of needs) and to develop a scale for the TAT to measure it. A series of studies (e.g., Meyer & Karon, 1967; Mitchell, 1968,1969; Nichols, 1970) have validated this concept, and showed "pathogenesis" of parents to vary with the seriousness of the pathology, as well as to differentiate parents of schizophrenics from parents of normals. Moreover, "pathogenesis" of psychotherapists for schizophrenic patients (VandenBos & Karon, 1971) was negatively correlated with improvement in treatment. While this measure has potential for identifying parents whose children will be at risk, no such effort has yet been attempted for possible preventive interventions.

The parental pressures that make patients vulnerable to schizophrenia are unconsciously motivated and usually do not involve conscious destructive intent. It often requires careful observation of spontaneous sequences of interaction or projective tests to reveal them. But the patients that Dr. Gochman and her co-workers are helping are so grossly disturbed that their patterns of mothering are obviously impaired, and the effects of such grossly impaired mothering cannot help but be devastating. Dr. Gochman points the way to interrupting the most easily demonstrable mechanism for the transmission of schizophrenia.

Moreover, the problems of the mothers also originate in infancy, and represent unsolved issues, whose replaying in later derivatives did not lead to better resolutions, but to continued re traumatization. Thus, therapeutic intervening in the mothering of their infants resonates with the patient's most central problems and has a benign effect on the pathology itself, that is, the mother's central issues.

In my experience, postpartum psychotic reactions have not been due to the meaning of the pain of childbirth. Rather, the mother had suffered severe deprivation in the relation with her own mother, and there had been a reversal of the mother-child roles, experienced orally as an unfillable emptiness. The reversed mother-child role was often re-experienced with the husband. Pregnancy with its bodily sensation of being increasingly filled in an unfamiliar way aroused a new hope of fulfillment. Birth was then experienced as unbearable emptiness and loss of hope, precipitating a psychotic reaction (Rosberg & Karon, 1959). However, the meanings of the pain of childbirth described by Dr. Gochman represent an addition to our knowledge of the causes (and hence prevention) of pathological reactions to this normal life event.

Her description of prototypic problematic mothering patterns is useful. Her seemingly casual statement that sensory or motor disabilities in the child or parent may also create at risk situations reminds me of the schizophrenic mother of eight, who was described by her husband as a good mother until each child was two, at which point she lost interest and wanted another infant. Her fantasy was that each child was her, reborn perfect. When the child started to be independent and clearly seemed imperfect, she needed another infant. Unfortunately, one child was born with a physical defect, and the mother suffocated the infant.

We are indebted to Dr. Gochman for pointing the way to effective interruption of the transmission of agony from one generation to the next, describing the mothering patterns, and beginning to outline appropriate interventions. Her work must be imitated and extended in other settings so that the unintended sins of the grandparents will not be visited upon even the second generation thereof.

REFERENCES

Bleuler, M. (1971). Some results of research in schizophrenia. In R. Cancro (Ed.), In the schizophrenic syndrome: An annual review (Vol. I. pp. 3-16). New York: Brunner/Mazel.

Fraiberg, S., Adelson, E., & Shapiro, V. (1975). Ghosts in the nursery. Journal of Child Psychology, 14, 387-421.

Hollingshead, A.B., & Redlich, F.C. (1958). Social class and mental illness. New York: Wiley.

Lidz, T. (1973). The origin and treatment of schizophrenic disorders. New York: Basic Books.

Meyer, R.G., & Karon, B.P. (1967). The schizophrenogenic mother concept and the TAT. Psychiatry, 30, 173-179.

Mitchell, K.M. (1968). An analysis of the schizophrenic mother concept by means of the TAT. Journal of Abnormal. Psychology, 73, 571-574.

———— (1969). Concept of "pathogenesis" in parents of schizophrenic and normal children. Journal of Abnormal Psychology, 74, 423-424.

Nichols, N. (1970). The relationship between degree of maternal pathogenicity and severity of ego impairment in schizophrenic offspring. Unpublished Ph.D. dissertation, University of Michigan.

Rogler, L.H., & Hollingshead, A. B. (1965). Trapped: Families and schizophrenia. New York: Wiley.

Rosberg, J., & Karon, B. (1959). A contribution to the understanding of post-partum psychosis. In B. Karon & G. R. VandenBos (1982), Psychotherapy of schizophrenia: The treatment of choice. New York: Jason Aronson.

Singer, M., & Wynne, L. (1965). Thought disorder and family relations of schizophrenics: IV. Results and implications. Archives of General Psychiatry, 12, 201-212.

Spitz, R. (1965). The first year of life. New York: International Universities Press.

Srole, L., Langner, T.S., Michael, S.T., Kirkpatrick, P., Opler, M.K., & Rennie, T. A. (1978). In L. Srole & A. K. Fischer (Eds.), Mental health in the metropolis. New York: New York University Press.

VandenBos, G.R., & Karon, B.P. (1971). Pathogenesis: A new therapist dimension related to therapeutic effectiveness. Journal of Personality Assessment, 35, 252—260.

Vaughn, C. E., & Left, J. P. (1976). The influence of family and social factors on the course of psychiatric illness. British Journal of Psychiatry, 129, 125-137.

CHAPTER 21
A Clinical Note On The Specific Nature of an "Oral" Trauma

Bertram P. Karon

The apparent discrepancies between clinical case studies and experimental investigations are disturbing to those of us who believe that there is only one psychology of man, whatever the source of the data.

The importance of oral experiences and traumata in the production of character traits and neurotic and psychotic symptoms has been stressed by Freudian psychoanalysis (Abraham, 1954; Fenichel, 1945, pp. 62-66). The role of these determinants seems to be manifest in case history material, and in many recent modifications of Freudian theory, oral problems are given even greater emphasis (Bergler, 1949; Klein, Heiman, & Money-Kyrle, 1955; Silverberg, 1952). Nonetheless, the bulk of the experimental work, as Orlansky (1949) has noted, does not seem to confirm the importance suggested by theory. It may therefore be worthwhile to discuss the relevant aspects of a patient whose adult symptoms showed clear indications of "oral" pathology but seemed to have no childhood basis for such problems. The nature of his oral trauma may help to clarify the disparity between psychoanalytic reconstructions and experimental findings.

The term "orality" is used in psychoanalysis to refer to the mouth and its functions—especially eating, drinking, sucking, and biting—to the dynamic characteristics connected with these (e.g., dependency is seen as being connected with the experience of being fed), and to the first psychosexual "stage" of early infancy, when these functions of the mouth are assumed to be the most important activities in the life of the child. The term is thus used to refer both to problems which originate in this early period of life and to problems having to do with mouth functions. According to Fenichel, one would expect oral pathology to be prominent in the symptoms of someone who had been excessively deprived of oral gratification, excessively indulged in the oral period, or excessively indulged in the oral period and excessively frustrated in the succeeding stage.

Both in theoretical discussions and in attempts to investigate the importance of "oral" experiences, attention has frequently been focused upon whether or not the child was breast-fed or how early he was weaned. More recently, it has been realized that an abrupt weaning at any age is more traumatic than a gradual one, no matter when it takes place (Sears & Wise, 1950).

Destructive oral experiences have been said many times to play an essential role in the development of schizophrenia (Beliak, 1948, 1958; Fenichel, 1945, pp. 415-452; Rosen, 1953; Sechehaye, 1955). A 32-year-old male chronic paranoid schizophrenic patient who illustrates this contention has been described in a previous paper (Karon & Rosberg, 1958), but the basis for his oral trauma was not spelled out in that brief account.

This patient's delusions were such that any psychoanalytically oriented psychotherapist would have concluded that he suffered severe problems of an obviously oral nature and that he must have undergone an oral trauma of considerable impact. For example, the patient was afraid of being poisoned. He would not drink milk at the beginning of the therapy and confided that: "The Athenian girls are laughing at me. They say their breasts are poisoned."

One day a woman with a rather well-endowed bosom walked by him. He made frantic wiping gestures from his side. Afterwards he said: "She approached me with her breast, and I got a pain in my side."

Despite these symptoms, it was possible to verify that this patient had been breast-fed for a full year and had been gradually weaned. Where, then, could there be an oral trauma?

On one occasion, his mother (who had read some of the literature of psychoanalysis) said to him: "Didn't I give you enough milk? Didn't I give you enough to drink?" The patient stared into space and replied: "The cow gave her calf milk and then kicked it. She shouldn't do that. It's something that happened hundreds of times in the history of the world."

In this delusion of the cow who kicked her calf (the patient, of course, denied that it had anything to do with him) is the key to the oral trauma. It did not consist of being deprived of the breast or of being weaned too early or too abruptly. The oral trauma consisted of a sequence of interactions: The child got fed and then got hurt. The "poisoned" milk seems not to be due to any characteristic of the milk itself, but to the fact that the mother resented any demand upon her to feed the child so that immediately after feeding him, she got angry. The child then felt the impact of her hostility and was hurt. "Poison" is simply something you eat, and you get hurt afterwards.

This sequence—child eats, mother gets angry, child feels hurt—was not something which happened once or twice in the patient's life. It was not something that happened to him only during a specific period of childhood. It was something that started when he was an infant and continued all his life. Even at the age of 32, it was observable. The mother took care of the treatment home for a period of time so as to save expenses. She seemed to be making every conscious effort to help her son. The therapist was startled to notice that after every meal she cooked for her son, she had an argument with him. If she did not cook the meal, there was no argument. Thus, it was not merely a single childhood experience, but the continuous re-enactment of the trauma that prevented it from ever being overcome.

It must not be supposed that this was in any way a conscious process for the mother. Consciously, she was doing everything she could for her son. She was unaware of her constant pattern—feed, get mad—which seemed obvious to an observer. Each evening the content of the argument dealt with something else.

Her emotional inability to feed is exemplified by the fact that after raising two children and after many years of married life, her cooking was barely palatable, not only according to the patient but according to the therapist's judgment as well. Her needs were exemplified in the very beginning of the treatment when she complained of her obviously sick son: "He always took and never gave; it's about time he gave a little." Actually, the patient had been forced to give in a number of different ways—his gifts to his mother, his writings, his paintings, etc. (Karon & Rosberg, 1958).

Since it is typical of the schizophrenogenic mother that she cannot tolerate the demand to need, to take care of, to nurture, it is likely that this repeated pattern of activity—feed, get mad—is frequently present in such cases. The important point is that the oral trauma is not merely a single childhood event, but the continuous re-enactment of the traumatic sequence.

The patient, while under therapy, lived in a private house with treatment personnel and with his mother.

Without being aware of it, the mother continuously imprinted the notion that after eating comes the pain. Is it any wonder then that the patient is afraid of being poisoned?

Thus, the apparent discrepancy between clinical case studies and experimental findings seems to be due to the fact that "oral trauma" has been interpreted as referring to a single specific event—usually weaning. This is not entirely the fault of the investigators since psychoanalytic theory is usually presented as if the key to symptom and character formation lies in such isolated events. The present case suggests that the important "oral" variables are the persisting patterns of interactions, including the mother's involuntary and unconscious reaction to the demand for nurturance. Isolated events, like weaning, are easily influenced by "enlightened" child care education or by conscious good intentions without removing the destructive character of the total relationship. It seems likely that when attention is directed to the continuing relationship between mother and child, the discrepancies between clinical and experimental data will disappear.

REFERENCES

Abraham, K. On the first pre-genital stage of the libido. In, Selected papers on psychoanalysis. New York: Basic Books, 1954. Pp. 248-279.

Bellak, L. Dementia praecox. New York: Grune & Stratton, 1948.

——— Schizophrenia. New York: Logos, 1958. Beugler, E. The basic neurosis. New York: Grune & Stratton, 1949.

Fenichel, O. The psychoanalytic theory of neurosis. New York: Norton, 1945.

Karon, B. P., & Rosberg, J. Study of the motherchild relationship in a case of paranoid schizophrenia. Amer. J. Psychother., 1958, 12, 522-533.

Klein, Melanie, Heiman, Paula, & Money-Kyrle, R.E. New directions in psychoanalysis. London: Tavistock, 1955.

Orlansky, H. Infant care and personality. Psychol. Bull., 1949, 46, 1-48.

Rosen, J.N. Direct analysis. New York: Grune & Stratton, 1953.

Sears, R.R., & Wise, G.W. Relation of cup-feeding in infancy to thumb-sucking and the oral drive. Amer. J. Orthopsychiat., 1950, 20, 123-160.

Seciieiiaye, Marguerite A. Symbolic realization. New York: International Univer. Press, 1955. Silverberg, W. V. Childhood experience and personal destiny. New York: Springer, 1952.

CHAPTER 22
Cognitive Fears and Psychoanalytic Phobias
Bertram P. Karon, PhD and Anmarie J. Widener, MSW, PhD

Today any unreasonable or excessive fear is diagnosed as a phobia. That is very different from the original psychoanalytic definition of a phobia. This difference in terminology leads to confusion and a clear difference in recommended treatments. In the words of the American Psychiatric Association's (2000) *Diagnostic and Statistical Manual of Mental Disorders* (4th ed., text rev.; *DSM-IV-TR*), a specific phobia is a "marked and persistent fear that is excessive or unreasonable, cued by the presence or anticipation of a specific object or situation . . ." (p. 449).

For many psychiatrists, a judgment of excessive or unreasonable in terms of objective reality makes sense because their treatment will be a medication that diminishes the capacity to experience anxiety. The source of the anxiety is irrelevant. However, for most psychotherapists, both psychodynamic and cognitive, medication is not an adequate treatment except as a temporary palliative. Given that cognitive therapy is, to some extent, a historical development from behavioral therapy, it is not surprising that the judgment of "unreasonable" or "excessive" for many cognitive therapists tends to be made in terms of objective reality. But for psychoanalysts and psychoanalytic therapists, a phobia has a more specific meaning. The fear must be unreasonable or excessive given the conscious life experiences of the individual.

Thus, unusually dangerous or painful experience that leads to an unusual fear does not produce a phobia in psychoanalytic terms. Neither would a lifetime of being told by a parent that something was dangerous, even though objectively it was not dangerous, lead to a phobia nor would identifying with a parent who had an unreasonable fear. These would all be considered fears, not phobias. Most of what is currently being described as phobias are actually fears. And fears respond well to cognitive therapy (e.g., desensitization).

The Psychodynamic Diagnostic Manual (PDM), on the other hand, states that "to be considered a phobia in the traditional sense, there must be evidence that the exaggerated fear (symptom) expresses the way the individual organizes internal experience" (PDM Task Force, 2006, p. 104). Even more clearly, in the section on child and adolescent symptoms, it states ". . . the individual with the phobia is usually not able to explain how he or she became afraid of this benign object, which we assume may unconsciously symbolize anxieties about separation, change, time, or death. We assume that this process is held in unconscious memory by psychological defenses" (PDM Task Force, 2006, p. 241).

This is important because a statement is often made that cognitive therapy routinely and quickly is effective for phobias and is the empirically validated treatment of choice (e.g., Craske, Antony, & Barlow, 2006; Gersley, 2001; Mayo Clinic Staff, 2011; Winerman, 2005). In fact, desensitization (which has been given several names) and its variants is a learning-based treatment which is empirically effective both in clinical work and in laboratory research and is very effective for fears that are consistent with the conscious learning history of the individual. In psychoanalytic words, it is very effective for fears. Psychoanalytic therapists also recommend it for fears. In addition, cognitive therapists may teach patients to think differently about their fears (Mayo Clinic Staff, 2011) but they do not help them discover unconscious meanings. Unfortunately, there are some psychoanalytic therapists who also seem not to know the difference between fears and phobias.

Freud recommended that, at some stage, every phobic patient must be encouraged to do what they are afraid of. But Freud said that with phobic patients, it was not important whether they succeed at first because the attempt will stir up the related issues and make it easier to discover their unconscious meaning.

There has long been established laboratory research (Haggard, 1943) as well as clinical experience that desensitization is effective for fears that are consistent with conscious experience but not effective for fears that are not consistent with the conscious learning history of the individual. They do not decondition. But they do decondition quickly when the subject or patient learns what he or she is actually afraid of. Thus, psychoanalytic work is very helpful for phobias that involve unconscious meanings.

Three Cases of Real Phobias

A patient with neurosis in psychoanalysis was afraid of flying. The fear of flying may be a fear or a phobia. Despite successfully enduring several flights, this patient's fear of flying did not diminish. During her most recent flight, she defended against her anxiety by a minor dissociation. She felt she could look down from above, on herself, as a passenger during the flight. She was not psychotic and did not believe she had actually left her body.

The fear of sexual excitement is not the most frequent meaning of the fear of flying, despite the fact that Freud described flying as a common symbol in dreams for sexual excitement, and the novel Fear of Flying which was based on this idea. Rather, it is most commonly based on the fear of being confined in an enclosure from which there is no escape, entirely dependent on the good judgment and skill of one person in charge (V. Jensen, personal communication, 1970). This turned out to be true for this patient. This patient's associations led to her mother driving the car with her three little girls in the back seat. When they irritated her, she would turn and hit them. The patient reported not having been afraid of being hit, but being very scared when that her mother turned around to hit them while continuing to drive the car. After discussing this and relating it to flying, the patient's fear of flying disappeared quickly.

A patient with neurosis after 5 years of psychoanalysis was told that it seemed that we had dealt with most of what needs to be worked on, and we should consider interruption. (Like many therapists, we believe the word "interruption" is more useful than the word "termination" because patients find it less threatening and it implies to them that they could return if necessary, which makes life without a therapist less scary.)

The next week she had a new symptom that she had never experienced before. She was terrified of crossing bridges. She had neither had an accident on a bridge nor had she known anyone else who have had an accident on a bridge. One would have to be a very stupid psychoanalyst not to be able to guess what bridge she was afraid to cross, but the patient made no connection.

However, her associations to her fear of bridges led to her fear of separating from her therapist, as well as her wish to separate, which in turn led to her fears of separating from her father and mother, as well as her wishes to separate from them, and their threats, explicit and implicit, of the dangers of separating from them. But that was not the major issue. There were childhood experiences in which her alcoholic father would come home and reach under the cover and fondle her. She did not know what to make of it. She did not think he had sexually molested her, although she was not sure. At first she said she was not scared of him, but then said that she would go to the bathroom before he came home, lock herself in, and stay there until he was asleep. She had never told anyone about these experiences or her feelings about them, too ashamed to discuss them even though she had been in helpful once-per-week therapy for 2 years as an adolescent, and had now been seen for 5 years in three times a week psychoanalysis.

After discussing in her analysis these experiences with her father and her feelings about them, she not only lost her fear of bridges but also successfully interrupted (i.e., terminated) her analysis. Obviously, at some level it was important to her that she not cross the bridge of terminating therapy until she had been able to discuss this important childhood problem and its meanings for her.

A patient with psychosis in psychoanalytic therapy was terrified of putting on his socks. He had had no scary experiences with socks. His associations led to the socks being a round hole that he put his foot in, and he was scared. His associations then led to the round opening being like a vagina, his mother's vagina, which he was afraid would injure him. Our discussion ended his fear of putting on his socks. This patient with severe psychosis then continued to explore his myriad of delusional ideas and symptoms in long-term psychoanalytic therapy. The meanings of his delusion that he was going to be forced to have intercourse with his mother or with a woman symbolic of her, and his fears of injury and castration by the vagina, as well as a wish for castration, have been described previously (Karon & Rosberg, 1958a, reprinted in Karon & VandenBos, 1981, pp. 362-369; Karon & Rosberg, 1958b, reprinted in Karon & VandenBos, 1981, pp. 337-353). His problems were resolved after a total of 5 years of treatment, 2 years on a 5 day per week basis as an inpatient, and 3 years as an outpatient. (Psychoanalytic therapists, like most competent therapists, of course, do not treat just one symptom, but everything that needs attention.) His recovery has been enduring for at least 30 years when last heard from despite his earlier 16 years of psychosis (during 8 of which he was hospitalized) before he began psychoanalytic psychotherapy without medication in a long-term residential treatment center. Unfortunately, such long-term psychotherapy for patients with psychosis is even rarer now than it was in the 1950s.

The importance of the distinction between fears and phobias is clear for psychoanalysts and psychoanalytic therapists. Cognitive therapists who have a "phobic" patient who does not respond to cognitive therapy will find it helpful to evaluate whether the patient's conscious learning history is consistent with the fear, and if it is not, to consider a consult with a psychoanalytic colleague, or even a referral.

Summary

Most of what are currently called phobias are actually fears, and they respond well to cognitive or exposure therapy. But patients with true phobias, fears that are discrepant from their conscious learning experiences and that involve unconscious meanings, do not respond to cognitive therapy but do respond well to psychoanalysis and psychoanalytic therapy. Three very different patients have been presented as illustrations of the unconscious meaning being made conscious as the treatment of choice for phobias.

REFERENCES

American Psychiatric Association. (2000). Diagnostic Statistical Manual of Mental Disorders (4th ed., text rev.). Washington, DC: Author.

Craske, M.G., Antony, M.M., & Barlow, D.H. (2006). Mastering your fears and phobias. New York, NY: Oxford University Press.

Gersley, E. (2001, November 17). Phobias: Causes and treatments. AllPsychONLINE.

Haggard, E.A. (1943). Experimental studies in affective processes: I. Some effects of cognitive structure and active participation on certain autonomic reactions during and following experimentally induced stress. Journal of Experimental Psychology, 33, 257-284.

Karon, B.P., & Rosberg,]. (1958a). The homosexual urges in schizophrenia. Psychoanalysis and the Psychoanalytic Review, 45, 50-56.

Karon, B.R, & Rosberg,]. (1958b). Study of the mother-child relationship in a case of paranoid schizophrenia. American Journal of Psychotherapy, 12, 522-533.

———— & VandenBos, G. R. (1981). Psychotherapy of schizophrenia: The treatment of choice. New York, NY: Jason Aronson.

Mayo Clinic Staff. (2011). Phobias. Treatments and drugs. Retrieved from http://www.mayoclinic.com/health/phobias/DS00272/DSECTION=treatments-and-drugs

Psychodynamic Diagnostic Manual Task Force. (2006). Psychodynamic diagnostic manual. Silver Spring, MD: Alliance of Psychoanalytic Organizations.

Winerman, L. (2005). Figuring out phobia. American Psychological Association: Monitor on Psychology, 36(7), 96.

CHAPTER 23
How Do You Talk to a Patient About Medication
Bertram P. Karon, PhD ABPP

As a psychotherapist and psychoanalyst, I always tell a new patient who is on psychiatric medication, "I will never ask you to give up anything you need. But the odds are that if you keep talking to me you will eventually go off medication."

They are usually surprised. Previous mental health professionals have usually insisted that they take their medication. Their family doctors may have prescribed the medication. Their family usually has insisted that they take their medication. Frequently, the patients do not believe that I mean what I say. A number of patients have seen me for six or eight weeks before they admitted that they had gone off their medication some time before they began seeing me, but were afraid to tell me so.

If they are not on psychiatric medication, I will not bring up the subject unless they do. However, these days most patients are on psychiatric medication before they seek psychotherapy. Usually, their own experience, if they take it seriously, is that it hasn't helped them. Otherwise, they would not be seeking your help. If they say, "It has saved my life," I say, "Terrific!" If we keep talking, the down side of the medications will come to light and can be discussed in therapy, but I don't bring it up until the patient does, or describes side effects that the patient does not know are side effects of their medication. These days I will suggest they go off gradually, as recommended by Peter Breggin and David Cohen in their book, *Your Drug May Be Your Problem.*

Of course, if I am giving a public lecture (whether to a class, a professional group, or the general public), there will be no chance to discuss it further. I would still say, "Terrific, but not all people are that lucky." I would then proceed to discuss the evidence.

If the patient who is not on psychiatric medication brings up the subject, or who seems like someone who might become litigious, I review the evidence briefly. I may start by saying, "some people would treat you with medication alone, some people would treat you with medication and psychotherapy, but if you see me, we will work with psychotherapy alone, because that's the most effective treatment." I may cite sources like Robert Whitaker's *Anatomy of an Epidemic,* Peter Breggin and David Cohen's *Your Drug May Be Your Problem,* Grace Jackson's *Drug-Induced Dementia*, or, if the problem is schizophrenia, my book, Karon and

VandenBos, *Psychotherapy of Schizophrenia: The Treatment of Choice*. I usually mention that Breggin and Jackson are psychiatrists, because that makes the criticisms of medication more credible. How much detail I go into with a patient depends on what the patient wants to know. Some patients don't care, and are willing to go along with my recommendations without question, and others want more information.

If possible, get their prescribing physician to cooperate with you in reducing the medication. Usually, they will cooperate in reducing the medication, bit by bit. By this time, I have cooperating psychiatrists will do anything I suggest, but this was not the case for a long time. I have sometimes said to a psychiatrist whom I did not know, "you may never have worked with a patient in intensive psychotherapy, and if you are uncomfortable with it, we can get a different psychiatrist. But I would like this patient to be gradually reduced in a medically responsible way." This has worked when I have tried it.

In a public lecture, I will say, "some people are helped by psychiatric medication in the short run, unfortunately, not as many as the ads suggest, but they also may have serious side effects, and they habituate, that is, they tend to have less helpful effect as time goes by. But more seriously, almost all of them have severe withdrawal effects when you try to get off them and are disasters in the long run if you don't get off them." These days I cite Robert Whitaker's data. About antidepressants I will say that they greatly increase the risk for suicide, and if you are on SSRIs and feel like killing yourself, or someone else, it is not you it is the medication, and you need to get it reduced, changed, and/or start psychotherapy. Contact the psychiatrist who prescribed the medication immediately. I mention the British action against using SSRIs on children and adolescents because of the dramatic increase in suicides as compared to no treatment at all, and the fact that these medications are not helpful to children and adolescents, and the more recent warnings adopted by the FDA against using these medications with people under 25. I also cite the fact that 30% of normal adult volunteers with no psychiatric problems or history of treatment, when blindly administered SSRIs become acutely suicidal, which wears off when the medication wears off.

Several patients who were doctors or nurses repeatedly brought up the subject of medication, and complained that I was not using it with them, even though they had agreed initially. Each time I would give a reasonable lecture on why it was not a good idea in my opinion. But it would be brought up again.

One physician patient who was particularly annoying in this way (implying that not using medication was incompetence since I was a psychologist, even though he had been treated unsuccessfully by several psychiatrists for years, all of whom used medication with or without psychotherapy) spent an hour on the subject, with my repeating the same rational replies I had made in every previous session in which he had raised this issue. At the end of the hour, he was very angry at me, which I initially understood as anger at my not using medication despite his insistence.

Later, it dawned on me that was not what was going on. The next session I began by saying that in the last session, he had raised the issue of medication and I had given him my usual lecture, and he was very angry at me, and he should have been angry at me, because I was stupid. "I wonder if you raise the issue of medication when there is something else we need to talk about that you don't want to talk about. You know what I will do. Now what is it that we should have been talking about." And there was something important and troubling that he should have been talking about.

That turned out to be true every time he subsequently raised the subject of medication, and it was also true of my other medical patients who repeatedly raised the issue of medication.

This is how I talk about medication with patients and also in lectures. I hope it is helpful to you unless you can figure out a better way.

CHAPTER 24
Preventing Relapse in Smokers Who Quit
Bertram P. Karon, PhD and Anmarie Widener, MSW, PhD

It is axiomatic that many, if not most, smokers who attempt to give up smoking relapse. It takes most smokers 8-11 tries, according to Cheryl Healton of the American Legacy Foundation, an antismoking group, as cited in the *New York Times* (Konrad, 2010). Despite this, in 1986, the American Cancer Society reported "over 90% of the estimated 37 million people who have stopped smoking in this country since the Surgeon General's first report linking smoking to cancer have done so unaided" (Chapman & MacKenzie, 2010, para. 1). Population studies have shown "unaided cessation" to be the most common method used by most successful ex-smokers (Chapman & MacKenzie). Yet, intervention studies have shown that those who try to quit without the use of medication or counseling have an abysmal 4%—6% success rate (Munsey, 2008). When medication and counseling are used (or used in combination), studies have shown only about one third successfully quit smoking after 2 years of treatment (Eisenberg et ah, 2010; Ellerbeck et ah, 2009). In those who successfully quit for a period of time, studies have shown that most of self-directed quitters (95%) will relapse within 1 year; furthermore, 60%-80% of those who enroll in a treatment program will relapse (Brandon, 2010). It could be, as noted in population studies, that "early failure" may be a sign of initial efforts that are not serious attempts (Chapman & MacKenzie).

There is a simple, inexpensive procedure for quitting smoking that prevents relapse. It has been used by one of us (Karon) for more than 40 years with patients, students, and others. We have not previously published this, because we practice psychoanalytic therapy or psychoanalysis, which does not usually treat patients for a single symptom but, rather, for all symptoms. Smoking has not been the most serious symptom for any of them, although it has been treated when raised by the patient. We have tended to write about symptoms which seemed life threatening, crippling, or of greater importance to the patient or therapist (Karon & VandenBos, 1981; Widener, 1998). However, smoking shortens life spans and can cause costly and serious diseases. Smoking cessation, if taken seriously, can increase health quality and decrease health care costs overall. In today's national efforts to curb health care costs while increasing health care and health quality, smoking cessation can be a key component of our nation's health reform. It is of increasing concern to individuals; indeed, even our current president, President Obama, during his election year and since, continues to try and quit smoking (Rosenbaum, 2008) not only for his own health needs but also to act as a role model for all of us.

This procedure is based on facts and theory about memory, best described by Tomkins in his book *Affects, Imagery, and Consciousness, Volume 4* (1992). According to Tomkins' theory, if human beings experience something in a complex context and then do not experience it for a while, when we next experience it, we tend to reintegrate the whole experience in all its complexity. In the case of smoking, while we smoke, we feel the cigarette in our lips as well as our hands, we smell the smoke, we taste the smoke, and we react to the nicotine. However, when we give up smoking, we do not experience the feelings, smells, or tastes of cigarettes. The next time that we experience any of these singly, we tend to re-experience the whole experience including the strong wish to smoke. That is when we relapse.

Nicotine cravings have been found to be triggered more by environmental cues than by how long it has been since you last smoked (Dar, Rosen-Korakin, Shapira, Gottlieb, & Frenk, 2010). This "discontinuity in addiction," as Tomkins calls it (1992), can also be found in over-eating habits, and David Kessler, author of *The End of Overeating* (2009) referred to it as "conditioned hyper-eating." Kessler explores "cued" neurological activation which causes us to crave certain foods high in fat, sugar, and salt; and he explains how psychological and sensory stimuli can condition us to eat these foods high in fat, sugar, and salt. When people are cued through media or smells or images or even anticipation of these palatable foods, their brain is activated and they begin to crave the food.

Taking these facts and theory into account, if we can give up smoking while re-experiencing the feeling, smell, and taste of the cigarette, we will be free of the return of the strong wish to smoke.

The Procedure

First of all, one must decide that he or she wants to stop smoking. If the person is not ready to quit smoking and does not wish to quit smoking, if he or she believes smoking is not dangerous to his or her health, then no technique will work. If one believes that smoking can lead to a decrease in longevity as well as other serious health problems, and if one values health and life over death and disease, then one can make the distinctions he or she needs to make to reprogram his or her mind.

The first step in the smoking cessation procedure is to decide how much you smoke. For most smokers, that is a pack a day. Then, for one entire month, buy your regular supply each day. Whenever you want to smoke, take a cigarette, light it, and as soon as it is going, put it out. You can take another cigarette immediately. However, put it out immediately, too. One smoker went through five cigarettes in a row.

Sometime during the month, you will forget to put out a cigarette. It is critical to realize that this is normal. You have smoked many cigarettes in your life, and now you have smoked one more. Now that you remember that you are giving it up, put it out. This is like the alcoholic who tries to give it up, feels good about it, then falls off the wagon, and feels as if it is hopeless. That is why it is important for his or her sponsor (if he or she is in Alcoholics Anonymous) to tell him or her that most people who give up alcohol fall off the wagon at some point; but now that he or she remembers, sober up and stay sober. This continued hope for success is one important factor that can help the alcoholic stay sober.

By the end of the month, you will be free of smoking, and you will not relapse.

Why It Fails

There have been no systematic controlled studies on the cessation of smoking using this technique. However, it has worked for most patients who have raised the issue in private practice for 45 years. Patients have been adults, both male and female, with a range of neurotic, borderline, and psychotic problems. It therefore seemed worth sharing.

There are some cases that fail. The most common are people who have ambivalent feelings about giving up smoking. For those who do not wish to give up smoking at all, no technique will work for them. There were also two patients who said they could not do this procedure and made no attempt. However, both of them stopped smoking without using this technique. One was diagnosed with throat cancer, and the other had a heart attack. Both were told by their doctors that it did not kill them this time; but it will the next time. Both of them stopped smoking after that. Unfortunately, the throat cancer recurred; but the heart attack patient had no further heart attacks and has lived a long life so far.

A good internist said that he tells his patients that, at any age, the odds of dying of cancer, heart attack, or stroke within the next 10 years are twice as high if you smoke. When you are young, the odds are small; when you are older, the odds are worse. He is frequently successful at getting his patients to make a decision to quit smoking. This decision to quit is critical.

One way of discussing the issue is to simply say that if smoking is worth dying for, do not give it up. If it is not worth dying for, then one should give it up. However, when you discuss the issue, you should be accurate as to the dangers, or willing to refer the patient to accurate sources of information. Of course, in psychotherapy, we respect the right of the patient to disagree with us, and we have raised the issue of smoking cessation only after the patient did first. However, in lectures to students, we have described the data on dangers of smoking, and this way of stopping, without being asked.

A way for a patient to fail with this technique is to maintain that it is a waste of money to buy cigarettes that you will not smoke and, therefore, cease to carry out the procedure prematurely. However, if the patient were told to buy a drug for 1 month that was equally expensive but that would help them quit smoking (if that is what they wanted), almost all of them would gladly do it. Saving on cigarette money in the short run is just a way to try to fail.

Tomkins' Theory

Tomkins' theory of memory was not published until after his death in the fourth volume of *Affects, Imagery, and Consciousness* (1992, pp. 225-228). The first three volumes of his most important book were published over a 30-year span while he was still alive.

A simple example of this theory of memory can be tested by anyone. If you write your name as slowly as possible, you will find that you tend to write it, not as you do now, but as you did when you were first learning to write. Some people even change the way they write specific letters, if they wrote those letters differently when they were first learning to write. This is because you have not written your name slowly since the days when you were first learning to write. This example, although simple and clear, is not practically important. However, the application to smoking is.

Tomkins and Karon discussed casually in 1955 that Tomkins' theory had implications for smokers, but neither went into detail at that time. At the time, Tomkins said that there was little interest in the psychological factors in smoking addiction in the funding agencies, but only in the physiological factors. Nonetheless, both Tomkins and Karon came to similar conclusions as to the implications of Tomkins' theory for smoking. However, the description in Tomkins (1992) volume IV of what it would be like to give up smoking while tasting and holding the cigarette is somewhat more agonizing and heroic than most smokers find it to be. Tomkins, attending to the affects, describes a man's "addiction transformation," as he successfully attempts to quit smoking:

This is the moment of truth for him. If he can tolerate himself at such a moment, he can govern himself, grow stronger, and win the reward of the smile of joy that the rapid reduction of negative affect evokes as an incremental bonus. From this point on, it will become easier rather than harder as the positive affect evoked by mastery combines with and attenuates each succeeding paler version of negative affect. At the end of the first week, this man's battle is almost won; his vulnerability to backsliding is constantly being reduced by the large number of graded combinations of positive and negative affects that will eventually make it possible for him to retrieve the pre-smoking traces of looking at a cigarette, as well as being unaware of the satisfactions of past smoking and the dissatisfactions that such remembered rewards generate during periods of experienced deprivation. (p. 227)

The following are illustrative case examples.

Case 1

A man in his late 20s gave up smoking. He had smoked sporadically since the age of 10, and smoked regularly from his freshman year in college. He smoked cigarettes, cigars, and a pipe at various times. At the age of 26, he gave up smoking. He stayed off smoking for nearly a year.

A friend invited him for dinner, along with several other friends. The meal was good and the company was pleasant. At the end of the meal, the host handed out cigars, which all the guests smoked. It tasted good, and his smoking habit was reinstated. Two years later, he tried this procedure. It worked. Approximately 2 years after that, he was at a cocktail party, something he had not done since he gave up smoking. Someone offered him a cigarette. He reached out, started to take a cigarette, and as it reached his mouth, rather than wanting to smoke, he remembered he had given up and put it down. The desire to smoke did not return.

He has not smoked since. More than 30 years have passed.

Case 2

In 2010, the second author counseled a young man in his mid-20s to use this technique to quit smoking. The young man had asked for counseling after experienced symptoms of dizziness and headache had not been able to be attributed to any physical reason; his doctor suggested counseling, assuming there might be a psychosomatic reason for his symptoms.

The man reported casually that he smoked, as he was describing his other problems. This man had been smoking about a pack a day since his college days (for about 8 years). He was explained of this technique only after he had said that he wanted to quit smoking, but was not able to do so successfully so far. On the third day of trying this smoking cessation technique, he reported having success but stating, "It feels a bit weird." When asked to describe what was weird about it, the man stated, "People keep looking at me like I'm crazy because I light a cigarette and then immediately put it out. But other than that, it's fine; yeah, it's working."

After 3 months, the young man had not smoked and reported the desire to smoke had not returned. The counseling ended and there was no follow-up. Incidentally, his symptoms of dizziness and headache also remitted.

Case 3

The second author told this technique to a man in his late 20s who had gone into counseling after the break-up of a relationship. His ex-girlfriend, who had left him, had been "into health," he reported; he felt one of the reasons she left him was that he had "developed bad health habits." He described starting to smoke only after he volunteered with the Peace Corps (a 27-month tour of duty) and had been sent to an Eastern European country where, he reported, "everyone smokes all the time, every day, everywhere, even the kids." He had been smoking for 1 year at the time he started counseling, and reported smoking about a half to three quarters of a pack a day. He reported that cigarettes were not only important socially in that country, but were also very cheap, so it was difficult to not smoke. However, he described feeling like he "got away from who [he] truly was," which according to him, was a "super health conscious person." He had a strong desire to quit smoking, not only for his own health and ego issues, but also for his belief that it would help him reconcile with his ex-girlfriend.

The second author described the smoking cessation technique to him. He was very interested in the theory behind the technique and found it made a lot of sense. He said knowing that information on "triggers" of differently encoded memory (sight, taste, smell, feel, cues, etc.) helped him to understand why he had not quit yet. He later reported not smoking any cigarettes "even when my best friends are smoking" and "when the social occasion is such that it is very hard not to smoke."

After 6 additional months, his therapy ended. He had not smoked for those 6 months and reported "no desire" to smoke. Incidentally, he had successfully grieved the loss of his relationship and had no continued hope for reconciliation with his ex-girlfriend.

Medication

The authors have used this procedure without medication. Additionally, in the case histories described earlier, none of the persons who used this technique were taking any form of medication. This technique to quit smoking has worked on a case-by-case level. Today, many, if not most, smokers use medication to help them quit. Theoretically, there does not seem to be any reason why it could not be combined with medications, but we have no research data or clinical observations on this issue. The use of antidepressants has been studied to some extent as an aid to quitting, but the combined use of antidepressant medication with this technique has not been researched. Moreover, we would be skeptical of the use of antidepressants as an aid to quitting, given the recent data raising serious questions about both the effectiveness and the safety of antidepressants despite their popularity (Breggin, 2008).

Conclusion

Smoking is a public health problem, but most smokers have trouble giving it up. Even then, many of them relapse. This procedure for preventing relapse is simple, and it works. It is useful for therapists who work with smokers and even for smokers who quit on their own.

REFERENCES

Brandon, T. (2010). Random sample. Monitor on Psychology, 41 (3), 22.

Breggin, R.R. (2008). Medication madness: A psychiatrist exposes the dangers of mood-altering medications. New York: St. Martin's Press.

Chapman, S., & MacKenzie, R. (2010). The global research neglect of unassisted smoking cessation: Causes and consequences. Public Library of Science Medicine, 7(2) el000216. doi: 10.1371/ journal. pmed. 1000216

Dar, R., Rosen-Korakin, N., Shapira, O., Gottlieb, Y., & Frenk, H. (2010). The craving to smoke in flight attendants: Relations with smoking deprivation, anticipation of smoking, and actual smoking. Journal of Abnormal Psychology, 119(1), 248-253.

Eisenberg, M.J., Blum, L.M., Filion, K.B., Rinfret, S., Pilote, L., Paradis, G., et al. (2010). The efficacy of smoking cessation therapies in cardiac patients: A meta-analysis of randomized controlled trials. Canadian Journal of Cardiology,26(2), 73-79.

Ellerbeck, E.F., Mahnken, J.D., Cupertino, A.P., Cox, L.S., Greiner, K. A., Mussulman, L. M., et al. (2009). Effect of varying levels of disease management on smoking cessation: A randomized trial. Annals of Internal Medicine, 150(7), 437-446.

Karon, B.R., & VandenBos, G.R. (1981). Psychotherapy of schizophrenia: The treatment of choice. New York: Aronson.

Kessler, D.A. (2009). The end of overeating: Taking control of the insatiable American appetite. New York: Rodale.

Konrad, W. (2010, January 9). For the New Year, cost-effective options to stop smoking. The New York Times, p. B6.

Munsey, C. (2008). Help your clients kick the habit. Monitor on Psychology, 39(10), 38-40.

Rosenbaum, R. (2008, December). Give the guy a butt! Let Obama smoke in the White House. USA Today, 10.

Tomkins, S.S. (1992). Affect, imagery, consciousness: VoL 4. Cognition: Duplication and transformation of information (pp. 225-228). New York: Springer Publishing.

Widener, A.J. (1998). Beyond Ritalin: The importance of therapeutic work with parents and children diagnosed ADD/ADHD. Journal of Child Psychotherapy, 24(2), 267-281.

CHAPTER 25
Some Clinical Notes on the Significance of the Number Four
Bertram P. Karon, Ph.D.

The importance of the number four within the framework of Jungian theory is well-known[1,4] (and see, in particular, *Mysterium Coniunctionis*[5,pp 164-321]). Jung points to the quatemity of the four mental functions (the two pairs of opposite functions: thinking vs. feeling, and sensation vs. intuition) which play such a central role in his theories. He also documents in detail the attractiveness and power attributed in many different cultures and periods to the manifestations of this archetype. Such manifestations are: the number four itself, the quaternio, the square, the circle divided into four parts, and the four-armed cross (for example, the Christian cross). According to Jung, this is an archetype of almost unequalled potency, importance, and interest, and, like all archetypes, it is put forth by Jung as evidence of the racial unconscious, inasmuch as it is postulated to exist in all cultures.

An alternative view with respect to universal symbolism, and one to which the present author subscribes, is that certain human problems are universal because of the biological nature and common experience of human beings. Where there are simple and readily available objects and ideas which are peculiarly apt for the expression of certain emotional themes, and where these objects and ideas are widespread over the earth's surface, their use as symbols of these emotional themes will be similarly widespread. For example, snakes (or ideas of snakes) are to be found in almost all parts of the world. Snakes are somewhat penisshaped, capable of rigidity and extensibility, alive (that is, outside the control of the ego), and dangerous. Is it then surprising to find that an uneducated village girl in India employs the snake in her dreams as an unmistakable penis symbol,[9] just as surely as any neurotic in western society?[7] (See also French's excellent discussion of water symbolism.[8])

This view of universal symbolism, which obviates the necessity for postulating a "racial unconscious," follows directly from Ferenczi's description of the ontogenetic development of symbolism.[9] Although such a view is not identical with Freud's original formulations,[10] it is compatible with the symbolic interpretations he presented. These interpretations, while more mundane and restricted to the psychosexual sphere than those of Jung, have also proved more capable of experimental verification.[11,12] Of course, despite generally found symbolic meanings, certainty as to the meaning which any particular individual attaches to a symbol can be attained only by an intensive study of that individual.

In Freud's view of symbolism, the symbol serves a specific disguise function.[10'p'164] Its function is not only to express the unconscious, but at the same time to preserve the meaning of what is being expressed from reaching consciousness. It is this dual function which accounts for the use of the symbol. This disguise-function has been disputed not only by the Jungians, but by others who see the symbol as simply a primitive language without 'any disguise-function necessarily involved, for example, Fromm[13] and Hall.[14'15*pp'80'100] However, the Freudian position once more seems to have experimental verification.16 Rosen, in developing "direct analysis," a psychoanalytic therapy of psychosis,[17'pp-3-4] extended this insight of Freud's to the symbols of the psychotic. As part of the direct analytic technique, direct interpretations are made of unconscious content, to undo the disguise-function of the psychotic delusions. A correct interpretation renders the patient's previous psychotic resolution ineffective, and makes possible a healthier resolution with the help of the therapist. Therefore, a knowledge of symbolism is a valuable tool for the direct analytic therapist.

The number three, according to Freud, is "in a class by itself" as a penis symbol.[18'p-146] It takes on this commonly found significance from the universal biological fact that the male genitalia has three parts. But what of the number four? Freud presents no interpretation for this symbol and there seemed to be no obvious referent to the present author other than those suggested by Jung.

In Jacobi's lectures on number symbolism at the Jung Institute,[19] odd numbers were described as masculine, and even as feminine. Three was described as the first "real number." Its meanings include such diverse referents as "the child," masculinity, and activity. Four was described as "three plus one," the quaternity which in turn is the "root and source of changing nature."

Jung himself describes the meanings of the quaternity as completion, wholeness, the totality of the four mental functions, and "the container and organizer of all opposites ... the possibility of order in wholeness."[4-p-317] It may represent a totality with the four elements unintegrated within it, or it may represent integrated totality, unity, integration, and the self. Along with the closely related symbol of the circle, it is the "hallmark of the individuation process,"[4-p-321] that process which is the aim, according to Jung, not only of psychotherapy but of all mental life; and the archetype of the quaternity refers both to the past and the future.

Such a meaning would account for its compellingness as a symbol. Jung is unequivocal about the fact that this meaning is not dependent on experience but is inherited as part of the racial unconscious: "... for the latter [the quaternity] is not a human invention at all but a fact which existed long before consciousness..."[4'p-227]

It was, therefore, with great interest that the author noticed that the number four played a large part in the systematic delusions of a paranoid schizophrenic under direct psychoanalytic therapy.[17] The patient considered himself God, the "infinity being." He was arranging the world so that "everything be best." ("Best," it turned out, meant breast. "The mystics told me about the connection," he said, "many years ago, but I don't think about such things any more.")

The patient divided mankind into four parts: "the poor and bad" and "the good and best"; the same four-part division was applied to inanimate objects and to ideas. He made it clear that he wanted to deal only with the last two and have nothing to do with the first two of these subdivisions. He never differentiated the poor from the bad or the good from the best; nevertheless, he resisted the idea that there were only two subdivisions and insisted on four.

There were four sexes: male, female, male-female, and femalemale. Each of these could be subdivided into four more sub-sexes labeled the same as the major sexes. In fact each of these 16 could again be subdivided into four more, again with the same labels, making 64 "if you want to be technical." There were also four dimensions: space, time, space-time, and time-space.

There were also four divisions of the world: mankind, animal, vegetable, and mineral. There were four ways men could be inspired to do good things: for themselves, for all people, for the world (including animal, vegetable, and mineral) and for him (God).

There were four earthly punishments he (God) could inflict on men: pain, suffering, obstruction, and social limitation; plus four degrees of damnation: eternal damned, accursed damned, worse damned, and temporary damned. There were four times: infinity past, infinity present, infinity future, and infinity eternal. There were four activities: thinking, believing, knowing, doing. In fact, the patient would insist that anything could, and should, be looked at from the standpoint of the four dimensions. Two phrases which recurred in his delusional monologues (in which he was "making the world best") were "four ways infinity from every present point in time" and "four ways infinity best."

The four activities (thinking, believing, knowing, doing) did indeed sound very Jungian; perhaps one should give the patient credit for tapping the collective unconscious instead of seeking a concealed psychodynamic problem. Thinking and believing might very well be the patient's equivalent of Jung's thinking and feeling. Similarly, knowing might be the equivalent of intuition. But doing hardly seems the equivalent of Jung's sensation, so Jung was abandoned as a source of enlightenment in favor of the patient himself.

The patient explained that, as God, he was also, of course, the greatest of philosophers. All of modern philosophic thinking would be impossible without his great discovery, which was none other than the "fourth dimension" (by this, he meant a fourth dimension to everything). You cannot, he would say, really think about anything unless you think in four dimensions. In three dimensions you can't find anything. People who "think in threes" are lost; they cannot do anything.

"If I say anything three times, it comes out all rotten. If I add a fourth, it comes out best." One day he was talking about childhood games, and devised a compulsive ritual which he explained as, "Step three times, then turn it into four."

One day he gave the author a lecture on numerology. When he was asked what the number four meant, he replied, "That's difficult. A square. A way of action. Perfect. Saturn number. Heavy —holding down. Perfect is turning threes into fours."

In this last sentence, the mystery was solved: "Four" meant simply "not three." But why not two or five rather than four?

In the patient's "lecture" on numerology, two was described only as "a feminine number," representing the breasts, and apparently the dangerous aspect of them. (After having reacted with fear to the approach of a woman with a well-endowed bosom, he explained his reaction as, "She came near me with her breast and I had a pain in my side; she was ruining me.")

The number one was also unacceptable, since it symbolized the same thing for the patient that three did. Five, on the other hand, was described cryptically as simply an "activity number"; it was perfectly acceptable. An alternative expression, and one apparently synonymous with "four ways infinity best" is "four, five infinity best." The patient got upset if four was changed to a lower number; he did not object to its being changed to a five. His reactions to other numbers depended on the special significance of the particular number: He, himself, never used anything but threes, fours—including 16 (four times four), 64 (four times four times four), and 256 (four to the fourth power)—and fives in his delusions. The lower numbers (one and two) are also avoided because someone might add something to change them into threes; four is the least number for which this cannot be done (and with abstract ideas no one can take away an element). Further, the patient can easily change any three into a four by the addition of another element, as when he added to the three more obvious times —infinity past, infinity present and infinity future—a fourth, infinity eternal.

There remain only two more steps in establishing the thesis that the number four represented the denial of the penis (and of sexuality in general) for this patient: first, to show that three is for him a penis symbol, and, second, to relate the denial of the penis (and of sexuality in general) to his pathology.

In his "lecture" on numerology, his explanation of the number three was: "Success. Jupiter [it developed that Jupiter was the god, not the planet] has threes." Jupiter, it became clear from the rest of his material, represented the patient's father. Whenever Jupiter appeared in hallucinations, he appeared as three gods —either as three Jupiters, or as one Jupiter accompanied by two lesser gods. The clinching evidence for the significance of the number three for this case came one day when the patient was sitting contemplating three pencils which he held in one hand. The writer took the middle one, and the patient yelled in distress, "Give me back my penis."

As to whether this denial of masculinity makes sense, the patient hid his penis with his hand when talking to people. In the middle of a fairly friendly conversation when he was responding freely, the writer asked him what the number four meant, why everything had to come in fours. He immediately stopped talking and put his hand over his penis. He would make no further response to the question.

Hiding the penis represented both an attempt to hide the existence of the penis and to protect it from castration (of which he was afraid, partly because of his own desire for castration).

He referred to himself as a middle-aged woman, or woman-man. He said he was not a homosexual, but a Lesbian. He then said that all sex was bad, it was not "best," he would not have anything to do with it. When urinating, he squatted like a woman rather than urinate standing. During one visit from his mother, the first thing he said was "Gloria Vanderbilt [a mother symbol] is stabbing me in the back," accompanying the statement with a wiping motion from his anus. After she left, he said he was a Lesbian. When the interpretation was offered to him that he thought his mother would love him if he were a woman, he replied that his mother was perfect, but that she liked young girls like Gloria Vanderbilt. Another time he brought up his mother's preference for young girls and was asked whether she was a Lesbian. "No," he said, "she's a different kind of thing. She's a homosexual and I'm a Lesbian."

"Are you a Lesbian?"

"No," he said.

"Why?"

"You'll get mad."

"Why?"

"I'm going to learn, Greer Garson will teach me. Greer Garson and me will be Lesbians. We will go and get some young girls together. Greer Garson has a penis which she hides."

"Do you have a penis?"

"No ... I mean, yes."

The question was repeated a couple of times, and each time he first said, "No," hesitated, and then said, "Yes."

When talking to his mother he generally referred to himself as a woman and to her as a man. Still, he could not accept his desire to he a woman for fear of the castration involved—although he wished for it. He was terrified and wished to escape to a realm where there were no penes (and hence no sexuality). He was afraid of being touched by either sex. Interestingly enough, whenever Hera—who represented his mother—occurred in his hallucinations there were always four Heras—four goddesses.

In brief, he felt that his mother resented his being a man, that this accounted for her hostility. Denying that he had a penis ("turning threes into fours") was one of his persistent symptomatic attempts to gain what he felt he lacked-—the unconditional, unreserved love of his mother as symbolized by the good breast ("makes the world best").*

Patients are always capable of teaching us what we wish to know about the unconscious, if only we are willing to listen. The problems which this patient symbolized by the number four are certainly common enough to suggest what the significance of this symbol may be for other humans, normal and pathological. In conclusion, the question may be raised whether it is a coincidence that the theory of Carl Jung, which originated in the denial of the importance which Freud ascribed to sexuality,[20,pp-19'44' 67'9S] should take as its cornerstone the symbol four.

Acknowledgment

The writer wishes to express his appreciation to Per Ostman for corroborating the clinical observations; to Eobert Firestone, Anton S. Morton, Jack Eosberg, and Alden E. Wessman for helpful suggestions; and to John N. Eosen, under whose supervision the patient was treated.

*The significance of the number four was derived entirely from the consistency of the observations; the meaning adduced for this symbol was not presented to the patient until after the paper was complete. Nevertheless, from the standpoint of "direct analysis,"[17, pp.] the best evidence for the correctness of an interpretation presented to a psychotic patient is a marked change in the pathology. It is worth while noting, therefore, that this interpretation, unlike others which had been offered to the patient, did, in fact, have a marked effect: The number four, with which the patient had been concerned continuously for years, disappeared from his delusional system when it was interpreted as a denial of his penis and of sexuality in general.

REFERENCES

Jacobi, Jolande: The Psychology of Jung. Tale. New Haven. 1949.

Jung, C.G.: Collected Papers on Analytical Psychology. Bailliere, Tindall & Cox. London. 1920.

———— : Psychology   and Alchemy. Pantheon. New York. 1953.

———— : The   Practice of Psychotherapy. Pantheon. New York. 1954.

———— : Mysterium   Ooniunetionis. Rascher. Zurich. 1955.

Alexander, V.K.: A case study of a multiple personality. J. Abnor. and Soc. Psychol., 52:272-276, 1956.

Abraham, K.: A complicated ceremonial found in neurotic women. Selected Papers on Psychoanalysis. Yol. I, pp. 157-163. Basic Books. New York. 1953.

French, T.H.: The Integrative Process in Dreams. The Integration of Behavior, Vol. II. University of Chicago. Chicago. 1954.

Ferenczi, S.: The ontogenesis of symbols. Sex in Psychoanalysis. Pp. 276-

281. Selected Papers, Vol. I. Basic Books. New York. 1950.

Freud, S.: The Interpretation of Dreams. Macmillan. New York. 1950.

Bettelheim, S., and Hartmann, H.: Parapraxes in Korsakow psychoses. In: The Organization and Pathology of Thought. Pp. 288-307. D. Rappaport, editor. Columbia. New York. 1951.

Farber, L.H., and Usher, C.: An experimental approach to dream psychology through the use of hypnosis. Psychoan. Quart., 12:202-216, 1943.

Fromm, E.: The Forgotten Language. Rinehart. New York. 1951.

Hall, C.S.: A cognitive theory of dream symbols. J. Gen. Psychol., 48:169-186, 1953.

———— : The Meaning of Dreams. Harper. New York. 1953.

Clark, R.A, and Sensibar, Minda R.: The relationship between symbolic and manifest projections of sexuality with some incidental correlates. J. Abnor. and Soc. Psychol., 50:327-334, 1955.

Rosen, J.N.: Direct Analysis. Grune & Stratton. New York. 1953.

Freud, S.: A General Introduction to Psychoanalysis. Garden City Publishing Company. Garden City. 1943.

Jacobi, Jolande: The symbolism of numbers. Unpublished lectures delivered at the C.G. Jung Institute, Zurich, January 28 and February 4, 1955, as part of her course, "Pictures from the Unconscious." (Notes transcribed and made available to the author through the courtesy of Dr. I.E. Alexander of Princeton University.)

Jung, C.G.: The Theory of Psychoanalysis. Nervous and Mental Disease Publishing Company. New York. 1915.

CHAPTER 26
Artistic Creation As Adaptive Ego Function and Not Regression In The Service of the Ego

Bertram P. Karon, Ph.D.

Artistic creation is a complex adaptive ego function, which all of us possess, but only some of us develop to a high degree of efficiency as a means of coping with internal and external reality. It serves a variety of needs, conscious and unconscious. But it is not regression, although some of the needs expressed are regressed needs. The meaning of the artistic work should not be the focus of analytic work unless that is the problem that brought the patient into treatment, which is rarely the case. Typically, artistic creation is the area in which the artist functions best and with which the artist neither seeks nor requires help. Contrary to popular belief, it is not necessary to be disturbed to be an artist; rather, if one is an artist, one will use one's talent to cope with that disturbance. The artist-to-be often shows a compulsive need to practice his or her art several hours every day long before he or she has any clear idea that he or she can pursue his or her art as a career, or earn a living by it, or have it appreciated by the rest of the world. Therapists need to be sensitive enough not to interfere with such apparently impractical, but truly valuable "compulsions."

I don't show my writing to my friends before it is done. They think I want their advice or criticism. If I thought they could write better than me, they would be writing. Now I only show them my work after my agent has sold it. Then they know I don't want their advice. I don't want their help or criticism. I just want them to love me for it."

It is my view, based on one writer and three painters I have had as patients, and one classical musician who is a good friend, that artistic creation is not regression, but a complex ego function that all of us have, but only some of us develop to a high degree of efficiency as a means of coping with internal and external reality.

It is not the case that one has to be psychopathological to be artistically gifted, but rather that if one has severe problems and is an artist, one uses this ego function to cope with one's problems. Thus, Beethoven stopped writing music in those rare times when he was happy; luckily for the world he was usually intensely depressed and only his music made life bearable (E. Sterba and R. Sterba, 1954). But had his life not been so miserable, the odds are that he would have learned to write music even without needing it to cope with misery. After all, Mendelssohn was a relatively happy man (Blunt, 1974) and still wrote first rate music, if not the caliber of Beethoven.

Beethoven is a good example of the futility of psychologists theorizing about art or analyzing an artist without being an artist. One of the classic vocational aptitude tests, the Seashore Musical Aptitude Test, is nothing but a pitch discrimination test. Early in Beethoven's career, a careful examination might have discovered subtle flaws in his hearing, presaging the gradual encroachment of deafness. One can well imagine one of our colleagues saying, "Well, Ludwig, whatever else you do, you should not seriously consider a career as a musician."

Indeed, without knowing Beethoven's story, would any of us predict that a deaf man could compose music, let alone that he would be brilliant at it? Beethoven himself did not know that he would compose his greatest works after he was deaf. The Heiligenstadt Testament, a letter he wrote to his brother, reveals his agony over who would hire a deaf composer, and over his dread of the consequences of his increasing loss of hearing. What would life be worth to a Beethoven who could not compose, play, or hear music?

It is art that makes life worthwhile to the artist. George Orwell tolerated the unpleasantness of his early life by telling himself the story of his life while he lived it. Later he told it to the rest of us in thin but masterful disguise (Woodcock, 1966).

Somerset Maugham has a short story about a writer who is suffering from a personal tragedy and who talks to a better writer about his suffering: "I'm broken and done for. I'm finished."

"Why don't you write a story about it? ... You know that's the great pull a writer has over other people. When something has made him terribly unhappy, and he's tortured and miserable, he can put it all into a story and it's astonishing what a comfort and relief it is" [1921, p. 704].

The lesser writer can't bring himself to do that; but the better writer would. Whatever happened to him, he could make something of value of it by writing a story. (It is obvious which writer represented Maugham.)

Artists are, of course, as varied as other people. While artistic creation is not regression, the needs expressed may be regressed, as in Michelangelo's apparent search for the breast in his search for the perfect piece of marble (R. Sterba and E. Sterba, 1956). Or in the musicians whose mothers write a piece of music which they practiced all day, then play for her delight. Or in the sculptor who continually tells scatalogical jokes, as long as he is with people who would not be offended by them, and whose favorite medium is clay, with which he produces powerful and beautiful productions.

I have treated three painters with psychoanalysis or psychoanalytic therapy. They did not come into treatment for help with their art; indeed, they were at their best when they were painting. (I believe this is typical of artists who come into treatment.) They neither needed nor wanted help with their painting. It was the rest of their life that was a mess. One patient was depressed, one suffered primary impotence, and the third was a chronic paranoid schizophrenic, who had spent half of the previous 15 years of his life in hospitals. The other half was the result of his ingenuity at escaping from hospitals; as far as I knew he had never been formally discharged by a medical staff before escaping

Ernst Kris (1952) advised against analyzing an artists art, for fear of disrupting the artists ability to create, by making him or her too self-conscious about the unconscious determinants of the work. Richard Sterba, in discussing a psychotic violinist, recommended that she should have a therapist who had no interest in music, since the only thing anyone had ever shown interest in was her extraordinary musical talent. A therapist with a strong interest in classical music would be too easily distracted from what needed attention to what everyone always attended to; it would be an easy and effective resistance.

The paranoid schizophrenic painter was the patient who first taught me that artistic creation was not regression. Painting was clearly his most highly developed ability. Although he did not like it, this patient could tolerate talking crazy, acting crazy, and being regarded as crazy by others, but on those rare occasions when his psychosis impaired his ability to paint, he was devastated.

We are all familiar with the fact that when non-artists become psychotic, they produce so-called schizophrenic art, that is, more or less abstract productions similar to expressionism, surrealism, dada, cubism, and so forth, depending upon the bent of the patient. However, this extremely talented man painted only literal and realistic renditions. It took a while for me to realize that the most important task for this man was holding onto reality, and that he used his most adaptive skill in the service of this need. It was only after he was no longer psychotic that he allowed himself to paint in abstract modes—when holding onto external reality and trying to ascertain what external reality was were no longer the most urgent issues.

It may well be that non-artist patients, whose capacity to reproduce accurate perceptions of reality is at best insufficient due to lack of talent and training, cannot use art for that purpose, but can use it to attempt to cope with the inadequately understood inner forces, unconscious memories, and psychotically distorted renderings of past and present reality that assail them.

The one aspect of his painting this patient wanted to discuss was his use of color. As he described it, "Michelangelo says I am a better draughtsman than he is, but he is a better colorist."

"When did he say that?" I asked.

"This morning."

Indeed, his paintings at that time were all in shades of brown and black.

The patient began one session by asking me, "What's the connection between painting and shitting? They say there is a connection between painting and shitting."

I did not ask him who they were, whether they were real people, someone he had read, or hallucinatory voices. Rather, I made the connection he seemed to be asking for.

"Sometimes little kids, when they are being toilet trained, think they are doing something nice for mother and they think of the shit as a gift. Then they discover mother doesn't really like the shit, even though she has been asking for it. Then they may substitute smearing brown and black substances on a piece of canvas and give her that."

After that hour, his colors improved and were no longer confined to shades of brown and black. This was the only time we discussed his painting, and that was because he raised the subject, made the connection, and only needed to have it spelled out more clearly.

At one point this patient gave me one of his paintings. I was impressed by the talent it demonstrated. But in the next session he asked for it back. I returned it to him, and he proceeded to destroy it in front of me.

I must admit mourning the loss later, particularly when seeing other professionals with examples of "schizophrenic" art their patients had produced hanging in their offices. I recalled the truly impressive work that my patient had both given me and destroyed. It was only years later that I realized that, unwittingly, on my part at least, this had been one of the most important and helpful hours in his treatment. As is so often the case, the art was a gift and communication to his mother. But she was too willing to take it, all of it, which was frightening and annoying. He had displayed talent early in life, and his mother, throughout his childhood, would go through his notebooks every night, and take out any poem, story, drawing, or painting that was complete. He would at times cry and ask to keep them, saying they were his. She said no, that she only did this for his own good, that she wanted to show people his work so that they would see how good it was.

Even as an adult he did not believe other people could appreciate his talent without his mother's intercession. In fact, he received very few direct compliments on his work, and did not know how impressed others were by his talent. But his mother, who frequently showed his work, continuously received approbation for his obvious talent throughout his life.

"Nobody thinks I'm worthwhile. If it were not for my mother, nobody would think I was worthwhile. Maybe if they thought I was God, they would have to think I was worthwhile," he said, describing a basis for one of his persistent delusions.

The second painter was neurotically depressed. He was a highly regarded man who painted realistically and despised abstract art, but was too polite to say that when it might hurt someone's feelings. Nonetheless, he did not realize the high esteem in which he was regarded until it was forced on his attention. Thus, he was sure that the faculty of a university department despised him and resented his teaching there, since he had never gone to college, but to an art school. Fortunately, he attended the faculty meetings regularly. At one of them, a colleague whom he did not know introduced himself and said, "I just want to let you know how lucky we feel that you are spending this year with us."

The only aspect of his painting that entered into the treatment was his feeling that he was insufficiently prolific. Since there is no objective standard, it was easy to maintain a feeling of inadequacy, even though it seemed unrealistic to me. However, his wife confirmed to him the inadequacy of his productivity. She was older than he, and played the role of a guilt-inducing maternal object to be placated, whose standards one could never satisfy. The work of analysis proceeded without regard to the content of this artist's work.

The third artist originally saw me for primary impotence. His art was abstract, and of a sort that I did not understand, which was useful for him since I was not tempted to discuss his work. He would interrupt the treatment for several weeks at a time, saying, "I have to paint." Usually this was in preparation for a show. During these periods, he would paint from the time he woke in the morning until he was exhausted and went to sleep, leaving the house only to get food or other provisions.

Only a fool would have attempted to insist on his coming to treatment at these times, and he would have ignored any such advice in any event. When these periods of intense work ended, he would resume the treatment, as well as the rest of his life.

Although I did not understand his work, and we never discussed it, artists who knew his work remarked in my presence that they felt his work had improved while he was in treatment.

He had grown up in a lower middle-class family in a large city. His father had been psychotic and did not work. His mother supported the family. Neither his family nor his friends had any interest in art. Indeed, most of the people in his neighborhood, including friends and relatives, considered him strange, if not outright crazy, for giving up his secure job in the post office to pursue further training and a career in art.

The only people who supported his interest were his art instructors. They recognized his potential and encouraged him to develop it. The further he went, the more his instructors felt he should go on. With their help he obtained a fellowship that enabled him to get a Master's degree in Fine Art. Nonetheless, most of the people he grew up with would still not understand why he gave up a secure job in the post office to become an artist.

He only came for treatment for his impotence after he was earning a living as an artist, and it was clear that that was a reasonable and stable career choice. One of the secondary gains of his impotence was that it enabled him to pursue his talent. If he had not been impotent, he would undoubtedly have married, had children (he was Catholic), and felt duty-bound to stay with his secure job at the post office to fulfill his family obligations rather than pursue the development of his talent. It was only after his career seemed stable that it was safe to consider losing the symptom.

He was originally seen once per week in psychoanalytic therapy. After about a year or so, I interpreted a fear of being drained through the penis, an infantile terror about which psychotic patients had taught me.

The patient dropped out of treatment. In subsequent years I frequently considered my mistake: Had the interpretation been in error? Had I been forcing a favorite insight on material it did not fit? Was the timing wrong? Or the phrasing? Was there something else going on that

I had missed?

Two years later, this patient passed me on the street and said, "I really should come in and see you again." But he didn't. Several years after that, however, he made an appointment and resumed treatment to help with other issues in his life. He began the first hour saying, "My symptom entirely disappeared. That's why I never came back." His not telling me related both to his hostility to his controlling psychotic father, his guilt at openly defying his father, and his wish to separate from the father or kill him, but all of these issues became clear only much later.

This man said something about his life that was unique. When he was working at the post office, he began painting several hours every day. He had not yet made a commitment to pursue art as a career or even to develop his talent. He had not yet decided to finish his education, let alone finish it in such an impractical field as art. If you had asked him if he thought he could earn a living as a painter, he would have said no. "But I began to paint four hours or more every day. I don't know why I did it. I just had to do it. I think I would have gone crazy if I didn't do it." And he continued to do this, for the rest of his life.

A similar statement was made to me by a friend who is an internationally respected classical musician. We had been friends in college, but we had lost contact with each other. One day, as I listened to classical music on the radio, I was struck by the beauty of a solo performance. I was startled when the announcer named my friend as the performer. A visit to a record store revealed that his records were on sale even in Lansing, Michigan, and that it was not a coincidence of name, but my old college friend. What startled me was that while I knew he loved classical music and had musical training, I did not know he played the instrument for which he is famous.

Over a period of years, I was able to attend a number of his concerts and renew our friendship. Finally, I had the courage to ask him the question that had been bothering me.

"I thought I knew you in college. But in all the time I knew you, you never once mentioned playing the instrument for which you are now famous."

"That's because I never played it until my senior year in college. After college I got married and got a job as a record librarian in a radio station, but in a rock station. Meanwhile I not only played the instrument, but I went to hear every soloist on it that I could, and talked to them about technique. I asked my family to help me buy a really good instrument, and every day after spending all day deciding between 'Rock Around the Clock' and 'Blue Suede Shoes,' I would come home and spend five hours a day playing it. I don't know why my wife put up with it, but she did. I had to play it five hours every day. I don't know why. I think I would have gone crazy if I didn't. After several years I was playing for a dinner guest just for amusement, who insisted I play more and then arranged a radio concert for me. After that my career was launched."

At the time when my patient and my friend talked to me, it was clear that they were in the right careers, both from their personal standpoints and from the standpoint of value to society. By hindsight it is obvious that there was no way they could have spent their time more valuably than the many hours each day that they compulsively spent painting or playing music. The best indicator of a writer is that he writes, of a painter that he paints, and of a musician that he plays or composes. But at the time they started and for a long time afterward, these artists had no clear idea what they would do with their talent, would have said that they did not think they could earn a living with it, had no conscious intention of trying, and certainly had no idea that their work would be valued and appreciated by critics and the public.

I cannot help wondering whether, if they had entered treatment during this period of their lives, we therapists would have had enough sense to leave them alone, to allow them without interference to act on this apparently "senseless" compulsion for hours on end, this compulsion that seemed unrelated to solving any real problem in their life.

I suspect that we might not have had enough foresight. On the other hand, I suspect they might not have let us interfere, no matter what we said. At least I hope so.

REFERENCES

Blunt, W. (1974), On Wings of Song: A Biography of Felix Mendelssohn. New York: Scribner. Kris, E. (1952), Psychoanalytic Explorations in Art. New York: International Universities Press. Maugham, S. (1921), The human element. In: The Complete Short Stories of Somerset Maugham, Volume I: East and West. Garden City, NY: Doubleday, pp. 671-704.

Sterba, E., & Sterba, R. (1954), Beethoven and His Nephew, tr. W. R. Trask. New York: Pantheon.

—— (1956), The anxieties of Michelangelo Buonarroti. Internat. J. Psycho-Anal., 37: 325-330.

Woodcock, G. (1966), The Crystal Spirit: A Study of George Orwell. Boston: Little, Brown

CHAPTER 27
Repressed Memories and World War II: Lest We Forget!
Bertram P. Karon and Anmarie J. Widener

The war neuroses of World War II (WWII) provide ample evidence that repression does indeed occur, and that the recovery of these traumatic memories and their related affects led to remission of symptoms. Moreover, these recovered memories were of events that had occurred. An illustrative case history from WWII is described. This well-documented body of data, well-known at the time, seems to have been forgotten in current discussions concerning repressed memories.

It is astounding that so many authoritative statements by contemporary psychologists and psychiatrists refer to repression and repressed memories as a myth (e.g., Holmes, 1992; Ofshe & Watters, 1994; Steele, 1994; Wakefield & Underwager, 1992). They state that repressed memory is an arcane idea for which no clear empirical evidence exists. If there are so-called recovered memories, they are held to be the result of dubious, pseudo-psychotherapeutic interventions.

Laboratory experiments from the 1930s (Diven, 1937; Haggard, 1943) to the present (e.g., Mathews & Wertheimer, 1958; Shevrin, 1978; Shevrin, Williams, Marshall, & Hertel, 1992) have shown evidence for repression, but today's skeptics are either unfamiliar with this research or possibly find it unconvincing. Behavioral therapists and many cognitive therapists have never seen clear evidence of repressed memories because the types of psychotherapy they practice do not routinely reveal such evidence. Of course, the new generation of exclusively biological psychiatrists work in a way that does not require obtaining such evidence. However, psychodynamic psychologists feel that they are constantly exposed in their clinical work to clear evidence of repressed memories. That is, patients typically say they do not remember things that, as the treatment progresses, they do remember. As these memories occur, related symptoms remit.

According to Gardner (1993), "better trained, older psychiatrists" (p. 374) do not believe that there is any evidence for amnesia other than on an organic basis (i.e., concussion or other brain damage syndromes). It is often pointed out that children who have observed the murder of their parents clearly retain the memory, which seems to imply that psychologically painful experiences do not get repressed. Lenor Terr, however, has reported that repeated traumas are more often repressed than a single traumatic event (Terr, 1991). Linda Williams (1994) studied women who had been sexually abused in childhood, where the event was clearly documented at the time of the trauma. She found that 38% of the women had no memory of the event 17 years later.

World War II Repression

There is a mass of convincing empirical data on repression that is relatively easily available but seems to have been forgotten. In World War II (WWII), there were literally hundreds of documented battlefield neuroses that involved the repression of traumatic combat experiences (e.g., Grinker & Spiegel, 1945; White, 1964). Professionals who worked in the Veterans Administration (VA) after WWII frequently saw such patients. Charles Fisher (1945) reported treating 20 cases of amnesia caused by repressed battlefield trauma. Each case of traumatic recovered memory could be corroborated by people other than the patient. Kardiner and Spiegel (1947) reported cases of men who, after years of incapacitation, recovered memories that had been forgotten and then recovered from their incapacitating symptoms. One important reason that this mass of data does not immediately come to mind is that there are very few living clinical psychologists who were working as therapists in the VA in the 1940s. Another reason may be that the data itself have been repressed.

Today, these WWII patients would be diagnosed with post-traumatic stress disorder (PTSD). These patients would have no memory of the traumatic battlefield event but would have symptoms, typically of conversion hysteria. Usually, there were other WWII servicemen there who described the traumatic combat experience. The only one who could not remember the experience was the patient with PTSD. When, in psychodynamic therapy, the traumatic experiences—including the patient's affect during the trauma—were reexperienced consciously (i.e., were no longer repressed), the hysterical symptoms disappeared. In order to speed up therapy, there were experimental uses of hypnosis and of sodium pentathol interviews to undo the repression and recover the memories in brief therapy. It was reported that using such procedures allowed the rapid recovery of the patient to pretraumatic functioning. The heightened suggestibility of the patient under hypnosis or pentathol was not considered a problem because the therapist frequently knew many of the realistic details of the combat trauma from other people. Hence, the problem of creating false memories was never a serious issue.

Clinical Example

The following clinical example illustrates a typical combat hysterical neurosis of WWII involving repression of the combat trauma:

Several years after the end of WWII, a veteran who had been treated by the neurology service of a VA hospital for a paralyzed arm was referred to the VA's psychology service. The neurologists concluded the paralysis was not organic but hysterical. A psychoanalytic psychologist, Edward Karon, treated the patient in psychoanalytic psychotherapy twice a week. After approximately 6 months of treatment, the patient mentioned, "You know, I once got a medal."

The next session, the patient brought in a newspaper clipping and began to talk about a WWII airplane crash reported in that paper. The following session, the patient began to describe the crash. He was the tail-gunner in a two-man bomber. Because of the cramped quarters in the tail turret of two-man bombers, tail-gunners were chosen to be small in size. The pilot, his friend, was over 6 feet tall and over 200 pounds. After a bombing mission, the plane crashed on its return to the landing field in England. The first three planes from this squadron crashed when landing; then this plane crashed; and the next two planes in that squadron also crashed. Reasonably enough, it was suspected that the planes had been sabotaged.

Because there were three wrecks already on the landing field, the pilot did not attempt to land on the runway. Instead, he attempted to land in a farmer's field. When the plane crashed, the tail-gunner broke an arm but was conscious. The plane was on fire; when the fire hit the gas tank, it would explode.

The tail-gunner freed himself from the wreckage and yelled for help from the several farmworkers who witnessed the crash. But they would not help because they knew the plane was going to blow up. His friend, the pilot, was unconscious and had broken both his legs. The tail-gunner tried to free his friend, but he could not because of the size and weight of the unconscious man. He yelled again for help, but no one came. He knew the plane was going to blow up, but the farmworkers could have rescued the two of them in minutes. He tried again to rescue his friend. He wanted to run, but he did not. With his one good arm, bit by bit, he moved the larger and heavier man out of the plane. He yelled again for help, but no one moved. Bit by bit, he pulled his friend with great difficulty, yelling for help. Eventually, an ambulance came, and he thought the ambulance crew would rush in and quickly move them to safety. But the ambulance crew knew the plane was going to blow up and circled the plane at a distance of 50 feet. When, inch by inch, he had pulled his friend 25 feet from the plane, the ambulance crew ran in and rescued them.

The tail-gunner was awarded a medal for his bravery. The pilot who had been unconscious during the whole event, eventually regained the use of both legs and was able to return to combat. The tail-gunner's broken arm completely healed. However, his other arm was paralyzed from then on, even after the war was over. Furthermore, he had no conscious memory of the crash or of saving his friend. He had repressed it.

During this psychotherapy session, he had remembered the details of his experience, including his heroic efforts and conscious terror. At the end of the session, his clothes were wringing wet with perspiration. But for the first time since that event, he had partial movement in his arm.

The hysterical paralysis psychodynamically represented a defense against ever experiencing the horror of that plane crash again. Like all of us would be, he was terrified and wanted to run from the plane to save himself. But his conscience could not let him abandon his friend, no matter how terrified he was or how dangerous the situation. His unconscious was protecting him: If he had broken both arms, he would have had no choice. There would have been no way to save his friend, and, therefore, it would have been all right to run for his life.

However, the unconscious is not realistic. This symptom protected him only from an exact repetition of the trauma, a future danger that would never occur. The war was over. Even if the war had continued and there was another crash, his paralyzed arm would only save his life if his non-paralyzed arm was again broken. Because the memory was repressed, it could not be corrected by accurate information about the present.

He did not gain full use of his arm, however, until the secondary gain of his symptom was also dealt with. As Sigmund Freud first pointed out, once a patient develops a symptom, it will be used for neurotic purposes in addition to those that led to its origin. This patient found it impossible to work at his occupation with a paralyzed arm. Being unable to work involuntarily was a way of expressing hostility to his wife. (In the 1940s and 50s, the traditional American family head-of-household and chief wage earner was the husband; being unable to work was a good way of expressing hostility to his wife.) One year of psychoanalytic psychotherapy sufficed not only to remove this symptom, but also to enable him to function effectively at work and at home.

In short, the war neuroses of WWII provide ample evidence that repression does indeed occur, and that the recovery of these traumatic memories and their related affects led to remission of symptoms. Moreover, these recovered memories were of events that had unquestionably occurred. Current controversies concerning repressed memories are always discussed without reference to this well-documented body of data, which was well-known at the time but seems to have been forgotten. The mental health professions, just as much as individual patients, need to remember their past in order to be effective in the real world.

REFERENCES

Diven, K. (1937). Certain determinants in the conditioning of anxiety reactions. Journal of Psychology, 3, 291-308.

Fisher, C. (1945). Amnestic states in war neurosis: The psychogenesis of fugues. The Psychoanalytic Quarterly, 14, 437-468.

Gardner, M. (1993). The false memory syndrome. Skeptical inquirer, 17, 370-375.

Grinker, R.R., & Spiegel, J.R (1945). Men under stress. New York: McGraw-Hill.

Haggard, E.A. (1943). Some conditions determining adjustment during and readjustment following experimentally induced stress. In S. S. Tomkins (Ed.), Contemporary psychopathology (pp. 529-544). Cambridge, MA: Harvard University Press.

Holmes, D.S. (1992). The evidence for repression: An examination of sixty years of research. In J. L. Singer (EdRepression and dissociation (pp. 85-102). Chicago: University of Chicago Press.

Kardiner, A., & Spiegel, H. (1947). War stress and neurotic illness. New York: Hoeber.

Mathews, A., & Wertheimer, M. (1958). A "pure" measure of perceptual defense uncontaminated by response suppression. Journal of Abnormal and Social Psychology, 57, 373-375.

Ofshe, R., & Watters, E. (1994). Making monsters: False memories, psychotherapy, and sexual hysteria. New York: Charles Scribner's Sons.

Shevrin, H. (1978). Evoked potential evidence for unconscious mental processes. A review of the literature. In A.S. Prangishvili, A.S., Sherozia, & F.V. Bassin (Eds.), The unconscious: Nature, functions, methods of study (pp. 610-625). Tbilisi, U.S.S.R.: Metsnierba.

Shevrin, H., Williams, W.J., Marshall, R.E, & Hertel, R.K. (1992). Event-related potential indicators of the dynamic unconscious. Consciousness & Cognition: An International Journal, I, 340-366.

Steele, D.R. (1994). Partial recall. Liberty, 7(3), 37-47.

Terr, L.C. (1991). Childhood traumas: An outline and overview. American Journal of Psychiatry, 148, 10-20.

Wakefield, H., & Underwager, R. (1992). Recovered memories of sexual abuse: Lawsuits against parents. Behavioral Sciences and the Law, 10, 483-507.

White, R.W. (1964). The abnormal personality. New York: Ronald Press.

Williams, L.M. (1994). Recall of childhood trauma: A prospective study of women's memories of child sexual abuse. Journal of Consulting & Clinical Psychology, 62, 1167-1176.

Section 3:
SUPERVISION AND TRAINING

CHAPTER 28
Supervising Therapists Treating the Severely Mentally Ill
Bertram P. Karon, Ph.D.

A patient of Gaetano Benedetti (1987) described it well. There was a corpse. Benedetti went into the land of the dead to get the corpse. Benedetti did not want to be there. According to the patient, Benedetti does not like the land of the dead. It scares him. He likes the land of the living. But he went in anyway to get the corpse. He did not try to just bring the corpse out, because you cannot. He dragged the corpse deeper into the land of the dead and through the land of the dead and out the other side. And the corpse came to life, and the corpse, said the patient, was me.

How do you teach a student to go into the land of the dead for a patient, go deeper with the patient, and come out the other side? How do you get a student to accept that being uncomfortable is a necessary part of the process, and that not being certain of what is going on is a sign of a good therapist?

Certainly not from a manual. To work with the severely disturbed is to be frightened, angry, depressed, bored, discouraged, or confused because the patients are frightened, angry, depressed, bored, discouraged, or confused, although patients also deal with their confusion by clinging to premature closure. When patients complain that psychotherapy is making them confused, I always say, "Good. You are not sick because you are confused, you are sick because you are sure of things which are not true."

(Much of psychopathology consists of believing things that are not true. In addition to delusions, hallucinations, and obvious transferences, are false beliefs learned from one's family or others, and reasonable, but wrong, conclusions based on trying to make sense of unusual experiences. These false beliefs usually solve an immediate problem but in the long run make a satisfying life impossible.)

Rarely are student therapists told that being confused is normal, in fact, essential to successful work with severely disturbed patients. Moreover, good therapy with severely disturbed patients almost always involves improvisation. If what we try works, we continue it. If it does not work, we stop and try something else.

The rest of this chapter consists of discussions of conscious resistance (the most important difference between working with psychotics and working with neurotics), supervisory technique, frequency of sessions, phrasing of interpretations, the difference between supervision and psychotherapy, useful didactic material, and the difference between psychoanalysis and psychoanalytic therapy.

Conscious Resistance and Therapist Confusion

What is most confusing to any therapist is that severely disturbed patients not only do not understand their experiences, they do not tell you even what they do understand. They do not trust you. This is the most important difference between neurotics and psychotics.

Case X. 1

A ten-year-old paranoid schizophrenic boy illustrated most clearly this difference between treating a severely disturbed patient, and treating a neurotic. After being in treatment between 8 to 12 months, he described a dream. I commented about it, but the patient said nothing. I added, "Well, maybe I'm wrong."

A slight smile appeared on the patient's lips, "How often do you think you've been wrong, Doc?"

"I don't know. Perhaps half the things I say to you don't fit."

Broader smile, "You haven't been wrong yet, Doc."

What a beautiful statement about a positive transference! But this was the first time that he had ever indicated that anything had been correct.

Those of us who have worked only with less disturbed patients or neurotics are not prepared for such massive conscious resistance. With less disturbed patients, we usually are told when we are correct or when things improve. We may even get feedback in the form of angry denials or accusations of stupidity for correct interpretations. But such reactions are helpful in guiding the therapy. What is not usual is no apparent reaction at all, a characteristic of the psychotically disturbed.

Severely disturbed patients may not want to tell you accurately what their symptoms, experiences, thoughts, fantasies, or feelings are, for fear that such disclosures will get them in trouble, or get you to insist on an unhelpful, inappropriate, or even destructive treatment. This is not only transference from unhelpful parents; it is also a transference from unhelpful mental health professionals.

Previous Mental Health Professionals

A group of patients, who were participating in peer counseling sessions that they found useful, described their reason for seeking out peer counseling; "If you are really hurting, really angry, really depressed, feel like killing yourself, you can't tell a mental health professional, they don't want to hear it, they will do something to shut you up or quiet you down. Only another patient will let you talk when you are really hurting." It would be comforting if one could dismiss their statements as unrealistic. They ought to be unrealistic, but unfortunately they are not. All of these patients reported similar experiences with professionals, even though no patient should ever be treated that way.

Some of this may have been due to the professionals' reaction (e. g., fear, anger, loathing, etc.) to the patients' bizarre symptoms, lack of cooperativeness, apparent lack of control, or apparent dangerousness, as well as to the wrong theories and inadequate resources available to the professional. But the professional's motives are not important. What is important is the effect on the patient. The patient needs to be able to consciously think about what happened and be able to talk about the fact that it was destructive. Otherwise the patients will usually assume without questioning that they themselves were solely responsible for their mistreatment and that whatever other professionals did was justified. Even if patients believe the professionals were not justified, the patients usually believe that you will defend the bad things other professionals did, and that you will require the patient to pretend that their mistreatment was justified. It is important to let the patient know that you are interested in the truth and helping the patient to cope with the truth, whatever it is. They will not really believe you initially, but they will begin to consider the possibility that you might mean what you say.

Of course, you cannot be sure what happened when you were not there, but you can start with the patient's version (which usually is true), and you and the patient will discover inaccuracies together. This is no different from discussing any other destructive experiences.

But many mental health professionals do not want to know about painful experiences. They really do dismiss bad life experiences as delusional and shut the patient up when the patient wants to talk about them, especially if the patient wants to talk about his or her experiences with strong feelings. Such professionals are more comfortable with treatments which diminish feelings or that do not require listening or understanding at all. That is why it is important to train a new generation of therapists who will let patients talk.

Parents and Conscious Resistance

I have never worked with a psychotic whose life, once I understood it as it was experienced, would not have driven me crazy. Psychotics are more sick than neurotics because their lives have been more painful. John Read and his colleagues (e.g., Read, Goodman, Morrison, Ross, & Aderhold, 2004; Read & Ross, 2003) have documented the abundant evidence that serious disorders can usually easily be found to have arisen from horrible life experiences. Thus, for example, the incidence in persons with schizophrenia of both childhood sexual abuse and of childhood physical abuse is far higher than in the general population or among patients with other psychiatric diagnoses.

Parents are often concerned they will be blamed for their child's disorder. Of course, some parents have been obviously hurtful and destructive. But most parents of schizophrenics are admirable people who will go to great lengths to attempt to get help for their children. While there are always destructive life experiences in the etiology of schizophrenia, sometimes these experiences have nothing to with their parents. Where parents have been hurtful, it is often the result of bad professional advice, an automatic repetition of their parents' mistakes or of their own childhood traumas (e.g., Fraiberg, 1977), or even a reaction, later, to the child's symptoms. Frequently, parenting mistakes are the result of unconscious defenses, as demonstrated by a series of Thematic Apperception Test studies (Karon & Widener, 1994; Meyer & Karon, 1967), which like all unconscious defenses are unchangeable until brought into awareness, and consequently are not matters of good or evil, but simply a problem to be solved. Parents of schizophrenics also have been found to tend to discourage the use of people outside the family as sources of information and corrective identifications. For most people, these extra-familial influences are correctives that diminish the bad effects when their parents make mistakes (as all parents do). While discouraging extra-familial influences may lead to greater family harmony, it has the unintended effect of enormously magnifying the bad effects of any parental mistakes.

For most patients, there was a succession of small hurts, each of which changed the conscious and unconscious fantasies that gave meaning to subsequent experiences. The psychotic symptoms are always a reasonable reaction to the events of the patient's life as subjectively experienced, but not necessarily as an outside observer would evaluate them.

When parents ask what caused their child's disorder, it is helpful to say, truthfully, that you do not know and ask them what they think. They often will tell you.

Case X. 2

The parent-child experiences that lay the basis for conscious resistances (not wanting to tell the therapist even what you know and understand) in severely disturbed patients was best described by the mother of a schizophrenic six-year-old boy. I discussed the issue of punishment with her. I asked whether she could use some method of punishment other than hitting him.

She said, "You don't understand, doctor. He never lets us know what he likes. If we knew what he liked, we would take it away from him, of course. But he never lets us know what he likes."

In addition to being afraid that the information will be used by the therapist to hurt them, severely disturbed patients often do not want to tell you how bad their lives have been and in what way, because it feels like disloyalty to the only parents they had, and to whom they still feel loyal. Of course, as Ronald Fairbairn (1954) so insightfully described, the most terrifying idea to anyone is that our parents were really bad in some way. Then there is no hope. But, if what seemed bad is the result of our own transgressions, that seems safer, because then there is hope. In Fairbairn's words, it is better to be morally bad than for things to be unconditionally bad. But then many people cannot change, because they would discover that their parent would not change.

Even when patients complain of their parents, it is often with the hope (usually unconscious) that the professional will tell them they are wrong and urge them to take responsibility for their own defects rather than blame others. That is why when the therapist does not blame the patient, but points out the weaknesses of a parent, or even simply accepts the patient's complaints about their parents, some patients becomes angry or afraid, rather than being relieved. It is also, according to Fairbairn, why some patients irritate you or try to get you to mistreat them. Then they can maintain the belief that, at least as compared to everybody else, including their therapist, their parents were good.

Supervisory Technique

Far more important than the technique of supervision is whether the supervisor has anything to teach. You cannot teach what you do not know. If you are not a competent clinical psychoanalyst, you cannot supervise psychoanalysis adequately. If you do not practice psychoanalytic therapy well, you cannot supervise psychoanalytic therapy adequately. If you do not know how to work with severely disturbed patients, the patients will not benefit from the treatment you supervise (e. g., May, 1968). While supposed experts like to talk about supervisory technique, no supervisory technique will work if the supervisor is teaching what he or she does not know, and any supervisory technique is likely to be helpful to the novice if the supervisor is knowledgeable.

In supervision, particularly with early students, the supervisor is a safety net. The student has the security that there is backup for any crisis. The supervisor, however, does not take over the case. I tell supervisees that they know much more about their patients than they can ever communicate to me, and they must use their best judgment, even if they are wrong, and then tell me about it, and what happened. "Supervision," I usually tell supervisees, "is not a substitute for your own judgment. But I can tell you what I hear, and what I would do, and if you cannot think of anything better to do, you can always do what I would do. And, of course, I expect you to review with me everything you do and what happened."

A supervisor can be helpful in providing a solid basis from which the student can operate, and can let the supervisee know that a lack of clear information about the progress of the treatment is to be expected, but if the student continues to use his or her own best judgment and does reasonable things, most patients will get better, and they will let you know eventually what is going on and that you are helping them. Not understanding and making mistakes is inevitable, but learning with the patient what you need to know to cure them is what psychoanalytic therapy is all about.

A supervisor should make it safe for the student to experience uncomfortable feelings including fear, anger, depression, and inadequacy as well as confusion, and should let the student know that not only are such uncomfortable feelings inevitable and simply part of the process, but they are a useful source of information .

Case X . 3

A chronic catatonic schizophrenic man in his twenties had been unsuccessfully treated as a child at several residential centers for disturbed children, underwent a short period of unsuccessful psychoanalytic therapy as an adolescent, and then was unsuccessfully treated at several well-known hospitals. He had been continuously hospitalized at his latest hospital for years. He was mute and immobile, had to be force fed, and was urinally and anally incontinent, although he defecated only approximately once every six weeks. He would come out of his catatonic pseudo-stupor (catatonics in fact are aware of everything that is going on), yell one word, "You!" or "Room!" or "Dear!" and then swing violently. He might hit himself, or the furniture, or you. He did not seem to care if he hit himself, but he had broken furniture. He also had broken the jaws of several attendants at a previous hospital. Consequently, he was usually kept in restraints.

I was scared of him. Because of his lack of toilet training, he was also disgusting. But I realized that in addition to being scared and disgusted, I did not like him. It was more than being scared and disgusted, those were rational feelings. I did not like him.

My associations led to my childhood. He reminded me of some other boys. "Dirty little bastards," who used to beat me up. After a while I grew big, so they stopped beating me, but they continued to beat other boys. At that point it was obvious that it was not fair to hate my patient because of what other "bastards" had done to me as a child.

But then I began to think. "Dirty little bastards." In fact, they were not big guys. Maybe they were scared. My patient was not a big man, although he was muscular.

The next time he started to get angry and seemed about to be violent, I said, "I know how scared you are. Why don't you use my strength to protect you?" He quieted right down, and his violence was never a problem in his treatment after that, because the same reassurance would consistently defuse his violence. Later I learned that as a child he had been thrown out of some of the residential treatment centers for beating up other children.

The attendants at his current institution (who were all former college football players) were amused. "Your strength? Do you know what he could do to you?" As an out of condition intellectual, I did. That is why I was scared of him. But the patient desperately wanted someone to protect him.

Supervisory Posture

Supervisees identify with supervisors. If they are treated kindly and supportively, they tend to treat their patients kindly and supportively. If their difficulties and pain as therapists are shared, they can share the patients' pain and difficulties. If the supervisor is cold or punitive, students become cold or punitive. If the supervisor is curious, accepting of the human condition, sees the value in "mistakes," is comfortable with the unconscious, and expects students to be first-rate, then the students tend to value their curiosity, learn from their mistakes, learn about the unconscious, and become first-rate.

I recall my first supervisory hour with Richard Sterba. It was my second psychoanalytic control case. After driving 100 miles on a Sunday, feeling both anxious and excited, I presented the case material. His first supervisory comment was, "Do you mind if I make a suggestion?" And he waited for an answer.

I was startled. "Of course. Please."

He then said, "I would have said it differently," and proceeded to suggest a far more therapeutic phrasing of the interpretation.

But in that first supervisory intervention, before he communicated specific information, he communicated a feeling of respect for the other person, which hopefully I internalized.

Of course, one must also serve as a kindly superego and parent figure. Supervisees need to know that if a crisis occurs that they cannot handle, they have immediate access to someone who will be there. Even when their handling of the crisis is appropriate, they need a kindly superego who will tell them that it was appropriate and allow them to tolerate their anxiety (and even learn from it about themselves and the patient). Indeed, even experienced professionals sometimes need that kind of sharing when dealing with crises or the apparent lack of progress of severely disturbed patients. In the face of difficult resistances, and the pessimism of colleagues, supervisees need the optimism of the supervisor that if one does as reasonable a job as one can, the odds are the patient will respond. Supervisees also need to know that their experience of the treatment as difficult occurs because it is difficult work. The pessimism and alarmism of most of their professional colleagues is a function of the latter's experience of working, as most mental health professionals do, with inadequate training. If supervisees are treating the kind of patient whose defenses do not permit him or her to communicate that the therapist is being helpful, the support and evaluation of an experienced supervisor becomes essential. Supervisees need to be reminded that most appropriately treated patients benefit greatly, that the patient cannot give the feedback you would like, but that their procedures and interpretations seem appropriate and should be continued or should be modified in specific ways, and why.

Feedback

The supervisor should also tell the supervisee to pay attention to feedback when it occurs. Often, the ward staff, if the patient is hospitalized, or family members, if the patient is living with them, will tell you about improvements. Repeated psychological testing, if it is available, can be useful. Sometimes the patient will tell you about improvement by describing other people as having become nicer. The patient may even tell you about improvement paradoxically by complaining about things that could not be problems if the patient had not made considerable improvement.

Case X. 4

"Goddammit, Karon, you're not helping me. I'm going to lose my B-average, and you don't care, and you're not helping me!"

But if this patient was taking college courses, and had a B average to lose, she had made enormous improvements. Initially her minister and her boss had brought this schizophrenic woman to my office instead of the state hospital.

"I don't enjoy sex and I get involved with the wrong kind of men. And you're not doing anything about it!"

This patient believed, when she started therapy, that no man would be interested in her. But if a man were interested in her and wanted sex and she said no, the man would kill her. That is what men do. But if she had sex, she believed, the sex would kill her.

For her to be having sex without enjoying it and to be involved with the wrong kind of men were both serious problems, but she had to have made enormous progress to have those problems.

Once a supervisee has continued the treatment of a difficult patient, about whom other professionals have been pessimistic, until the patient has palpably improved, the successful treatment of a severely disturbed patient can be a benign trauma from whose effects the supervisee never recovers.

Frequency of Sessions

For any therapy with any patient, it is my experience that the more time available, the easier it is for both patient and therapist. Unfortunately, the therapist's schedule, the patient's schedule, the need to charge a fee, and the limited financial resources available all lead to briefer therapy, both in time and in number of sessions per week. Every genuine therapist feels the conflict between wanting to help as many people as possible and wanting to do a therapy that is thorough and helpful. But we know best how to do that in ways that take time. Every genuine therapist also knows the conflict between wanting to be available to everyone irrespective of financial status and wanting to live in the way that a decent income permits, or, if part of an agency, the need to maintain the fiscal solvency of the agency, particularly if the agency provides real help.

Of course, even worse are the consequences of "managed care." Decisions about number of sessions are made on the basis of financial considerations by people neither primarily concerned with, nor capable of evaluating, what is in the best interests of the patient.

There is, as far as I know, no systematic research on the effects of number of sessions per week per se on the nature and content of the hour or on the course of the treatment. The nearest to a systematic study was the report of Alexander and French (1946) that reducing the number of sessions per week seemed more compatible with effective treatment than cutting down the calendar time. People take time to grow. Technically, Alexander & French suggested that in once or twice per week therapy more of the transference reactions outside the therapy hour had to be analyzed as opposed to analyzing the transference neurosis itself, that is, transference reactions within the therapeutic session.

Under even the most stringent institutional restrictions, I would recommend strongly that the first week of treatment for psychotic individuals should be five sessions, although the length of the session may be shortened to half an hour. Even if the treatment is going to be continued on a once per week basis, the patient needs to know you are there, the therapeutic alliance needs to be established, and the therapist and patient need to have a chance for the transference and countertransference dynamics to begin to be apparent. I have never been able to help a patient at a frequency of less than once per week, although

I have tried it either to save the patient's money, or to accommodate a patient's schedule. Consequently, I share that information and insist that the patient must be seen at least once per week if I am going to supervise the case, and preferably twice per week. For psychoanalytic candidates, of course, I insist on a minimum of three times per week.

During periods of crisis or when the patient is undergoing unusual stress the frequency may be increased. The Michigan State Psychotherapy Research Project (Karon & VandenBos, 1981) found that most of even the most severely disturbed of a group of chronic inner city schizophrenics were able to function outside the hospital within eight weeks of psychoanalytic therapy five days per week without medication. Benedetti and Furlan (1987) reported from Italy and Switzerland a series of 50 severely schizophrenic patients treated with intensive psychoanalytic therapy by supervisees with excellent results in 80% of the cases. The patients were seen for two to five sessions per week for 3 to 10 years; median frequency was three times per week, median length of treatment was five years.

Surprisingly, in the Michigan State project, those economically poor inner city severely schizophrenic patients who came in intermittently during crises, did as well as those who came in regularly once per week. If you are poor, the reality problems are so huge that psychotherapy seems like a luxury. The therapist may know, but the patient does not, that their reality problems would be easier to handle if they saw their therapist. But during crises, if seen immediately, the patients work hard, and change. When the crisis is over, the therapists were ready to continue in a traditional way, but the patients disappeared, only to reappear with a later crisis. These patients taught me the importance and the value of psychoanalytic crisis therapy. Even when they come in during a later crisis, it takes more stress before they break down again, and they again make good use of the crisis therapy to continue growing.

Fears that too intensive a frequency will cause too much regression, particularly for borderline patients, are common. But it is not the frequency per se, which is disabling, but the character of the sessions. An unresponsive therapist, a cold and condemning therapist, or a therapist who sits behind the patient and does not talk are disasters for a severely disturbed patient. Such therapists simply repeat earlier traumas. Deeply disturbed patients, as well as some who are not deeply disturbed, usually experience silent or unresponsive therapists (who believe they are simply being neutral) as rejecting them. The patients may experience a non-talking therapist or one who sits behind the patient and is quiet as someone who does not want to relate to them, or, if they are psychotic, sometimes as someone who is not there. If the patients come from criminal or delinquent sub-groups, they do not trust anyone they cannot see.

It is essential that the therapist or analyst be willing to provide as much structure and support as the defenses of the patient require. This is not a one-time diagnostic judgment, but a reaction in each hour to the patient as he or she experiences that therapy hour, so that the patients' ability to cope with the anxieties aroused by their memories and transference reactions are not exceeded.

One particularly destructive pattern is the therapist who at first encourages the patient to be open about everything and to go deep into themselves and their lives. The therapist may even be initially supportive and helpful. But when the patient opens up and reveals deep parts of themselves, the therapist's defenses give out. Then the therapist tries to get the patient to shut up. The therapist may suddenly become punitive. If even one's therapist cannot stand one's life or feelings, what chance has the patient to face the terrors alone? The therapeutic hour becomes a trauma, and the patient gets sicker rather than improving.

It is not uncommon to hear that too few sessions are so unhinging that the patient had better not be treated psychotherapeutically at all, but medicated, punished, advised, or left alone. The problem, as before, is the character of the session. The most frequent danger with too low a frequency is that nothing of importance will happen. Not only is it harder for the therapist to obtain the necessary information about the therapy to guide the process optimally, but the lack of supportive contact makes independent growth seem too scary for the patient. In my experience, a low but acceptable frequency is once per week.

Low Frequency Forced by Patients.
Case X. 5

Sometimes a low frequency of sessions is forced by the defenses of the patient. One psychotic depressive woman moved to her parents' house instead of to a hospital. They lived some 40 miles away and could only bring her once a week. This turned out to be an advantage. Like many psychotic depressives, this lady was irritating. It was possible for her to have a reasonable, kind, but active therapist once a week; although by the end of most of her early hours my countertransference was such that

I usually felt enraged at her. By the next week, however, she once more had a rational and kind therapist for most of her hour. The treatment progressed to a satisfactory outcome. Not only did her psychosis remit, but she handled her five children more appropriately, had a better relationship with her husband, including a better sexual relationship, and held a part-time job successfully for the first time in her marriage. In part because of their better relationship, her husband became more effective and was able to earn more money, which was important for their way of life. But given the intensity of my emotional reaction, it is questionable that such a benign outcome would have been possible if she had been seen more frequently, particularly at the beginning.

Case X. 6

An ambulatory paranoid patient, with a delusion that there was a rumor that he was a homosexual, was unable to work. Previous therapy had enabled him to finish schooling and embark on a professional career (not in the psychological professions). However, this rumor had followed him, he said, from city to city, and now was preventing him from being able to practice his profession. Despite offers to cut his fee, he insisted on being seen not more than half an hour once per week because he "could not afford any more." He would sit in the furthest corner of the room, and stated that he had "no thoughts, no feelings, no dreams. What do you want to talk about?" It was possible nonetheless to help him, in the minimal weekly time he permitted, to be able to work, to relate to friends, and to date, with the "rumor" gradually subsiding.

When he would not talk about his thoughts or his feelings or his dreams, I decided to try the Thematic Apperception Test . Each session I gave him one card, asked him to tell a story, and then asked him to associate to the story. He was able to cooperate. By the time all the cards were exhausted, a real psychotherapeutic process was well underway. While the treatment was terminated prematurely by the therapist's standards, with many neurotic traits remaining and far short of our analytic ideal, the treatment was a success by the patient's standards, was well worth the time involved, and has led to stable functioning and a successful professional career for years, to date.

Case X. 6

An ambulatory depressive had been in treatment for 20 years with various psychiatrists, some of whom were psychoanalysts, but all of whom medicated him, sometimes accompanied by psychotherapy. He was still depressed and was referred to me. He was told that, given the length of his problems, he should be seen a minimum of three times a week, and that while no firm estimate could be made, he would need to be in treatment at least two or three years. He was irate: "You are just trying to run a bill on me. I know. I have friends who work in an HMO. They treat people in 16 sessions. That's all anyone needs. And I'm not coming in more than once a week." He was told that, while I disagreed, I would certainly do what I could for him in the time he allowed.

At the tenth session, I reminded him that he had only six more sessions, and asked how he felt about it. He was furious that I would not see him more than 16 sessions. After he berated me, he was told that if he felt that strongly, I would continue treating him. Shortly thereafter he became furious that I refused to see him more than once a week. After allowing him to berate me, I told him I would be willing to see him twice a week. After a few months he became furious that I refused to see him more than twice a week. Again, after allowing his rage, I agreed with his demand for three times a week. The analytic treatment then proceeded successfully with, of course, the difficulties usual for severely depressed, hostile patients.

He would get angry at my rigidity because I would not treat him with medication. Patients get to know our weak spots. I informed him each time he raised the issue that if he would prefer to be treated with medication I would be glad to refer him to a competent medicating psychiatrist who would prescribe the right medication at the right dosage and monitor side effects carefully. If he would prefer a combination, I would refer him to a competent medicating psychiatrist who would prescribe the right medication at the right dosage, but who also talks with his patients. Or if he wanted to work hard, he could stay and work with me.

"Won't you work with me if I get medication."

"No, but I'll be here after you've tried it, if you want to come back." I then gave him a brief lecture on the evidence to explain my position.

He would always get furious at my rigidity. But he continued in treatment. Eventually I realized what was actually happening, and said to him, "Last session you raised the issue of medication, and I gave you my little lecture as I always do, and you were furious at me. And you should have been furious at me, because I was stupid. I think you raise the subject when there is something important to talk about that you do not want to talk about, and you know I will give my regular comment. What is it we should have been talking about?"

There was something important, and whenever afterwards he raised the issue of medication, there was always something more important to talk about. Raising the issue of medication when there is something more important to talk about is a resistance frequently used by patients who are physicians or nurses.

The general therapeutic principle is that if you know something of importance to the patient's well being that you think the patient does not know, you tell them. If, as often happens, they want to make use of the information but cannot, then the two of you can investigate why. But it is usually not necessary to give them the information more than once.
I wondered how he could have been in treatment, including therapy, for 20 years and still be so depressed. He told me at the end of treatment that none of his psychiatrists, including the psychoanalysts, had ever related his depression to the way his mother or his father had related to him. "I guess they helped me. I limped through life more or less, but I guess I have never really been in therapy until now."

Phrasing

A condemning therapist obviously is traumatic, but it is important to remember that even neurotic patients tend to experience every interpretation as an accusation. That is why the phrasing of an interpretation is critical. Thus, for example, a well-meaning therapist may say something about the patient having a sexual or angry feeling. The therapist believes he or she is being kind and is giving the patient permission to have that feeling, or letting the patient know that such a feeling is normal or justified. But that is not what patients hear. They implicitly add "and you shouldn't" to anything the therapist says. Therefore the therapist must try to phrase interpretations and comments so that they cannot be twisted into accusations of crime. Phrasings like, "Anyone would feel..." or "It would only be human to feel..." help. Almost anything, no matter how anxiety provoking, can be discussed from the standpoint of the defense: "I wonder if you are afraid that you might..." The phrase "I wonder if..." structures the intervention as not a contest of wills nor an authoritarian verdict of doom, but as an idea to be considered, and even possibly rejected. A rejected interpretation, if it is correct, will come back at a later time with new material or when the patient has had time to think about it.

Therapists often are annoyed that patients at a later time will say "I had a new idea," and then discuss something the therapist said earlier that was rejected initially. In most cases the patient really has forgotten the origin of the idea. The student needs to know that, while the student's feeling annoyed is normal, the origin of the idea is of no importance, and should not be an issue. The patient does not need another parent who will not let them have any ideas of their own, but insists that anything good comes from the parent.

Even the word "why" is usually heard by patients as a condemnation. After all, when parents ask "Why did you do that?," it is usually a rebuke and not a request for information.

One difficult thing for a therapist to talk about in therapy is when the patient is genuinely annoying. It may be important to discuss, but on a transference basis it may be too frightening for a patient to think his or her therapist is angry at the patient. One possibility is to phrase it as "If I were not your therapist, I would be annoyed (or angry) when you..."

Case X . 7

A deeply depressed woman described not being able to stand her 3 year old grand-daughter, who was not always easy to control, like most 3 year olds. She talked as if it was normal not to like a 3 year old. I can tolerate and deal with many irritating ideas and actions, including felonies, and attempted assaults on me, but I found this outrageous. I did not immediately comment, because I was too angry to be able to intervene helpfully. It was too important not to talk about in her treatment, but deeply depressed people do not need to be told they are bad. It took me two weeks to think through a way of raising the issue without traumatizing the patient: "There is something puzzling. You are basically a kind person. You may disagree with me, but you are basically a kind person. But your feelings toward your granddaughter are discrepant from that. It seems to me that something must have happened to you when you were her age, when you were three years old."

"But you know I can't remember anything from that age."

"Yes, but that doesn't mean nothing happened or that it did not have an effect. We tend to react to bad things that happened to us when our children or grandchildren are the same age we were when it happened."

She insisted that she could not remember anything, and we talked about that period without achieving closure, although she reported possible bad events that she had heard of that period. Her mother was going through obvious stresses in the dissolution of her marriage. The patient considered the possibility that her mother might have found her independence and uncontrollability hard to bear (the aspect of her granddaughter she reported as making the child dislikable). After our discussion, she noticed and reported that her granddaughter seemed irrationally to like being with her, wanted to sit next to her in the car, and liked her stories. Their relationship progressed to a healthy one.

The Sequence of Training

Most people who think about the issue of the ideal training of a psychoanalytic therapist recommend that the novice should first experience a thorough personal psychoanalysis, then conduct traditional psychoanalyses of neurotics under supervision, and then be trained in briefer psychoanalytic therapies or in working with more severe patients. Thus, the therapist will really understand, from his or her own analysis, what therapy is about, learn from supervised analyses what would come to the surface if there were sufficient time and a cooperative patient, and then be able to utilize this in briefer psychoanalytic therapy and in working with difficult patients.

Almost nobody goes through the sequence of training in that rational order. For example, no graduate student in our program practices psychoanalysis, in the narrow sense. The only practitioners I supervise in psychoanalysis are psychologists and social workers in the community, who are in private practice or community agencies, have been analyzed, and have taken seminars in analytic technique and wish eventually to be trained as psychoanalysts. Graduate students, often without any prior personal therapy, begin by doing brief psychoanalytic therapy. Most of the competent ones obtain some personal psychotherapy before they finish graduate school, but, primarily for financial reasons, do not begin personal psychoanalysis until they are out in the field.

Before we despair, however, we should note that the first generation of psychoanalysts, whose contributions display a level of insight, creativity, and therapeutic competence far above what is usual today, went through what we would consider haphazard training. Of course, these were bright, creative, highly motivated individuals, who lived psychoanalysis

(Richard Sterba, personal communication). They learned as much as possible about psychoanalysis in the broadest possible sense. You may argue, as Robert Knight (1954, pp. 24-25) has, that they were less well adjusted than the present generation, but better analysts. Knight argues that his generation of candidates was motivated to learn as little as possible about psychoanalysis, get through their training quickly, and open an office, and this led to a necessary proliferation of explicit requirements. But this very proliferation of explicit requirements appeals to that kind of candidate he deplores, while discouraging the creative individuals to whom psychoanalysis appealed earlier.

Many of our current creative psychoanalysts have gone through unusual routes in their training. The question is: does the irrational route that we have created in graduate school make any sense at all? Given the unfortunate frequency of faculty in Psychology, Psychiatry, and Social Work who know little about psychotherapy and who discourage learning about psychotherapy, the obvious answer is any sequence of training is better than no training.

Selection

I believe in self-selection. I have found it works best to supervise only students or professionals who choose to be supervised by me. This is now a general rule in our Psychological Clinic. I like the kind of clinicians, whether students or practicing professionals, who get themselves into the dilemma: "I think I can help this patient, but my colleagues/supervisors/ setting says that it should be interrupted or can't be done, and I think they are wrong, but I need supervision from someone experienced. Maybe I'm wrong (although I don't think so), or maybe I'm getting in over my head, but this patient is treatable, and they are not going to treat him or her, if I don't. You [Karon] are the only one I know who would encourage me to treat this patient."

Since my own patients rarely see me for fewer than two years, I require that students I supervise make a commitment to be available to the patient for a minimum of two years, even though that is not the academic requirement. In addition to being a reasonable requirement, it weeds out those who are not highly motivated. (One bright graduate student asked me if it was all right if he saw a sever borderline patient five days a week. Surprised that a graduate student wanted to work that hard, I agreed since he was insightful, highly motivated, and seeing me in supervision once per week. He did a brilliant job of psychoanalytic therapy.)

Supervision of Therapy

There are many disagreements about the philosophies and techniques of supervision. In particular, how much of the student's dynamics do you delve into, how much is it didactic, how much do you focus only on the patient, should you use audiovisual aids or observe the actual interview?

The supervisor, I believe, should remember he or she is not the student's therapist. While the anxieties involved in doing psychoanalytic therapy are contained by the supervisor, the supervisor does not delve into the student's dynamics. The opposite stance is experienced by the student as intrusive, punitive, and scary. It is useful to say, "I wonder if there is a personal issue here, that you might want to discuss with your therapist. Think about it and you decide. You don't need to discuss it with me." For a student not in therapy: "I wonder if this isn't making you anxious. This is very difficult material (or this is a very difficult person). This might be a good time to start your own therapy. You don't need to discuss your personal issues with me, but think about it."

The injunction "you don't need to discuss it with me" allows students the privacy and maturity they need and allows them to discuss freely some aspects of it if they choose. They usually do choose to discuss what seems most pertinent.

If you really think the dynamics are critical to discuss, it may be brought up as, "Some people have a problem with ...and that would lead them to do ...". The important principle is not to be experienced as intrusive or punitive, because that will make it impossible for the student to be honest in the future.

I rarely use mechanical aids. In my project in treating schizophrenics with psychoanalytic therapy, the early hours of both the experienced therapists and the trainees were viewed on videotape and discussed for training purposes. That was initially useful. It was also reassuring to the novice in dealing with unpredictable patients if their sessions were being simultaneously watched by colleagues who could intervene if necessary.

Nonetheless, the student therapists on the Michigan Psychotherapy Research Project then, and the students at the university since then, reported that they generally did not find the discussion of their tapes remarkably helpful, but they reported that observing my tapes was helpful. In my graduate seminar on the Psychotherapy of Psychosis,

I either treated a patient in front of the group (usually with a one-way mirror) or had them observe videotapes of the treatment of a psychotic patient. The model of my correct interventions helps, but even more they notice that I am sometimes tired, distracted, insensitive, and have countertransference reactions, and, despite that, even difficult patients obviously improve. Therefore, the psychotherapy of the deeply disturbed cannot be a trick that only some gifted, superbly trained individual can practice, but something that intelligent and respectful human beings who want to be helpful can learn to do.

In my experience the traditional supervision hour, with the student recounting from notes is, in general, best. I request that the notes be written after the hour, as Freud (1912) recommended, not during it. What the students bring up is what is puzzling to them, and then anything you say has an effect in changing their understanding and technique. Your insights meet their need, help resolve their anxieties or curiosities. When you bring up something from a tape, it does not have the same effect in facilitating their learning, because it does not meet their needs. It must be admitted that one psychopathic student was able to lie to me successfully in ordinary supervision hours. But supervision is not police work. For the bulk of students this is the optimal way to go. One cannot corrupt the teaching process because one liar can take advantage of you.

In supervision of psychoanalysis, the supervisee is more experienced, so less time need be spent on basic mechanics that the supervisee has already learned. More time is available to listen to the subtle aspects of the fantasy material, which are usually more available in the presentations of experienced therapists during the supervision hour, and the supervisee is more sensitive to the transference and countertransference issues. Most often experienced supervisees are held back by one formulation of the material, including the transference and countertransference, which has prevented them from hearing a different, more relevant formulation. But the difference in supervision is one of degree, that is, the process of supervision is basically the same except that, the more experienced and knowledgeable the supervisee, the more one can focus on subtler issues. Of course, supervisees at any level vary widely in what they already know.

As Richard Sterba has pointed out (personal communication), supervision is easier than psychotherapy because the supervisee's unconscious almost always organizes the material so that only the addition of the last link is needed, even though the supervisee seemingly does not consciously understand what the material is all about.

Didactic Material

Those who choose to be supervised by me already have a strong interest in psychoanalysis. Obviously, I expect even the most inexperienced student to have read Freud's *Introductory Lectures* (1916-1917) and *New Introductory Lectures* (1933). I ask them to read his papers on technique (1963), and at least one paper of mine, "The tragedy of schizophrenia without psychotherapy" (Karon, 2003). I then require them to read Fromm-Reichmann's *Principles of Intensive Psychotherapy* (1960), if they have not already done so, and David Malan's book on brief therapy, *Individual Psychotherapy and the Science of Psychodynamics* (1979). I have never had a novice therapist who did not get enthusiastic about that book.

Any other reading will be based on the individual case. If the patient has psychotic features, obviously I assign my book (Karon & VandenBos, 1981). The best paper I know on the treatment of manic-depressive patients is Teixeira (1992), although I also like Karon (2005).

There is, of course, some didactic material that is so essential that it gets discussed with every psychotherapy student. They need to know at least the following:

If the patient is schizophrenic, that schizophrenia is a chronic terror syndrome. All the symptoms of schizophrenia are manifestations of or defenses against terror.

There is no schizophrenic language but each patient has a language we must learn.

That apparently weak affect is actually chronic terror, which blanches out other affects.

That inappropriate affect is usually socially inappropriate, not inappropriate to the patient's subjective experience.

Catatonic stupor is not a stupor, but a biologically evolved chronic terror state, the last stage of defense for prey in the clutch of predators, a state in which enormous pain can be inflicted with no apparent response, but the animal or human is fully conscious of everything that is going on. Indeed, patients will tell you they felt like they would die if they moved, and they usually respond to a verbal reassurance, "I won't let anyone kill you."

Hallucinations are waking dreams, fully understandable by Freud's theory of dreams, with minor modifications (e.g., there are no universal meanings to symbols, only frequently occurring meanings), and the analysis of hallucinations is as useful in therapy as the analysis of dreams. While dreams and hallucinations may occur in any sensory modality, in schizophrenia the primary modality is auditory, although other sensory modalities may also be involved.

Delusions have four major bases (Karon, 1989):

Transference to the world at large –like the obvious meaning of the two alien giants – a green male and a silver female – whom a patient needed to find and have a relationship with, because they controlled the world.

Defenses against pseudo-homosexual impulses.

Strange meanings to concepts that are found within a particular family, but which the patient erroneously believes everyone knows and believes.

The need to have a more or less consistent view of oneself and one's world. If one has unusual experiences, both in reality and in one's symptoms, the resultant beliefs seem bizarre, but they are never more bizarre than is necessary. Since this is a normal process, used for abnormal problems, a non-frightened, non-humiliating therapist can suggest better alternatives based on our better knowledge of the real world, other people, and, most of all, of how the human mind works.

With severely depressed patients, it is important to know that they tend to use isolation as a defense. If you ask them what happened just before their depression, or other symptom, started, they will typically say, "Nothing." If you insist that they were alive, that something must have been happening, they will say, "Nothing important." If you insist they tell you the unimportant things, they will typically tell you things that would depress anyone.

Just because the patient or other professionals say the patient is depressed, does not mean you know what their affect really is. Find out. It may be sadness, guilt, shame, distress, self-contempt, anger, anxiety, undifferentiated negative affect, or no feelings at all. Psychotic depressives often have no conscious affect, apparently repressing the pain. When they begin to feel sad or weep, they are usually getting better.

There is no such thing as a spontaneous panic attack or anxiety or an endogenous depression. The affect is always appropriate – if you are anxious, there is something to be scared of; if you are depressed there is something to be depressed about; if you are angry, there is something hurting you. If it is not conscious, it is unconscious. If it is not in the present, it is in the past and something in the present symbolizes it.

Patients who talk about suicide should be taken seriously. Hopelessness is a necessary but not a sufficient cause for suicide. Nonetheless, the therapist must create hope that through therapy a relation is possible and the problems are in principle solvable. Since suicide is often aggressive retaliation, consciously or unconsciously, the therapist must let the patient know that it really does not hurt the intended victim that much. Suicide often involves the projection of one's superego into someone else. That is why suicidal patients almost always tell someone, implicitly asking "Do I deserve to live or die?" and if the other person does nothing, that patient interprets that as deciding they deserve to die. Therefore the therapist must indicate by word and action that they do not believe the patient deserves to die. Finally, suicide is often the result of a belief that the patient's parent wanted the patient dead, and that needs to be explored.

It is well known that some depressed patients seem to be getting better, but then kill themselves. It is usually stated that they did not have enough energy before. That is not what is going on. According to Atwood (1972), some patients decide to solve their problems by killing themselves. They seem to be getting better, and then they carry out their solution.

If depressed patients are actually getting better, they develop more insight into why they were depressed. If they are going to kill themselves, they seem to be getting better, but they have no more insight into why they were depressed.

If they are actually getting better, they talk more about the future. If they seem to be better, but are going to kill themselves, they do not talk more about the future, because they do not have a future.

If they are getting better, they will talk about suicide, if you bring up the subject. If a depressed person seems to be getting better but is actually going to kill him or her self, they will not talk about suicide, or they will tell you unemotionally that they are going to kill themselves.

If all three indices are in the right direction, they are getting better; if all three are in the wrong direction, they are going to kill themselves, unless you intervene. Hospitalization is a resource. Having someone stay with the patient continuously is a resource. Electro-convulsive therapy (ECT) is not a resource. It defers suicide (until enough of the patient's memory returns), but does not prevent it. The fear of ECT is often a precipitant of suicide. Moreover, the patient has to live with permanent after-effects (Breggin, 1997; Robertson & Pryor, 2006). Anti-depressant medication is a two-edged sword. It may make some patients less suicidal, but it makes others more suicidal (Breggin & Cohen, 1999; Jackson, 2005). Almost all psychiatric medications have strong withdrawal effects, which often give the patient and the treating professionals the feeling that no matter how badly they feel, they would be worse off without their medication, because they become markedly more ill if they try to stop too quickly. Jackson (2005) provides the most accurate description of the biochemical nature of currently used psychiatric medications, evidence for their effects and effectiveness, side effects, and withdrawal effects. Breggin and Cohen (1999) offer the best guide for how to safely withdraw from anti-anxiety medication, anti-depressants, anti-psychotics, and mood stabilizers, both in general and with respect to specific medications. It is my view both from clinical experience as well as available research findings (Karon & VandenBos, 1981) that for any patient the most effective treatment is psychoanalytic therapy with a knowledgeable therapist without medication, if the patient, the therapist, and the setting can tolerate it. If the patient asks for it (which is rare), or if the therapist cannot tolerate severe symptoms or disorganized patients, or if the setting (e.g., hospital, family) cannot tolerate them, medication may be used. Medication may also be used to cope with a crisis. But in either case it should always be considered a temporary solution, and the medication withdrawn as the patient can tolerate it. Research (e.g., Karon & VandenBos, 1981) shows that is a good way to work. Psychotherapy plus continuing medication is better than medication alone, but not as effective in the long run as psychotherapy alone, or psychotherapy with initial medication which is withdrawn as the patient can tolerate.

Psychoanalysis and Psychoanalytic Therapy

I stress the continuity between psychoanalysis and psychoanalytic therapy. Since the 1940s psychoanalytic therapy has been distinguished from psychoanalysis proper. In the earlier literature (e.g., Sterba, 1935), "psychoanalytic therapy" was used simply to indicate that what was being discussed was psychoanalysis as therapy, or its therapeutic action. Freud, while decrying "wild analysis" (1910), was not rigid as to the technique he utilized, as evidenced by his case histories, for example, the "Rat Man" (1909), or the techniques he accepted in his students and colleagues (e.g., Aichhorn, 1936). One of my early psychoanalytic instructors defined psychoanalytic therapy as being as much like psychoanalysis as the defenses of the patient, the time available, and the skill of the therapist permit. That has always seemed to me a proper definition.

The continuity that is implied is real. As my students have pointed out, I am apt to use the phrase "real treatment" to mean "psychoanalysis or psychoanalytic therapy," as in the sentence, "After years of medication, behavior modification, cognitive therapy, and so forth, the patient finally began real treatment."

Both psychoanalysis and psychoanalytic therapy treat a person, never just a single symptom. All problems are treated in terms of their importance to the patient, whether or not they correspond to conventionally labeled symptoms, and whether or not they were the presenting complaint.

Any psychoanalysis that is not good therapy cannot be good psychoanalysis. Psychoanalytic theories provide the basis for proper technique, whether standard or modified. Suitable modifications, or parameters, of psychoanalysis and psychoanalytic therapy are always used by competent clinicians, as required by the defenses of the patient. Where the dividing line between psychoanalysis and psychoanalytic therapy is drawn varies from writer to writer. It may be that psychoanalysis is "any investigation that takes seriously the unconscious and repression, resistance and transference," or any technique that consists of doing what needs to be done, to the best of your ability, on the basis of a psychoanalytic understanding of the patient and the treatment process, two definitions that I like. Or, more restrictively, only if the patient in addition is seen at least three, four, five, or six days a week, on a couch, facing away from the analyst, and suffers from neurotic or certain characterological problems. Or only if structural change is produced, or only if a full "transference neurosis" occurs and is resolved, or only if the sole therapeutic agent is interpretation, narrowly defined. Thoma and Kachele (1987) point out how difficult such criteria are to use scientifically, and the clear continuity between various psychoanalytic therapies and psychoanalysis, and how everything that is learned about psychoanalysis illuminates the psychoanalytic therapies and everything that is learned about the psychoanalytic therapies illuminates the process of psychoanalysis.

It really makes no difference in treatment where you draw the dividing line, as long as the technique used, whether called psychoanalysis or psychoanalytic therapy, is appropriate to the defenses of the patient, in the best judgment of the analyst or therapist.

Final Comment

Bruno Bettelheim (1983) once said, "If you treat the patient with common courtesy, and treat them the way you would want to be treated, you will almost always do the technically correct thing." And I would add, "If you treat the supervisee with common courtesy, and treat them the way you would want to be treated, both you and they will almost always do the right thing."

REFERENCES

Aichhorn, A. (1936). Wayward youth. London: Putnam.

Alexander, F., French, T.M., et al. (1946). Psychoanalytic therapy: Principles and applications. New York: Ronald Press.

Atwood, G. (1972). Note on a relationship between suicidal intentions and the depressive mood. Psychotherapy: Theory, Research, and Practice, 9. 284-285.

Benedetti, G. (1987). Psychotherapy of schizophrenia. New York: New York University Press.

Benedetti, G., & Furlan, G.M. (1987). Individual psychoanalytic psychotherapy of schizophrenia. In G. Benedetti, Psychotherapy of schizophrenia. New York: New York University Press, pp. 198-212.

Bettelheim, B. (1983). Supervision of a borderline patient. University of Detroit Advanced Psychotherapy Workshop, Detroit, MI.

Breggin, P.R. (1997). Electroshock for depression. In Brain-disabling treatments in psychiatry: Drugs, electroshock, and the FDA (pp. 129-156). New York: Springer.

——— & Cohen, D.R. (1999). Your drug may be your problem: How and why to stop taking psychiatric medications. Cambridge, MA: Perseus Books.

Fairbairn, R.W.D. (1954). An Object-Relations Theory of Personality. New York: Basic Books.

Fenichel, O. (1945). The Psychoanalytic Theory of Neurosis. New York: Norton.

Freud, S. (1909). Notes upon a case of obsessional neurosis. Standard Edition, 10, 153-318. London: Hogarth Press, 1955.

——— (1910). "Wild" psychoanalysis. Standard Edition, 11, 219-230. London: Hogarth Press, 1957.

———— (1912). Recommendations to physicians practicing psychoanalysis. Standard Edition, /2, 109-120. London: Hogarth

———— (1916-1917). Introductory lectures. Standard Edition, /5-/6. London: Hogarth Press, 1961-1963.

———— (1933). New introductory lectures on psychoanalysis. Standard Edition, 22. London: Hogarth Press, 1964.

———— (1963). Therapy and technique. New York: Collier Books.

Fromm-Reichmann, F. (1960). Principles of intensive psychotherapy. Chicago: University of Chicago Press.

Jackson, G.E. (2005). Rethinking psychiatric drugs: A guide for informed consent. Bloomington, IN: AuthorHouse. Karon, B. P. (1989). On the formation of delusions. Psychoanalytic Psychology, 6, 169-185.

Karon, B.P. (2003). The tragedy of schizophrenia without psychotherapy. Journal of the American Academy of Psychoanalysis and Dynamic Psychiatry, 31, 89-118.

———— (2005). Recurrent psychotic depression is treatable by psychoanalytic therapy without medication. Ethical Human Psychology and Psychiatry, 7, 45-56.

———— & VandenBos, G.R. (1981). Psychotherapy of schizophrenia: The treatment of choice. New York: Aronson.

Knight, R.P. (1954). The present status of organized psychoanalysis in the United States. In R. P. Knight & C. R. Friedman (Eds.), Psychoanalytic psychiatry and psychology (pp. 7-26). New York: International Universities Press.

Malan, D. (1979). Individual psychotherapy and the science of psychodynamics. London: Butterworth.

May, P.R.A. (1968). Treatment of schizophrenia: A comparative study of five treatment methods. New York: Science House.

Read, J., & Ross, C.A. (2003). Psychological trauma and psychosis: Another reason why people diagnosed schizophrenic must be offered psychological therapies. The Journal of the American Academy of Psychoanalysis and Dynamic Psychiatry, 31, 247-268.

———— Goodman, L., Morrison, A.P., Ross, C.A., & Aderhold, V. (2004). Childhood trauma, loss, and stress. In J. Read, L. R. Mosher, & R. P. Bentall (Eds.), Models of madness: Psychological, social, and biological approaches to schizophrenia (pp. 223-252). New York: Brunner-Routledge.

Robertson, H., & Pryor, R. (2006). Memory and cognitive effects of ECT: informing and assessing patients. Advances in Psychiatric Treatment, 12, 228-238.

Sterba, R. (1935). Psychoanalytic therapy. In The collected papers (H. Daldin, Ed.), pp. 71-86. Croton-on-Hudson, NY: North River Press, 1987.

Teixeira, M. (1992). Psychoanalytic theory and therapy in the treatment of manic-depressive disorders. Psychoanalysis and Psychotherapy, 11, 81-96.

Thoma, H., & Kachele, H. (1987). Psychoanalytic practice. Berlin: Springer Verlag.

CHAPTER 29
Psychoanalysis, Psychoanalytic Therapy, and the Process of Supervision
Bertram R Karon, Ph.D.

Since the 1940s psychoanalytic therapy has been distinguished from psychoanalysis proper. In the earlier literature (e.g., Sterba, 1935), "psychoanalytic therapy" was used simply to indicate that what was being discussed was psychoanalysis as therapy, or its therapeutic action.

Freud, while decrying "wild analysis" (1910), was not rigid as to the technique he utilized, as evidenced by his case histories, for example, the "Rat Man" (1909), or the techniques he accepted in his students and colleagues (e.g., Aichhorn, 1936).

One of my early psychoanalytic instructors defined psychoanalytic therapy as being as much like psychoanalysis as the defenses of the patient, the time available, and the skill of the therapist permit. That has always seemed to me a proper definition.

The continuity that is implied is real. As my students have pointed out, I am apt to use the phrase "real treatment" to mean "psychoanalysis or psychoanalytic therapy," as in the sentence, "After years of medication, behavior modification, cognitive therapy, and so forth, the patient finally began real treatment."

Any psychoanalysis which is not good therapy cannot be good psychoanalysis. Psychoanalytic theories provide the basis for proper technique, whether standard or modified. Suitable modifications, or parameters, of psychoanalysis and psychoanalytic therapy are always used by competent clinicians, as required by the defenses of the patient.

"Parameter-phobia" among analysts is the result of an internalized punitive psychoanalytic superego based on experiences with one's real psychoanalytic supervisors fused with remnants of the preexisting primitive sadistic superego. It should not be necessary to say, but it is necessary to say, that the concept of "parameters" does not refer to crimes, but to consciously conceptualizing the rationale for technical procedures, so that you can consciously evaluate their effectiveness and keep track of the inevitable countertransference distortions.

Where the dividing line between psychoanalysis and psychoanalytic therapy is drawn varies from writer to writer. It may be that psychoanalysis is "any investigation that takes seriously the unconscious and repression, resistance and transference," or any technique that consists of doing what needs to be done, to the best of your ability, on the basis of a psychoanalytic understanding of the patient and the treatment process. Or only if the patient is seen at least three, four, five, or six days a week, on a couch, facing away from the analyst, and suffers from neurotic or certain characterological problems. Or only if structural change is produced, or only if a full "transference neurosis" occurs and is resolved, or only if the sole therapeutic agent is interpretation, narrowly defined. It really makes no difference in treatment where you draw the line, as long as the technique used, whether called psychoanalysis or psychoanalytic therapy, is appropriate to the defenses of the patient, in the best judgment of the analyst or therapist.

Thoma and Kachele (1987) point out how difficult such criteria are to use scientifically, and the clear continuity between various psychoanalytic therapies and psychoanalysis, and how everything that is learned about the psychoanalytic therapies illuminates the process of psychoanalysis proper, and that what is learned in psychoanalysis is relevant to understanding the psychoanalytic therapies.

For any therapy with any patient, it is my experience that the more time available, the easier it is for both patient and therapist. Unfortunately, the therapist's schedule, the patient's schedule, the need to charge a fee, and the limited financial resources available all lead to briefer therapy, both in time and in number of sessions per week. Every genuine therapist feels the conflict between wanting to help as many people as possible and wanting to do a therapy that is thorough and helpful, and we know best how to do that in ways that take time. Every genuine therapist also knows the conflict between wanting to be available to everyone irrespective of financial status and wanting to live in the way that a decent income permits, or, if part of an agency, the need to maintain the fiscal solvency of the agency, particularly if the agency provides real help.

There is, as far as I know, no systematic research on the effects of number of sessions per week per se on the nature and content of the hour or on the course of the treatment. The nearest to a systematic study was the report of Alexander and French (1946) that reducing the number of sessions per week seemed more compatible with effective treatment than cutting down the calendar time. Technically, they suggested that in once or twice per week therapy, more of the transference reactions outside the therapy hour had to be analyzed as opposed to analyzing the transference neurosis itself.

Certainly, under even the most stringent institutional restrictions, I would recommend strongly that the first week of treatment for psychotic individuals should be five sessions, although the length of the session may be shortened to half an hour. Even if the treatment is going to be continued on a once per week basis, the patient needs to know you are there, the therapeutic alliance needs to be established, and the therapist and patient need to have a chance for the transference and countertransference dynamics to begin to be apparent.

It is not uncommon to hear fears that too intensive a frequency will cause too much regression, particularly for borderline patients. But it is not the frequency per se which is disabling but the character of the sessions. In particular, it is essential that the therapist or analyst be willing to provide as much structure and support as the defenses of the patient require. This is not a one-time diagnostic judgment, but a reaction in each hour to the patients as they experience that therapy hour, so that the patients' ability to cope with the anxieties aroused by their memories and transference reactions are not exceeded. Again, it is not uncommon to hear that too few sessions are so unhinging that the patient had better not be treated psychotherapeutically at all, but medicated, punished, advised, or left alone. Again, the problem is the character of the session. The greatest danger is that nothing of importance will happen with too low a frequency, although it is true that with a low frequency, it is harder for the therapist to obtain the necessary information about the therapy to guide the process optimally.

Sometimes the low frequency is forced by the defenses of the patient, however. One psychotic depressive patient moved to her parents' house instead of to a hospital. They lived some 40 miles away and could only bring her once a week. This turned out to be an advantage. Like many psychotic depressives, this lady was very irritating. It was possible for her to have a reasonable, kind, but active therapist once a week, although by the end of her hour my countertransference was such that I usually felt enraged at her. By the next week, however, she once more had a rational and kind therapist for most of her hour. The treatment progressed to a very satisfactory outcome—not only did her psychosis remit, but she handled her five children more appropriately, had a better relationship with her husband, including a better sexual relationship, and held a part-time job successfully for the first time in her marriage. In part because of their better relationship, her husband became more effective and was able to earn more money, which was important for their way of life. But given the intensity of my emotional reaction, it is questionable that such a benign outcome would have been possible if she had been seen more frequently, particularly at the beginning.

One ambulatory depressive of 20 years standing was told that he should be seen a minimum of three times a week, and that while no firm estimate could be made, he would need to be in treatment at least two or three years. He was irate: "You are just trying to run a bill on me. I know. I have friends who work in an HMO. They treat people in 16 sessions. That's all anyone needs. And I'm not coming in more than once a week." He was told that, while I disagreed, I would certainly do what I could for him in the time he allowed.

At the tenth session, I reminded him that he had only six more sessions, and asked how he felt about it. He was furious that I would not see him more than 16 sessions. After he berated me, he was told that if he felt that strongly, I would continue treating him. Shortly thereafter he became furious that I refused to see him more than once a week. After allowing him to berate me, I again conceded to his wish to be seen twice a week. After a few months he became furious that I refused to see him more than twice a week. Again, after allowing his rage, I agreed with his demand for three times a week. The analytic treatment then proceeded with the difficulties usual for severely depressed, hostile patients.

An ambulatory paranoid patient, with a delusion that there was a rumor that he was a homosexual, was unable to work. Previous therapy had enabled him to finish schooling and embark on a professional career (not in the psychological professions). This rumor had followed him, however, from city to city. Despite offers to cut his fee, he insisted on being seen not more than half an hour once per week because he "could not afford any more." He would sit in the furthest corner of the room, and stated that he had no thoughts, what did the therapist want to talk about? It was possible nonetheless to help him, in the minimal time he permitted, to be able to work, to relate to friends, and to date without the "rumor" recurring. While the treatment was terminated prematurely by the therapist's standards, with many neurotic traits remaining and far short of our analytic ideal, the treatment was a success by the patient's standards, was well worth the time involved, and has led to stable functioning for years (as of now).

Most people who think about the issue of the ideal training of a psychoanalytic therapist recommend that the novice should first experience a thorough personal psychoanalysis, then conduct traditional psychoanalyses under supervision, and then be trained in briefer psychoanalytic therapies. Thus, the therapist will really understand, from his or her own analysis, what therapy is about, learn from supervised analyses what would come to the surface if there were sufficient time, and then be able to utilize this in briefer psychoanalytic therapy.

Almost nobody goes through the sequence of training in that rational order. For example, no graduate student in our program practices psychoanalysis, in the narrow sense. The only practitioners I supervise in psychoanalysis are psychologists and social workers in the community, who are in private practice or community agencies, have been analyzed, and have taken seminars in analytic technique and wish eventually to be trained as psychoanalysts. Graduate students, often without any prior personal therapy, begin by doing brief psychoanalytic therapy. Most of the competent ones obtain some personal psychotherapy before they finish graduate school, but do not begin personal psychoanalysis until they are out in the field, primarily for financial reasons.

Before we despair, however, we should note that the first generation of psychoanalysts, whose contributions display a level of insight, creativity, and therapeutic competence far above what is usual today, went through what we would consider haphazard training. Of course, these were bright, creative, highly motivated individuals, who lived psychoanalysis. They learned as much as possible about psychoanalysis in the broadest possible sense. You may argue, as Robert Knight (1954, pp. 24-25) has, that they were less well-adjusted than the present generation, but better analysts. Knight argues that his generation of candidates was motivated to learn as little as possible about psychoanalysis and get through their training, and this led to the proliferation of explicit requirements. But this very proliferation of explicit requirements appeals to that kind of candidate he deplores, while discouraging the creative individuals to whom psychoanalysis appealed earlier.

Many of our current creative psychoanalysts have gone through unusual routes in their training. The question is: does the irrational route that we have created in graduate school make any sense at all?

I have found it useful to supervise only students (or professionals) who choose to be supervised by me. This is now a general rule in our Psychological Clinic. Those who choose to be supervised by me already have a strong interest in psychoanalysis. Obviously, I expect even the most inexperienced student to have read Freud's *Introductory Lectures* (1916-1917) and *New Introductory Lectures* (1933), his papers on technique (1963), and at least one paper of mine. I then require them to read Fromm-Reichmann's *Principles of Intensive Psychotherapy* (1960), if they have not already done so, and David Malan's book on brief therapy, *Individual Psychotherapy and the Science of Psychodynamics* (1979). I have never had a novice therapist who did not get enthusiastic about that book. Indeed, graduate students uniformly object, "Why did you make us read Fenichel? It's all in here anyway, only much clearer."

Any other reading will be based on the individual case. If the patient has psychotic features, obviously I assign my book (Karon &VandenBos, 1981).

I stress the continuity between psychoanalysis and psychoanalytic therapy. I like the kinds of clinicians, students or the more experienced, who get themselves into the dilemma: "I think I can help this patient, but my colleagues/supervisors/setting says that it should be interrupted or can't be done, and I think they are wrong, but I need supervision from someone experienced. Maybe I'm wrong (although I don't think so), or maybe I'm getting in over my head, but this patient is treatable, and they are not going to treat him or her, if I don't. You are the only one I know who would encourage me to treat this patient."

Since I believe in self-selection, I tell prospective student trainees that I expect them to see any patient I supervise at least twice a week. Moreover, since my own patients rarely see me for less than two years, I require that students I supervise make a commitment to be available to the patient for a minimum of two years, even though that is not the academic requirement. In addition to being a reasonable requirement, it weeds out those who are not highly motivated. (One bright student asked me if it was all right if he saw a patient five days a week, and did a brilliant job of psychoanalytic therapy with a severe borderline.)

There are many disagreements about the philosophies and techniques of supervision. In particular, how much of the student's dynamics do you delve into, how much is it didactic, how much do you focus only on the patient, should you use audiovisual aids or observe the actual interview?

But far more important than the technique of supervision is whether the supervisor has anything to teach. You cannot teach what you do not know. You cannot supervise what you do not practice. If you are not a competent clinical psychoanalyst, you cannot supervise psychoanalysis adequately. If you do not practice psychoanalytic therapy well, you cannot supervise psychoanalytic therapy adequately. No supervisory technique will work if the supervisor is teaching what he or she does not know, and any technique is likely to be helpful to the novice if the supervisor is knowledgeable.

In supervision, particularly with early students, the supervisor is a safety net. The student has the security that there is backup for any crisis. The supervisor, however, does not take over the case. Students cannot possibly communicate everything they know about a case. And it is the students' responsibility to act on their own best clinical judgment, even if they are wrong. What the supervisor provides is: "This is what I hear, what I might do, and if you cannot do any better, you can always do or say what I would have. And, of course, I expect you to review everything you do."

The supervisor is not the student's therapist. While the anxieties involved in doing psychoanalytic therapy are contained by the supervisor, the supervisor does not delve into the student's dynamics. The opposite stance is experienced by the student as intrusive, punitive, and scary. It is useful to say, "I wonder if there is a personal issue here, that you might want to discuss with your therapist. Think about it and you decide. You don't need to discuss it with me." For a student not in therapy: "I wonder if this isn't making you anxious. This is very difficult material (or this is a very difficult person). This might be a good time to start your own therapy. You don't need to discuss your personal issues with me, but think about it."

The injunction "you don't need to discuss it with me" allows students the privacy and maturity they need and allows them to discuss freely some aspects of it if they choose. They usually do choose to discuss what seems most pertinent.

Supervisees identify with supervisors. If they are treated kindly and supportively, they tend to treat their patients kindly and supportively. If their difficulties and pain as therapists are shared, they can share the patients' pain and difficulties. If the supervisor is cold or punitive, students become cold or punitive. If the supervisor is curious, accepting of the human condition, sees the value in "mistakes," is comfortable with the unconscious, and expects students to be first-rate, then the students tend to value their curiosity, learn from their mistakes, learn about the unconscious, and become first-rate.

I recall my first supervisory hour with Richard Sterba. It was my second control case. After driving 100 miles on a Sunday, feeling both anxious and excited, I presented the case material. His first supervisory comment was, "Do you mind if I make a suggestion?" And he waited for an answer.

I was startled. "Of course. Please."

He then said, "I would have said it differently," and proceeded to suggest a far more therapeutic phrasing of the interpretation.

But in that first supervisory intervention, before he communicated specific information, he communicated a feeling of respect for the other person, which hopefully I internalized.

Even the novice students in our program who are supervised by me have done some counseling or psychotherapy, and so it is my job to reach them where they are and broaden and deepen their knowledge and technique. This is, of course, true no matter at what stage they are in their training. For professionals in private practice who seek me out, I find I have to encourage them to consider seeing the patient more intensively, or using a couch when it is appropriate. Just as there is a resistance in some therapists to using "parameters" appropriate to the defenses of the patient, there is also a resistance in others to using classical technique when it would obviously be helpful.

Of course, one must also serve as a kindly superego and parent figure. Supervisees need to know that if a crisis occurs that they cannot handle, they have immediate access to someone who will be there. Even when their handling of the crisis is appropriate, they need a kindly superego who will tell them so and allow them to tolerate their anxiety (and even learn from it about themselves and the patient). Indeed, experienced professionals sometimes need that kind of sharing. In the face of difficult resistances, and the pessimism of colleagues, supervisees need the optimism of the supervisor that if one does as reasonable a job as one can, the odds are the patient will respond. Supervisees also need to know that their experience of the treatment as difficult occurs because it is difficult work, and the pessimism and alarmism of colleagues is a function of the latter's experience of working, as most mental health professionals do, with inadequate training. If supervisees are treating the kind of patient whose defenses do not permit him or her to communicate that the therapist is being helpful, the support and evaluation of an experienced supervisor becomes essential. Supervisees need to be reminded that most appropriately treated patients benefit greatly, that the patient cannot give the feedback you would like, but that the procedures and interpretations seem appropriate and should be continued or should be modified in specific ways.

Once a supervisee has continued the treatment of a difficult patient, about whom other professionals have been pessimistic, until the patient has palpably improved, this serves as a benign trauma from whose effects the supervisee never recovers.

I rarely use mechanical aids. In my project in treating schizophrenics with psychoanalytic therapy, the early hours of both the experienced therapists and the trainees were viewed on videotape and discussed for training purposes. That was initially useful. It was also reassuring to the novice in dealing with unpredictable patients that the sessions were being simultaneously watched by colleagues who could intervene if necessary.

The students then, and the students at the university, did not find the discussion of their tapes remarkably helpful, but do report observing my tapes as helpful. The model of correct interventions helps, but even more, they notice that I am sometimes tired, distracted, insensitive, and have countertransference reactions, and despite that, even very difficult patients obviously improve. Therefore, it cannot be a trick that only some gifted, superbly trained individual can practice, but something that intelligent human beings who want to be helpful can learn to do.

It is my experience that the traditional supervision hour, with the student recounting from notes is best. I request that the notes be written after the hour, as Freud (1912) recommended, not during it. What the students bring up is what is puzzling to them, and then anything you say has an effect in changing their understanding and technique. Your insights meet their need, help resolve their anxieties or curiosities. When you bring up something from a tape, it does not have the same effect in facilitating their learning, because it does not meet their needs. It must be admitted that one psychopathic student was able to lie to me successfully in ordinary supervision hours. But supervision is not police work. For the bulk of students this is the optimal way to go. One cannot corrupt the teaching process because one liar can take advantage of you.

In supervision of psychoanalysis, the supervisee is more experienced, so less time need be spent on basic mechanics. More time is available to listen to the subtle aspects of the fantasy material, which is more available, and the supervisee is more sensitive to the transference and countertransference issues. Most often experienced supervisees are held back by one formulation of the material, including the transference and countertransference, which has prevented them from hearing^ different, more relevant formulation. But the difference in supervision is one of degree.

As Richard Sterba has pointed out (personal communication), supervision is easier than psychotherapy because the supervisee's unconscious almost always organizes the material so that only the addition of the last link is needed, even though the supervisee seemingly does not consciously understand it.

Bruno Bettelheim (1983) once said, "If you treat the patient with common courtesy, and treat the patient the way you would want to be treated, you will almost always do the right thing." And I would add, "If you treat the supervisee with common courtesy, and treat them the way you would want to be treated, both you and they will almost always do the right thing."

REFERENCES

Aichhorn, A. (1936). Wayward youth. London: Putnam.

Alexander, F., French, T.M., et al. (1946). Psychoanalytic therapy: Principles and applications. New York: Ronald Press.

Bettelheim, B. (1983). Supervision of a borderline patient. University of Detroit Advanced Psychotherapy Workshop, Detroit.

Freud, S. (1909). Notes upon a case of obsessional neurosis. Standard Edition, 10, 153-318. London: Hogarth Press, 1955.

———— (1910). "Wild" psychoanalysis. Standard Edition, 11, 219-230. London: Hogarth Press, 1957.

———— (1912). Recommendations to physicians practising psychoanalysis. Standard Edition, 12, 109-120. London: Hogarth Press, 1958.

———— (1916-1917). Introductory lectures. Standard Edition, 15-16. London: Hogarth Press, 1961-1963.

———— (1933). New introductory lectures on psychoanalysis. Standard Edition, 22. London: Hogarth Press, 1964.

———— (1963). Therapy and technique. New York: Collier Books. Fromm-Reichmann, F. (1960). Principles of intensive psychotherapy. Chicago: University of Chicago Press.

Karon, B.P., & VandenBos, G.R. (1981). Psychotherapy of schizophrenia: The treatment of choice. New York: Aronson.

Knight, R.P. (1954). The present status of organized psychoanalysis in the United States. In R.P. Knight & C.R. Friedman (Eds.), Psychoanalytic psychiatry and psychology (pp. 7-26). New York: International Universities Press.

Malan, D. (1979). Individual psychotherapy and the science of psychodynamics. London: Butterworth.

Sterba, R. (1935). Psychoanalytic therapy. In The collected papers (H. Daldin, Ed.), pp71-86. Croton-on-Hudson, NY: North River Press, 1987.

Thoma, H., & Kachele, H. (1987). Psychoanalytic practice. Berlin: SpringerVerlag.

CHAPTER 30
Becoming a First-Rate Professional Psychologist Despite Graduate Education

Bertram P. Karon

Professional psychology is exciting, creative work. Graduate schools often discourage, bore, and wear down the student. Research is made painful; research training all too often does not lead to doing research as a professional. The system punishes faculty for taking the time to acquire adequate clinical training or experience. Inadequate faculty are pessimistic about therapy, diagnosis, consultation, and private practice. Experimental psychologists often keep students from being exposed to clinical psychology, for fear that it will interest them. One should publish when one has something important (data or theory) to share. If one can understand the irrational parts of the system, one can surmount them and enjoy contributing to the field as a therapist, researcher; and/or teacher.

There are only two good reasons for being a psychologist. The first is that you would like to help people, particularly if you are a clinician. The second is that you are curious. Psychology is an addiction that, one hopes, graduate students have already acquired and of which they are unlikely ever to be cured.

When graduate students apply to graduate school, they think psychology is interesting. They know that they do not yet know the field, but they know the faculty does; and the faculty will help them to become first-rate psychologists.

Very soon, graduate students notice other things. Some faculty are pessimistic about the future of psychology. Faculty do not always agree with each other or with the professional literature the students already know. This is not as troubling as the fact that some faculty discourage intellectual interests. They may not want to become familiar with some of the professional literature (and may even disapprove of the student being familiar with it). Moreover, the amount of work is enormous the first year, but it gets easier later. Nonetheless, a great deal of this work seems irrelevant and, sometimes, meaningless. What is going on?

Two books describe graduate education insightfully and make it easier for graduate students to survive. *White Collar: The American Middle Class* is a study of white-collar professions by the sociologist C. Wright Mills (1953). He likens the university to a feudal system wherein junior faculty swear fealty to senior faculty in return for protection and graduate students swear fealty to junior faculty in return for protection. Many of the requirements of graduate education. Mills maintains, are "dragons." Dragons have no purpose except to be slain; that is, they are tests of motivation to prove how difficult it is to get knighthood (or the doctorate) and, therefore, how valuable those people must be who already have it (the faculty).

One factor that Mills did not describe was not a major issue in the 1940s. Today, what is more important than seniority for status and political power is grant money. Faculty are retained, promoted, and given tenure on the basis of grant money above all else. This means that whatever is fashionable with the granting agencies gets priority, and pure research does not (Negin, 1993). Biological research in psychopathology and treatment is now supported far more extensively than is research in psychotherapy, particularly psychodynamic psychotherapy (e.g., Breggin, 1991; "Schizophrenia-related grants," 1993). Psychology departments thus become overloaded with biological researchers. Moreover, teaching and professional competence become secondary at best.

In *On Method: Toward a Reconstruction of Psychological Investigation*, David Bakan (1967) argued that whatever systems consistently do is what they are intended to do. This may or may not coincide with what the system officially says it does. Clinical programs frequently do not teach first-rate clinical skills. One of the reasons given is that doctoral programs in psychology were originally designed to train researchers, not clinicians. But the modal number of publications past the doctoral thesis for psychologists in all subfields of psychology is zero.

Bakan argued that the real (if unspoken and perhaps unconscious) intention of the system is to ensure that the student will never become a competitor of the faculty. Research in graduate school often is made so intellectually uninteresting and so painful in its execution that, when the ex-graduate student has a free choice, he or she will not choose to do research. Ironically, the oversimplified paradigms imposed on doctoral research are such that few American Departments of Psychology would grant a doctorate for any research that Erik Erikson or Jean Piaget ever did. Yet Erikson was a full professor at prestigious universities, and any American university would have raised its scientific status by having either of these men as a full professor.

Once it is realized that those aspects of graduate education that seem irrational are, indeed, irrational (i.e., not rationally related to helping the student become a first-rate psychologist) and that this is true not only of the Department of Psychology at one university, but also of all graduate departments at all universities, then it is easier for the student to cope with that irrationality and to make a conscious decision about whether the system or the student will win. After all, students win if they persevere, get their doctorate, and become faculty members; then they may impose some rationality on that part of education they can control (the courses they teach and that part of the program over which they have some control).

Of course, the apparently irrational aspects of graduate education may not have so involuted or Machiavellian an explanation. It may simply reflect the fact that helping a student do interesting, important, or creative research, or enhancing the student's intellectual development or clinical skills, has nothing to do with getting the faculty member's grant research done (the activity on which the faculty member's salary and advancement may depend). Many faculty members have difficulty resisting such pressures.

It is also the case that you cannot teach what you do not know. Although this certainly applies to research and theoretical training, it is particularly true of clinical training. Faculty members frequently have taken university jobs before they have had a chance to develop first-rate skills. They are usually punished for taking the time to develop further clinical competence and rewarded for activities that preclude their developing further clinical skills. Behavioral and cognitive approaches are more readily investigated by traditional experimental paradigms and, therefore, are more likely to yield publishable articles. It is not an accident that academic clinical psychologists are twice as likely to be behavioral or cognitive rather than psychodynamic; however, practicing clinical psychologists are one and a half times as likely to be psychodynamic as they are to be behavioral or cognitive (Association for Advancement of Behavior Therapy Membership Directory, 1992-1993; Directory of the American Psychological Association, 1993; National Register of Health Service Providers in Psychology, 1991-1992).

However, clinical experience teaches that, in the real world, psychodynamic approaches are more helpful than is taught by behavioral and cognitive faculty. The mono-symptomatic patient—who is most frequently researched and is most responsive to behavioral approaches—represents a minority of psychotherapy patients: Eighty percent of patients in most settings have two Axis I or Axis II diagnoses from the *Diagnostic and Statistical Manual of Mental Disorders* (3rd ed. rev. [DSM 1987]; American Psychiatric Association, 1987); 60% have three or more (Miranda & Dwyer, 1993; Persons, 1993; Shea, 1993; Wolfe, 1993). Multi-symptomatic patients respond better to a psychoanalytic treatment (which treats patients, not symptoms). This is not to say that behavioral or cognitive approaches are not helpful, it is just to say that the relative merits as taught in most graduate programs do not reflect the observations and opinions of experienced practitioners.

During a session titled "For Graduate Students Only" at an annual meeting of Division 29 (the Division of Psychotherapy) of the American Psychological Association, one graduate student described his supervisor, during the second year of practicum, getting depressed because he thought he had not helped anyone in therapy. The graduate student, trying to be supportive, said that he thought the faculty member had been helpful. That one graduate student had such an experience was not disturbing. What was disturbing was that all around the room were graduate students nodding their heads; if they had not had that particular experience, they could well imagine having that experience with their faculty.

Even for a career in research in clinical psychology, you need to master clinical skills. In studies of diagnostic procedures-such as the Rorschach or the Thematic Apperception Test (TAT)—the most important variable is whether the diagnosticians have training and experience in using that diagnostic procedure to predict that criterion (Karon, 1968,1978). Similarly, the best predictor of the findings of an outcome study of any psychotherapy is whether there is anyone on the project who knows how to do that kind of therapy with that kind of patient (e.g., Karon, 1989; Karon & VandenBos, 1981).

Some faculty think the way to train researchers is not to train them as clinicians. Most incoming graduate students, however, want to be clinicians, and most psychologists will not do research after they have received their doctorate. Nonetheless, some do end up as good researchers, if the faculty does not kill their curiosity. For example, two ex-graduate students, the Gurs, whose work on the measurement of cerebral blood flow and localization of function is well-known, were not trained by a neuroscience program; in fact, they were trained as very competent psychodynamic clinicians whose scientific curiosity led them to the field to which they are now contributing.

The pressure to be a hypocrite begins from the moment a student applies for graduate school. It used to be that if you admitted you wanted to be clinician (that is, a psychotherapist), you would be turned down by most, if not all, graduate programs. To get into graduate school, you would have to lie and say that you wanted to do research with a clinical background. I thought we were beyond that period. Alas, however, for most Ph.D. programs today, it is still necessary to tell that lie.

Most students, undergraduate as well as graduate, are primarily interested in the parts of psychology that are related to clinical psychology, to psychotherapy, and to psychoanalysis. Sixty percent of psychologists are now practitioners (Directory of the American Psychological Association, 1993). Undergraduate courses, however, still try to avoid these topics or try to treat them in a superficial and uninformed way. Eysenck's (1952) study, which claimed that psychotherapy does not work, is full of methodological flaws, and yet it is still taken at face value. The Smith, Glass, and Miller (1980) meta-analysis, which accurately summarized all available studies, concluded that psychotherapy clearly helps; yet it is still given scant space. Moreover, psychoanalysis is usually treated as if none of its theories have been validated in experimental situations, even though there have been solid experimental validations of many psychoanalytic theories. The books by Kline (1972) in England and by Fisher and Greenberg (1977) in the United States both summarize much of these data, and yet they are rarely mentioned. There are other examples of such imbalance (e.g., Karon & O'Grady, 1970; Meehl, 1954).

It is important for graduate students to know that faculty are not necessarily the best judge of what is important. Faculty members can share what they think is important; however, students have to supplement this with their own interests. First-rate graduate students cannot be put in little slots, but have far-ranging curiosities. Faculty can contribute in part by calling attention to what the faculty member has found important and valuable and in part by getting out of the way.

Graduate schools not only make students choose which field of psychology they wish to be in before they get there, but they also ask, if students choose clinical psychology, whether they are going to be adult or child clinicians before they get to graduate school. This is convenient for administrators who want to deal with graduate students as if they were pegs in a board, but it has nothing to do with education. The truth is that graduate students do not know what they want to do with their lives when they apply to graduate school, let alone in what particular subfield of psychology they are most interested.

In my own career development, I was sure that I could never be a psychotherapist because I thought therapists were people who intuitively understood others; and I knew I was frequently out in left field. However, it seemed clear to me that it was unlikely that I would do meaningful research in personality or clinical psychology without clinical training. In my internship I found that, although therapy was difficult and anxiety provoking, it was also interesting. Furthermore, my patients improved; and I began writing original clinical articles. I soon discovered I was a therapist. Moreover, post-doctorally I knew I could never be a psychoanalyst after hearing psychoanalysts whose theories were so abstract that I could not relate them to anything a human being might experience. This surprised me because, as a graduate student, when I wondered "Why am I here?" I would go to the library and read some article by Freud that was new to me; I would always conclude that there was something that interested me in psychology. Only then could I go back to the physiology of the inner ear or factor analysis or whatever I needed to learn to get through the program. When I discovered psychoanalysts who were kind, intellectually honest, and therapeutically effective, I fell in love with psychoanalysis again. Although I had to arrange my own training, and my writings are not orthodox, I am surprised to discover I am now accepted as a psychologist-psychoanalyst.

I was interviewed for a faculty job at Dartmouth, and they offered me the job, but my thesis advisor said, "You'll never finish, if you take a job now," so I turned it down. A year later, my thesis was finished, and the same job opened up. I badly wanted a job, and tried very hard to be what I thought was their kind of psychologist: ultrarigorous and non-speculative. They turned me down. (I later learned that if I had been myself, I might well have gotten the job.) A faculty member who heard my colloquium wrote to a friend of mine, "Your friend is certainly bright, but he will never make an undergraduate lecturer." Nonetheless, my students tell me that is possibly what I do best.

Finally, I had given up hope that I would ever be a college professor about a month before I received a letter from Michigan State University telling me that there was an opening and, if I was interested, to submit a vita and a statement of my research interests. I decided to be absolutely honest: I told them that I was interested in evaluating the effectiveness of psychoanalytic therapy for schizophrenics and investigating unconscious fantasies. I figured that would scare them enough so that I would not have to make a decision. Much to my surprise, it led to my current position. I remind myself of these things whenever I am tempted to judge someone else early in their career.

There are two ways to be a great psychologist. The first is to be a fashion expert; that is, to do what is fashionable. The best of these psychologists are able to anticipate early each fashion so as to ride the crest of the wave. They may even decry those psychologists who led the last intellectual fashion, never mentioning that they themselves were prominent among "those psychologists."

The other way to be a great psychologist is to do what you think is important whether or not it is fashionable and whether or not your colleagues agree with you. If it is important to you, it will eventually be important to the field. Those psychologists who do what they think is important are sometimes in fashion and paid attention to and at other times are completely out of fashion and ignored, but these are the psychologists who make the real contributions. All too often graduate students are taught explicitly or implicitly to do research on anything except what is important to them. There was a period when I used to insist that any graduate student who wanted me to be on their master's or doctoral thesis committees must waste a half hour with me before we even began to talk about their proposal. I would ask, "Is there anything in this field you would like to know the answer to? Don't worry about whether there is any way to answer it or whether it's practical. Is there anything you would like to know the answer to?" Usually there was something interesting and important that the student had dismissed as being not worthy or possible to investigate but that was no more difficult to investigate than the trivial topic the student had chosen for his or her thesis project.

I remember asking one graduate student if there was anything to which he would like to know the answer. He said, "Yes, I'd like to know why people kill each other." I shared my clinical experience, and he told me what he knew. "Do you have access to murderers?" I asked. "Sure," he said, "I work at a maximum security prison." He was a graduate student in counseling psychology and had no training in the use of the TAT, so I explained it to him. I suggested he test 3 murderers and 3 non-murderer inmates. He thought whether they were psychotic or not might be important, so he tested 2 psychotic murderers and 2 non-psychotic murderers as well as 2 psychotic and 2 non-psychotic non-murderers. As we went over the protocols, some of the issues we had discussed plainly emerged.

He then tested samples of 20 and 20 and found that clinical exprience was validated. The most important difference was that the murderers could not tolerate conscious anger. Secondary findings were that they were less likely to be physically aggressive than the other inmates, but if physical aggression occurred, the aggression was more likely to be lethal in quality (e.g., shooting or knifing as opposed to beating up); they tended to be less tolerant of conscious affect in general; they had a model of violence in childhood; and the most frequent motive for murder was sexual jealousy. As he said to me when working on the study (McKie, 1971), "You know, research is interesting!"

It is true that an academic career is a publish or perish world. Consequently, you should start publishing in graduate school, or whenever you can. It makes you marketable in the academic world, research settings, and even in clinical settings. However, there are some things graduate students and other psychologists need to know; the most important is that you do not need anyone's permission to publish. All you need is to write an article and submit it in the format requested by that journal. All too often, having to get the okay from someone on the faculty simply means adding another editor; and the more different editors an article has to go through before being accepted, the less likely it is to be accepted. Particularly if you write clinical articles, you may not be supported by your faculty, but you may have something of value to communicate. The best criterion for writing an article is that you have important information to communicate. Science is not a private affair. When you know something that is more than what the average psychologist in your field knows, you have a duty to communicate it. Sometimes faculty members can be helpful by suggesting improvements or encouraging graduate students to publish.

Should you decide to publish, you cannot afford to be thin-skinned. The editor will send your article to be reviewed by two to four consultants. Reviewers vary widely in their values, in their knowledge, and in what they think they know but in fact do not. Although the merit of the article does influence their judgments, there is a lottery factor.

It is not uncommon to have an article rejected by a journal with a low rate of rejections and accepted by a journal with a high rate of rejections. One of my favorite rejections was from the British Journal of Medical Psychology. The reviewer wrote, "This article proves nothing but the enthusiasm of the authors." At that time I wondered whether my clinical articles were of any value. Irving Alexander, a distinguished psychologist, suggested I send my articles to someone who might understand them and see if they were of value. I sent them to Ronald Fairbairn, the Scottish psychoanalyst whose work I thought was brilliant. I received no answer and dismissed it with thoughts of how brash it was for a newly graduated psychologist whose work is unknown to write to this brilliant and famous man and impose on his time. A year later, however, I received a handwritten note stating he had been ill and had misplaced my articles; he then discussed them seriously and incisively. He disagreed cogently with the position of one of the articles, but he very much liked the other article. The article he liked was the one that had been turned down with a devastating review. Ironically, Fairbairn was a consultant for that journal but obviously not the one who had reviewed my article.

A second favorite is a rejection letter I received signed by Anna Freud, saying this was an excellent article and they were sure some journal with aims that were similar but not identical to the aims of their journal would publish it. Again, I remember asking Irving Alexander what that meant, and he said, "It means you are not a member of the club."

My third favorite rejection letter was for a critique article written with David Saunders. The editor rejected the article as not worth publishing. What makes this noteworthy is that the rejection letter was received a little over 1 year after they had published our article (Karon & Saunders, 1958). I have even had the experience of being told, 10 years after article of mine was published, how important it was by a man who had forgotten that he had once reviewed that article and recommended against its publication.

The most common thing to happen when you submit an article is for it to be rejected. It is important not to be discouraged. Although it is not a strong correlation, the trend seems to be that the better an article is, the more journals reject it before it gets published. The meaning of this trend becomes evident when I give you my formula for guaranteeing your article will be accepted. First, investigate something trivial. Second, investigate it by a technique that is well-known and frequently used. (Here you can see the wisdom of choosing something trivial: If you investigate something important, you may have to use an unusual experimental or investigative procedure or data analysis to be able to investigate exactly what you want to investigate.) Third, find exactly what everyone would predict you would find. Your article will be published, because it will not upset any of the reviewers. Of course, your research will be trivial. If you study something important, or use an unusual proce-dure, or find something unexpected, you may have difficulty publishing it precisely because your article is important and unorthodox.

When I get a letter of rejection, I read it and get furious. I then lay it aside for at least 24 hours, reread it, and then reread my article to see if the criticisms bear any resemblance to what I said. I usually am furious again and put it aside again. The third time I read the criticisms and go over my article so as to judge whether any of the criticisms are justified (e.g., I may have been misleading in the way I have described something). I then make any changes that I think might improve the article and send it to the next journal. It is not unusual for the next journal's reviewer to be most upset by changes that were made at the suggestion of the previous journal's reviewer. I have found that, in general, it is rarely worthwhile to make substantive changes on the basis of rejection letters.

If the article is accepted as is, I feel elated, but, unfortunately, that is a rare event. However, it is more frequent as you get older.

When an article is accepted, it is usually with suggested or required changes. My initial reaction is to feel good. Then I read the suggested changes and usually feel furious. Twenty-four hours later, I reread the suggested changes and then reread my article. At that point, I am usually furious again. The third time, I read the suggested changes again and reread my article to see if I can make the suggested changes without ruining the article. It is almost never a question of improving it. Either the changes make no real difference or they make it worse. If they do not make it too much worse, I will accept them to not go through the fuss of submitting it again. Sometimes there will be one or two changes that are so destructive or wrong-headed that I try arguing with the editors, and sometimes I succeed in getting them to understand. Of course, there are editors who make constructive suggestions, or who allow the author to decide whether the suggestions improve the article, or even who publish the article as submitted, but they are rare.

Many graduate students will become or are college professors. Let me make some suggestions, because most of the people who want to teach you how to teach are not good teachers themselves. The one thing students will not forgive a teacher is not knowing what they are talking about: They should not forgive you. Faculty should talk about not only what they know, but also about what interests them in particular. The only way to justify the lecture system is to remember that a great deal of human learning is by identification. When an instructor talks about what fascinates him or her, the students get carried along and often find themselves fascinated by things hitherto dull. If the instructor is bored with the material, however, what chance does a student have?

In any course it is impossible to cover all the relevant information. If you do not talk about what you know the most about and what interests you, you are cheating the students. You are holding back what you really have to offer them, knowledge. If there is nothing in your field that really interests you, then you are in the wrong field.

When I first taught personality, I did not talk about the effects of discrimination on Blacks and Whites, even though I had done research on it. I felt that was my peculiar interest. I soon discovered from the students' questions, however, that what fascinated me fascinated many other people. Furthermore, the students said they were excited that they studied with someone who actually did research himself. Of course, all faculty members have done research, but we often feel we ought not to talk about our own work. Paradoxically, that is precisely what students find most interesting.

If possible, use primary sources because secondary sources (particularly introductory textbooks in any field) leave the excitement out. They usually are written by second-rate minds (the first-rate minds are doing original work) and hide the fact that the geniuses in any field disagree about fundamentals. The field is usually presented as if everything were clear ; if the students are confused, this leads them to believe it is because they are stupid. Students find it exciting to know that science is not that simple, that experts disagree, and that something may not be obvious to them precisely because it is not obvious to the "experts."

A textbook does provide organization and a view of what one term or semester's work in that area might well cover. Particularly if you are not used to teaching that course, it can be useful. Because almost all textbooks are dull, however, I recommend that you read what you have assigned the student and talk around it—tell the students where the textbook is wrong, or has left out something important, or does not know the latest relevant scientific information.

Silvan Tomkins, the distinguished personality theorist, told me that originally he had tried to prepare students for graduate school in his undergraduate course in personality, but that later he found, by talking to those students with whom he felt he had succeeded (who had completed graduate school and done original work), that that was not important. What was important was whether he had gotten them intrigued with studying the human personality. If he had, they did whatever they had to do to go to graduate school and to complete it. If they never became intrigued with studying the human personality, nothing mattered.

As scientists and as teachers, psychologists often try to rule out observational data as irrelevant, ignoring those other sciences, like astronomy and biology, where observational data play a large role. The strange definitions of science that psychologists have put forth to eliminate Freud from psychology would eliminate Darwin from biology, a move that no biologist would tolerate.

The case history method of detailed clinical observation is ignored, even though it has been the most productive investigative technique in our field. As is true of most clinicians, 80% of what I value in my knowledge of human psychology has been learned through my clinical observations, other clinicians' reports of their clinical observations, or distillates of their clinical observations by people like Freud, Sullivan, Fairbairn, and others. Only 20% of what I value has been learned by all the other investigative techniques in psychology put together.

Boring, a historian of psychology, used to describe Freud's way of working as largely mistaken but then concluded that he was the most important single contributor to experimental psychology. This is possible, but not probable. What seems more probable is that good rules in developing a scientific theory from laboratory data might be different from the good rules in developing a scientific theory from case history data. In both cases, a scientific theory must be disprovable in principle by obtainable data. A scientific theory to be tested by case history data should be formulated so that a single observation can invalidate it. Probabilistic theories cannot be disproved by case histories. In addition, you must, as Freud did, continue to gather case histories and revise your strongly formulated theories, as each case history disproves something. By the time Freud saw five cases, he described phenomena that had not been previously described and that have since been validated and entered the general body of knowledge in psychology.

You will see, however, or have seen, five cases very early in your career. Please take your own observations seriously. There is a great deal going on that is important that has not yet been described.

To use a metaphor, it has been said that elephants move surprisingly quietly in the wild. If you are in the forest, and an elephant is not interested in knocking down trees, you may not notice him. That does not mean, however, that an elephant is a subtle phenomenon. The woods of human experience are full of elephants that have not yet been adequately described. When we look through laboratory experiments for subtle effects, we may not notice the elephants. In the clinical situation, if an elephant walks by, we may well notice him. This may be why so much has been learned from clinical experience.

The other reason is that relevant data may only be available in the clinical situation, such as the observations of human thought processes made manifest only in the psychoanalytic situation of free association.

What you yourself observe is what is real and is just as valid and important as what Freud or Adler or your faculty mentor has observed.

Early in my career, I was surprised to discover that male adolescent reformatory inmates who had acute schizophrenic reactions and who were seen immediately would pull out of the psychotic state with 1 week of daily psychotherapy sessions without medication and could then be continued in psychotherapy on a weekly basis while continuing their ordinary activities. This contrasted sharply with my experience with chronic patients who had been subjected to electroconvulsive therapy and other organic treatments and who changed very slowly. It also contrasted with the long course of psychosis that would ensue when these acute patients were transferred to a hospital that provided medication without psychotherapy. Understandably, I was excited by this observation.

An older psychologist, who thought he was giving me good advice, said, "Stop telling people you're curing schizophrenia. Nobody cures schizophrenics, and you just make people mad at you." Silvan Tomkins' reaction, however, was, "Really? What do you think accounted for it?" which was a much more useful response.

There is a problem that afflicts experimental as well as clinical psychologists. Again and again, I have seen psychologists investigate a problem or theory, starting with something tangential to major concerns. As they follow it up, they get into more and more interesting issues with far-ranging implications. Strangely, when they are led to the point at which further investigation would call into question the major theories of this field, just when it should be most interesting, the line of investigation is dropped. (I understand this as a scientific variant of the Oedipus complex: "I am qualified to ask little questions, but only the grown-ups are allowed to ask the big questions; when I must challenge the grown-ups, or become their equal, I must step asking questions.") As clinicians, students may be given misinformation in graduate school. They will be taught *DSM-III-R* or the fourth edition of the *DSM* (American Psychiatric Association, 1994) as if it were science and not politics; but such diagnoses as are found in these texts predict only 5% to 10% of the outcome of psychotherapy (Beutler & Grawe, 1990). They are helpful to our colleagues in biological psychiatry, however, because they tell them on what page of the Merck Manual of Diagnosis and Therapy (Berkow, 1992) to look up this year's recommended medication. Using such guides, students will be taught pseudo-biological explanations that will be found false in the next 20 years. Students will be told that medications cure things that they do not cure.

Graduate students may be told that psychotherapy does not work: It does. They may be told they cannot make it in private practice: They can. The demand for private practitioners who are competent is still enormous. The more people there are in practice, the greater the demand. This is understandable by taking seriously unfashionable data: the Midtown Manhattan study (Srole, Langner, Michael, Opler, & Rennie, 1962) that found that 80% of Americans are at least seriously neurotic. There is an enormous amount of palpable misery out there, and psychologists can do something about it.

At the present time the prime profession offering psychotherapy is the clinical psychologist, and the most frequent setting is private practice. We have problems about making help available to the poor, but psychologists can help to solve that problem. The recent change in the Medicare law, caused by psychologists, is going to open up whole new areas to solve as everyone over the age of 65 in the United States can for the first time afford psychotherapy.

Right now psychiatrists generally get little or no training in psychotherapy (Breggin, 1991). Although they can make more money as pill-pushers, the accumulating evidence is that pills are at best second-rate treatment (Fisher & Greenberg, 1989), and the dangerous side effects (Breggin, 1983,1991) are becoming better and better known. Psychiatrists now complain in most large cities that patients do not want to see them, but ask for psychologists because the patients believe that only psychologists will talk to them, and psychiatrists will not (e.g., "Canadian survey," 1989; Sanua, 1993). Prescription privileges for psychologists might be bad for patients, because someone had better practice psychotherapy.

Only the clinical psychologist has the flexibility to develop further the current effective brief therapies and the willingness to make the commitment that intensive psychotherapy requires. Psychotherapy today, and probably forever, is not a simple set of rules, like plumbing. If it were, most of us would be bored and do something else. Freud's metaphor of the chess game is still apt, except that the patient is not an opponent: Each therapy, like a chess game, is unique, and one can only specify in detail the beginning game, the ending game, and some rules of strategy. What we learn from therapy, we use to change our basic theory. I am convinced that, in addition to economic motives, this is a major source of resistance by medical analysts to the training of psychologists as psychoanalysts.

Physicians tend to approach a theory like engineers. The theory is true, and the ingenuity of the physician is to apply it to a specific case.

Psychologists tend to approach a theory like a scientist: A theory is a point of departure that may be modified at any time on the basis of further observations. That is unsettling to many physicians. The psychologists who have been accepted as psychoanalysts by their American medical colleagues have tended to be those whose modifications were accepted. The recent lawsuit opening up the American Psychoanalytic Association and the development of independent institutes providing first-rate psychoanalytic training to psychologists throughout the country will be good for psychoanalysis, because psychologists are scientists. It will be good for psychology, too, because it will bring psychoanalysis back into the mainstream of psychology.

When I reached the point of taking graduate preliminary examinations, I started reading in four areas—psychometrics, social, personality, and abnormal psychology. I leaned toward abnormal psychology, but a friend said, "Don't you realize that all of that literature will have to be rewritten in the next 20 years?" My immediate thought was, "Precisely."

Nearly everything in this field still needs to be rewritten in the next 20 years. My advice to future graduate students: Do not let anyone stop you.

I want to thank my former graduate students and particularly the late Anne Cunningham, who nominated me and contacted others. To understand graduate or undergraduate education, however, you have to take seriously that a great deal of human learning is by identification. The graduate instructors to whom I owe the most, and with whom I have identified the most, were Silvan Tomkins, Irving Alexander, and Roy Heath. They set models for me, from which my students have greatly benefitted.

I wish to express my deep appreciation to Anmarie Widener for her critical comments and editorial assistance.

REFERENCES

American Psychiatric Association. (1987). Diagnostic and statis-tical manual of mental disorders (3rd ed., rev.). Washington, DC:

American Psychiatric Association. (1994). Diagnostic and statisti-cal manual of mental disorders (4th ed.). Washington, DC:

Association for Advancement of Behavior Therapy Membership Directory. (1992-1993). New York: Association for Advancement of

Behavior Therapy.

Bakan, D. (1967). On method: Toward a reconstruction of psy-chological investigation. San Francisco: Jossey-Bass.

Berkow, R.(Ed.).(1992). Merck manual ofdiagnosis and therapy (16th ed.). Rahway, NJ: Merck and Company.

Beutler, L. E., & Grawe, K. (1990, June). A cross-cultural com-parison of differential improvement rates. In L. E. Beutler (Chair), Indicators of differential treatment outcomes. Symposium con-ducted at the meeting of the Society for Psychotherapy Research, Wintergreen, VA.

Breggin, P.R. (1983). Psychiatric drugs: Hazards to the brain. New York: Springer.

———— (1991). Toxic psychiatry. New York: St. Martin's Press.

Canadian survey uncovers public perceptions about psychiatry: Stigma is hard to kill. (1989, May 19). Psychiatric News, pp. 2,14. Directory of the American Psychological Association. (1993). Washington, DC: American Psychological Association.

Eysenck, H.J. (1952). The effects of psychotherapy: An evalua-tion. Journal of Consulting Psychology, 16, 319-324.

Fisher, S., & Greenberg, R.P. (1977). The scientific credibility of

Freud's theories and therapy. New Vbrk: Basic Books.

Fisher, S., & Greenberg, R. P. (1989). The limits of biological treat

Karon, B.P. (1968). Problems of validities. In A. I. Rabin (Ed.), Projective techniques in personality assessment: A modern in-troduction (pp. 85-111). New York: Springer.

———— (1978). Projective tests are valid. American Psy-chologist, 33, 764-765.

———— (1989). Psychotherapy versus medication for schizo-phrenia: Empirical comparisons. In S. Fisher & R. Greenberg (Eds.), The limits of biological treatments for psychological dis-tress: Comparisons with psychotherapy and placebo (pp. 105-151). Hillsdale, NJ: Erlbaum.

———— & O'Grady, P. (1970). Quantified judgments of mental health from the Rorschach, TAT, and clinical status interview by means of a scaling technique. Journal ofConsulting and Clinical Psychology, 34, 229-235.

———— & Saunders, D.R. (1958). Some implications of the Eysenck-Prell study of "The inheritance of neuroticism": A cri-tique. Journal of Mental Science, 104, 350-358.

———— & VandenBos, G R. (1981). Psychotherapy of schiz-ophrenia: Treatment of choice. New York: Jason Aronson.

Kline, P. (1972). Fact and fantasy in Freudian theory. London: Methuen.

McKie, R.R. (1971). A clinical study: Relationships of anger and fear to aggression, in murderers and in non-violent offenders. Unpublished doctoral dissertation, Michigan State University, Department of Counseling, Personnel Services, and Education-al Psychology.

Meehl, P.E. (1954). Clinical versus statistical prediction: A theo-retical analysis and a review of the evidence. Minneapolis: Uni-versity of Minnesota Press.

Mills, C.W. (1953). White collar: The American middle classes. New York: Oxford University Press.

Miranda, J., & Dwyer, S. (1993, June). Adapting psychotherapy outcome research to clinical reality. In J. B. Persons (Chair), Adapting psychotherapy outcome research to clinical reality. Symposium conducted at the meeting of the Society for Psycho-therapy Research, Pittsburgh, PA.

National Register of Health Service Providers in Psychology. (1991-1992). Washington, DC: Council for the National Register of Health Service Providers in Psychology.

Negin, E. (1993). Why college tuitions are so high. The Atlantic, 277(3), 32.

Persons, J.B. (1993, June). Adapting psychotherapy outcome re-search to clinical reality. In J. B. Persons (Chair), Adapting psy-chotherapy outcome research to clinical reality. Symposium conducted at the meeting of the Society for Psychotherapy Re-search, Pittsburgh, PA.

Sanua, V.D. (1993, August). Perceptions of psychologists and psychiatrists. In J. Waters (Chair), The public image of psychol-ogy: Love, hate or ambivalence. Symposium conducted at the 101st Annual Convention of the American Psychological Asso-ciation, Toronto, Ontario, Canada.

Schizophrenia-related grants—fiscal year 1991. (1993). Schizo-phrenia Bulletin, 19, 171-194.

Shea, M. T. (1993, June). Adapting psychotherapy outcome re-search to clinical reality. In J. B. Persons (Chair), Adapting psy-chotherapy outcome research to clinical reality. Symposium conducted at the meeting of the Society for Psychotherapy Re-search, Pittsburgh, PA.

Smith, J. C., Glass, G. V., & Miller, T. I. (1980). The benefits of psy-chotherapy. Baltimore: Johns Hopkins Press.

Srole, L., Langner, T. S., Michael, S. T., Opler, M., & Rennie, T. (1962).

Mental health in the metropolis: The midiown Manhattan study (Vol.1). New \brk: McGraw-Hill.

Wolfe, B. E. (1993, June). Discussion. In J. B. Persons (Chair), Adapting psychotherapy outcome research to clinical reality. Symposium conducted at the meeting of the Society for Psycho-therapy Research, Pittsburgh, PA.

In Conclusion

CHAPTER 31
Insights, Hope, Kindness, And Confusion:
Odyssey af a Psychoanalyst
Bertram P. Karon, PhD

Insights from the author's previous systematic research and psychoanalytic observations are summarized. In a nationwide Gallup sample, segregation was found destructive to African Americans and Whites, although differently so. Clinical experience delineated the number 4 as a symbol, the helpfulness of psychoanalysis, and meanings of schizophrenic symptoms. Thematic Apperception Test (TAT) pathogenesis (unconsciously based hurtful parenting) differentiated both parents of schizophrenics and inadequate therapists. A controlled project demonstrated that 70 sessions of psychoanalytic therapy were more helpful than medication with respect to schizophrenic thought disorder, hospitalization, and living a more human life. Masked clinical judgments from Rorschachs, TATs, and interviews were found to be valid. Clinical papers described treating lower socioeconomic status patients, not eating, the 4 bases of delusions, and the necessity to be kind, tolerant, stubborn, and confused and to avoid abstractions.

For the American Psychological Association centenary, Division 39 asked me to give a paper on the state of the art of psychoanalysis; its title was "Science, Hope, and Kindness in Psychoanalytic Technique" (Karon, 1989b), because all three aspects are important. Although all of the research techniques in psychology have been useful, psychoanalytic clinical observations, including free association, have yielded the most information about what it means to be human.

My introduction to psychoanalysis came from my brother, who shortly after World War II treated my uncle. This apparent breach of the rules came about because my uncle, a bright but uneducated man, developed a functional heart condition, which incapacitated him. He did not leave the house, lay in bed most of the day, was exhausted after walking 20 feet, and seemed to be having heart attacks nearly every day. A famous Harvard psychiatrist, Myerson, told him that if he were a wealthy man, he would recommend psychoanalysis, but since he was not wealthy, he recommended a course of shock treatment, and if that did not work, a lobotomy. My uncle went to the library and read about shock treatment and lobotomy, and what he read scared him. My brother, visiting home after discharge, told us about participating in an experimental program in Boston during the early days of World War II in which two students from each of six universities were chosen from their freshman biology class; they were given some analysis, extra courses, and supervision, and half of them turned out to be good therapists. The program was ended, with the recommendation that the therapists go to medical school and become psychiatrists or, if the new profession of clinical psychology became accepted, become psychologists. My brother served in the Army (the Signal Corps), but after the war he finished college and eventually became a clinical psychologist.

He saw my uncle twice a week for 6 months and then had to leave town to finish his education. During treatment my uncle lost his heart symptoms, developed asthma, lost his asthma, developed a stomach ulcer, lost that symptom, and developed migraine headaches. Approximately once a month he would have to leave work early with a migraine headache. He said, "This psychoanalysis stuff is all bullshit. I feel as bad as I ever did." Then he walked over to a sign (he had a sign shop)—a sign so heavy that at 16 I would not have tried to move it—picked it up, and moved it across the room. His marriage and life satisfaction also had obviously improved, despite his comment.

My thought was that if a drug had produced that change, we would be reading about it as a miracle drug. Moreover, if a drug had produced the changes, he would be considered three cures and a failure, rather than one patient whose symptoms had changed; whether he was an improvement or a failure depended on whether the new symptoms were better or worse than the old ones.

My brother said that if I wanted to understand what it was all about, I should read Freud's *Introductory Lectures* (1917/1963), a book from which I have never recovered and which consequently I have made many thousands of undergraduates read, telling them it is the best single book in the field of psychology, a book that all the bright people assume you know as background to their work. Reading it I remember thinking, "How does Freud know so much about me? I've never told anybody."

As a Freshman at Harvard, I took a course with Gordon Allport, who had qualms about some of Freud's ideas but felt that students needed to know about psychoanalysis. Nonetheless, he defined psychoanalysis as "that psychology that goes down deepest, stays down longest, and comes up dirtiest." I took a course with Edward Boring, the experimental psychologist, who said that if all Freud did was make psychologists take seriously the concept of unconscious processes, that alone would make him the most important contributor to experimental psychology for the next 100 years. I also took a course with B. F. Skinner, who had us read three books: one of his own, a book by his students praising him, and Freud's *Introductory Lectures*. He said that if you want to be a psychologist there were two people you should know about: Skinner and Freud. Skinner was right that if a scientific theory was meaningful it could be defined in terms of relationships between observables, and he was ingenious in defining Freud's concepts behaviorally. But the relationships are so subtle that no one would discover them by thinking only behaviorally. Once you have read Freud, there is no doubt who was the more subtle and creative mind. One of my students later quoted me to Skinner, who said, "Those were the early days. I don't assign Freud anymore."

I was lucky enough to take courses with Henry Murray, Robert White, and the sociologist Talcott Parsons, all of whom took Freud seriously.

I did an undergraduate honors thesis on early childhood memories, just so I could get a chance to work with Gordon Allport. He had me read Alfred Adler, which did me no harm at all. I mentioned to one of my friends that some of these childhood memories (gathered by a written questionnaire) sounded like Freudian dreams. He said, "Why don't you interpret them?"

So laughingly I did, making predictions for the Allport-Vernon Scale of Values and the Gough Scale of Masculinity-Femininity. When I tested them, these predictions were more statistically significant than anything else in the study. I was embarrassed and put in a two-page apologia for using Freudian symbols seriously, but they did work, and as an empiricist I had to report it.

I had so much trouble writing that thesis that I told one of my readers, Robert White, that I thought I should not go to graduate school: "What good is a psychologist who can't write up his work?" White, like the psychoanalyst he was, ruined my life by saying that was not a good enough reason for not going to graduate school. He suggested I could always collaborate, with someone else doing the writing. I have collaborated, but I always end up doing the writing anyway.

Over 140 publications and two books later, I still have trouble writing. But it cheered me to learn that most people have trouble writing, including Ernest Hemingway. According to his son, he would wake up at 5:00 every morning, creep quietly to his office, work until 10:00 without talking to anyone, and then come down to breakfast as if he had just woken up. He would begin drinking immediately and made a show of wasting his life and not working, because he was so ashamed of how little he produced in 35 hours a week of hard work. If Hemingway had trouble writing, the rest of us have no need to feel bad about it.

I had taken an experimental psychology course with Walter Tomans, who told me that I had promise but that I needed a theoretical orientation. He said there was only one body of theory that had any hope of dealing with all of the experimental and clinical data of psychology, and that was some form of modem psychoanalytic theory. I asked "Like who?" He said, "Like Kris, Hartmann, Rappaport, French, and Alexander." I asked what I should read by them; he told me, and I read them before graduate school. Although I disagree with many of their solutions, it was impossible afterward to take seriously any psychologist who said that psychoanalysis had nothing to say about the important issues.

I was sure I would never become a clinician because I thought clinicians were people who intuitively understood others, and I knew I was frequently out in left field. I went to graduate school in psychometrics because I seemed to be good at it, and there was a fellowship you could live on at Princeton. I told them, although I do not think they believed me, that I was not really interested in psychometrics but that most people who were any good at studying the human personality seemed to have trouble with mathematics. There might be useful quantitative tools, and it might be useful to have someone interested in personality who knew them. They said the only person they had in personality was Silvan Tomkins and asked if I would like to meet him.

Silvan (the only faculty member at Princeton that all the graduate students referred to by first name) talked to me for over an hour. When I mentioned my early memory research and Freudian symbols, he said, "Of course, people react to the symbols," and cited experimental research and clinical data, published and unpublished, that no one at Harvard had ever mentioned. He knew more of the literature than anyone I had met before or have since. Others have told me there was a 15-year period when he read every journal in the field—meaning psychology, psychiatry, and psychoanalysis. He once told me he had had a severe reading block. Throughout school he would read with a handkerchief, and the sweat would pour off his face. I knew that despite this, he had gotten a bachelor's degree from the University of Pennsylvania, been kicked out of graduate school in psychology for being interested in studying values, completed a PhD in philosophy at Penn, and returned to psychology when he was invited by both Henry Murray and Robert White to join their research group at Harvard—all of this with a severe reading block. While with the

Murray group, he got into psychoanalysis and, among other things, lost his reading block. My guess is that he went on a reading binge for the rest of his life—"You mean reading is this easy!"

I was also reassured years later when he told me he had stopped reading every journal because there were now so many that it was impossible, even for him.

In graduate school, whenever I wondered, "Why am I here? I'm bored by most of this," I would go to the library and read an article by Sigmund Freud that I had not read, and I always concluded there was something in this field that interested me. Freud can be wrong, but he is never stupid.

I got as far as prelim exams and was not sure what area to do it in— psychometrics (I had taken a full program in this field), social, personality theory (which Tomkins wanted me to take), or abnormal. The abnormal reading list was twice as long as any other, but the first reading I did for it was Freud's five volumes of the *Collected Papers,* Anna Freud, and Fenichel. By that time I was hooked; this was what I wanted to think about.

I was going to do a dissertation on Tomkins's theory, but while we were talking, he made a casual comment about the nationwide data gathered to standardize the Tomkins-Horn Picture Arrangement Test, that someone could use those data to study the effects of segregation. The next day I mentioned that sounded interesting. He said, "Does that interest you more than working on my theory?"

Embarrassed, I said, "Actually, yes."

He said, "Then do it." And he helped me get a grant. I remember that when I think of all the faculty who cannibalize their students' work.

My first research publication was in psychometrics: an empirical evaluation of different ways of equating scales. Soon after, an article came out of a can of beer with a friend. A graduate student in sociology asked if I knew anything about Q-technique and would I read an article using it to test demographic transition theory. He was going to write a critique because the authors misunderstood the theory. Their main argument was that the theory predicted two factors that did not appear in the factor analysis and that factors not predicted by the theory did occur. However, their misuse of Q-technique was such that if the predicted factors had been in the original data, their analysis would have eliminated them from the factor matrix, and their analysis was guaranteed to produce spurious factors by chance. We said so in print.

David Saunders and I wrote a methodological critique of an article by Hans Eysenck, the spuriously rigorous psychologist, who published an article comparing identical and fraternal twins and concluded that 80% of the variance of neuroticism was genetic. The article was cited in supposedly rigorous reviews of the literature, such as the American Handbook of Psychiatry. But we discovered he had used the wrong formula; using the correct one reduced the number to 50%, and correcting his arithmetic mistakes reduced it to 30%, which itself is probably an overestimate, given the unlikely assumptions of the statistical indices used in such studies, even when correctly computed (Karon & Saunders, 1958).

I decided that almost every one who had really contributed to the study of personality was a clinician and that therefore if I was serious, I should do a clinical internship. I said that to Tomkins, who said, "Of course, you should do a clinical internship." I did not tell him I was convinced I would make a terrible clinician. I wrote to three internships, intending to take whichever one accepted me, but all three did.

I had read John Rosen's book on treating schizophrenia, and had heard him talk. I wrote to him, asking if he would take a psychologist for training. Of the three opportunities, this was the most controversial. I asked two psychoanalysts I trusted about him. One said, "He has brilliant intuitions about the oral period. If I were a young man, I would work with him a year myself." The other said, "He's a character disorder and you can't believe a word he says." Unfortunately, they were both right.

Luckily, I have an aggressive streak, and I resigned six times during that year, because it was the only way to get Rosen to keep his word and not get in the way. Two psychologists, Jack Rosberg and Bob Firestone, were already there for training, although Firestone left after a couple of months. They were helpful and honest. We argued, took ourselves seriously, and went back to the patients for the real data in the field. There were three months when Rosberg and I were the only therapists there, while Rosen and the less seriously disturbed patients and their attendants went to Florida.

During that year I discovered that clinical work was exciting, although difficult, scary, and depressing as well. My patients were improving, despite the fact that every patient there had already failed at the best and most expensive hospitals in America. If you took psychoanalysis seriously, what the patients said made sense. Alone and with Jack Rosberg, I began to write clinical papers.

The first was on the discovery of the meaning of the number 4 as a symbol—learned from a paranoid schizophrenic patient who had been obsessed with the number 4 for many years (Karon, 1958). It represented a denial of the number 3—an escape to a world where there were no penises and no sexuality, and therefore his mother would love him. These obsessions disappeared when they were interpreted.

The second was on the meaning of postpartum psychoses, based on the material from a chronic postpartum schizophrenic patient who got better (Rosberg & Karon, 1959). The birth was experienced as a traumatic loss of what was inside her body, which had felt like the gradual achievement of longed-for but seemingly impossible oral gratification.

The third was on the mother-child relationship in a case of paranoid schizophrenia where the treatment material could be related to observations of the mother and her interaction with her son while she took care of the treatment house in which he lived (Karon & Rosberg, 1958b).

The fourth was on the oedipal material in an apparently deteriorated schizophrenic (Rosberg & Karon, 1958). The oedipal material was obvious; however, it did not have the usual meaning but rather symbolized earlier, primarily oral conflicts. It was this patient who first taught me about the draining fantasy.

The fifth, based on several patients, was about apparent homosexual impulses in schizophrenics and dealt with their pregenital sources, including draining fantasies, the wish to be one's own mother, and the belief that their mother would love them if they were the other gender (Karon & Rosberg, 1958a). By this time I was sure I was a therapist, but I wasn't sure I was a psychologist, because the American Psychological Association and its Division 12 (Clinical Psychology) were opposed to psychologists doing psychotherapy. So too were most state psychological associations.

I had collected data on segregation—Tomkins-Horn Picture Arrangement Tests from high school samples in the Bronx, Trenton, New Jersey, New Orleans, and rural Mississippi—as well as using the nationwide Gallup standardization sample gathered by John Miner and Silvan Tomkins. Luckily, I was able to use John Tukey to help me solve the problems of research design and data analysis that I could not solve myself. The study demonstrated rigorously that segregation had effects on the human personality that could not be attributed to chance, education, race, vocabulary IQ, degree of industrialization, population density, rural-urban residence, or gender. Further, most of these effects represented impaired functioning.

This was important, because although most researchers described the effects as hurtful, there were some African Americans who claimed that to be Black in the United States was so bad that the differences between North and South were trivial, and there were other people, primarily White researchers who had grown up in the South, who claimed that the segregated system was better for African Americans because they knew what to expect, as compared with the uncertainties of discrimination in the North.

Under segregation there was an increase among African Americans in the feeling that people would go out of their way to make trouble for you, a reflection of the fact that segregation and its legal and extralegal concomitants were ways in which people did make trouble for African Americans. There was an increased use of the defense mechanism of denial to deal with problems concerning anger and aggression—denial of (i.e., not recognizing) a picture showing people picking on the hero, denial of physical aggression, and denial of aggressive thoughts. There was no general increase in the use of denial for other problems, like physical injury. There was also an increase in consciously suppressed anger. The system of segregation hurt, but if an African American man or woman acted angry, that could bring down terrible retribution on the individual and his or her loved ones, so there were increases in both conscious and unconscious defenses against anger. There was an increase in the number of people who could not feel feelings. We cannot hold back one feeling; the battle against anger can lead to feeling nothing. There was also an increase in people whose affects were labile, changeable. Although this is more descriptive than representing pathology, it probably reflects the problem with anger that is repressed and breaks through. There was a suggestion of a work problem—an effort to overcome difficulties in work, but the effort wears out. Getting and holding a job were the big problems for African Americans, but in the South there was also the feeling that you would not be allowed to succeed even if you did work hard.

Within the South, African Americans from rural Mississippi, where the system of segregation was most severe, showed more psychological scars than most of the sample, and African Americans from New Orleans, where the system was less severe than in most of the South, showed less psychological scars than most of the sample. Even if we cannot make a perfect world, making one that is less evil will decrease the human cost proportionately.

In the North, African Americans who had lived all of their life in the North showed less of these effects than those who had lived some of their life in the South, demonstrating that we carry the effects of our childhood with us all of our lives. Indeed, those who had lived all of their life in the North were surprisingly healthy given that the neighborhoods they lived in were not ideal communities by any standard. In the South of the 1950s, however, segregation hurt, but society said it was not wrong. In the North, African Americans knew they were in a battle that they had not won, but they had not lost, either. They knew that anyone who was bad to them was bad. Facing the truth about a bad situation preserves a sense of ego integrity, which wards off much of the harmful effect of a bad situation. It really is true that if you have the courage to face the truth, the truth really does, to a large extent, set you free.

I had data and wanted to analyze the effects of segregation on Whites. I sent in 17 grant applications and was turned down on all of them. It was the McCarthy era, and as one turn-down said, "We have done all that we are going to do on civil rights." Nonetheless, I did analyze the data and found rigorously that Southern Whites were injured by segregation, but in ways different from African Americans.

The problem of race relations in the Border South of the 1950s was more serious than in the North, but Whites in the Border South talked about it openly as a problem, whereas Whites in the North in the 1950s tended to talk as if there was no problem in the North. The consequences for Whites seemed to be equal. On the social level as on the personal level, a more serious problem dealt with openly seemed to have equal effects as a less serious problem dealt with by denial.

But Deep South Whites, who had more of a problem of race relations than the Border South Whites but handled it by denial, showed effects. There was a marked decrease in wanting to work hard or strive to get ahead; the segregation culture undercut achievement motivation. The feeling that if Whites had to try to get ahead by outworking or competing with African Americans as equals, they could not undercut the motivation to work hard. There was a marked increase in submissive authoritarianism—there was not an increase in potential Hitlers but an increase in people who would follow a potential Hitler. The society that controlled Blacks also controlled Whites, accustoming them to being controlled. There was an increase in compulsive negativism—people who need to do exactly the opposite of what the people they are with want them to do. This is a neurotic attempt to prove to oneself that one is not controlled.

All of this was published in my book *Black Scars: A Rigorous Investigation of the Effects of Discrimination, With an Appendix on Southern Whites* (Karon, 1975).

After I finished that book, I took a job at a reformatory for male adolescents in New Jersey. The first week I was there, I was told by the assistant superintendent to arrange an emergency transfer to the state hospital for a prisoner. He was listed as being in treatment with the psychiatrist, a medical psychoanalyst, who was there 1 day a week and would not be there that week. As a matter of principle, I insisted that no inmate would be transferred without his therapist's permission. The boy was psychotic and in isolation. An hour and a half sufficed to pull him out of the psychotic state and return him to his work assignments. I saw him for the next 4 days. When the psychiatrist returned, he did not want to treat the prisoner, so I did.

I set up a policy of five daily sessions of psychotherapy without medication before any transfers would be considered. Every patient was no longer psychotic by the fifth session. Further psychotherapy continued on at least a once-a-week basis while the inmate carried out his work assignments.

No patient had to be transferred for reasons of psychosis during the 6 months when I was chief psychologist. Before and after that 6 months, one or two patients a month were transferred to the state hospital with a diagnosis of schizophrenia. In the 1950s the average length of stay of medicated schizophrenics was 2 years, before being returned to the reformatory.

I was startled at how quickly the patients pulled together. In my internship with Rosen, I had only treated chronic patients who had been medicated for years and usually shocked, and they changed slowly. These reformatory patients were in my office within a day or two of becoming blatantly psychotic, had not been given electroconvulsive therapy, and were rarely medicated.

An older psychologist, when I talked about this experience, said to me, "Stop telling people you are curing schizophrenics. No one cures schizophrenics, and you only make people angry at you when you say that." He thought he was giving me good advice.

When I told Silvan Tomkins, his reaction was more helpful. "What do you think accounted for it?" The answer to that question is discussed below.

Research in Philadelphia using a modified Blacky test demonstrated that the castration fears in male schizophrenics involved both parents, but the fear of being castrated by mother was more frightening and defended against by the fear of the father (Karon, 1964). However, I found that the modal set of castration fears in normal males tended to be similar, although not as devastating (Karon, 1970).

At Michigan State, I investigated the schizophrenogenic mother concept. Clinical experience indicated that there was no single set of overt behaviors so common as to lead to consistent findings, but unconscious dynamics were consistent. This is measurable by the Thematic Apperception Test (TAT) scale I termed "Pathogenesis," the degree to which, without being aware of it, a person does not take into account the needs of someone dependent on him or her when the dependent person's needs potentially conflict with the more dominant person's needs. The concept was theoretically defined, and the first masked study showed almost no overlap between mothers of schizophrenic individuals and mothers of normal individuals. Further replications showed consistently that mothers of normal children scored about 30% pathogenic (apparently the percentage of potential conflicts in which the parent does not take the child's needs into account) and mothers of schizophrenics averaged 75% pathogenic. No parent is perfect or perfectly hurtful, but a lifetime of living with a pathogenic parent makes one vulnerable. Nichols (1970) found that the severity of pathology and of the thought disorder in adult male schizophrenics correlated with the pathogenesis score of their mothers. Mitchell (1974) found that fathers of schizophrenics were also elevated in pathogenesis. There are also findings for child-abusive parents and that the school performance and functioning of adolescent girls correlated negatively with the pathogenesis scores of their parents. (All of this research is reviewed in a later publication, Karon & Widener, 1994.)

My most important research is undoubtedly the Michigan State Psychotherapy Research Project, which randomly assigned schizophrenics from inner city Detroit to three groups: psychoanalytic therapy without medication, psychoanalytic therapy with medication, and medication appropriately used plus support. The outcomes were blindly evaluated by a recorded clinical status interview by an experienced analyst not connected with the treatment. Clues to treatment were deleted by a secretary, and the tapes were blindly rated by clinical psychologists. In addition, the Rorschach, the TAT, the Wechsler Intelligence Scale, the Drasgow-Feldman Visual-Verbal test (a measure of schizophrenic thought disorder), and Porteus mazes were used as outcome measures.

A psychological scaling technique was used to reduce clinical judgments of emotional health (from the clinical interviews, the Rorschach, and the TAT, each separately) to numerical values on a ratio scale. The Thorndike-Gallup Vocabulary scale was used to control for IQ.

The first findings were that subjective clinical judgments by competent clinicians are valid (Karon & O'Grady, 1970). Ratings of mental health made independently from the clinical status interview, Rorschach, and TAT correlated with each other and with other indices of mental health but, most important, correlated between -.50 and -.70 with days in the hospital in the 6 months after the ratings were made. This was replicated, with the same findings. The interviews, Rorschachs, TATs, and ratings were gathered for research and were not available to the ward chiefs and hospital staff who determined when the patients were discharged. Of course, there was a sensible research design, using masked evaluations and a psychological scaling method (as in psychophysics) to map subjective clinical judgments onto meaningful numerical ratings, so that if the clinical judgments were valid, this could be demonstrated rigorously. Further, the interviewer and the tester were clinically skilled, and the raters were bright graduate students with appropriate clinical training. Pathogenesis of therapists, measured from their TATs, correlated with poorer outcome for patients, indicating unconscious difficulties for therapists as well as parents (VandenBos & Karon, 1971).

The most important finding was that an average of 70 sessions of psychoanalytic therapy over a 20-month period led to more improvement in the thought disorder, quicker discharge, lower re-hospitalization, greater decrease in symptoms, and a more human way of life than did medication. Psychoanalytic therapy accompanied by medication was better than medication alone, but not as helpful as psychoanalytic therapy without medication at all or with initial medication that was withdrawn as rapidly as the patients could tolerate. Thomas Tierney, the other experienced therapist and supervisor, did not like talking with disorganized patients, but he was honest with them: "The medication does not cure anything, it just makes things bearable so we can talk. The only thing that will cure you is your understanding." He would then withdraw the medication as rapidly as he felt the patients could tolerate. Much to my surprise, that turned out to be a good way to work.

Both Tierney and I had over 10 years' experience in working psychoanalytically with schizophrenic patients and were experienced in treating lower socioeconomic status patients and African American patients. The inexperienced therapists were graduate students in clinical psychology or psychiatric residents; they wanted to learn to do this kind of therapy, respected their supervisors, were given careful training and supervision, and were paid for their time.

In the American studies that are cited as evidence that psychoanalytic therapy is not as helpful as medication (e.g., Grinspoon, Ewalt, & Shader, 1972; May, 1968), the therapists were psychiatric residents who had no training in psychotherapy or who had training in treating a different kind of patient with a different kind of therapy; they were supervised by "experienced therapists" who had never treated a schizophrenic by psychotherapy, and they were given no extra pay for the time on the project but were told to work on it if they wanted to complete their residency or to continue their affiliation with the hospital (so they resented the work). The McLean study (Gunderson et al., 1984) concluded that supportive therapy was better for schizophrenics than uncovering therapy, because more of the completing patients were able to work. But the major finding was ignored: Three out of four patients in both groups avoided the project therapists and did not complete the project (Karon, 1984). That is because the therapists in both groups were required to insist that the patients take their medication.

The inexperienced therapists on our project were told that they did not have to work with the supervisor to whom they were assigned if they did not want to, but to have a cup of coffee with their assigned supervisor if they had qualms. In each case, the student came away with the feeling that this was someone from whom they could learn.

There were problems in carrying out this research. The patients were primarily African American and the therapists were all White, reflecting the psychiatric residents at Detroit Psychiatric Institute and the graduate students at Wayne State and Michigan State universities in the 1960s. The Detroit race riot occurred in the middle of the project, making patients feel guilty about getting help from White people. One patient told me, however, that she had discussed me with her neighbor, and they decided I was a Black man passing for White since "Whites don't talk the way you do."

My grant was administered by a National Institute of Mental Health psychologist whose research reputation was based on a study finding that only medication and not psychotherapy was helpful to schizophrenics. Somehow there seemed to be administrative problems—like requiring us in the middle of treatment to stop paying the psychiatric residents for their time because it was against American Psychiatric Association policy. Luckily, after a short interruption but before the therapists had become too demoralized, Tierney discovered that this policy had been changed some time before we had been asked to disrupt the treatment.

I later learned that other disruptions occurred in the hospital because we made the regular hospital staff uncomfortable. In general when professionals realize that if they take your findings seriously they will have to change what they do, their hostility tends to rise, even if they were initially eager for you to bring your research to their setting.

Psychotherapy with medication led to earlier behavioral control, but there was less change in the thought disorder. But change in the thought disorder was the best predictor of long-term improvement. At the time, we thought that the slowed underlying change was because medications suppress affective reactions, and emotional reactions in the therapeutic hour are part of what changes people. Since then we have also become aware of the evidence that so-called antipsychotic medications are also neurotoxic.

At this point I realized that I had allowed the University to be destructive to me. I was writing only the kinds of papers that have chi-squares and analyses of variance and not writing clinical papers, which are what I most value and was most likely to read.

I returned to writing clinical papers, including one with VandenBos that I still value on the resistances specific to lower socioeconomic status patients and the related countertransference problems (Karon & VandenBos, 1977). The most important idea was that there are only two types of therapists: those who have never been poor, who feel guilty about not suffering, and those who have been poor but have become not poor by hard work and deferring gratifications, for whom the patient represents themselves, if they had been lazy or bad. In both cases, the unconscious impulse is to get rid of the patient who makes us feel guilty or who represents our bad self.

Then we wrote a paper on treating patients who will not or cannot eat. The key is not to panic but to have the therapy hour at a meal where you eat and the patient can if they would. The material is easier to get to and more helpful.

It took 10 years after the work was done to complete our book, *Psychotherapy of Schizophrenia: The Treatment of Choice* (Karon & VandenBos, 1981), containing both clinical insights and observations and our rigorous empirical evaluations. In it there is a chapter originally titled "Special Issues in Psychotherapy," covering homicide, suicide, lower socioeconomic status patients, gender and ethnic issues, drugs and alcohol problems, criminals, and patients who cannot eat or cannot sleep. The editors insisted it be cut out because it did not deal specifically with schizophrenia. Our insistence that one or more of these issues occur in every case made no difference. So we added two words, "Of Schizophrenia," to the title, made no other changes, and the editors accepted it. But the chapter is about these issues in general, and we recommend it as helpful to any therapist irrespective of diagnostic category.

My paper on the formation of delusions (Karon, 1989a) contained perhaps the most important clinical insight—that there are four major bases of delusions: (a) transference to the world at large; (b) defenses against pseudohomosexual impulses, as Freud (1911/1958) wrote about in the case of Schreber; (c) strange meanings of concepts taught within a particular family; and (d) the universal need to have a more or less integrated view of oneself and one's world, even if one has strange experiences. Because the paranoid system is not a pathology but a normal process used to cope with pathological problems, a non-frightened, non-humiliating psychoanalytic therapist can listen carefully, respectfully point out discrepancies, and supplement the patient's knowledge with the therapist's more accurate knowledge of the world, of other people, and, most important, of the workings of the human mind.

Since then I have published a computer survey of the empirical data on the effectiveness of psychoanalytic therapy for schizophrenics. Psychoanalytic therapy works. In addition to my study, Benedetti and Furlan (1987), even without a control group, and Revere, Rodeffer, Dawson, and Bigelow (1983), with a control group, are impressive. Benedetti and Furlan reported very good results in 80% of severe schizophrenics treated psychoanalytically; median treatment was three times per week for 5 years.

Unfortunately, I discovered that clinical practice was not so much influenced by the real data but by drug company advertising and political influence on the government and professional organizations. Consequently, I reluctantly got involved in the politics of Division 39, but Division 39 has been helpful.

Widener and I (Karon & Widener, 1994) published a review of research, both mine and others', showing that there really are parents whose children are more vulnerable to schizophrenia, as well as clinical data. We also published several articles citing both clinical observations and research data showing that repression and recovered memories of traumas really exist (e.g., Karon & Widener, 1999). That would seem like a silly point, except that members of the False Memory Society keep maintaining that repression does not exist, because their reason for being is to defend in court parents who have been accused of child abuse, and they do not seem very concerned about whether they are telling the truth.

Three more clinical papers seem important to me: The first (Karon, 1998) pointed out the importance in psychoanalysis and psychoanalytic therapy not only of insight but of internalizing the therapist who must create hope, be kind, be stubborn in not accepting defeat in the therapeutic endeavor, and above all, tolerate being confused. All of us have been intimidated by seemingly certain colleagues, but their patients do not do well. The confused therapist provides a model for the patient that being confused is acceptable; that therapist is open to new insights.

The analyst is internalized as a more rational, kinder, and more hopeful conscience, and as a healthier model for the ego, for how a human being might be. Of course, like the adolescent, the patient will discard those of our quirks that are not helpful.

The second paper (Karon, 2002) pointed out that analyzability is the wrong question; the right question is what do we need to do to make it possible to analyze this patient. The third (Karon, 2003a) returned to Ferenczi's (1919/1953) "for example": that what is powerful and therapeutic in psychoanalysis is what is specific and concrete. Psychoanalysts, as well as patients, use their abstractions to escape their anxiety, but doing so is a disservice to the patient.

Finally, the recent paper I am most proud of (Karon, 2003b) was the Frieda Fromm-Reichmann memorial lecture at the Washington School of Psychiatry. It surveys our knowledge of schizophrenia, but its title tells the story, "The tragedy of schizophrenia without psychotherapy."

Psychoanalytic ideas and techniques are very powerful for a wide range of patients. There is a great deal of helpable misery out there, and it is a tragedy for any patient when psychoanalysis or psychoanalytic therapy is not available.

REFERENCES

Benedetti, G., & Furlan, P. M. (1987). Individual psychoanalytic psychotherapy of schizophrenia. In G. Benedetti (Ed.), Psychotherapy of schizophrenia (pp. 198-212). New York: New York University Press.

Ferenczi, S. (1953). "For example" in psychoanalysis. In Further contributions to the theory and technique of psychoanalysis (pp. 184-186). New York: Basic Books. (Original work published 1919)

Freud, S. (1958). Psychoanalytic notes on an autobiographical account of a case of paranoia (dementia paranoids). In J. Strachey (Ed. & Trans.), The standard edition of the complete psychological works of Sigmund Freud (Vol. 12, pp. 9-80). London: Hogarth Press. (Original work published 1911)

———— (1963). Introductory lectures on psychoanalysis. In J. Strachey (Ed. & Trans.), The standard edition of the complete psychological works of Sigmund Freud (Vol. 15, pp. 1-239; Vol. 16, pp. 241^196). (Original work published 1917)

Grinspoon, L., Ewalt, J.R., & Shader, R.I. (1972). Schizophrenia, pharmacotherapy, and psychotherapy. Baltimore: William & Wilkins.

Gunderson, J.G., Frank, A.F., Katz, H. M., Vannicelli, M.L., Frosch, J.P., & Knapp, P. H. (1984). Effects of psychotherapy in schizophrenia: Part II. Comparative outcomes of two forms of treatment. Schizophrenia Bulletin, 10, 564-598.

Karon, B.P. (1958). Some clinical notes on the significance of the number four. Psychiatric Quarterly, 32, 281-288.

———— (1964). An experimental investigation of parental castration phantasies in schizophrenic patients. British Journal of Psychiatry (Journal of Mental Science), 110, 206-212.

———— (1970). An experimental investigation of parental castration phantasies. British Journal of Psychiatry, 117, 69-73.

———— (1975). Black scars: A rigorous investigation of the effects of discrimination, with an appendix on Southern Whites. New York: Springer.

———— (1984). The fear of reducing medication and where have all the patients gone? Schizophrenia Bulletin, 10, 613-617.

———— (1989a). On the formation of delusions. Psychoanalytic

Psychology, 6, 169-185.

———— (1989b). The state of the art of psychoanalysis: Science, hope, and kindness in psychoanalytic technique. Psychoanalysis and Psychotherapy, 7, 99-115.

———— (1998). What produces deep-seated change in psychotherapy? Internalizing the tolerant, kind, confused, and stubborn therapist and insight. Psychotherapy in Private Practice, 17, 9-15.

———— (2002). Analyzability or the ability to analyze. Contemporary Psychoanalysis, 38, 121-140.

———— (2003a). Abstractions, the psychoanalyst's escape from psychoanalysis: Ferenczi's "for example" revisited. Psychoanalytic Review, 90, 363-379.

———— (2003b). The tragedy of schizophrenia without psychotherapy. Journal of the American Academy of Psychoanalysis and Dynamic Psychiatry, 31, 89-118.

———— & O'Grady, P. (1970). Quantified judgments of mental health from the Rorschach, TAT, and Clinical Status Interview by means of a scaling technique. Journal of Counseling and Clinical Psychology, 34, 229-235.

———— & Rosberg, J. (1958a). The homosexual urges in schizophrenia. Psychoanalysis and The Psychoanalytic Review, 45, 50-56.

———— & Rosberg, J. (1958b). Study of the mother-child relationship in a case of paranoid schizophrenia. American Journal of Psychotherapy, 12, 522-533.

———— & Saunders, D.R. (1958). Some implications of the Eysenck-Prell study of "The inheritance of neuroticism": A critique. Journal of Mental Science, 104, 350-358.

———— & VandenBos, G.R. (1977). Psychotherapeutic technique and the economically poor patient. Psychotherapy: Theory, Research, and Practice, 14, 169-180.

———— & VandenBos, G.R. (1981). Psychotherapy of schizophrenia: The treatment of choice. New York: Jason Aronson.

———— & Widener, A.J. (1994). Is there really a schizophrenogenic parent? Psychoanalytic Psychology, 11, 47-61.

———— & Widener, A.J. (1999). Repressed memories: Just the facts. Professional Psychology: Research and Practice, 30, 625-626.

May, P.R.A. (1968). Treatment of schizophrenia: A comparative study of five treatment methods. New York: Science House.

Mitchell, K.M. (1974). Relationship between differential levels of parental "pathogenesis" and male children's diagnosis. Journal of Clinical Psychology, 30, 49-50.

Nichols, N. (1970). The relationship between degree of maternal pathogenicity and severity of ego impairment in schizophrenic offspring (Doctoral dissertation, University of Michigan, 1970). Dissertation Abstracts International, 31, 5003B.

Revere, V.L., Rodeffer, C.J., Dawson, S.D., & Bigelow, L.B. (1983). Modifying psychotherapeutic techniques to meet the needs of chronic schizophrenics. Hospital and Community Psychiatry, 34, 361-362.

Rosberg, J., & Karon, B.P. (1958). The Oedipus complex in an apparently deteriorated case of schizophrenia. Journal of Abnormal and Social Psychology, 57, 221-225.

———— & Karon, B.P. (1959). A direct analytic contribution to the understanding of postpartum psychoses. Psychiatric Quarterly, 33, 296-304.

VandenBos, G.R., & Karon, B.P. (1971). Pathogenesis: A new therapist dimension related to therapeutic effectiveness. Journal of Personality Assessment, 35, 252-260.

APPENDIX

Appendix

Bibliography of
Bertram P. Karon, Ph.d.

Articles

1. Van Nort, L. & Karon, B.P. (1955). Demographic transition re-examined. American Sociological Review, 20, 523-527.

2. Karon, B.P. (1955). Personality factors which may be associated with the development of mathematical ability. Educational Testing Service Research Memorandum.

3. ——— (1956). Stability of equated test scores. Journal of Experimental Education, 23, 181-195.

4. Van Nort, L. & Karon, B.P. (1956). Reply to Weinstein. American Sociological Review, 21, 371-373.

5. Karon, B.P. & Cliff, R.H. (1958). The Cureton-Tukey technique for equating test scores. Educational Testing Service Research Bulletin.

6. ——— & Saunders, D.R. (1958). Some implications of the Eysenck-Prell study of "The inheritance of neuroticism": A critique. Journal of Mental Science, 104, 350-358.

7. ——— (1958). Some clinical notes on the significance of the number four. Psychiatric Quarterly, 32, 281-288.

8. ——— & Rosberg, J. (1958). Study of the mother-child relationship in a case of paranoid schizophrenia. American Journal of Psychotherapy, 12, 522-523.

9. Rosberg, J. & Karon, B.P. (1958). The Oedipus complex in an apparently deteriorated case of schizophrenia. Journal of Abnormal and Social Psychology, 57, 221-225.

10. Karon, B.P. & Rosberg, J. (1958). The homosexual urges in schizophrenia. Psychoanalysis & Psychoanalytical Review, 45, 50-56.

11. ——— & Alexander, I.E. (1958). A modification of Kendall's Tau for measuring association in contingency tables. P4sychometriks, 23, 377-383.

12. ——— (1959). The reviewer missed the point. The Crisis, 216-218. Fifth

13. Macht, L.B., Alexander, I.E. & Karon, B.P. (1959). Lewin's level

of aspiration model applied to occupational preference. Human Relationships, 33, 296-304.

14. Rosberg, J. & Karon, B.P. (1959). A direct analytic contribution to the understanding of post-partum psychoses. Psychiatric Quarterly, 33, 296-304.

15. Karon, E.S. & Karon, B.P. (1959). Differentiation and differential counsel of two types of neurotic personalities. Journal of Psychology, 47, 231-234.

16. Karon, B.P. (1960). A clinical note on the significance of an "oral" trauma. Journal of Abnormal Psychology, 61, 480-481.

17. Karon, E.S. & Karon, B.P. (1961). Techniques of primitive witchcraft in modern psychotherapy. Acta Psychotherapy and Psychosomatics, 9(6), 393-400.

18. Karon, B.P. (1964). An experimental investigation of parental castration phantasies in schizophrenic patients. British Journal of Psychiatry (Journal of Mental Science), 464, 67-73.

19. ——— (1964). A note on the treatment of age as a variable in regression equations. American Statistician, 18, 27-28.

20. ——— (1964). Suicide as the wish to hurt someone else, and resulting treatment techniques. Journal of Individual Psychology, 26, 206-212.

21. ——— (1964). Effect of segregation and integration on children's personality (Discussion of paper by Kenneth Clark). School Integration, Bureau of Educational Research, Michigan State University, 16-25.

22. Sheppard, E. & Karon, B.P. (1964). Systematic studies of dreams: The relationship between ratings of the manifest content of dreams and associations to dream elements. Comprehensive Psychiatry, 1, 27-43.

23. Karon, B.P. (1965). The resolution of acute schizophrenic reactions: A contribution to the off fifth development of non-classical treatment techniques. Psychotherapy: Theory, Research, and Practice, 27-43.

24. ——— (1966). Reliability: Paradigm or paradox, with especial reference to personality tests. Journal of Projective Techniques and Personality Assessment, 30, 223-227.

25. Meyer, R. & Karon, B.P. (1967). A study of the schizophrenogenic

mother concept by means of the TAT. Psychiatry, 30, 173-179.

26. Long, F. & Karon, B.P. (1967). Rorschach validity as measured by the identification of individual patients. Journal of Projective Techniques and Personality Assessment, 33. 20-24.

27. Karon, B.P. & O'Grady, P. (1969). Intellectual test changes in schizophrenic patients in the first six months of treatment. Psychotherapy: Theory, Research, and Practice, 6, 88-96.

28. ———— & O'Grady, P. (1970). Quantified judgments of mental health from the Rorschach, TAT, and Clinical Status Interview by means of a scaling technique. Journal of Counselling and Clinical Psychology, 34, 229-235.

29. ———— (1970). An experimental study of parental castration phantasies. British Journal of Psychiatry, 117, 69-73.

30. ———— & VandenBos, G.R. (1970). Experience, medication, and the effectiveness of psychotherapy with schizophrenics. British Journal of Psychiatry, 116, 427428.

31. ———— & VandenBos, G.R. (1971). Pathogenesis: A new therapist dimension related to clinical effectiveness. Journal of Personality Assessment, 35, 252-260.

32. ———— (1973). The price of privilege: The effects of the American caste system on the Deep South white. Social Behavior and Personality, 1(2), 161-168.

33. ———— & VandenBos, G.R. (1972). The consequences of psychotherapy for schizophrenic patients. Psychotherapy: Theory, Research and Practice, 9, 111120.

34. ———— (1972). Black and white development. (Review of S. Hauser. Black and white identity formation: Studies in the psychosocial development of lower socioeconomic class adolescent boys.) Contemporary Psychology, 17, 445-446.

35. Glatt, C. & Karon, B.P. (1974). A Rorschach validation study of the ego regression theory of psychopathology. Journal of Counselling and Clinical Psychology, 42, 569-576.

36. Karon, B.P. & VandenBos, G.R. (1974). Thought disorder in schizophrenia, length of hospitalization, and clinical status ratings: Validity for the Feldman-Drasgon Visual-Verbal test. Journal of Clinical Psychology, 30, 264-266.

37. ———— (1974). Psychotherapy with schizophrenics--a reply.

Schizophrenia Bulletin, 9, 10-11.

38. VandenBos, G.R. & Karon, B.P. (1975). Medication and/or psychotherapy for schizophrenics: Which part of the elephant have you touched? International Mental Health Research Newsletter, 17(3), 1-13.

39. Karon, B.P. (1975). All in the family. (Review of T. Lidz. Origin and Treatment of Schizophrenic Disorder.) Comtempory Psychology, 20, 473-475.

40. ——— & VandenBos, G.R. (1975). Treatment costs of psychotherapy as compared to medication for schizophrenics. Professional Psychology, 6, 293-298.

41. ——— & VandenBos, G.R. (1975). Issues in current research on psychotherapy vs. medication for schizophrenics: Methodological issues in research. Psychotherapy: Theory, Research and Practice, 12, 143-148.

42. ——— (1975). "You've got to look in the right place": A response to Wender, Rosenthal & Kety. Contempory Psychology, 20, 987.

43. ——— & VandenBos, G.R. (1976). Cost/benefit analysis for schizophrenic patients treated by psychologist psychotherapists, psychiatrist psychotherapists, and medication (without psychotherapy). Professional Psychology, 7, 107-111.

44. ——— (1976). "You still have to look in the right place": A further response to Wender, Rosenthal, & Kety. Contempory Psychology, 21, 74.

45. ——— (1977). You have to read more than the chapter headings. Contemporary Psychology, 22, 476.

46. ——— (1977). Reply to Henderson. Contemporary Sociology, 6, 406-407.

47. ——— & VandenBos, G.R. (1977). Psychotherapuetic technique and the economically poor patient. Psychotherapy: Theory, Research, and Practice, 14, 169-180.

48. ——— (1978). Projective tests are valid. American Psychologist, 33, 764-765.

49. ——— & VandenBos, G.R. (1978). Psychotherapy with schizophrenics requires relevant training. National Institute of Mental Health Schizophrenia Bulletin, 4, 480-483.

50. ——— & VandenBos, G.R. (1978). A suggestion for treating

psychotic patients who won't eat. Hospital & Community Psychiatry, 29, 641-645.

51. Siegel, S.N., Hoffman, L., Ensroth, J., Woodward, R.D. & Karon, B.P. (1979). Long-term psychotherapy: Its scope and its insurability. MPS position statement, adopted by MPS Council, December 14, 1978. Michigan Psychiatric Society Update, 1, 1-6.

52. Karon, B.P. (1980). The treatment of schizophrenia by short-term psychotherapy. In Gochman (Ed.), Institutional innovations for patient transition from hospital to community: The Proceedings of the Eighth Annual Oberholzer Day Convocation, (pp 20-45). Washington: NIMH.

53. Ratner, S.G., VandenBos, G.R., Denny, M.R. & Karon, B.P. (1981). The adaptive significance of the catatonic stupor in humans and animals from an evolutionary perspective. Academic Psychology Bulletin, 3, 273-279.

54. Karon, B.P. (1982). Truth therapy and lie therapy. (Review of R. Langs. The Psychotherapeutic Conspiracy. New York: Aronson.) Contemporary Psychology, 28, 464.

55. ——— (1983). Review of J.S. Strauss, M. Bowers, T.W. Downey, S. Fleck, S. Jackson, & I. Levine (Eds.), The psychotherapy of schizophrenia. Journal of Nervous and Mental Disease, 171, 53.

56. ——— (1983). The indispensability of medication. American Psychologist, 38, 503.

57. ——— (1984). The fear of reducing medication, and where have all the patients gone? Schizophrenia Bulletin, 10, 613-617.

58. ——— (1984). A type of transference based on identification with an abusing parent. Psychoanalytic Psychology, 1(4), 345-348.

59. ——— (1984). Omission in review of treatment interactions. Schizophrenia Bulletin, 11(1).

60. ——— (1985). The treatment of acute schizophrenic patients in private practice. The Independent Practitioner, 5(2), 18-19.

61. ——— (1985). Missoppfatninger om psykoterpai med schizofrene. Agrippa--psykiatrisk tekster, 7(3), 154-171.

62. ——— (1986). Medication and psychotherapy. Psychiatric Times, 12(2), 20,12, 16.

63. ——— (1986). Psychiatrists, psychologists, medication, and psychotherapy. The Psychotherapy Bulletin, 20(3), 7-8.

64. ———— (1986). Discussion of preventive therapy for high risk mothers and children. Dynamic Psychotherapy, 4, 40-43.

65. ———— (1987). Current misconceptions about psychotherapy with schizophrenics. Dynamic Psychotherapy, 5(1), 3-15.

66. ———— (1987). Psychotherapy and psychosis: The treatment of acute schizophrenic patients in private practice. British Journal of Psychotherapy, 4(2), 135-147.

67. ————, Revere, V.L., Gochman, S.I. & Parson, E.R. (1987). What gene? APA Monitor, 18(8), 5.

68. Crisp, P. & Karon, B.P. (1987). Mystification and projective identification in psychotherapy with schizophrenics. Psichiatria e Psicoterapia Analitica, 6(2), 211-222.

69. Karon, B.P. (1988). Some current resistances to psychoanalysis. PsychologistPsychoanalyst, 8(3), 20-21.

70. Karon, B.P. (1989). Let us not emulate the father of Oedipus. PsychologistPsycholoanalyst, 9(1), Winter, 23-24.

71. Karon, B.P. (1989). On the formation of delusions. Psychoanalytic Psychology, 6(2), 169-185.

72. Karon, B.P. (1989). The state of the art of psychoanalysis: Science, hope, and kindness in psychoanalytic technique. Psychoanalysis and Psychotherapy, 7(2), 99-115.

73. Karon, B.P. (1990). The fear of understanding schizophrenia and the avoidance of the acutely disturbed college student. Journal of American College Health, 39(2), 61-72.

74. Karon, B.P. (1990). Problems of psychotherapy under managed health care. Psychotherapy in Private Practice, Monograph supplement.

75. Karon, B.P. (1990). Psychoanalysis, psychoanalytic therapy, and the process of supervision. Current Issues in Psychoanalytic Practice. Monograph No. 2. Psychoanalytic Approaches to Supervision, 147-156.

76. Karon, B.P. (1990). Hazards to patients and psychologists in the golden prescription pad. Physicians Weekly, December, 1-2.

77. Karon, B.P. (1990). Defense mechanisms in schizophrenia. Gradiva: Journal of the Sociedad Psicoanalitica de Mexico A.C., in press.

78. Karon, B.P. (1990). The specific determinants of a negative therapeutic reaction. Psychoanalysis and Psychotherapy, 8, 137-144.

79. Karon, B.P. (1990). "The future of Psychoanalysis lies with the Psychologist". Psychologist-Psychoanalyst, 12(4), 1-3.

80. ——— (1991 if). Prescription privileges and the fear of not medicating. Psychologist-Psychoanalyst, 11(1), 1-4.

81. ——— (1991). "Try To Get Along With Each Other." Psychologist-Psychoanalyst, 11(2), 1-4

82. ——— (1991). Psychoanalysis and truth. Psychologist-Psychoanalyst, 11(3), 1-3.

83. ——— (1991). Psychoanalysis and war. Psychologist-Psychoanalyst, 11 (Special Supplement), 1-2.

84. ——— (1991). Artistic Creating. Psychologist-Psychoanalyst, 11.

85. ——— (1991). Should psychologists prescribe certain drugs? No. The Public Citizens Health Research Group Health Letter. 7(1), 2.

86. ——— (1992). The fear of understanding schizophrenia. Psychoanalytic Psychology, 9(2), 191-212.

87. ——— (1992) Review of Breggin, P.R., Toxic Psychiatry: Why Therapy, Empathy, and Love Must Replace the Drugs, Electroshock, and BiochemicalTheories of the "New Psychiatry". New York: St. Martin's Press, 1991, Psychologist Psychoanalyst, 12, 32-33.

88. ———, (1992). Problems of psychotherapy under managed health care. Psychotherapy in Private Practice, 11(2), 55-63.

89. ——— (1992) Parents and schizophrenia. The APA Monitor, 23(4), 3,46.

90. ——— (1993) The psychotherapy of schizophrenia. Center for Psychological Studies Newsletter, 6(2), 2-3.

91. ——— (1993) Karon responds to Lane's article. Center for Psychological Studies Newsletter, 6(2), 5-6.

92. ——— & Widener, A. J. (1994). Is there really a schizophrenogenic parent? Psychoanalytic Psychology, 11, 47-61.

93. ——— (1994). Artistic creation as adaptive ego function and not regression in the service of the ego. Psychoanalysis and

Psychotherapy, 11, 80-85.

94. Kaley, H., Kaplan, S., Karon, B., Liff, Z. (1994). Getting elected: When, how, what. Psychologist Psychoanalyst, 14(3), 5.

95. Karon, B.P. (1994). False memory syndrome. Skeptical Inquirer, 18, 213.

96. ——— (1994). The prescription privilege and Division 39. Psychologist Psychoanalyst, 14(4), 16-18.

97. ——— (1995). Provision of psychotherapy under managed health care: A growing crisis and national nightmare. Professional Psychology: Research and Practice: 26(1), 5-9.

98. ———(1995). Becoming a first rate psychologist despite graduate education. Professional Psychology: Research and Practice, 26(2), 211-217.

99. ——— & Teixeira, M.A. (1995). "Guidelines for the Treatment of Depression in Primary Care" and the APA response. American Psychologist, 50, 453-455.

100. ———, (1995). "Obecny stan opieki psychiatrycznej w USA" (The current status of mental health care in United States Psychiatria Polska, XXIX(2), 273-278.

101. ———, (1996). A "successful" murderer. The Round Robin, XI (3), 17-19.

102. ——— (1996). On being abducted by aliens. Psychoanalytic Psychology, 13, 417-418.

103.——— (Nov. 4, 1996). Depression treatment exceeds   medication. Lansing State Journal, 5A.

104. ———, & Whitaker, L.C. (1996). Psychotherapy and the fear of understanding schizophrenia. The Psychotherapy Patient, 9, No. 3/4, 23-41.

105. ——— (June 9, 1997). Anxiety causes, care confusing for many. Lansing State Journal, 5A.

106. ———, & Whitaker, L.C. (1997). Brain damage is better than having to understand schizophrenia: Medication and other organic treatments. Journal of College Student Psychotherapy, 11(4), 33-55. Fifth

107. ——— & Widener, A. J. (1997). Repressed memories and World War II: Lest we forget! Professional Psychology:

Research and Practice, 28, 338-340.

109. ———— (1998). What produces deep-seated change in psychotherapy? Internalizing the tolerant, kind, confused, and stubborn therapist and insight. Psychotherapy in Private Practice, 17, 9-15. Fifth

110. ———— (1998). 1993-1995. Newsletter of the Michigan Psychoanalytic Council.

111. ———— (1999). Multiple voices: A virtual discussion. Journal of Psychotherapy Integration, 7, 249-252.

112. ———— (1999). The tragedy of schizophrenia. The General Psychologist. 32(1), 3-14.

113. ————, & Widener, A.J. (1999). Repressed memories: Just the facts. Professional Psychology: Research and Practice, 30, 625-626.

114. ————, & Widener, A.J.(1999). The tragedy of schizophrenia: Its myth of incurability. Ethical Human Science and Services, 1(3), 1-17.

115. ———— (2000) Treatment of severely disturbed patients in private practice. Psychologist-Psychoanalyst, 20(2), 40-43.

116. ———— (2000). The clinical interpretation of the Thematic Apperception Test, Rorschach, and other clinical data: A reexamination of statistical vs. clinical prediction. Professional Psychology: Research and Practice, 31, 230-233.

117. ————, & Widener, A.J. (2000) The tragedy of schizophrenia:Its myth of incurability. Acta Psychiatrica Scandinavica, 102, No. 404, 25-26.

118. ———— & Widener, A.J. (2001). Repressed memories: Avoiding the obvious. Psychoanalytic Psychology, 18, 161-164. 119. ———— (2001). The fear of understanding schizophrenia and iatrogenic myths. Journal of Contemporary Psychotherapy, 31, 15-20.

120. ———— (2002). Analyzability or the ability to analyze. Contemporary Psychoanalysis, 38, 121-140.

121. ————(2003). The tragedy of schizophrenia without psychotherapy Journal of the American Academy of Psychoanalysis and Dynamic Psychiatry, 31, 89-118.

122. ———— (2003). Abstractions, the psychoanalyst's escape from

psychoanalysis: Ferenczi's "For example" revisited. Psychoanalytic Review, 90, 363-379.

123. ——— (2003). Psychotropic medication and psychotherapy. The Round Robin, 18(1), 21-22.

124. ——— (2003). [Review of the book, L.C. Whitaker, Understanding and preventing violence: The psychology of human destructiveness]. Psychologist-Psychoanalyst, 23(2), 55.

125. ——— (2004). Hope, kindness, confusion, insight, and stubbornness: The odyssey of a psychoanalyst. Psychoanalytic Psychology, 21, 541-553.

126. ——— (2005). Recurrent psychotic depression is treatable by psychoanalytic therapy without medication Ethical Human Psychology and Psychiatry, 6, 45-56.

127. ——— (2005) Silvan S. Tomkins. SPA Exchange, 17(2), 12-13.

128. ——— (2005). [Review of the book, Ricardo C. Ainslie (2004) Long Dark Road: Bill King and Murder in Jasper, Texas] Psychologist-Psychoanalyst, 25(3), 77-78.

129. ——— (2005). Can biological and psychological interventions be integrated in the treatment of psychosis? Probably not. Bulletin of the Michigan Psychoanalytic Council, 1,29-34.

130. ——— (2006). Introduction to special section on treatment of psychoses by psychotherapy. Psychotherapy Research,16, 188-189.

131. ——— (2006). Can biological and psychological interventions be integrated in the treatment of psychosis? Probably not. Ethical Human Psychology and Psychiatry, 8, 225-228.

132. ——— (2007). The use of hallucinations in the treatment of psychotic patients. Ethical Human Psychology and Psychiatry, 9, 155-164.

133. ——— (2007). Supervising therapists treating the severely mentally ill. Bulletin of the Michigan Psychoanalytic Council, 3, 3-25.

134. ——— (2007). Does adding medication to psychotherapy for depression improve or worsen outcome? Journal of College Student Psychotherapy, 21, 179-198.

135. ——— (2007). Trauma and schizophrenia. Journal of Psychological Trauma, 6, 127-144.

136. ———(2008). An "incurable" schizophrenic: The case of Mr. X. Pragmatic Case Studies in Psychotherapy [Online], 4, Article 1, 1-24.

137. ——— (2008). Psychotherapy of schizophrenia works. Pragmatic Case Studies in Psychotherapy], 4, Article 5, 55-61.

138. ——— (2008). Trauma and schizophrenia. Bulletin of the Michigan Psychoanalytic Council, 4, 104-122.

139. ———, & Karon, M.K. (2010). Review of Linda Andre's (2008) Doctors of Deception: What They Don't Want You to Know about Shock Treatment. Psychologist-Psychoanalyst, 30(1), 23-24.

140. ——— (2010). Review of Robert Whitaker's (2010) Anatomy of an Epidemic: Magic Bullets,Psychiatric Drugs, and the Astonishing Rise of Mental Illness in America. Psychologist-Psychoanalyst, 30(3), 35-37.

141. ———, & Widener, A.J. (2011). Preventing relapse in smokers who quit. Ethical Human Psychology and Psychiatry, 13, 76-82.

142. ——— (2011). Who am I to treat this person? What it feels like to treat a seriously disturbed patient. Bulletin of the Michigan Psychoanalytic Council, 7, 2-24.

143. ——— (2011). Re: Jacqueline Sanders's Reminiscence of Bruno Bettelheim. Division/Review, 1(2),38. Div. 39, APA.

144. ——— (2011). Interpersonal therapy. Society for Interpersonal Theory and Research (SITAR) Newsletter, 12(2), 11-13.

145. ——— (2012). How do you talk to a patient about medication? ISEPP Bulletin--Number 1, 15-16. International Society for Ethical Psychiatry and Psychology.

146. ———, & Widener, A.J. (2012). Educating graduate students. Ethical Human Psychology and Psychiatry, 14, 134-139.

147. ——— (2012). Review of Peter Breggin's Psychiatric Drug Withdrawal. Ethical Human Psychology and Psychiatry, 14, 150-151.

148. Waiess, E. A., & Karon, B.P. (2012). The traumatic flashback as one basis of misunderstanding between patients and law enforcement officers. Ethical Human Psychology and Psychiatry, 14,192-198.

149. Karon, B.P., & Widener, A.J. (2013). Cognitive fears and psychoanalytic phobias. Ethical Human Psychology and Psychiatry, 15, 59-63.

150. ———— (2014). Suicide. ISEPP Bulletin--Number 2, 10-11. International Society for Ethical Psychiatry and Psychology.

151. ———— & Widener, A. J. (2014). Adolescent hostility toward therapists. Ethical Human Psychology and Psychiatry, 16, 194-200.

Books

Karon, B.P. (1958). The Negro personality. New York: Springer.

———— (1975). Black scars. New York: Springer (Revision of 1958).

———— & VandenBos, G.R. (1981). Psychotherapy of schizophrenia: The treatment of choice. New York: Aronson.

———— & VandenBos, G.R. (1985). Psykoterapi med schizofrene. Oslo: Universitetsforlaget AS.

———— & VandenBos, G.R. (1985). Psykoterapi vid schizofreni: Overstattning av gun zetterstrom. Stockholm: Wahlstrom & Widstrand.

Edited Books

Tomkins, S.S. (1962). (B.P. Karon, Ed.), Affect, Imagery, and Consciousness. Vol. I. New York: Springer.

———— (1963). (B.P. Karon, Ed.), Affect, Imagery, and Consciousness, Vol. II. New York: Springer.

Chapters

Karon, B.P. (1968). Problems of validities. In A.I. Rabin (Ed.), Projective techniques in personality assessment. New York: Springer.

Nikelly, A.G. & Karon, B.P. (1971). Suicide. In A.G. Nikelly (Ed.), Techniques for behavior change. Springfield: Charles C. Thomas.

Karon, B.P. & VandenBos, G.R. (1971). Experience, medication, and the effectiveness of psychotherapy with schizophrenics. In R. Cancro (Ed.), The Schizophrenic Syndroe: An Annual Review, (734-742). New York: Brunnor/Mazel.

Sheppard, E. & Karon, B.P. (1978). Systematic studies of dreams: The relationship between ratings of the manifest content of dreams and associations to dream elements. In S. Fisher and R.P. Greenberg (Eds.), The scientific evaluation of Freud's theories and therapy: A book of readings. New York: Basic Books.

Karon, B.P. & VandenBos, G.R. (1979). Der Einfluss der psychoterapeutischen Erfahrung auf den Therapieeffekt. In P. Matussek (Ed.), Psychoterapie Schizophrener Psychosen, (251-266). Hamburg: Hoffman and Campe.

——— & VandenBos, G.R. (1979). Cost/benefit analysis: Psychologist vs. psychiatrist for schizophrenics. In C. Kiesler and N. Cummings (Eds.), Psychology national health insurance: A sourcebook, (288-297). Washington: American Psychological Association.

——— (1981). The thematic apperception test. In A.I. Rabin (Ed.), Projective techniques in personality assessment (2nd Ed.), (85-120). New York: Springer.

VandenBos, G.R. & Karon, B.P. (1981). The treatment of severely disturbed patients, with attention to the relative cost-effectiveness of psychotherapy and medication. In B. Christiansen (Ed.), Does psychology return its costs? (77-99). Oslo, Norway: Norwegian Research Council.

Karon, B.P. (1985). Introduction. In R.F. Morgan (Ed.), Electric shock (vii-xi). Toronto: IPI Publishing.

——— (1989). Psychotherapy versus medication for schizophrenia: Empirical comparisons. In S. Fisher & R.P. Greenberg (Eds.), The limits of biological treatments for psychological distress: Comparisons with psychotherapy and placebos (105-150). Hillsdale, NJ: Lawrence Erlbaum.

——— (1990). Psychoanalysis, psychoanalytic therapy, and the process of supervision. In R. C. Lane (Ed.), Psychoanalytic approaches to supervision (pp. 147-156). New York: Brunner/Mazel.

——— (1992). Introduction. In R.F. Morgan (Ed.), Electric Shock; The Case Against. Toronto: IPI Publishing.

——— (1992). Discussion of Pekka Tienari's Paper. In Andrzej Werbart and Johan Cullberg (Eds.), Psychotherapy of Schizophrenia: Facilitating and Obstructive Factors (pp. 173 178). Scandinavian University Press.

——— (1992) Foreword. In H. Toch, Violent Men. Washington, DC: American Psychological Assn.

——— (1993). The formation of delusions. In G. Benedetti & P. Furlan (Eds.). The Psychotherapy of Schizophrenia: Effective

Clinical Approaches -Controversies, Critiques & Recommendations (pp. 61-68). Seattle, Toronto, Gottingen, Bern: Hogrefe & Huber.

———— (1994). The future of psychoanalysis. In R. Lane & M. Meisels (Eds.) A History of the Division of Psychoanalysis of the American Psychological Association (pp. 351-365). Hillsdale, NJ: Erlbaum.

———— & Widener, A. (1994). Psychodynamic therapies in historical perspective; "Nothing human do I consider alien to me." In B. Bongar & L.E. Beutler (Eds.) A Comprehensive Textbook of Psychotherapy: Theory, and Practice (pp 24-47). Oxford: Oxford University Press.

———— & Teixeira, M. (1995). Psychotherapy for schizophrenia. In J. Barber & P. Crits-Christoph (Eds.) Dynamic Therapies for Psychiatric Disorders (Axis I) (pp. 84-130). New York: Basic Books.

———— (1995). In search of truth. In J. Modrow, How to Become a Schizophrenic: The Case Against Biological Psychiatry (pp. xi-xiv). Everett, WA: Apollyon Press.

———— (1995) Effective psychoanalytic therapy of schizophrenia and other severe disorders. In VandenBos, G.R., Frank-McNeil, J., Norcross, J.C. & Freedheim, D.K. (eds.) The Anatomy of Psychotherapy. (pp. 83-97). Washington, DC: American Psychological Association.

———— & Whitaker, L.C. (1996). Psychotherapy and the fear of understanding schizophrenia. In P.R. Breggin & E.M. Stern (Eds.) Psychosocial Approach to Deeply Disturbed Persons. (pp. 23-41). New York, selected different Haworth.

———— & VandenBos, G.R. (1998). Schizophrenia and psychosis in elderly populations. In I.H. Nordhus, G.R. VandenBos, S. Berg, & P. Fromholt (eds.), Clinical Geropsychology, 219-230. Washington, DC: APA Books

Karon, B.P. (1998). "The struggle is not yet over." In R. Prince (ed.) The Death of Psychoanalysis: Murder, Suicide, or Rumor Greatly Exaggerated. Northvale, NJ: Aronson.

———— & Teixeira, M.A. (2002) Schizophrenia. In E. Erwin (ed.) The Freud Encyclopedia: Theory, Therapy, and Culture (pp. 502-504). New York: Gardner.

Silver, A-L., Koehler, B., & Karon, B. P. (2004). Psychodynamic therapy of schizophrenia: Its history and development. In J. Read, L. R. Mosher, & R. P. Bentall (Eds.). Models of Madness: Psychological, Social, and Biological Approaches to Schizophrenia (pp. 209-222). Hove, UK, and New York: Brunner-Routledge for ISPS.

Karon, B.P. (2007). Trauma and schizophrenia. In S. N. Gold & J. D. Elhai (Eds.) Trauma and Serious Mental Illness (pp. 179-198). Binghamton, NY: Haworth.

————— (2007). Does adding medication to psychotherapy improve or worsen outcome of depression? In L. Whitaker & S. E. Cooper (Eds.) Pharmacological Treatment of College Students with Psychological Problems,(pp. 179-198). Binghamton, NY: Haworth.

————— (2007). Supervising therapists treating the severely mentally ill. In A. K. Hess, K. D. Hess, & T. H. Hess (Eds.) Psychotherapy Supervision: Theory Research and Practice, Second Edition (pp. 359-379). Hoboken, NJ: Wiley.

————— (2008). Pathogenesis Index. In S. R. Jenkins (Ed.) A Handbook Of Clinical Scoring Systems for Thematic Apperception Techniques (pp. 347-364). New York: Taylor & Francis.

————— (2008). Scoring manual for the Pathogenesis Index. In S. R. Jenkins (Ed.) A Handbook Of Clinical Scoring Systems for Thematic Apperception Techniques (pp. 365-384). New York: Taylor & Francis.

————— & Silver, A.L. (2009). Foreword. In D. Garfield & D. Mackler (Eds.) Beyond Medication: Therapeutic Engagement and Recovery from Psychosis (pp. xi-xix). Hove, East Sussex & New York,: Routledge.

————— (2009). All I know about Peter Breggin). In G. Breggin & ICSPP (Eds.) The Conscience of Psychiatry (pp. 14-23). Ithaca, NY: Lake Edge.

Koehler, B., Silver, A.L. & Karon, B.P. (2013). Psychodynamic approaches to psychosis: Defenses against terror. In J. Read & J. Dillon(Eds.). Models of Madness: Psychological, Social, and Biological Approaches to Schizophrenia, Second Edition (pp. 238-248). Hove, UK, and New York: Taylor & Francis (Routledge) for ISPS.

www.ingramcontent.com/pod-product-compliance
Lightning Source LLC
Chambersburg PA
CBHW060304030426
42336CB00011B/927